lone

Naples, Pompeii & the Amalfi Coast

Naples, Pompeii & Around
p36

The Islands
p105

The Amalfi Coast
p140

Salerno & the Cilento
p176

THIS EDITION WRITTEN AND RESEARCHED BY
Cristian Bonetto, Helena Smith

Mar 2016

Contents

MERCATO DI PORTA
NOLANA, NAPLES P51

PIZZA P240

LONELY PLANET/GETTY IMAGES ©

ANGELA SORRENTINO/GETTY IMAGES ©

Contents

MARINA CORRICELLA,
PROCIDA P137

UNDERSTAND

SURVIVAL GUIDE

SPECIAL FEATURES

Welcome to Naples, Pompeii & the Amalfi Coast

Naples, Pompeii and the Amalfi Coast are the Italy of your wildest dreams, a rich, intense, hypnotic ragù of Arabesque street life, decadent palaces, pastel-hued villages and aria-inspiring vistas.

Cultural Riches

Few parts of Europe can match Campania's cultural conundrums. Should you spend the morning waltzing through chandeliered Bourbon bedrooms or the frescoed villa of a Roman emperor's wife? And which of Caravaggio's canvases shouldn't you miss: the multiscene masterpiece inside Naples' Pio Monte della Misericordia or the artist's brooding swan song inside the city's belle époque Palazzo Zevallos? Campania's blockbuster heritage will set your imagination alight with its chariot grooves and temples, bombastic frescoes and heart-stirring sculptures.

Food, Glorious Food

Campania is the country's culinary showoff, home to Italy's top pizza, pasta, mozzarella, tomatoes, citrus and seafood. It's like a never-ending feast; bubbling, wood-fired pizza in Naples, long lunches at Cilento *agriturismi* (farm stays), and lavish pastries at celebrity-status Amalfi Coast *pasticcerie* (pastry shops). Should you tuck into *coniglio all'Ischitana* (Ischian-style rabbit) at a rustic island trattoria? Pick up some famous *colatura di alici* (anchovy essence) in Cetara? Or just kick back with a crisp Falanghina and debate who has the creamiest buffalo mozzarella – Caserta or Paestum?

Southern Charm

Passionate, effusive and often generous to a fault, Campanians have a way of making other Italians seem just a little uptight. Despite the demands of modern life, there is always time for an impromptu espresso at the local bar or a bite of juicy gossip on a sun-bleached piazza. One minute you're choosing produce at a street market, the next you're in the middle of a feverish discussion about the weather, the in-laws or Napoli's on-field performance. Noone is a stranger for long, and a casual *chiacchiera* (chat) could easily land you at the bountiful table of your new best friend.

Natural Highs

Mother Nature went into overdrive in Italy's south, creating a thrilling playground of rugged mountains, steaming fumaroles, and ethereal coastal grottoes. Crank up the pulse rate exploring bat-filled grottoes at the Grotte di Castelcivita, cave diving off the Capri coast, or feeling the earth's subterranean wrath at the Solfatara Crater. Need to bring it down a notch? Horse-ride the slopes of Mt Vesuvius, sail the Amalfi Coast or simply soak at a thermal beach on Ischia. The options may be many, but there's one constant: a landscape that is beautiful, diverse and just a little magic.

Why I Love Naples, Pompeii & the Amalfi Coast

By Cristian Bonetto, Author

My family might hail from Italy's north, but my heart is tied tightly to Naples, Pompeii and the Amalfi Coast. This is the nation at its most intense, a place of brawny espresso in scorching cups and hairpin coastal roads. The region thrives on drama, from avaricious *palazzi* replete with scandalous tales to ghostly ruins in the shadow of Vesuvius. That the Bay of Naples resembles a giant amphitheatre is hardly coincidental. Bursting with twists, turns and inimitable pathos, no other corner of the *bel paese* makes me feel so incredibly alive.

For more about our authors, see page 288

Above: Marina Grande, Capri (p113)

Naples, Pompeii & the Amalfi Coast

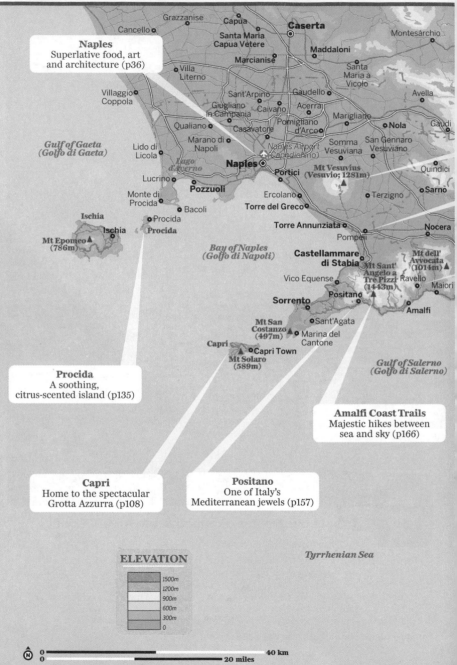

Naples
Superlative food, art
and architecture (p36)

Procida
A soothing,
citrus-scented island (p135)

Amalfi Coast Trails
Majestic hikes between
sea and sky (p166)

Capri
Home to the spectacular
Grotta Azzurra (p108)

Positano
One of Italy's
Mediterranean jewels (p157)

ELEVATION

	1500m
	1200m
	900m
	600m
	300m
	0

Tyrrhenian Sea

0 — 40 km
0 — 20 miles

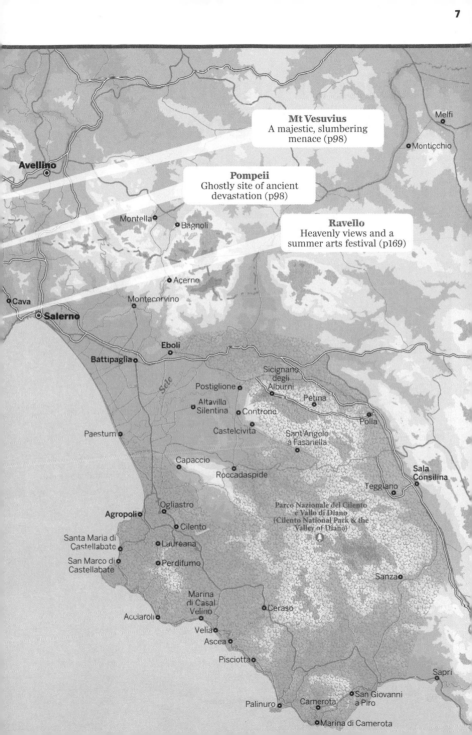

Mt Vesuvius
A majestic, slumbering menace (p98)

Pompeii
Ghostly site of ancient devastation (p98)

Ravello
Heavenly views and a summer arts festival (p169)

Melfi

Monticchio

Avellino

Montella

Bagnoli

Montecorvino

Acerno

Cava

Salerno

Eboli

Battipaglia

Sele

Postiglione

Sicignano degli Alburni

Petina

Altavilla Silentina

Controne

Polla

Castelcivita

Sant'Angelo a Fasanella

Paestum

Capaccio

Roccadaspide

Sala Consilina

Teggiano

Agropoli

Ogliastro

Cilento

Parco Nazionale del Cilento e Vallo di Diano
(Cilento National Park & the Valley of Diano)

Santa Maria di Castellabate

Laureana

San Marco di Castellabate

Perdifumo

Sanza

Marina di Casal Velino

Ceraso

Acciaroli

Velia

Ascea

Pisciotta

Sapri

Palinuro

Camerota

San Giovanni a Piro

Marina di Camerota

Naples, Pompeii & the Amalfi Coast's
Top 10

Neapolitan Street Life

1 There's nothing like waking up to the sound of a Neapolitan street market (p86), whether it's rough-and-ready Porta Nolana market or the city's oldest, La Pignasecca. A feast for the senses, it's as close to a North African bazaar as it is to a European market: fruit vendors raucously hawking their wares in Neapolitan dialect, swordfish heads casting sidelong glances at you across heaps of silvery sardines on ice, the irresistible perfume of crunchy *casareccio* (homestyle) bread, and the just-baked *sfogliatelle* (ricotta-filled pastries). Mercato di Porta Nolana, Naples (p49)

Pompeii

2 A once-thriving Roman town frozen for all time in its 2000-year-old death throes, the ruins of Pompeii (p98) are a haunting reminder of Mother Nature's merciless force and the fleeting nature of life itself. Wander Roman streets, the grassy, column-lined forum, the city brothel, the 5000-seat theatre and the frescoed Villa dei Misteri while pondering Pliny the Younger's terrifying account of the tragedy: 'Darkness came on again, again ashes, thick and heavy. We got up repeatedly to shake these off; otherwise we would have been buried and crushed by the weight'.

LONELY PLANET/GETTY IMAGES ©

MARTIN CHILD/GETTY IMAGES ©

STU SALMON/GETTY IMAGES ©

FRANK CHMURA/GETTY IMAGES ©

Amalfi Coast Trails

3 The charms of the Amalfi Coast stretch way beyond the glittering baubles of the coastal towns. Venture inland and you'll find meandering footpaths that, prior to 1840, were the only way people got around on dry land. Orange groves, pine trees, wild orchids and crumbling ruins flank the trails amid landscapes that shift and change. Yet one thing remains constant: the breathtaking coastal views. If you are seeking something suitably divine, succumb to the Sentiero degli Dei (p166), the 'Walk of the Gods'.

Procida

4 Wind-swept and citrus-scented, tiny Procida (p135) oozes old-school southern-Italian appeal. Faded gelato-hued houses crowd the marina as the evocative introduction to an island where tourism has remained remarkably low-key – a tourist office only opened here in 2012. Narrow, strung-with-washing lanes beckon strollers to the backstreets, secret swimming spots make for summertime bliss, and crumbling historic sights add a quiet sense of mystery. You may well eat some of the best fish of your trip here, served so fresh it's almost flapping. Above right: Marina Corricella, Procida

Grotta Azzurra

5 Capri's craggy coast is studded with more than a dozen sea caves, most of them accessible and spectacular, but none as justifiably famous as the Grotta Azzurra (p113; Blue Grotto). The cave is made particularly spectacular by its magical, iridescent blue light. What's the secret, you ask? It's all in the refraction of sunlight through the water, reflected off shimmering white sand. The result is an electric-blue marvel Walt Disney could only have dreamt of. Accessing the cave is an experience in itself: on a little wooden rowboat complete with singing captain.

Ravello

6 Ravello (p169) exudes a tantalising sense of beauty, idle luxury and the past – its illustrious legion of lovers including Virginia Woolf and Truman Capote. Perched above the Amalfi Coast, the town bristles with sumptuous churches, palaces and villas. Among the latter is Villa Rufolo, its romantic gardens famously inspiring the German composer Wagner. In commemoration, a summer festival of classical music is held on its terrace, a fabulous event best booked ahead. Ravello's setting is sublime, framed by lush countryside stippled with citrus and olive groves.

Positano

7 Pearl of the Amalfi Coast, Positano (p157) is scandalously stunning, a picture-perfect composition of pastel-coloured houses tumbling down towards a deep indigo sea. This easy beauty also informs its skinny, pedestrian streets, lined with chic boutiques for fussy fashionistas. If fabulous food inspires you more than fine fabrics, swoon over seafood at the superb La Cambusa (p161). Just don't forget neighbouring Praiano (p163), a tranquil corner on this clamorous coast where locals, rather than tourists, fill the piazza benches and bars.

Palazzo Reale di Capodimonte

8 It's just as well that Charles IV of Bourbon built big: his mother, Elisabetta Farnese, handed down one serious booty of art and antiquities – a sumptuous, sprawling feast of epic canvases and tapestries, elegant sculptures and dainty ceramics, with just a splash of contemporary paintings and installations. Palazzo Reale di Capodimonte (p65) might be one of Italy's less famous collections, but it's also one of its best, showcasing names such as Raphael, Titian, Caravaggio, Masaccio and El Greco.

FRANCESCO IACOBELLI/GETTY IMAGES ©

LONELY PLANET/GETTY IMAGES ©

Museo Archeologico Nazionale

9 A treasure chest of ancient art, propaganda and erotica, Naples' Museo Archeologico Nazionale (p51) is one of the world's most important archaeological museums. It's here that you'll find the breathtaking *Toro Farnese* (Farnese Bull), the largest sculptural group to have survived from antiquity, as well as exquisitely detailed mosaics and glassware, and vibrant frescoes that once adorned the region's elegant ancient villas. It wouldn't be a Roman affair without a little debauchery, waiting for you in the museum's infamous Gabinetto Segreto (Secret Chamber).

Mt Vesuvius

10 Guilty of decimating Pompeii and Herculaneum in AD 79, Mt Vesuvius (p98) looms over the Bay of Naples like a beautiful, unpredictable beast. Though well behaved since 1944, it remains mainland Europe's only active volcano, soaring a lofty 1281m above three million Neapolitans. Its slopes are part of the Parco Nazionale del Vesuvio, an area laced with soothing nature trails. For the ultimate high, head to the summit, where you can peer into its mouth and scan the land from the Tyrrhenian Sea to the Apennine Mountains.

Need to Know

For more information, see Survival Guide (p259)

Currency
Euro (€)

Language
Italian

Visas
Generally not required for stays of up to 90 days (or at all for EU nationals); some nationalities need a Schengen visa.

Money
ATMs at Naples' Capodichino airport and major train stations; widely available in towns and cities. Credit cards accepted in most hotels and restaurants.

Mobile Phones
Most modern phones work; switch off data roaming to avoid exorbitant charges. Buy a local SIM card for cheaper rates on data roaming and local calls; contact your home service provider to ensure your phone is unlocked.

Time
Central European Time (GMT/UTC plus one hour)

When to Go

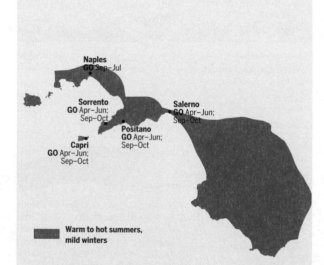

Naples
GO Sep–Jul

Sorrento
GO Apr–Jun; Sep–Oct

Salerno
GO Apr–Jun; Sep–Oct

Positano
GO Apr–Jun; Sep–Oct

Capri
GO Apr–Jun; Sep–Oct

Warm to hot summers, mild winters

High Season
(Jul–Aug)

➡ Queues and crowds at big sights, beaches and on the road, especially August.

➡ Many restaurants and shops close in Naples in August.

➡ A good period for cultural events in tourist areas.

Shoulder
(Apr–Jun & Sep–Oct)

➡ Good deals on accommodation.

➡ Spring is best for festivals, wildflowers and local produce.

➡ June and September generally deliver summer heat without the August crowds and traffic.

Low Season
(Nov–Mar)

➡ Prices at their lowest – up to 30% lower than high season.

➡ Many sights, hotels and restaurants closed in coastal and mountainous areas.

➡ Christmas feasting and colourful Carnevale celebrations.

Useful Websites

➡ **Lonely Planet** (www. lonelyplanet.com/italy) Destination information, hotel bookings, traveller forum and more.

➡ **In Campania** (www. incampania.com) Campania tourist bureau website.

➡ **Napoli Unplugged** (www. napoliunplugged.com) Sights, events, news and practicalities.

➡ **Positano** (www.positano. com) Information on sights, activities, accommodation, transport and more along the Amalfi Coast.

➡ **Capri** (www.capri.com) User-friendly site covering all aspects of Capri.

➡ **Trenitalia** (www.trenitalia. com) Italian railways website.

Important Numbers

Ambulance	☎118
Fire	☎115
Police	☎112/113
Italy's country code	☎39
International access code	☎00
International reverse charge assistance	☎170
Directory assistance	☎1254

Exchange Rates

Australia	A$1	€0.64
Canada	C$1	€0.67
Japan	¥100	€0.73
New Zealand	NZ$1	€0.58
UK	UK£1	€1.37
USA	US$1	€0.89

For current exchange rates see www.xe.com.

Daily Costs

Budget: Less than €100

➡ Dorm bed: €15–30

➡ Double room in a budget hotel: €50–100

➡ Lunch and dinner of pizza and pasta: €15

➡ Excellent markets and delis for self-catering

Midrange: €100–200

➡ Double room in a midrange hotel: €80–180

➡ Lunch and dinner in local restaurants: €25–50

➡ Three-day Naples Artecard pass €21

Top End: More than €200

➡ Double room in a four- or five-star hotel: €150–450

➡ Top restaurant dinner: €50–120

➡ Spa visit with treatment. €75

Opening Hours

Opening hours vary throughout the year. We've provided high-season opening hours; hours will generally decrease in the shoulder and low seasons. Be mindful that opening hours can be fickle at some smaller businesses.

Banks 8.30am 1.30pm and 2.45-3.45pm or 4.15pm Monday to Friday

Restaurants noon-3pm and 7.30-11pm or midnight

Cafes 7.30am-8pm or later

Clubs 11pm-5am

Shops 9am-1pm and 3.30-7.30pm (or 4-8pm) Monday to Saturday, some close Monday morning and some open Sunday

Arriving in Naples & the Amalfi Coast

Naples Capodichino Airport (NAP)

Alibus Airport Shuttle – €3 (€4 on board) to Stazione Centrale and Molo Beverello (hydrofoil terminal) every 20 to 30 minutes, 6.30am to 11.40pm

Taxi – €19 set fare to Piazza Municipio and adjoining Molo Beverello; journey time 20 to 30 minutes

Stazione Centrale, Naples

Metro – €1 (one-trip ANM ticket) to Municipio (Piazza Municipio) every eight to 14 minutes, around 6.15am to 10.30pm (to around 1am Friday and Saturday)

Taxi – €11 set fare to Piazza Municipio and Molo Beverello; journey time 15 to 20 minutes

Getting Around

Transport in the region is reasonably priced and relatively reliable in the main tourist areas.

Metro Line 1 connects Naples' Stazione Centrale to Piazza Municipio (for hydrofoil and ferry terminals), Via Toledo and Vomero. Line 2 runs to Pozzuoli.

Train Good for getting from Naples to Ercolano (Herculaneum), Pompeii, Sorrento, Salerno, Caserta and parts of the Campi Flegrei.

Bus Handy for travel along the Amalfi Coast and around Capri and Ischia. Some services reach sights in the Campi Flegrei.

Car Useful for reaching remote areas of the Cilento. Inadvisable in Naples year-round and along the Amalfi Coast in summer.

For much more on **getting around**, see p268 ➡

First Time Naples

For more information, see Survival Guide (p259)

Checklist

➡ Check the validity of your passport

➡ Check airline baggage restrictions

➡ Organise travel insurance (p261)

➡ Make bookings for accommodation, tours and entertainment

➡ Inform your credit/debit-card company of your travel plans

➡ Check whether you can use your mobile phone (p264)

➡ Find out what you need to hire a car (p271)

What to Pack

➡ Passport (and a photocopy of it, kept separately)

➡ Credit cards and driver's licence

➡ Phrasebook

➡ Italian electrical adapter

➡ Mobile (cell) phone charger

➡ Sunscreen, hat, sunglasses

➡ Waterproof jacket

➡ Comfortable shoes

➡ A detailed driving map

➡ Patience and a sense of humour

Top Tips for Your Trip

➡ Visit in late spring, early summer or early autumn for gorgeous weather without the peak-season crowds.

➡ Speak at least a few Italian words. A little can go a long way.

➡ Avoid restaurants with spruikers and mediocre tourist menus.

➡ Queue jumping is common in Italy; be polite but assertive.

➡ Be mindful of your possessions, especially in crowds and on transport.

What to Wear

Appearances matter in Italy. The concept of *la bella figura* (making a good impression) encapsulates the Italian obsession with looking good. In general, trousers (pants), jeans, shirts and polo shirts for men, and skirts or trousers for women, will serve you well in the city. Shorts, T-shirts and sandals are fine in summer and at the beach, but long sleeves are required for dining out. For the evening, think smart casual. A light sweater or waterproof jacket is useful in spring and autumn, and sturdy shoes are good for visiting archaeological sites. Dress modestly when visiting churches and religious sites, covering torso, shoulders and thighs.

Sleeping

If visiting in high season, the sooner you book the better – up to three months in advance for a July visit. For more information, see Accommodation on p195.

➡ **Hotels** All prices and levels of quality.

➡ **B&Bs** Often great value, ranging from rooms in family homes to self-catering studio apartments.

➡ **Farm stays** Perfect for families, *agriturismi* range from rustic farmhouses to luxe abodes with swimming pool.

➡ **Pensions** Similar to hotels, though *pensioni* are generally of one-to three-star quality and family run.

➡ **Hostels** You'll find both HI-affiliated and privately run *ostelli*, many also with private rooms.

Driving in Naples & the Amalfi Coast

Much of central Naples is off-limits to nonresident vehicles, and the combo of anarchic traffic and illegal parking attendants demanding tips will quickly ruin your holiday. Nonresident vehicles are prohibited on Capri for much of the year, and driving is largely discouraged on Ischia and Procida. Peak-season traffic can make driving along the Amalfi Coast stressful, though having your own vehicle here means ultimate flexibility. Driving is ideal in the Cilento region, allowing you to discover out-of-the-way towns and beaches. There are tolls on most motorways, payable by cash or credit card as you exit. For information on traffic conditions, tolls and distances, see www. autostrade.it.

Bargaining

Gentle haggling is common in markets; in all other instances you're expected to pay the stated price.

Tipping

Tipping is generally optional.

➡ **Taxis** Round up to the nearest euro.

➡ **Restaurants** Most restaurants have a *coperto* (cover charge; usually €1 to €3) and a *servizio* (service charge) of 10% to 15%. If service isn't included, consider a small tip.

➡ **Bars** Italians often place a €0.10 or €0.20 coin on the bar when ordering coffee; if drinks are brought to your table, tip as if you're in a restaurant.

MAXIME BERMOND/GETTY IMAGES ©

Naples at sunset

Language

Unlike in many other European countries, English is not widely spoken in Italy. Of course, in the main tourist centres you can get by, but in the countryside and off the tourist track you'll need to master a few basic phrases. This will improve your experience no end, especially when ordering in restaurants, some of which have no written menu. See the Language chapter (p273) of this book for all the phrases you need to get by.

Etiquette

Italy is a surprisingly formal society; the following tips will help you avoid any awkward moments.

➡ **Greetings** Shake hands and say *buongiorno* (good day) or *buona sera* (good evening) to strangers; kiss both cheeks and say *come stai*? (how are you?) for friends. Use *lei* (you) in polite company; use *tu* (you) with friends and children. Only use first names if invited.

➡ **Asking for help** Say *mi scusi* (excuse me) to attract attention; use *permesso* (permission) when you want to pass by in a crowded space.

➡ **Eating and drinking** When dining in an Italian home, bring wine or a small gift of *dolci* (sweets) from a local *pasticceria* (pastry shop). Let your host lead when sitting and starting the meal.

➡ **Gestures** Maintain eye contact during conversation and when toasting.

If You Like...

Fabulous Feasting

Pizza Italy's most famous export is best sampled in its spiritual home, Naples, at legendary pizzerias like **Starita** (p80).

Markets Lip-smacking produce and electric street life collide at Neapolitan street markets like **Porta Nolana** (p86) and **La Pignasecca** (p54).

Mozzarella di bufala Nosh on Italy's silkiest cheese at dedicated eateries like **Muu Muzzarella Lounge** (p78) and **Inn Bufalito** (p149), or visit a maker at **Tenuta Vannulo** (p191).

President A Michelin-starred wonder in Pompeii, where local history, produce, passion and creativity meet. (p104)

Donna Rosa Every soupçon of fame is justified at this Amalfi Coast institution. (p161)

Wine & The City Wine tastings and a bounty of cultural events in Naples. (p75)

Archaeological Treasures

Museo Archeologico Nazionale An incomparable booty of ancient sculptures, mosaics, frescoes and decorative arts in the heart of Naples. (p51)

Herculaneum Time stands still at this astoundingly well-preserved Roman town, complete with bathhouses, abodes, businesses and furniture. (p94)

Villa Oplontis Snoop around the reputed home of Emperor Nero's second wife, adorned with fabulous frescoes and a bigger-is-better pool. (p96)

Paestum Escape the hurly burly at these magical, millennia-old Greek temples, framed by fields and wildflowers. (p184)

Museo Archeologico Provinciale Star attraction at Salerno's archaeological museum is a 1st-century-BC bronze head of Apollo, fished out of the nearby sea in 1930. (p179)

Il Vallone dei Mulino Ruins of ancient wheat mills deep in a central Sorrento gorge. (p145)

Wild Beauty

Amalfi Coast More than just turquoise seas, the Amalfi Coast is laced with stunning, user-friendly walking trails. (p140)

Parco Nazionale del Cilento An extraordinarily untamed wonderland of crystal-clear streams, rivers and tumbling waterfalls. (p183)

Isole Faraglioni Capri's iconic limestone pinnacles rise from the sea like nymphs. (p111)

Grotta di Matermània Faded mosaics adorn this giant cave, used by the Romans as a sacred shrine. (p114)

Negombo Thermal pools, a private beach and beautiful botanical gardens put the luxe in alfresco downtime. (p131)

Mt Vesuvius A time-bomb volcano with nature trails and on-a-cloud views. (p98)

Inspiring Art

Palazzo Reale di Capodimonte From Botticelli and Caravaggio to American pop-art icons, this palace-museum is home to art-world royalty. (p65)

Galleria di Palazzo Zevallos Stigliano Caravaggio's ghostly epilogue heads a perfectly sized art collection in a jewel-box former bank. (p53)

Museo del Novecento Twentieth-century southern Italian art in a hulking Neapolitan fortress. (p64)

Naples Metro Let contemporary art transport you under the streets on Naples' just-expanded Metrò dell'Arte (Art Metro; p50).

Franco Senesi Two high-end galleries dishing up contemporary work from mostly Italian artists and sculptors. (p159)

Museo Pinacoteca Provinciale From the Renaissance to the 20th century, Salerno's top art museum has you covered. (p178)

Architecture

Reggia di Caserta An ambitious baroque epilogue with silver-screen credentials. (p74)

Duomo Swirling baroque frescoes and ancient mosaics co-exist in this architectural sonnet to Naples' patron saint. (p45)

Galleria Umberto I This glorious arcade in downtown Naples puts cookie-cutter modern malls to shame. (p55)

Cattedrale di Sant'Andrea Amalfi's zebra-stripe cathedral is a study in harmonious intercultural relations. (p166)

Palazzo dello Spagnuolo Not so much a staircase as an operatic tribute to the Neapolitan spirit. (p73)

Certosa di San Giacomo A 14th-century island monastery oozing old-school Caprese style. (p109)

Romantic Gardens

Ravello View the Amalfi Coast from the Belvedere of Infinity at **Villa Cimbrone** (p171) and swoon over classical tunes at **Villa Rufolo**. (p171)

La Mortella An Ischian tropical paradise inspired by the gardens of Granada's Alhambra. (p132)

Reggia di Caserta It's a case of more is more in the gardens of Caserta's gargantuan royal palace. (p74)

Villa Floridiana An elegant villa, a tortoise-filled fountain and dreamy sea and city views define this Neapolitan hillside hideaway. (p64)

Giardini di Augusto See what the Emperor saw at Augustus' decadent Capri playground. (p111)

Orto Medico Seek out a little-known cloister with healing herbs and a trickling fountain. (p49)

Top: Fountain at La Mortella botanical gardens, Ischia (p132)
Bottom: Classic Neapolitan margherita pizza (p240)

Month by Month

February

Short and accursed is how Italians describe February. It might still be chilly, but almond trees start to blossom and Carnevale season brightens things up with confetti, costumes and sugar-dusted treats.

Carnevale

In the period leading up to Ash Wednesday, many southern Italian towns stage pre-Lenten carnivals. Kids don fancy costumes and throw *coriandoli* (coloured confetti), elaborate *carri* (floats) are paraded down the street, and everyone indulges one last time before Lent. This is also the time for Carnevale treats like *chiacchiere* (crisp, fried pastry dough sprinkled with powdered sugar).

Festa di Sant'Antonino

Sorrento's patron saint is celebrated on 14 February with street stalls, fireworks and musical processions through the *centro storico* (historic centre). It's also the perfect time to tuck into Sorrento's famous *torta di Sant'Antonino;* a chocolate- and cream-filled tart.

March

The weather in March is capricious: sunny, rainy and windy all at once. Not surprisingly, the locals call it *Marzo pazzo* (Crazy March). The official start of spring is 21 March, but things only really start to open up for the main season during the Easter Holy Week.

Settimana Santa

Processions and passion plays mark Easter Holy Week across the Campania region. On Good Friday and the Thursday preceding it, hooded penitents walk through the streets of Sorrento. On tiny Procida, Good Friday sees wooden statues and life-size tableaux carted across the island.

May

Roses and early summer produce make May a perfect time to travel, especially for walkers. The weather is warm but not too hot and prices are good value. It's also patron-saint season.

Festa di San Gennaro

Naples' patron saint day sees the faithful flock to the Duomo to see San Gennaro's blood liquefy. If it does, the city is deemed safe from volcanic catastrophe. The miraculous event is repeated on 19 September and 16 December.

Maggio dei Monumenti

As the weather warms up, Naples puts on a mammoth, month-long program of art exhibitions, concerts, performances and tours. Many architectural and historical treasures usually off-limits to the public are open and free to visit.

Wine & the City

A two-week celebration of regional *vino* in Naples (www.wineandthecity.it), with free wine degustations, *aperitivo* sessions, theatre, music and exhibitions. Venues range from museums, castles and galleries to restaurants, shops and yachts.

June

Summer kicks off: the temperature cranks up quickly, *lidi* (beaches) start to open in earnest and some of the big summer festivals commence. The Anniversary of the Republic on 2 June is a national holiday.

☆ Napoli Teatro Festival Italia

Naples' theatre festival (www.napoliteatrofestival. it) delivers top-quality homegrown and foreign theatre, performance art and exhibitions over three weeks. Including both mainstream and fringe events, the festival takes place across the city, from theatres to metro stations.

🎽 Napoli Bike Festival

Neapolitans get in their saddles in early June for the city's burgeoning bike fest (www.napolibikefestival.it). Running over three days, activities include cycling tours, competitions, workshops and more.

☆ Ravello Festival

Perched high above the Amalfi Coast, Ravello draws world-renowned artists during its summer-long festival (www.ravello festival.com). Spanning everything from music and dance to film and art exhibitions, several events take place in the exquisite Villa Rufolo gardens from June to September.

July

School is out and Italians everywhere are heading to the coast or mountains for their summer holidays. Prices and temperatures rise. The beaches are in full swing, as are several major music and cultural festivals.

☆ Giffoni Film Festival

Europe's biggest children's film festival (www.giffoni filmfestival.it) livens up the town of Giffoni Valle Piana, east of Salerno. Attracting children and teens from across the world, the 10-day event includes screenings, workshops, seminars and big-name guests such as Mark Ruffalo and Robert De Niro.

🎆 Sagra del Tonno

Tiny Cetara plays host to this annual tuna festival, held over four days in late July or early August. Tuna dishes aside, you can taste-test the town's celebrated anchovies, made famous thanks to its *colatura di alici* (anchovy paste).

🎆 Festa di Sant'Anna

Ischia celebrates the feast day of Sant'Anna to spectacular effect on 26 July. The island's local councils build competing floats to sail in a flotilla, with spectacular fireworks and a symbolic 'burning' of Ischia Ponte's medieval Castello Aragonese to boot.

August

August in Campania is hot, expensive and crowded. Everyone is on holiday and, while it may no longer be true that everything is shut, many businesses and restaurants do close for part of the month.

🎆 Ferragosto

After Christmas and Easter, Ferragosto is Italy's biggest holiday. While it now marks the Feast of the Assumption, even the ancient Romans honoured their pagan gods on Feriae Augusti. The beaches are super crowded.

December

Despite the cooler days and longer nights, looming Christmas festivities warm things up with festive street lights, nativity scenes and Yuletide specialities.

🎆 Natale

The weeks preceding Christmas shine with religious events. Many churches set up nativity scenes known as *presepi*. People from across the country head to Naples to buy its famous *pastori* (nativity-scene figurines or statues) on and around Via San Gregorio Armeno.

Itineraries

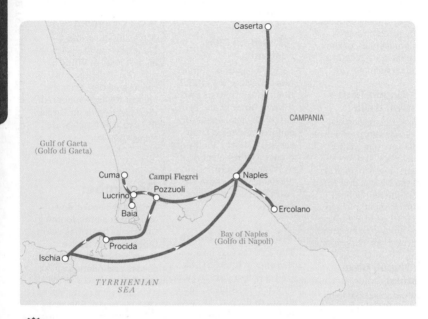

Palazzi, Ruins & Islands

The greater Naples area is home to some of Italy's oldest and most impressive human achievements, not to mention some of its most outstanding natural scenery. Follow this route for an intoxicating mix of archaeology, artistry and soul-stirring beauty.

Start with three action-packed days in **Naples**, taste-testing its famous pizza and swooning over its frescoed churches. On day four, consider a day trip to **Caserta**, home to a Unesco-lauded palace that upstages Versailles. Alternatively, shoot southeast to **Ercolano** to roam the extraordinary Roman ruins of Herculaneum. On day five, head west from Naples for a day in the Campi Flegrei, home to some of Italy's finest Graeco-Roman remnants. In **Pozzuoli**, check out Italy's third-largest Roman amphitheatre and the geologically freaky Solfatara Crater. Bathe like the Romans in **Lucrino**, see where emperors soaked in **Baia** or roam Greek ruins in **Cuma**. Come day six, catch a ferry across to **Procida** and spend a couple of days relaxing in stuck-in-time fishing villages and on secret beaches. Head to verdant **Ischia** on day eight, taking three days to explore its archaeology, gardens, castle and wineries, and treating yourself at one of its thermal spas. Refreshed and restored, sail back to Naples on day 10.

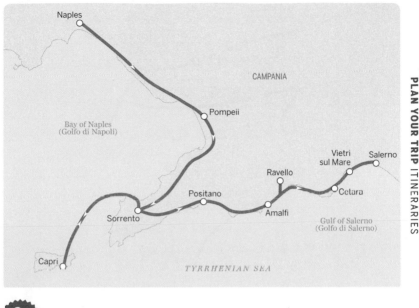

A Coastal Affair

Campania's fabled coastline is one of the world's most beautiful, inspiring countless artists, romantics and bon vivants. This itinerary takes in its most seductive highlights.

Start your sojourn with a trio of days in **Naples**, indulging in its artistic, architectural and culinary riches. Make time for at least two of the city's impressive museums, explore its markets and catacombs, marvel at the *Cristo velato* (Veiled Christ) sculpture in the Cappella Sansevero, and (in season) catch an aria at the majestic Teatro San Carlo. Spend day four turning back time at **Pompeii**, before evening cocktails in laid-back **Sorrento**. Spend the next day ambling Sorrento's streets, getting a crash course in craftsmanship at the Museo Correale and Museo Bottega della Tarsia Lignea, and finding peace in the cloisters of the Chiesa di San Francesco. Crank up the romance on day six by sailing across to **Capri**, giving yourself three days to fall madly in love with this fabled island. Glide into the dazzling Grotta Azzurra (Blue Grotto), ride up to Monte Solaro, and lose the hordes on side streets and bucolic walking trails.

On day nine, sail back to Sorrento and hit the hairpin turns and heavenly vistas of the Amalfi Coast. First stop: **Positano**. Check in for three nights, slipping on your Prada sandals and sauntering through the town's labyrinth of chic laneways. Sup on fresh seafood, hire your own boat, or tie up your hiking boots and get a natural high on the Sentiero degli Dei (Walk of the Gods). Spend day 12 in deeply historic **Amalfi**, exploring its architecturally eclectic cathedral and cloisters before continuing to sky-high **Ravello**, long-time haunt of composers, writers and Hollywood stars. Stay the night to soak up the town's understated elegance, and spend the following day taking in its villas and uber-romantic gardens. Continue east to the upbeat regional city of Salerno, your final stop. On the way, drop into **Cetara** to sample its famous tuna and anchovies and into **Vietri sul Mare** to shop for colourful local ceramics. Spend a day in **Salerno**, diving into its medieval core to savour the city's fabulous seafood, pastries and street life. Come evening, join the locals for a spot of bar-hopping bonhomie – the *perfetto* end to your coastal affair.

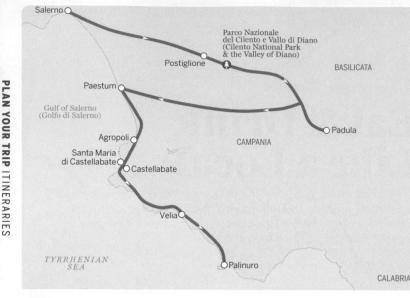

9 DAYS — The Cilento Trail

While the lure of Naples, Capri and the Amalfi Coast are irresistible, Campania heaves with lesser-known marvels. From Hellenic temples and cave-studded mountains to one of Italy's largest monasteries, this route leads down less-trodden paths.

Start your adventure in the underrated city of **Salerno**. Its cathedral is widely considered to be Italy's most beautiful medieval church, while its engrossing multimedia Museo Virtuale della Scuola Medica Salernitana tells the story of the city's medieval medical school, once one of Europe's most important. Head up to the Castello di Arechi for sweeping views, and to the revamped waterfront for a late-afternoon *passeggiata* (stroll). After dark, join the *salernitani* (Salerno locals) in the city's vibrant medieval heart for a little bar-hopping and *movida* (partying). On day two, bid Salerno *arrivederci* and head inland for three days in the rugged beauty of the **Parco Nazionale del Cilento e Vallo di Diano**, Italy's second-largest national park and a Unesco World Heritage Site. Base yourself at one of the park's *agriturismi* (farm stays) and explore the area's famous grottoes, namely the Grotte di Castelcivita and Grotte di Pertosa. Make sure to spend a few hours in the medieval town of **Postiglione** – home to an 11th-century Norman castle – and a morning or afternoon in **Padula**, famous for its mammoth Carthusian monastery, the Certosa di San Lorenzo. Not far from the Certosa is the fabled Valle delle Orchidee (Valley of the Orchids), whose 70-plus varieties of orchid create a dazzling blaze of springtime colour. One of the national park's more curious sites is Roscigno Vecchia, a veritable ghost town abandoned early last century.

On day five, head back towards the coast to gasp at the mighty Greek temples of **Paestum**, the oldest of which dates back to the 6th century BC. Spend the evening and the following morning in **Agropoli**, wandering its atmospheric *centro storico* (historic centre) before heading south to **Santa Maria di Castellabate** for superlative seafood noshing. On day seven, head up to the beautiful medieval town of **Castellabate** and wander its shamelessly charming laneways, then spend the afternoon exploring the ancient ruins of **Velia**. End your Cilento travels with a couple of lazy beach days in **Palinuro**, which, like Capri, lays claim to a dazzling Grotta Azzurra (Blue Grotto).

Plan Your Trip
Eat & Drink Like a Local

Naples, Pompeii and the Amalfi Coast are a culinary mecca, where impeccable produce and well-trained taste buds have created one of the world's most envied gastronomic landscapes. Whet your appetite with the following food-trip essentials.

Food Experiences

So much produce, so many classics, so little time! Fine-tune your culinary radar with the following musts.

Meals of a Lifetime

➡ **Donna Rosa, Positano** Home cooking gets an innovative, Michelin-starred makeover. (p161)

➡ **Il Focolare, Ischia** A rustic Slow Food gem showcasing homegrown island produce. (p135)

➡ **President, Pompeii** Confident, often playful takes on Campanian classics; worthy of its Michelin star. (p104)

➡ **Marina Grande, Amalfi** Fresh, fragrant, succulent seafood overlooking the beach. (p168)

Cheap Treats

➡ **Pizza** Both wood-fired and *fritta* (deep fried).

➡ **Fritture** Deep-fried snacks including *crocchè* (potato croquettes), best bought from *friggitorie* (fried-food take-away outlets).

➡ **Taralli** Crunchy, usually savoury ring-shaped biscuits, sold plain or in variations like *taralli mandorlati* (with almonds).

➡ **Sfogliatella** Cinnamon-scented ricotta pastries in *riccia* (filo) and *frolla* (shortcrust) varieties.

➡ **Gelato** The best gelato uses seasonal ingredients and natural colours.

The Year in Food

There's never a bad time to raise your fork in Campania. For more of food events, see p20.

Spring (Mar–May)

Asparagus, artichokes and Easter specialities. Celebrate the region's increasingly prolific *vino* at Naples' Wine & The City (p75).

Summer (Jun–Aug)

Eggplants, peppers, tomatoes and Cetara's Sagra del Tonno (p174). Bite into *albicocche vesuviane* (Vesuvian apricots) and *pere mastantuono* (mastantuono pears).

Autumn (Sep–Nov)

Mushrooms, chestnuts, black truffles and *mele annurche* (annurche apples). Plough through pasta at Minori's Gustaminori (p173), a food fest dedicated to Italy's favourite staple.

Winter (Dec–Feb)

Christmas and Carnevale treats, plus earthy stalwarts like *zuppa di castagne e fagioli* (chestnut and bean soup). Dig into sausages by a bonfire at Sorrento's Sagra della Salsiccia e Ceppone (p146).

Local Specialities

Each corner of the region boasts its own edible staples. Here are some of the best:

➡ **Naples** Thin-crust pizza, *spaghetti alle vongole* (spaghetti with clams), *pasta cacio e pepe* (pasta with caciocavallo cheese and pepper) and *sartù* (rice timbale with cheese, vegetables and meat). Snack on *pizza fritta* (fried pizza dough stuffed with charcuterie, cheese and tomato) and *supplì di riso* (fried rice balls). Desserts include *pastiera napoletana* (a citrus-scented ricotta tart).

➡ **Caserta** Internationally renowned for its moreish *mozzarella di bufala* (buffalo-milk mozzarella).

➡ **Capri** Light *insalata caprese* (mozzarella, tomato and basil salad) and calorific *torta caprese* (almond and chocolate cake). Wash it down with *limoncello* (lemon liqueur).

➡ **Ischia** Plunge into *spaghetti alla puttanesca* (spaghetti with olives, chilli, garlic and tomato sauce), *coniglio all'ischitana* (rabbit with garlic, chilli, tomato, herbs and white wine) and aromatic *vino* from local wineries like Casa D'Ambra.

➡ **Minori** Taste-test the town's pasta, especially its fresh *scialatielli* (thick ribbons of pasta) and *'ndunderi,* ancient Roman precursors of gnocchi.

➡ **Cetara** Savour Italy's best anchovies with *spaghetti con alici e finocchietto selvatico* (spaghetti with anchovies and wild fennel) and *colatura di alici* (anchovy essence).

➡ **Salerno and the Cilento** Drizzle Colline Salernitane DOP extra virgin olive oil and devour buffalo-milk mozzarella from Paestum. Other notable Cilento cheeses include goat's-milk *cacioricotta di capra* and cow's-milk *caciocavallo podolico*.

WHAT TO BOOK

Generally, all high-end and popular restaurants should be booked ahead, especially for Friday and Saturday evenings and Sunday lunch. In major tourist towns, always book restaurants in the summer high season and during Easter and Christmas. Cooking courses such as Sorrento Cooking School (p146), Mamma Agata (p171) and Gelateria David (p146) should also be booked ahead.

How to Eat & Drink Like a Local

Now that your appetite is piqued, it's time for the technicalities of eating *alla campana* (Campania style).

When to Eat

➡ **Colazione (breakfast)** Often little more than a pre-work espresso accompanied by a *cornetto* (Italian croissant) or a *sfogliatella* (sweet ricotta-filled pastry).

➡ **Pranzo (lunch)** Traditionally the main meal of the day. Standard restaurant times are noon to 3pm; many locals don't lunch before 2pm.

➡ **Aperitivo** Popular in Naples, post-work drinks see numerous bars offer tasty morsels for the price of a *spritz* between 6pm and 9pm.

➡ **Cena (dinner)** Traditionally lighter than lunch, though still a main meal. Standard restaurant hours are 7.30pm to 11pm (later in summer). Most locals don't dine before 8.30pm.

Choosing a Restaurant

➡ **Ristorante (restaurant)** Formal service and refined dishes and wines; perfect for special occasions.

➡ **Trattoria** A more casual version of a restaurant, with cheaper prices and regional specialities. Avoid places with 'tourist menus'.

➡ **Osteria** Historically, a tavern focused on wine; the modern version is usually an intimate trattoria or wine bar offering a handful of dishes.

➡ **Enoteca** Wine bars often serve snacks to accompany your well-chosen tipple.

➡ **Agriturismo** A working farmhouse offering accommodation, as well as food made with farm-grown produce.

➡ **Pizzeria** Great for a cheap feed and cold beer.

Plan Your Trip
Outdoor Activities

Naples and Campania lay claim to some of Italy's most dramatic and breathtaking terrain. For outdoor aficionados, the area is full of possibilities, from diving off the Amalfi Coast to trekking in rugged, ancient Cilento woods.

Walking & Hiking

From beachside strolls to hardcore hikes, Campania has it covered. Terrain around here can be stoney and extremely steep, and walkers should come prepared. Bring comfortable lace-up walking shoes or sturdy boots, a small day pack, sunscreen, sunglasses and a hat, plenty of water and some energy-stoking snacks. If you're planning a serious hike, let someone know the approximate duration and location.

Around Naples

For a walk on the wild side, head to Pozzuoli's Solfatara Crater (p89), where a trail circles the rim of a restless volcano; it's possible to take an atmospheric evening tour here. Further west, crater-turned-lake Lago d'Averno (p93) offers an altogether more tranquil, bucolic circuit.

On the other side of Naples, reaching the summit of Mt Vesuvius (p98) is easier than you may think, with regular shuttle buses connecting Ercolano-Scavi Circumvesuviana station to the summit car park. From here, it's a relatively easy 860m walk up to the summit, where your reward is a 360-degree panorama capturing Naples, its bay, and the distant Apennine mountains. The volcano is part of the **Parco Nazionale del Vesuvio** (Vesuvius National Park; www.epnv.it), a national park crisscrossed by nine nature *sentieri* (trails) of varying

Best Outdoor Experiences

Best Things to Do

Coastal grottoes Sail into Campania's dazzling sea caves.

Amalfi Coast hikes See the fabled coast from high mountain paths.

Thermal therapy De-stress in soothing natural hot springs.

Solfatara Crater Feel the fury at this hot-as-hell crater.

Mt Vesuvius Scale the slopes of the infamous volcano.

Punta Campanella Marine Reserve Dive down to meet some colourful local characters.

Grotte di Castelcivita Explore the caverns at Europe's oldest settlement.

Positano cruising Sail to a little-known archipelago for a sunset Campari.

Best Times to Go

April to June Walk among wildflowers.

July and September Water sports and warm-water diving without the August crowds.

lengths and intensity (www.vesuviopark. it). The most challenging and rewarding is the 6.7km Lungo la Strada Matrone (Rte 6). Starting from Via Cifelli, it heads up the volcano's southeastern slope to the summit. The park itself is a rich natural oasis, home to hedgehogs, moles, stonemartens and foxes, as well as around 140 species of bird, including spotted woodpeckers, hawks and imperial ravens.

Naples Trips & Tours (p98) runs horse-riding tours of the national park.

The Islands

To the surprise of many, both Capri and Ischia offer some spectacular walks that will see you enjoying the islands away from the beach crowds. Enjoyable though precipitous trails lead you out of Capri Town to a Roman villa and a natural rock arch, or for a more arduous route you can follow a chain of forts and take in the western coast. On Ischia, the best option to explore the thermally rich interior is to take a Geo-Ausfluge (p133) tour, conducted by a local geologist.

Parco Nazionale del Cilento e Vallo di Diano

Southeast of the Amalfi Coast, the Parco Nazionale del Cilento e Vallo di Diano serves up relaxing walks and more challenging hikes, reliable guides and excellent maps. This remarkable wilderness area is home to around 3000 registered botanical

species, as well as a number of rare birds, including the golden eagle and seacrow.

The park's most famous feature, however, is an incredible series of caves. Among these are the Grotte di Castelcivita (p184) and Grotta dell'Angelo, their Gothic-like stalagmites and stalactites yours to explore on daily speleological tours. Online, www.parks.it offers useful information on the region's national parks.

Beaches & Water Sports

Naples offers metropolitan beaches, but you're better off splashing about in the cleaner waters of the bay islands, or along the Amalfi and Cilento coasts. Water quality in the region is improving, with several strands receiving the Blue Flag clean beach award.

Private beaches are especially prevalent at summertime hot spots like Capri, Ischia and the Amalfi Coast, offering everything from on-site restaurants and bars to *ombrellone* (beach umbrella) and *lettino* (sunbed) hire. Admission is usually around €10. If you don't fancy paying for a place on the sand, look for a *spiaggia libera* (free beach). Usually signposted, these often consist of crowded, narrow stretches of beach close to the nearest road access or sometimes right beside the private beach. Some (but not all) free beaches come with shower and toilet facilities. Many of the region's best (and less crowded) swimming spots – for example, the Li Galli islands (off the Amalfi Coast), Fiordo Di Furore (east of Praiano) and Cavallo Morto (near Erchie) – are only accessible from the water; tourist offices can provide information on tours and boat hire.

There are plenty of options in the region for water sports. Kayak Napoli (p75) runs day and evening tours of the city coast, which take in old *palazzi* (mansions) and coastal caves. At Marina Piccola (p114) on Capri you can hire canoes to attempt a circuit of the island, if you're feeling strong.

TOP BEACHES
....

➡ **Baia di Ieranto** A spectacular beach at the tip of the Punta Penna peninsula south of Sorrento. (p149)

➡ **Baia di Sorgeto** Catch a water taxi to this toasty thermal beach on Ischia. (p134)

➡ **Spiaggia Marmelli** Retreat to a lush, soothing cove on the Cilento coast. (p193)

➡ **Spiaggia di Fornillo** Crystal-clear water awaits at this in-the-know alternative to Positano's main beach. (p159)

➡ **Santa Maria di Castellabate** Velvet-soft sand and powder-blue sea at a Cilento coast resort.(p190)

Spas & Springs

The Bay of Naples has been celebrated for its thermal waters for thousands of years, seducing everyone from Roman emperors to frazzled celebrities.

Easily reached on the Cumana train from Naples, the Terme Stufe di Nerone

Above: Hiker at the summit of Mt Vesuvius (p98)

Right: Isole Faraglioni limestone stacks off the island of Capri (p111)

JANOKA82-GETTY IMAGES ©

Snorkelling in the Bay of Naples

(p108) is one of the most famous thermal spas in the Campi Flegrei, complete with indoor and outdoor pools, terraced gardens, and saunas carved out of the region's trademark *tufo* rock. In the bay itself, Ischia is one of the world's richest, most diverse hydrothermal hot spots, with no fewer than 103 thermal springs, 67 fumaroles and 29 underground basins. Spa parks Negombo (p131) and Giardini Poseidon (p133) combine lush gardens with a booty of mineral pools and massage treatments and a private beach. Less luxurious but more historic is the Terme Cavascura (p135), complete with old Roman baths.

Boating & Sailing

The region has a proud maritime tradition and you can readily hire a paddle boat or yacht on the bay islands as well as on the mainland coast. Experienced mariners can island-hop around the Bay of Naples or along the Amalfi Coast on chartered yachts, while weekend boaters can explore hidden coves in rented dinghies, for which you need no experience – be sure you understand the instructions before you set off!

Every four years Amalfi hosts the **Regata delle Antiche Repubbliche Marinare** (Regatta of the Old Maritime Republics), an annual boat race between the once mighty maritime republics of Amalfi, Venice, Genoa and Pisa. Amalfi's turn will come around again in 2016.

Diving

Diving is a popular pursuit in Campania, and you'll have no trouble finding diving schools offering equipment hire, courses and dives for all levels. One of the region's best diving spots is the **Punta Campanella Marine Reserve**. Located at the tip of the Sorrento Peninsula, it's well known for its colourful marine fauna, small reefs and multicoloured seaweed. Other favourite dive sites include the WWII wrecks at Agropoli (p188), the turquoise waters around Capri (108) and the underwater grottoes of Marina del Cantone (p156).

Avoid August, when much of Campania's coastline is besieged by holidaymakers. Information on diving schools and areas is available from local tourist offices and online at www.diveitaly.com (in Italian).

Plan Your Trip
Travel with Children

With a little planning and some background information on the region's gripping history, Naples and the Amalfi Coast are guaranteed to hook young, curious minds. After all, this is the land of giant gladiatorial arenas, mysterious catacombs, hissing craters and bubbling beaches. Jump in!

Naples & the Amalfi Coast for Kids

Children are adored in Campania and welcomed almost anywhere. On the downside, the region has few special amenities for junior travellers, and the combination of Naples' breathless pace, the Amalfi Coast's twisting coastal road and the stroller-unfriendly cobbled stones at archaeological sites can prove challenging. With a little adaptation and an open mind, however, young families will find that Campania is a richly stimulating, rewarding destination.

Children's Highlights

Always ask at tourist offices about any family activities, festivals and events, and consider investing in a few children's history books to help their imagination along at archaeological sites. Most museums and sights offer discounted entry for kids, although some discounts are for EU citizens only. For more information, see Lonely Planet's *Travel with Children,* the Italy-focused website www.italiakids.com or the Naples-focused www.napoliperbambini. com (in Italian). For more general tips, check out www.travelwithyourkids.com and www.familytravelnetwork.com.

Best Regions for Kids

Naples, Pompeii & Around
Capital attractions: step back in time at Pompeii, Herculaneum and Oplontis, explore ancient cisterns, passageways and ghoulish cemeteries below lively city streets, get experimental at a science museum and sidle up to a sizzling geological freak.

The Islands
Beach babes: seek your own perfect swimming cove on a private boat on Procida, sail into a sparkling, magical grotto on Capri, or pool-hop at a sprawling thermal-spa resort on lush, volcanic Ischia.

The Amalfi Coast
Surf and turf: chill out on a summertime boat trip, get splash-happy at a coveted beach, hike high above the coastline, and take in a little history at a quirky paper museum in Amalfi.

Salerno & the Cilento
Wild and cultured: learn about ancient medicine at a multimedia museum, attend a children's film festival, or run wild in wide open spaces, riding rivers, feeding farm animals and sorting out your stalactites from your stalagmites.

Culture Vultures

➡ **MAV (Museo Archeologico Virtuale), Ercolano** Campania's ancient ruins brought back to life with holograms and videos. (p97)

➡ **Museo della Carta, Amalfi** Explore the region's proud papermaking tradition in a historic Amalfi paper mill. (p167)

➡ **Città della Scienza, Bagnoli, Naples** A super-fun science centre just west of Naples. (p92)

➡ **Museo Virtuale della Scuola Medica Salernitana, Salerno** An interactive museum dedicated to medieval medicine. (p179)

➡ **Giffoni Film Festival, Giffoni Valle Piana, Salerno** Europe's biggest children's film festival. (p21)

Thrills & Spills

➡ **Solfatara Crater, Pozzuoli** Mother Nature hissy fits at a shallow volcanic crater. (p89)

➡ **Negombo, Ischia** A thermal-springs park with mineral pools and thermal beach, plus massage and beauty treatments for frazzled parents. (p131)

➡ **Grotta Azzurra, Capri** Pixar has nothing on Capri's dazzling, other-worldly Blue Grotto. (p113)

➡ **Parco Nazionale del Cilento e Vallo di Diano, Cilento** River rafting, colourful grottoes and *agriturismo* (farm stay) complete with furry friends. (p183)

Time Travel

➡ **Pompeii** Ancient theatres, houses, shops, even a stadium. The ancient brothel will no doubt bemuse teens. (p98)

➡ **Herculaneum** Smaller than Pompeii and better preserved, with carbonised furniture and ancient shop advertisements. (p94)

➡ **Napoli Sotterranea, Naples** Head down a secret porthole into a magical labyrinth of Graeco-Roman passageways and cisterns. (p48)

➡ **Cimitero delle Fontanelle, Naples** It's Halloween every day at the ghoulish Fontanelle Cemetery, stacked with human skulls and bones. (p72)

Planning

When to Go

May, June and September are generally warm and sunny, without the summer peak crowds. Colourful floats and costumes make Carnevale (February or March) another good bet, while the region's famous *presepi* (nativity cribs) can help make December magical.

Where to Stay

Book accommodation in advance whenever possible. In hotels, some double rooms can't accommodate an extra bed for kids, so check ahead. If the child is small enough to share your bed, some hoteliers will let you do this for free.

➡ **Hostels and apartments** Good for multibed rooms, self-catering and lounge facilities.

➡ **Campgrounds** Buzzing in high season (summer), with many offering activities for kids of all ages.

➡ **Farm stays** Great for outdoor space; numerous *agriturismi* also come with cute, furry animals.

Where to Eat

➡ Most eateries, especially trattorias and pizzerias, welcome kids.

➡ If reserving a table, ask if they have a *seggiolone* (high chair).

➡ Children's menus are uncommon, though requesting a *mezzo piatto* (half plate) off the menu is usually fine.

Essentials

➡ Disposable nappies (diapers) are readily available at supermarkets and pharmacies. Pharmacies also stock baby formula in powder or liquid form, as well as sterilising solutions.

➡ Fresh cow's milk is sold in cartons in supermarkets and in bars with a 'Latteria' sign. UHT milk is popular, and in many out-of-the-way areas it's the only kind available.

Transport

➡ Cobbled streets, potholes and crowded transport make travelling with a stroller cumbersome; consider investing in an ergonomic baby carrier instead.

➡ Public-transport operators offer free travel for one child aged up to six if accompanied by a paying adult. An adult accompanying more than one child must purchase one ticket per every two children.

➡ Most car-hire firms offer children's safety seats at a nominal cost, but these should be booked ahead.

Regions at a Glance

Naples, Pompeii & Around

Food
History
Museums

Pizza & Pasta

Naples' loud and lusty streets serve up some of the nation's most famous flavours: coffee, pizza, pasta, Vesuvian tomatoes, *sfogliatelle* (sweetened ricotta pastries), *babà* (rum-soaked sponge cake) and a panoply of seafood to be devoured every which way you can.

Ancient Sites

Neapolitans abide by the motto *carpe diem* (seize the day). All around them, at Pompeii, Ercolano, Pozzuoli, Baia and Cuma, they are reminded that life is short and unpredictable. Even beneath their feet lurk reminders of long-lost lives, from subterranean markets to macabre funerary frescoes.

Museums & Galleries

Naples explodes with art and antiquities, from colossal Roman statues at Museo Archeologico Nazionale to Caravaggio at Palazzo Reale di Capodimonte. Beyond them is a long list of lesser-known treasures, including Teatro San Carlo's own theatre museum, MeMus.

p36

The Islands

Spas
Landscapes
Food

Thermal Spas

Ischia's thermal springs have been soothing weary muscles since ancient times. Find a little zen at a bubbling beach, soak in an old Roman bath, then get yourself wrapped and pummelled at a sprawling spa resort.

Superlative Scenery

From Capri's vertiginous cliffs and electric-blue grotto to Ischia's luxe gardens and vine-clad hillsides to Procida's peeling, pastel villages, beauty defines the details in the Bay of Naples. So aim your camera and make the peeps back home turn a deeper shade of green.

Island Flavours

Whether you're enjoying *torta caprese* (almond and chocolate cake) on a Capri piazza, slow-cooked rabbit at a rustic Ischian trattoria or just-caught fish on a Procida beach, expect to make some long-lasting culinary memories.

p105

The Amalfi Coast

Scenery
Activities
Culture

Coastal Beauty

Cloud-scraping cliffs, terraced vineyards, tumbling fishing villages in mood-lifting hues, not to mention those obscenely turquoise Tyrrhenian waters – views come at you from all angles on Italy's most stunning and celebrated coastline.

Natural Wonders

Above, below or at sea level, active types are spoilt for choice. Whether you fancy swimming or diving in crystal-clear seas, cove-hopping on a sailing boat or escaping the hordes on a hiking trail high above the sea, the Amalfi Coast is guaranteed to keep your heart rate up.

Art & Architecture

Contemporary painting and sculpture in Positano, medieval cloisters in Amalfi, classical overtures in ravishing Ravello: beyond the gleaming yachts, crowded beaches and Gucci-clad eye candy awaits a small but precious string of cultural riches.

p140

Salerno & the Cilento

Ruins
Nature
Food

Hellenic Ruins

Long before the Romans staked their claim, Greek sandals stomped around this turf. Pay tribute to the power and elegance of Magna Graecia (Greater Greece) at the stoic temples of Paestum and the bucolic ruins of Velia.

Rugged Escapes

Deep, dark woods, exhilarating rapids and cathedral-like caves littered with evidence of early human history: the Parco Nazionale del Cilento e Vallo di Diano is one of the country's biggest, wildest natural playgrounds and the ultimate spot for a back-to-nature Campanian adventure.

A Bountiful Larder

Luscious buffalo-milk mozzarella and peppery olive oil, perfect artichokes and velvety white figs, glistening seafood and plump, rum-soaked pastries – Salerno and the Cilento aren't short on lauded regional edibles.

p176

On the Road

Naples, Pompeii & Around

POP 3.1 MILLION

Best Places to Eat

➡ L'Ebbrezza di Noè (p79)

➡ Eccellenze Campane (p76)

➡ President (p104)

➡ Pizzeria Starita (p80)

➡ La Taverna di Santa Chiara (p77)

Best Ancient Sites

➡ Ruins of Pompeii (p98)

➡ Ruins of Herculaneum (p94)

➡ Catacomba di San Gennaro (p66)

➡ Complesso Monumentale di San Lorenzo Maggiore (p48)

Why Go?

Italy's third-largest city is one of its oldest, most artistic and most delicious. Naples' *centro storico* (historic centre) is a Unesco World Heritage Site, its archaeological treasures are among the world's most impressive, and its swag of vainglorious palaces, castles and churches make Rome look positively provincial.

Then there's the food. Blessed with rich volcanic soils, a bountiful sea and centuries of culinary know-how, the Naples region is one of Italy's epicurean heavyweights, serving up the country's best pizza, pasta and coffee, and many of its most celebrated seafood dishes, street snacks and sweet treats. Certainly, Naples' urban sprawl can feel anarchic, tattered and unloved. But look beyond the grime and graffiti and you'll uncover a city of breathtaking frescoes, sculptures and panoramas, of unexpected elegance, of spontaneous conversations and profound humanity. Welcome to Italy's most unlikely masterpiece.

When to Go

➡ May is arguably the best month to visit Naples and the surrounding area. The days are generally warm and the city buzzes with a string of special events. Among these is Wine & The City, a two-week celebration of *vino*, food and the art of living, as well as Maggio dei Monumenti, a month-long festival packed with cultural offerings, from art exhibitions to themed walking tours.

➡ June and September are also good bets, with summery days tailor-made for sightseeing and enjoying Naples' inimitable street life.

➡ Most Neapolitans take their annual break in the searing heat of August, during which many of the city's restaurants and shops close for two to four weeks.

Naples, Pompeii & Around Highlights

1 Marvelling at human ingenuity in the **Cappella Sansevero** (p38).

2 Seeing how the ancients lived at **Pompeii** (p98).

3 Eyeing up classical interiors and erotica at the **Museo Archeologico Nazionale** (p51).

4 Demanding an encore at Italy's grandest opera house, the **Teatro San Carlo** (p83).

5 Dabbling with Caravaggio, Warhol and regal excess at the **Palazzo Reale di Capodimonte** (p65).

6 Exploring a subterranean otherworld at **Catacomba di San Gennaro** (p66).

7 Combining cloisters and carriages with romantic views at **Certosa e Museo di San Martino** (p63).

8 Snooping around millennia-old properties at **Herculaneum** (p94).

9 Mingling, toasting and flirting at bobo hang-out **Piazza Bellini** (p49).

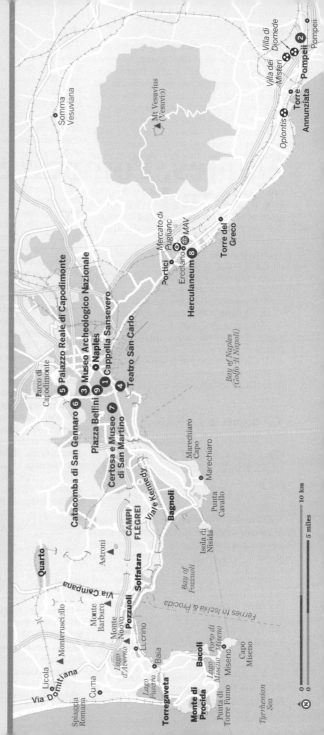

History

After founding nearby Cuma in the 8th century BC, the ancient Greeks settled the city in around 680 BC, calling it Parthenope. Under the Romans, the area became an ancient Miami of sorts: a sun-soaked spa region that drew the likes of Virgil. Dampening the bonhomie was Mt Vesuvius' eruption in AD 79.

Naples fell into Norman hands in 1139 before the French Angevins took control a century later, boosting the city's cred with the mighty Castel Nuovo. By the 16th century, Naples was under Spanish rule and riding high on Spain's colonial riches. By 1600, it was Europe's largest city and a burgeoning baroque beauty adorned by artists like Luca Giordano, Giuseppe de Ribera and Caravaggio.

Despite a devastating plague in 1656, Naples' ego soared under the Bourbons (1734–1860), with epic constructions such as the Teatro San Carlo and the Reggia di Caserta sealing the city's showcase reputation.

An ill-fated attempt at republican rule in 1799 was followed by a short stint under the French and a final period of Bourbon governance before nationalist rebel Giuseppe Garibaldi inspired the city to snip off the puppet strings and join a united Italy in 1860.

◉ Sights & Activities

◉ Centro Storico & Mercato

Secret cloisters, cultish shrines and bellowing *pizzaioli* (pizza makers): Naples' *centro storico* (historic centre) is a bewitching urban brew. Its three east–west *decumani* (main streets) follow the original street plan of ancient Neapolis. Most of the major sights are grouped around the busiest two of these classical thoroughfares: 'Spaccanapoli' (consisting of Via Benedetto Croce, Via San Biagio dei Librai and Via Vicaria Vecchia) and Via dei Tribunali. North of Via dei Tribunali, Via della Sapienza, Via Anticaglia and Via Santissimi Apostoli make up the quieter third *decumanus*.

Southeast of the *centro storico* lie the shabby, frenetic streets of the Mercato district, a fast and filthy mix of cheap hotels, Sri Lankan spice shops and rough-and-ready markets, including the lip-smacking Mercato di Porta Nolana.

★ **Cappella Sansevero** CHAPEL
(Map p40; ☑ 081 551 84 70; www.museosansevero.it; Via Francesco de Sanctis 19; adult/reduced €7/5; ◷ 9.30am-6.30pm Mon & Wed-Sat, to 2pm Sun; Ⓜ Dante) It's in this Masonic-inspired baroque chapel that you'll find Giuseppe Sanmartino's incredible sculpture *Cristo velato* (Veiled Christ), its marble veil so realistic that it's tempting to try to lift it and view Christ underneath. It's one of several artistic wonders that include Francesco Queirolo's sculpture *Disinganno* (Disillusion), Antonio Corradini's *Pudicizia* (Modesty) and riotously colourful frescoes by Francesco Maria Russo, the latter untouched since their creation in 1749.

Originally built around the end of the 16th century to house the tombs of the di Sangro family, the chapel was given its current baroque fit-out by Prince Raimondo di Sangro, who, between 1749 and 1766, commissioned the finest artists to adorn the interior. In Queirolo's *Disinganno*, the man trying to untangle himself from a net represents Raimondo's father, Antonio, Duke of Torremaggiore. After the premature death of his wife, Antonio abandoned the young Raimondo, choosing instead a life of travel and hedonistic pleasures. Repentant in his later years, he returned to Naples and joined the priesthood, his attempt to free himself from sin represented in Queirolo's masterpiece.

Even more poignant is Antonio Corradini's *Pudicizia,* whose veiled female figure pays tribute to Raimondo's mother, Cecilia Gaetani d'Aquila d'Aragona. Raimondo was only 11 months old when she died, and the statue's lost gaze and broken plaque represent a life cruelly cut short.

The chapel's original polychrome marble flooring was badly damaged in a major collapse involving the chapel and the neighbouring Palazzo dei di Sangro in 1889. Designed by Francesco Celebrano, the flooring survives in fragmentary form in the passageway leading off from the chapel's right side. The passageway leads to a staircase, at the bottom of which you'll find two meticulously preserved human arterial systems – one of a man, the other of a woman. Debate still circles the models: are the arterial systems real or reproductions? And if they are real, just how was such an incredible state of preservation achieved? More than two centuries on, the mystery surrounding the alchemist prince lives on.

Naples

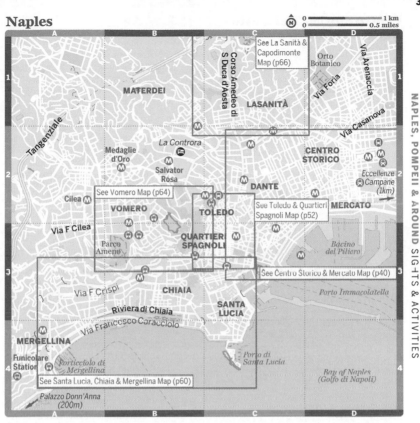

⭐ **Complesso Monumentale
di Santa Chiara** BASILICA, MONASTERY
(Map p40; ☎ 081 551 66 73; www.monasterodi
santachiara.eu; Via Santa Chiara 49c; basilica free,
Complesso Monumentale adult/reduced €6/4.50;
⊙ basilica 7.30am-1pm & 4.30-8pm, Complesso
Monumentale 9.30am-5.30pm Mon-Sat, 10am-
2.30pm Sun; Ⓜ Dante) Vast, Gothic and cleverly deceptive, the mighty **Basilica di Santa
Chiara** stands at the heart of this tranquil
monastery complex. The church was severe-
ly damaged in WWII. what you see today
is a 20th-century recreation of Gagliardo
Primario's 14th-century original. Adjoining
it are the basilica's **cloisters**, adorned with
brightly coloured 17th-century majolica tiles
and frescoes.

While the Angevin porticoes date back to
the 14th century, the cloisters took on their
current look in the 18th century thanks to
the landscaping work of Domenico Antonio Vaccaro. The walkways that divide the
central garden of lavender and citrus trees
are lined with 72 ceramic-tiled octagonal
columns connected by benches. Painted by
Donato e Giuseppe Massa, the tiles depict
various rural scenes, from hunting sessions
to vignettes of peasant life. The four internal walls are covered with soft, whimsical
17th-century frescoes of Franciscan tales.

Adjacent to the cloisters, a small and elegant **museum** of mostly ecclesiastical props
also features the excavated ruins of a 1st-cen-
tury spa complex, including a remarkably
well-preserved *laconicum* (sauna).

Commissioned by Robert of Anjou for his
wife Sancia di Maiorca, the monastic complex was built to house 200 monks and the
tombs of the Angevin royal family. Dissed as
a 'stable' by Robert's ungrateful son Charles
of Anjou, the basilica received a luscious
baroque makeover by Domenico Antonio
Vaccaro, Gaetano Buonocore and Giovanni
Del Gaizo in the 18th century before taking

Centro Storico & Mercato

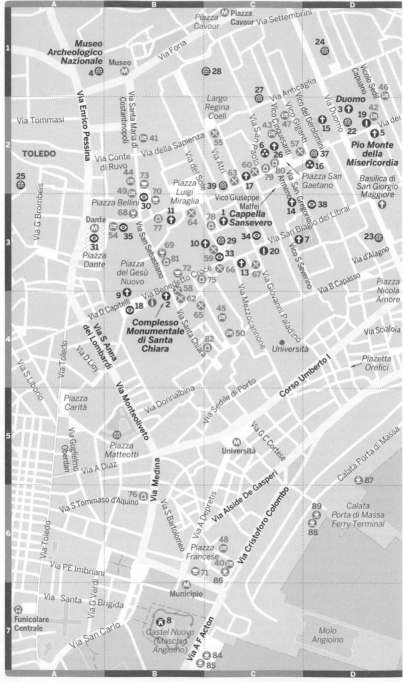

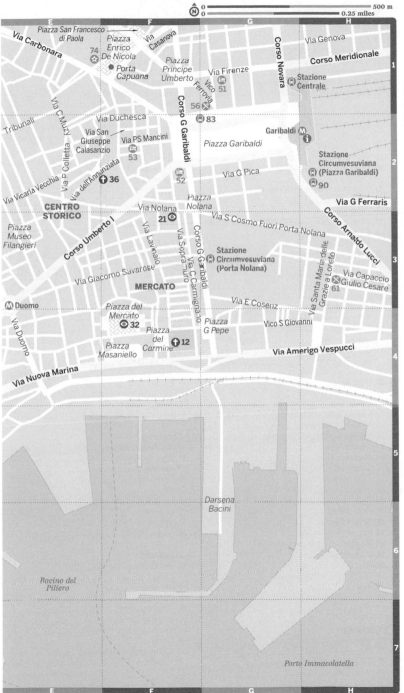

Centro Storico & Mercato

a direct hit during an Allied air raid on 4 August 1943. Its reconstruction was completed in 1953. Features that did survive the fire include part of a 14th-century fresco to the left of the main door and a chapel containing the tombs of the Bourbon kings from Ferdinand I to Francesco II.

Chiesa del Gesù Nuovo   CHURCH
(Map p40; ☑081 551 86 13; Piazza del Gesù Nuovo; ⏱7.15am-12.45pm & 4-8pm Mon-Sat, 7am-2pm & 4-9pm Sun; Ⓜ Dante) The extraordinary Chiesa del Gesù Nuovo is an architectural Kinder Surprise. Its shell is the Giuseppe Valeriani–designed, 15th-century facade of Palazzo Sanseverino, converted to create the 16th-century church. Inside, piperno-stone sobriety gives way to a gob-smacking blast of baroque that could make the Vatican blush: a vainglorious showcase for the work of top-tier artists such as Francesco Solimena, Luca Giordano and Cosimo Fanzago.

The church is the final resting place of much-loved local saint Giuseppe Moscati (1880–1927), a doctor who served the city's poor. Adjacent to the right transept, the Sale di San Giuseppe Moscati (Rooms of St Joseph Moscati) include a recreation of the great man's study, complete with the arm chair in which he died. Scan the walls for ex-votos, gifts offered by the faithful for miracles purportedly received.

The church flanks the northern side of beautiful Piazza del Gesù Nuovo, a favourite late-night hang-out for students and lefties. At its centre soars Giuseppe Genuino's lavish Guglia dell'Immacolata, an obelisk built between 1747 and 1750. On 8 December, the Feast of the Immaculate Conception, firemen scramble up to the top to place a wreath of flowers at the Virgin Mary's feet.

Piazza San Domenico Maggiore   PIAZZA
(Map p40; Piazza San Domenico Maggiore; Ⓜ Dante) Star of this operatic square is the 18th-century Guglia di San Domenico. The work of Cosimo Fanzago, Francesco Antonio Picchiatti and Domenico Antonio Vaccaro, the obelisk honours its namesake saint for stamping out the plague epidemic of 1656. Unfaithful Maria d'Avalos and her lover, Don Fabrizio, weren't quite as lucky – Palazzo dei Di Sangro is where Maria's jealous husband, Neapolitan musician Carlo Gesualdo, murdered the lovebirds in 1590.

Altogether more upbeat is the Gothic Chiesa di San Domenico Maggiore, whose curious nave flanks the piazza's northern edge. If you can see a face in the facade, you're not going crazy: it was an intentional add-on, created to jazz up the church's derrière after the piazza's creation.

Chiesa di San Domenico Maggiore   CHURCH
(Map p40; ☑081 45 91 88; Piazza San Domenico Maggiore 8a; ⏱8.30am-noon & 4-7pm Mon-Sat, 9am-1pm & 4.30-7.15pm Sun; Ⓜ Dante) Completed in 1324 on the orders of Charles I of Anjou, this was the royal church of the Angevins. Of the few 14th-century remnants surviving the church's countless revamps, the frescoes by Pietro Cavallini in the Cappella Brancaccio take the cake. The sacristy is also noteworthy, featuring a beautiful ceiling fresco by Francesco Solimena and 45 coffins of Aragon princes and other nobles.

In the Cappellone del Crocifisso, the 13th-century *Crocifisso tra La Vergine e San Giovanni* is said to have spoken to St Thomas Aquinas, asking him: '*Bene scripsisti di me, Thoma; quam recipies a me pro tu labore mercedem?*' (You've written good things about me, Thomas; what will you get in return?) – '*Domine, non aliam nisi te*' (Nothing if not you, O Lord), Thomas replied diplomatically. The first bishop of New York, Richard Luke Concanen (1747–1810), is also buried here.

Chiesa di Sant'Angelo a Nilo   CHURCH
(Map p40; ☑081 420 12 22; Vico Donnaromita 15; ⏱8.30am-1pm & 4.30-6.30pm Mon-Sat, 8.30am-1pm Sun; Ⓜ Dante) This modest 14th-century church houses one of the first great artworks to grace the Neapolitan Renaissance – the majestic tomb of Cardinal Brancaccio, the church's founder. Although considered a part of Naples' artistic heritage, the sarcophagus was actually sculpted in Pisa by Donatello, Michelozzo and Pagno di Lapo Partigiani. Taking a year to complete, the chiselled marvel was shipped to Naples in 1427.

Piazzetta Nilo   PIAZZA
(Map p40; Via Nilo; Ⓜ Dante) You'll stumble across two deities in this dusty little square. First is ancient-Egyptian river god Nilo: the marble Statua del Nilo was erected by Alexandrian merchants who lived in the area during Roman times. The sculpture mysteriously disappeared when the Egyptian expats moved out, turning up headless in the 15th century. Its recently restored bearded bonce was added in the 18th century.

Opposite the statue, Bar Nilo is home to a tongue-in-cheek shrine (Via San Biagio Dei Librai 129; ☉ 7.30am-8pm Mon-Sat, to 4.30pm Sun) to Argentine footballer and ex-Napoli deity Diego Maradona.

Stuck to an epic poem written in Maradona's honour is a small, wiry, black hair – 'Kapel Original of Maradona' reads the English label, a direct translation of the Italian *Capello originale di Maradona*. The small container is full of genuine Maradona tears...and shame on anyone who suggests it's only water. Note: you'll be expected to buy a coffee or drink in the bar.

Cappella del Monte di Pietà CHAPEL
(Map p40; ☑ 081 580 71 11; Via San Biagio dei Librai 114; 🚌 C55 to Via Duomo, Ⓜ Duomo) Closed indefinitely for restoration on our last visit, this imposing 16th-century complex was originally home to the Pio Monte di Pietà, an organisation set up to issue interest-free loans to impoverished debtors. Its most impressive asset is the perfectly preserved mannerist chapel and its four richly decorated side rooms. Flanking the entrance are two sculptures by Pietro Bernini, while above it sits Michelangelo Naccherino's *Pietà*. Inside, striking 17th-century frescoes by Belisario Corenzio take the breath away. Call for reopening updates.

Via San Gregorio Armeno STREET
(Map p40; 🚌 C55 to Via Duomo) Dismissed by serious collectors, this narrow street remains famous across Italy for its *pastori* (nativity crib figurines) nonetheless. Connecting Spaccanapoli with Via dei Tribunali, the *decumanus maior* (main road) of ancient Neapolis, its clutter of shops and workshops peddle everything from doting donkeys to kitsch celebrity caricatures. At No 8 you'll find the workshop of Giuseppe Ferrigno, whose terracotta figurines are the most famous and esteemed on the strip.

Chiesa e Chiostro di
San Gregorio Armeno CHURCH, CLOISTER
(Map p40; ☑ 081 420 63 85; Via San Gregorio Armeno 44; ☉ 9.30am-noon Mon-Fri, to 1pm Sat & Sun; 🚌 C55 to Via Duomo) Overstatement knows no bounds at this richly ornamented 16th-century monastic complex. The church packs a visual punch with its lavish wood and papier-mâché choir stalls, sumptuous altar by Dionisio Lazzari, and Luca Giordano's masterpiece fresco *The Embarkation, Journey and Arrival of the Armenia Nuns with the Relics of St Gregory*. Excess gives way to

soothing tranquillity in the picture-perfect cloisters, accessible through the gate on Vico Giuseppe Maffei.

Giordano's famous fresco recounts the 13th-century exile of nuns fleeing persecution in Constantinople. Once in Naples, the holy escapees set up this monastic complex, naming it after the Bishop of Armenia, San Gregorio, whose earthly remains they were carrying with them. More famously, though, they also kept the relics and dried blood of Santa Patrizia (St Patricia), who, having escaped from Constantinople, died in Naples sometime between the 4th and 8th centuries. Patricia's powdered blood is said to liquefy every Tuesday, unlike that of Naples' patron saint, San Gennaro, which can only manage it three times a year.

The cloisters feature a whimsical baroque fountain embellished with masks, dolphins and sea horses, and two exquisite statues portraying Christ and the Samaritan by Matteo Bottigliero. At the southern end is the convent's old bakery, which is still hung with cooking utensils. Close by is the Cappella della Madonna dell'Idria. Adorned with paintings by baroque artist Paolo De Matteis, the chapel is the only remnant of the original medieval convent.

From the cloisters you can enter the beautifully decorated *coro delle monache* (nuns' choir stall), which looks down on the church nave and altar. If you're lucky, you might catch a glimpse of the choir's 612-year-old wooden nativity scene, usually hidden away in a cabinet on the southern wall. Either way, take note of the discreet windows lining the oval cupola above the choir stall. These belong to a secret second choir stall, hidden so that even ill, bed-ridden nuns could attend mass.

Museo di Filangieri MUSEUM
(Map p40; ☑ 081 20 31 75; www.salviamoilmuseofilangieri.org; Via Duomo 288; admission €5; ☉ 9am-6pm Tue-Sat; 🚌 C55 to Via Duomo, Ⓜ Duomo) The kooky Filangieri Museum houses everything from Asian and European armour to ancient pottery and sumptuous paintings spanning the 15th to the 19th centuries. Much of the collection belonged to 19th-century prince Gaetano Filangieri, whose private, walnut-panelled *biblioteca* (library) afforded him commanding views of the newly restored Sala Agata (Agatha Hall). The hall is home to much of the collection, while the ground floor is used for cultural events, including classical-music concerts.

THREE PERFECT DAYS

Day 1: Cloisters, Classics & Camparis

Start with a burst of colour in the cloister of the **Basilica di Santa Chiara** (p39), be rendered speechless by Giuseppe Sanmartino's *Cristo velato* (Veiled Christ) in the **Cappella Sansevero** (p38), and wander Roman ruins under a Gothic beauty at **Complesso Monumentale di San Lorenzo Maggiore** (p48). Make a pit stop at **Di Matteo** (p77) for bubbling pizza or golden street food before musing over a Caravaggio masterpiece at **Pio Monte della Misericordia** (p45) and relishing Lanfranco's dome fresco at the **Duomo** (p45). That done, travel even further back in time at the **Museo Archeologico Nazionale** (p51). Round off the day with regional specialities at **La Taverna di Santa Chiara** (p77), followed by late-night drinks on **Piazza Bellini** (p49).

Day 2: Produce, Masterpieces & Seaside Dolce Vita

Pique the appetite with an early-morning stroll through **La Pignasecca** (p54) before swooning over art and interiors at **Palazzo Reale di Capodimonte** (p65) or the **Certosa e Museo di San Martino** (p63). Either way, head down to the shore in the afternoon, lunching boatside at **Trattoria Castel dell'Ovo** (p79) and taking in the views from a castle rooftop at neighbouring **Castel dell'Ovo** (p61). From here, it's an easy walk to Chiaia's chichi boutiques. Wardrobe revamped, sip and mingle with a local Falanghina at **Enoteca Belledonne** (p81) before dinner at **L'Ebbrezza di Noè** (p79), **L'Altro Loco** (p79) or the more casual **Muu Muzzarella Lounge** (p78).

Day 3: Volcanic Views & Victims

Head into the suburbs and up **Mt Vesuvius** (p98) for dizzying views and a face-to-face with its deceptively peaceful crater. Back down the slope, walk the ghostly streets of ancient **Pompeii** (p98) or **Herculaneum** (p94) before heading back to town in time for a (pre-booked) performance at the **Teatro San Carlo** (p83).

Among the collection highlights are Luca della Robbia's delicate sculpture *Testa di fanciullo imberbe* (Head of a Beardless Boy), Adriaen Hendricx van Ostade's humourous painting *Interno di taverna* (Inside a Tavern), and Giuseppe de Ribera's deeply psychological canvas *Santa Maria Egiziaca* (St Mary of Egypt).

The *palazzo* itself dates back to the late 15th century, its design heavily influenced by the architecture of Renaissance Florence. Incredibly, the widening of Via Duomo in the 1880s saw the building demolished and reassembled 20m further back.

★ **Pio Monte della Misericordia** CHURCH, MUSEUM
(Map p40; ☎081 44 69 44; www.piomontedella-misericordia.it; Via dei Tribunali 253; adult/reduced €7/5; ◷9am-2pm Thu-Tue; 🚌C55 to Via Duomo) The 1st floor of this octagonal, 17th-century church delivers a small, satisfying collection of Renaissance and baroque art, including works by Francesco de Mura, Giuseppe de Ribera, Andrea Vaccaro and Paul van Somer. It's also home to contemporary artworks by Italian and foreign artists, each inspired by

Caravaggio's masterpiece *Le Sette Opere di Misericordia* (The Seven Acts of Mercy). Considered by many to be the most important painting in Naples, you'll find it above the main altar in the ground-floor chapel.

Magnificently demonstrating the artist's chiaroscuro style, which had a revolutionary impact in Naples, *Le Sette Opere di Misericordia* was considered unique in its ability to illustrate the various acts in one seamlessly choreographed scene. On display in the 1st-floor gallery is the *Declaratoria del 14 Ottobre 1607*, an original church document acknowledging payment of 400 ducats to Caravaggio for the masterpiece.

On the opposite side of the street stands the Guglia di San Gennaro (Piazza Riario Sforza). Dating back to 1636, with stonework by Cosimo Fanzago and a bronze statue by Tommaso Montani, the obelisk is a soaring *grazie* (thank you) to the city's patron saint for protecting Naples from the 1631 eruption of Mt Vesuvius.

★ **Duomo** CATHEDRAL
(Map p40; ☎081 44 90 65; Via Duomo 149; baptistry €1.50; ◷cathedral 8.30am-1.30pm &

2.30-8pm Mon-Sat, 8.30am-1.30pm & 4.30-7.30pm Sun, baptistry 8.30am-1pm Mon-Sat, 8.30am-12.30pm & 5-6.30pm Sun; 🚍C55 to Via Duomo) Whether you go for Giovanni Lanfranco's fresco in the Cappella di San Gennaro (Chapel of St Janarius), the 4th-century mosaics in the baptistry, or the thrice-annual miracle of San Gennaro, do not miss Naples' cathedral. Kick-started by Charles I of Anjou in 1272 and consecrated in 1315, it was largely destroyed in a 1456 earthquake, with copious nips and tucks over the subsequent centuries.

Among these is the gleaming neo-Gothic facade, only added in the late 19th century. Step inside and you'll immediately notice the central nave's gilded coffered ceiling, studded with late-mannerist art. The high sections of the nave and the transept are the work of baroque overachiever Luca Giordano.

Off the right aisle, the 17th-century Cappella di San Gennaro (also known as Chapel of the Treasury) was designed by Giovanni Cola di Franco and completed in 1637. The most sought-after artists of the period worked on the chapel, creating one of Naples' greatest baroque legacies. Highlights here include Giuseppe de Ribera's gripping canvas *St Gennaro Escaping the Furnace Unscathed* and Giovanni Lanfranco's dizzying dome fresco. Hidden away in a strongbox behind the altar is a 14th-century silver bust in which sits the skull of San Gennaro and the two phials that hold his miraculously liquefying blood.

The next chapel eastwards contains an urn with the saint's bones and a cupboard full of femurs, tibias and fibulas. Below the high altar is the Cappella Carafa, a Renaissance chapel built to house yet more of the saint's remains.

Off the left aisle lies the 4th-century Basilica di Santa Restituta, subject to an almost complete makeover after the earthquake of 1688. From it you can access the Battistero di San Giovanni in Fonte. Western Europe's oldest baptistry, it's encrusted with fragments of glittering 4th-century mosaics. Alas, the Duomo's subterranean archaeological zone, which includes fascinating remains of Greek and Roman buildings and roads, remains closed indefinitely.

Museo del Tesoro di San Gennaro   MUSEUM
(Map p40; ☑ 081 29 49 80; www.museosangennaro.it; Via Duomo 149; admission €5; ☺ 9am-6pm Easter–mid-Jan, reduced hours rest of year; 🚍C55

to Via Duomo) If you're intrigued by Naples' cultish love affair with San Gennaro, eye up his glittering treasury at the Museo del Tesoro di San Gennaro, adjacent to the Duomo. Gifts made to Naples' patron saint include ambitious bronze busts, silver ampullae, and even a gilded 18th-century sedan chair used to transport his bust on rainy procession days. The star attraction, however, is Matteo Treglia's extraordinary 18th-century mitre, adorned with 3694 gems: 3328 diamonds, 198 emeralds and 168 rubies.

Upstairs, the Sacristia dell'Immacolata (Sacristy of the Immaculate Conception) shines with 17th-century frescoes by Luca Giordano and Giacomo Farelli. The frescoes in the adjoining Antesacrestia are the work of Francesco Maria Russo, their solid hues reminiscent of his more famous work inside Naples' Cappella Sansevero. Luca Giordano makes another appearance in the adjoining Sacrestia Nuova (New Sacristy), his signed ceiling fresco one of the few works the artist began *and* completed alone.

Complesso Monumentale
dei Girolamini   CHURCH, GALLERY
(Map p40; ☑ 333 4338049; Via Duomo 142; adult/reduced €5/2.50; ☺ 8.30am-7pm Mon, Tue, Thu & Fri, to 2pm Sat & Sun; 🚍C55 to Via Duomo) The Chiesa dei Girolamini features two facades, the more imposing of which is the 18th-century one facing Piazza dei Girolamini on Via dei Tribunali. Inside, disrepair is redeemed by numerous baroque delights, among them frescoes by Francesco Solimena and a pair of monumental marble angels by 18th-century sculptor Giuseppe Sanmartino, considered his finest works beyond his *Cristo velato* (Veiled Christ). The adjacent 17th-century convent features two beautiful cloisters and a small gallery with 16th- to 18th-century works by Neapolitan masters. The sprawling 16th-century complex is also home to the Biblioteca dei Girolamini (Girolamini Library). Dating back to 1586, it's the oldest library in Naples and the second-oldest in Italy. In 2013, the library made world headlines after its director, Marino Massimo De Caro, was indicted for looting its rare, precious collection of books. The library is currently closed to the public.

Museo Diocesano di Napoli   MUSEUM
(Map p40; ☑ 081 557 13 65; www.museodiocesanonapoli.it; Chiesa di Santa Maria Donnaregina Nuova, Largo Donnaregina; adult/reduced €6/4; ☺ 9.30am-4.30pm Mon & Wed-Sat, 9.30am-2pm

LOCAL KNOWLEDGE

BANKSY, STREET ART & NAPLES

The obvious drawcard on Via dei Tribunali's Piazza dei Girolamini may be its namesake baroque church (p46), but scan the wall of the building to the right and you'll discover an altogether more contemporary attraction: a stencil of the Madonna under a pistol. Typically Neapolitan in its intermingling of the sacred and the profane, the easily missed work is by celebrated street artist Banksy. The British artist's second work in Naples – an interpretation of Bernini's St Teresa with a McDonald's meal and Coca-Cola on her lap – was destroyed by a less talented graffiti writer in 2010.

Banksy's Madonna is one of many engaging, whimsical and downright provocative street-art creations in the city, whose homegrown talent includes the duo cyop&kaf (www.cyopekaf.org), Diego Miedo (www.diegomiedo.org) and Felice Pignataro (www.felicepignataro.org). If you're itching to explore the local scene, consider booking a three-hour walking tour of the city's kerbside creativity with **Napoli Paint Stories** (⏲333 1589423; napolipaintstories@gmail.com; per person €8; ⊙ varies, usually Sat & Sun). Usually run on weekends, the tours can be arranged in English by emailing in advance. For more information, check Napoli Paint Stories' Facebook page.

Sun; Ⓜ Piazza Cavour) What was once a baroque place of prayer is now a repository for religious paintings, triptychs and sculptures, many hailing from defunct churches. Notable works include Luca Giordano's final canvases (either side of the main altar), Paolo De Matteis' *St Sebastian Healed by St Irene*, and a young Francesco Solimena's fresco *The Miracle of the Roses of St Francis*, in the Coro delle Monache (Nuns' Choir). Accessed from the museum, the Gothic **Chiesa di Donnaregina Vecchia** houses Naples' largest cycle of 14th-century frescoes.

Attributed to various artists, including Pietro Cavallini and Filippo Rusuti, the frescoes line the walls of Donnaregina Vecchia's Nuns' Choir. Particularly striking are the technicolour scenes depicting the Martyrdom of St Ursula along the back wall. If you can peel your eyes off, look up to appreciate Pietro Belverte's early 16th-century coffered ceiling. Downstairs, a small, marble-clad cloister offers a clear view of Donnaregina Vecchia's original Gothic facade, while back inside the church, the austere Gothic nave is home to the mosaicked tomb of Mary of Hungary (c 1257–1323), a 14th-century masterpiece attributed to Tino di Camaino and Gagliardo Primario. Directly opposite the tomb, the Cappella Loffredo features fragments of vivid early 14th-century frescoes, including a wince-inducing scene of St John enduring a dip in boiling oil.

Classical-music concerts are occasionally held inside Donnaregina Nuova. Check the museum website or local press for upcoming events. Buy concert tickets at the venue.

MADRE
GALLERY

(Museo d'Arte Contemporanea Donnaregina; Map p66; ⏲081 1931 3016; www.madrenapoli.it; Via Settembrini 79; adult/reduced €7/3.50, Mon free; ⊙10am-7.30pm Mon & Wed-Sat, to 8pm Sun; Ⓜ Piazza Cavour) When *Madonna and Child* overload hits, reboot at Naples' museum of modern and contemporary art. Start on level three – the setting for temporary exhibitions – before hitting level two's permanent collection of painting, sculpture and installations from prolific 20th- and 21st-century artists. Among these are Olafur Eliasson, Shirin Neshat and Julian Beck, as well as Italian heavyweights Mario Merz and Michelangelo Pistoletto. Specially commissioned installations from the likes of Francesco Clemente, Anish Kapoor and Rebecca Horn cap things off on level one.

MADRE hosts a number of special events, including occasional DJ sets and parties. Check the museum's Facebook page (in Italian) for updates.

T293
GALLERY

(Map p40; ⏲081 29 58 82; www.t293.it; Via dei Tribunali 293; ⊙noon-7pm Mon-Fri; ⌕C55 to Via Duomo) Sneaky T293 is a fantastic surprise for fans of contemporary art. Hidden away up an anonymous stairwell, it has a knack for thought-provoking shows. Some past exhibitions have included painting, sculpture and installation art from some of the world's most exciting artists, among them Henrik Olai Kaarstein, Helen Marten and Martin Soto Climent. Check the website for exhibition details.

**Complesso Monumentale
di San Lorenzo Maggiore** ARCHAEOLOGICAL SITE
(Map p40; ☑ 081 211 08 60; www.sanlorenzomaggiorenapoli.it; Via dei Tribunali 316; church admission free, excavations & museum adult/reduced €9/7; ☺ 9.30am-5.30pm; ⬚ C55 to Via Duomo) Architecture and history buffs shouldn't miss this richly layered religious complex, its commanding basilica deemed one of Naples' finest medieval buildings. Aside from Ferdinando Sanfelice's petite facade, the Cappella al Rosario and the Cappellone di Sant'Antonio, its baroque makeover was stripped away last century to reveal its austere, Gothic elegance. Beneath the basilica, a sprawl of extraordinary ruins will transport you back two millennia.

Down here you can conjure up the Graeco-Roman city as you walk past ancient bakeries, wineries and communal laundries. At the far end of the *cardo* (road) are seven barrel-vaulted rooms that once formed part of a covered market.

The basilica itself was commenced in 1270 by French architects, who built the apse. Local architects took over the following century, recycling ancient columns in the nave. Catherine of Austria, who died in 1323, is buried here in a beautiful mosaicked tomb. Legend has it that this was where Boccaccio first fell for Mary of Anjou, the inspiration for his character Fiammetta, while the poet Petrarch called the

---

ℹ SIGHTSEE FOR LESS

If you're planning to blitz the sights, the Campania artecard (☑ 800 60 06 01; www.campaniartecard.it) is an excellent investment. A cumulative ticket that covers museum admission and transport, it comes in various forms. The Naples three-day ticket (adult/reduced €21/12) gives free admission to three participating sites, a 50% discount at others and free use of public transport in the city. Other handy options include a seven-day 'Tutta la Regione' ticket (€34), which offers free admission to five sites and discounted admission to others in areas as far afield as Caserta, Ravello (Amalfi Coast) and Paestum. The latter does not cover transport. Cards can be purchased online, at the dedicated artecard booth inside the tourist office at Stazione Centrale or at participating sites and museums.

---

adjoining convent home in 1345. The religious complex is also home to the Museo dell'Opera di San Lorenzo Maggiore and its intriguing booty of local archaeological finds, including Graeco-Roman sarcophagi, ceramics and crockery from the digs below. Other treasures include vivacious 9th-century ceramics, Angevin frescoes, paintings by Giuseppe Marullo and Luigi Velpi, and fine examples of 17th- and 18th-century ecclesiastical vestments.

Basilica di San Paolo Maggiore CHURCH
(Map p40; ☑ 081 45 40 48; Piazza San Gaetano 76; ☺ 9am-5.45pm Mon-Sat; ⬚ C55 to Via Duomo) Despite dating to the 8th century, this glorious basilica was almost entirely rebuilt at the end of the 16th century. Its huge, gold-stuccoed interior features paintings by Massimo Stanzione and Paolo De Matteis and a striking geometric floor by Nicola Tammaro. Top billing, however, goes to the sumptuous sacristy, lavished with luminous frescoes by baroque-meister Francesco Solimena. Built in 1603, the double staircase adorning the basilica's main facade is the work of Francesco Grimaldi. Much older are the two columns flanking the entrance, taken from the Roman temple to Castor and Pollux that stood on the site.

Napoli Sotterranea ARCHAEOLOGICAL SITE
(Underground Naples; Map p40; ☑ 081 29 69 44; www.napolisotterranea.org; Piazza San Gaetano 68; adult/reduced €10/8; ☺ English tours 10am, noon, 2pm, 4pm & 6pm; ⬚ C55 to Via Duomo) This evocative guided tour leads you 40m below street level to explore Naples' ancient labyrinth of aqueducts, passages and cisterns.

The passages were originally hewn by the Greeks to extract tufa stone used in construction and to channel water from Mt Vesuvius. Extended by the Romans, the network of conduits and cisterns was more recently used as an air-raid shelter in WWII. Part of the tour takes place by candlelight via extremely narrow passages – not suitable for expanded girths!

**Complesso Museale di Santa Maria delle
Anime del Purgatorio ad Arco** CHURCH
(Map p40; ☑ 081 21 19 29; www.purgatorioadarco. it; Via dei Tribunali 39; guided tours adult/reduced €4/3; ☺ guided tours every 30min 10.30am-1pm Mon-Fri, 10am-5pm Sat; Ⓜ Dante) Consecrated in 1638, the engrossing *chiesa delle cape*

di morte (church of the skulls) sits on two levels. While the upper church boasts fine paintings – nominally Luca Giordano's *The Death of St Alessio* and Massimo Stanzione's *Virgin with the Souls of Purgatory* – the lower church (only accessible by guided tour) is most famous as a hot spot for the cult-like worship of the *anime pezzentelle* (poor souls).

Between the 17th and early 19th centuries, the large, nameless grave at the centre of the lower church received the remains of countless locals who could not afford to be buried in the church. Heaving with anonymous bones, the hypogeum became an epicentre for the cult of the *anime pezzentelle,* in which followers adopted skulls and prayed for souls. It was hoped that once the souls reached heaven, they would offer graces and blessings as gratitude. Up to 60 masses were held here each day, and on All Souls' Day, queues leading into the underground vault would reach the Duomo, 450m away. Although burials on this site ceased soon after the declaration of the Edict of Saint-Cloud (a Napoleonic order banning burials within the city's borders), the wall shrines remained. The most famous of these belongs to 'Lucia' – a tiara-crowned skull named for a neon sign left at her shrine. According to legend, the skull was that of an 18th-century teenage bride, whose tragic death from tuberculosis saw her become the unofficial protector of young brides. To this day, you will find gifts of jewellery and bridal bouquets at her shrine, left by those who still believe in the cult.

The guided tour also takes in the upper church's sacristy, home to a small but beautiful collection of devotional art and ecclesiastical robes. The church is sometimes used for evening cultural events – check the website to see what might be in the wings.

Chiesa di San Pietro a Maiella   CHURCH
(Map p40; ☑ 081 45 90 08; Piazza Luigi Miraglia 25; ⊗ 8.45am-1pm Mon-Sat, 10.30am-noon Sun; ⓜ Dante) Dedicated to hermit Pietro del Morrone, who was promoted to Pope Celestine V in 1294, this church delivers a yin-and-yang combo of Gothic restraint and baroque exuberance. The chapel to the left of the presbytery features 14th-century frescoes by Giovanni Barrile, while the nave is capped by 10 superlative ceiling paintings by baroque artist Mattia Preti.

Further baroque touches are provided by Cosimo Fanzago, designer of the marble altar, polychromatic balustrade and transept flooring, as well as Massimo Stanzione, whose *Madonna Appearing to Celestine V* hangs in one of the side chapels on the right. The Conservatorio di Musica San Pietro a Majella di Napoli – one of Italy's finest music schools – occupies the adjoining convent.

Port'Alba   GATE
(Map p40; Via Port'Alba; ⓜ Dante) A Mediterranean Diagon Alley, Port'Alba is an atmospheric porthole into the *centro storico,* best experienced on weekday afternoons. Crammed with bookshops and stalls, it's the place for leather-bound classics, a dog-eared Manzoni or retro postcards and magazines. The gate, which leads through to Piazza Dante, was opened in 1625 by Antonio Alvárez, the Spanish viceroy of Naples.

At the eastern end of Via Port'Alba, southbound Via San Sebastiano is famous for its concentration of musical-instrument shops.

Piazza Bellini   PIAZZA
(Map p40; ⓜ Dante) One of the best spots to chill with a *spritz* is this free-spirited, bar-lined square. Featuring excavated ruins from the city's 4th-century Greek city walls, it's the classic go-to for bohemians and best experienced in the evening when it heaves with uni students, left-leaning crowds and a healthy dose of flirtatious glances. Generally speaking, bars at the western end of the square attract the bulk of locals, while those on the eastern side draw the out-of-town crowds.

Ospedale degli Incurabili   HISTORIC BUILDING
(Map p40; ☑ 081 44 06 47, 339 5446243; info@ ilfarodippocrate.it; Via Maria Longo 50; pharmacy tour €10; ⊗ pharmacy tour Sat mornings by appointment only, Orto Medico & Chiostro Santa Maria delle Grazie 9am-5pm; ⓜ Piazza Cavour, Museo) It's at this 16th-century hospital and monastic complex that you'll find the **Museo delle Arti Sanitarie** (Museum of the History of Medicine & Health; admission free, donation appreciated; ⊗ 9.30am-1.30pm Mon-Fri), a small museum packed with rare, historical surgical instruments, among them an 18th-century defibrillator, a portable pharmacy kit adorned with painted Roman landscapes, and an original *flagello della peste,* a beak-like wooden mask worn during the city's plagues. It's also here that you can book a guided tour of the neighbouring Farmacia Storica degli Incurabili, a breathtaking 18th-century apothecary.

Tours of the *farmacia* run on Saturday morning and can be booked online or by calling the museum (request an English-speaking guide). Divided into a glorious reception hall and a laboratory, the apothecary's lavish walnut shelves are lined with decorative majolica vases, while Pietro Bardellino's epic ceiling painting portrays an episode from Homer's *Illiad,* in which Machaon is curing the wounded Menelaus. A more unusual feature of the reception hall is a rococo inlay portraying an allegory of caesarean birth.

Some of Naples' finest baroque architects and artists worked on the apothecary: Domenico Antonio Vaccaro styled the facade, Bartolomeo Vecchione designed the interior, and Gennaro di Fiore engraved the shelves, the latter also collaborating with Carlo Vanvitelli at the Reggia di Caserta (p74). The majolica vases were painted by Lorenzo Salandra and Donato Massa (whose most famous tilework is found in the cloister of the Basilica di Santa Chiara; p39). Not surprisingly, the pharmacy is widely considered one of the city's finest examples of early 18th-century craftsmanship.

Both the museum and *farmacia* face the Cortile degli Incurabili (Courtyard of the Incurables), from which stairs lead up to the

ART IN TRANSIT

Underground art means just that in Naples, with many of the city's metro stations designed or decorated by top-tier artists, both homegrown and foreign. You'll find Mario Merz' blue neon digits at Vanvitelli; a witty Fiat installation by Perino & Vele at Salvator Rosa; and technicolour wall drawings by Sol LeWitt at Materdei. And that's before we mention the snapshots by heavyweight Italian photographers at Museo or Jannis Kounellis' eerie shoe installation at Dante.

Most of the city's 'Art Stations' are on the recently extended Line 1. Among the most striking is Università, brainchild of Egyptian-born industrial-designer Karim Rashid. True to Rashid's style, the station is a playful, candy-coloured ode to the digital age. White tiles clad the station entrance, each one printed with a word originating in the last century. In the station itself you'll find lenticular icons that change perspective and colour, a sculpture reflecting the nodes and synapses of the brain, platform steps decorated with abstracted portraits of Dante and Beatrice, even platform walls adorned with glowing, 'animated' artwork (stare persistently).

Even more breathtaking is Toledo station. Topping a CNN list of Europe's most impressive metro stations in 2014, its lobby features ruins from an Aragonese fortress and a spectacular wall mosaic by conceptual artist William Kentridge. Depicted in the latter is a medley of Neapolitan icons, from San Gennaro and a *pizzaiolo* (pizza maker) to the Museo Archeologico Nazionale's famous *Farnese Atlante* sculpture. Another Kentridge mural hovers above the escalators (it's said that the cat represents the artist himself). Toledo station reaches a depth of 50m below sea level, a fact not lost on the station's colour scheme, which goes from ochre (representing Naples' iconic tufa stone) to a dazzling blue as you descend the escalators. It's here, 'below the sea', that you'll find a spectacular mosaic porthole, streaming down light from the sky above. The porthole's light installation is by artist Robert Wilson, whose concourse 'Light Panels' ripple as you hurry past them.

Designed by architects Alvaro Siza and Eduardo Souto De Mura, Municipio station (opened in 2015) comes with its own museum space, home to some of the 3000 artefacts unearthed during the station's construction. Among the astounding finds are remnants of the city's ancient Greek and Roman ports, as well as Roman vessels. The base of a 14th-century Angevin tower – the Torre dell'Incoronata – is showcased in the station's concourse, beside a specially commissioned installation by Israeli artist Michal Rovner. The ancient and the cutting-edge also collide at Duomo station, where a street-level glass-and-steel bubble designed by Italian starchitect Massimiliano Fuksas sheds light on a Roman temple used for the Isolympic Augustan Roman Italic Games, a local version of Greece's ancient Olympics.

For more information on Naples' art stations, download the free PDF information sheets on the ANM (www.anm.it) website; click on the Metro Art/Le Stazioni dell'Arte link. Either way, grab a metro ticket, head underground and get inspired.

main hospital building. Enter it to access the wonderful Orto Medico (Medical Garden), lovingly adorned with medicinal plants and herbs. At its centre is a small fountain and a beautiful 400-year-old camphor tree. Walk a little further on and you'll stumble upon the smaller Chiostro Santa Maria delle Grazie, its lush tropical foliage framed by a frescoed, vaulted portico.

Mercato di Porta Nolana
MARKET

(Map p40; Porta Nolana; ☺8am-6pm Mon-Sat, to 2pm Sun; Ⓜ Garibaldi) Naples at its most vociferous and intense, the Mercato di Porta Nolana is a heady, gritty street market where bellowing fishmongers and greengrocers collide with fragrant delis and bakeries, industrious Chinese traders and contraband cigarette stalls. Dive in for anything from buxom tomatoes and mozzarella to golden-fried street snacks, cheap luggage and bootleg CDs. The market's namesake is medieval city gate Porta Nolana, which stands at the head of Via Sopramuro. Its two cylindrical towers, optimistically named Faith and Hope, support an arch decorated with a bas-relief of Ferdinand I of Aragon on horseback.

Chiesa di Santa Maria del Carmine
CHURCH

(Map p40; ☏081 20 11 96; Piazza del Carmine; ☺6.30am-noon Mon, Tue & Thu-Sat, to 1.30pm Wed, to 2pm Sun; ☐151, 154, ☐1, 4 to Via Nuova Marina) Its 17th-century *campanile* (bell tower) is Naples' tallest, and this iconic church is home to a famously nimble crucifix. Now hanging in a tabernacle beneath the church's main arch, the cross reputedly dodged a cannonball fired at the church in 1439 during the war between Alfonso of Aragon and Robert of Anjou. Equally miraculous is the 13th-century Byzantine icon of the *Madonna della Bruna,* held behind the main altar, and famously celebrated with fireworks each 16 July.

Indeed, the much-loved Chiesa di Santa Maria del Carmine is shrouded in legend. According to Neapolitan folklore, when Conrad (Corradino) of Swabia was charged with attempting to depose Charles I of Anjou in 1268, his mother, Elisabetta di Baviera, desperately tried to collect the money required to free her son. Alas, the money arrived too late, Conrad lost his head and his grief-stricken mamma handed the cash to the church (on the condition that the Carmelite brothers prayed for him every day). They agreed, the church went up and a monument to Conrad remains in the transept.

Just northwest of the church and Piazza del Carmine, the Piazza del Mercato has an even more macabre past. The starting point for the deadly plague of 1656, it was here that over 200 supporters of the ill-fated Parthenopean Republic of 1799 were systematically executed.

◉ Toledo & Quartieri Spagnoli

Constructed by Spanish viceroy Don Pedro de Toledo in the 16th century, *palazzo*-flanked Via Toledo (also known as Via Roma) is Naples' veritable high street and a popular strip for an evening *passeggiata* (stroll). With ever-busy Piazza Trento e Trieste at its southern end, it becomes Via Enrico Pessina further north, skimming past Piazza Dante and the Museo Archeologico Nazionale on its way towards lofty Capodimonte.

Directly west of Via Toledo lie the razor-thin streets of the Quartieri Spagnoli (Spanish Quarter), originally built to house Don Pedro's Spanish troops. Low on actual sights, its washing-strung streets harbour a handful of hidden delights, from cut-price drinking holes to the unmissable Pignasecca market. Squeeze in for a serve of pure *Napoli popolana* (working-class Naples).

★ Museo Archeologico Nazionale
MUSEUM

(Map p40; ☏081 442 21 49; http://cir.campania.beniculturali.it/museoarcheologiconazionale; Piazza Museo Nazionale 19; adult/reduced €8/4; ☺9am-7.30pm Wed-Mon; Ⓜ Museo, Piazza Cavour) Naples' National Archaeological Museum serves up one of the world's finest collections of Graeco-Roman artefacts. Originally a cavalry barracks and later seat of the city's university, the museum was established by the Bourbon king Charles VII in the late 18th century to house the antiquities he inherited from his mother, Elisabetta Farnese, as well as treasures looted from Pompeii and Herculaneum. Star exhibits include the celebrated *Toro Farnese* (Farnese Bull) sculpture and a series of awe-inspiring mosaics from Pompeii's Casa del Fauno.

Before tackling the collection, consider investing in the *National Archaeological Museum of Naples* (€12), published by Electa; if you want to concentrate on the highlights, audioguides (€5) are available in English. It's also worth calling ahead to ensure that the galleries you want to see are open, as staff shortages often mean that sections of the museum close for part of the day.

The basement houses the Borgia collection of Egyptian relics and epigraphs (closed indefinitely on our last visit). The ground-floor **Farnese collection** of colossal Greek and Roman sculptures features the *Toro Farnese* and a muscle-bound *Ercole* (Hercules). Sculpted in the early 3rd century AD and noted in the writings of Pliny, the *Toro Farnese,* probably a Roman copy of a Greek original, depicts the humiliating death of Dirce, Queen of Thebes. Carved from a single colossal block of marble, the sculpture was discovered in 1545 near the Baths of Caracalla in Rome and was restored by Michelangelo, before eventually being shipped to Naples in 1787. *Ercole* was discovered in the same Roman excavations, albeit without his legs. When they turned up at a later dig, the Bourbons had them fitted.

If you're short on time, take in both these masterpieces before heading straight to the mezzanine floor, home to an exquisite collection of **mosaics**, mostly from Pompeii. Of the series taken from the Casa del Fauno, it is *La battaglia di Alessandro contro Dario* (The Battle of Alexander against Darius) that really stands out. The best-known depiction of Alexander the Great, the 20-sq-metre mosaic was probably made by Alexandrian

Toledo & Quartieri Spagnoli

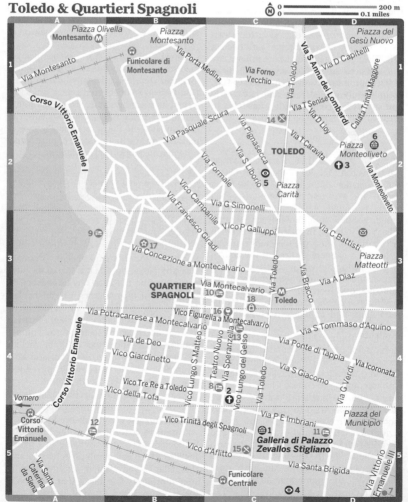

craftsmen working in Italy around the end of the 2nd century BC.

Beyond the mosaics, the **Gabinetto Segreto** (Secret Chamber) contains a small but much-studied collection of ancient erotica. Pan is caught in the act with a nanny goat in the collection's most famous piece – a small and surprisingly sophisticated statue taken from the Villa dei Papiri in Herculaneum. You'll also find a series of nine paintings depicting erotic positions – a menu for brothel patrons. Originally the royal library, the enormous **Sala Meridiana** (Great Hall of the Sundial) on the 1st floor is home to the *Farnese Atlante*, a statue of Atlas carrying a globe on his shoulders, as well as various paintings from the Farnese collection. Look up and you'll find Pietro Bardellino's riotously colourful 1781 fresco depicting the (short-lived) triumph of Ferdinand IV of Bourbon and Marie Caroline of Austria in Rome.

The rest of the 1st floor is largely devoted to fascinating discoveries from Pompeii, Herculaneum, Boscoreale, Stabiae and Cuma. Among them are whimsical wall **frescoes** from the Villa di Agrippa Postumus and the Casa di Meleagro, extraordinary bronzes from the Villa dei Papiri, as well as ceramics, glassware, engraved coppers and Greek funerary vases.

★**Galleria di Palazzo Zevallos Stigliano** GALLERY
(Map p52; ☑081 42 50 11; www.palazzozevallos.com; Via Toledo 185; adult/reduced €5/3; ⊙10am-6pm Tue-Fri, to 8pm Sat & Sun; Ⓜ Municipio)

Built for a Spanish merchant in the 17th century and reconfigured in belle époque style by architect Luigi Platania in the early 20th century, Palazzo Zevallos Stigliano houses a compact yet stunning collection of Neapolitan and Italian art spanning the 17th- to early-20th centuries. Star attraction is Caravaggio's mesmerising swan song, *The Martyrdom of St Ursula* (1610). Completed weeks before the artist's lonely death, the painting depicts a vengeful king of the Huns piercing the heart of his unwilling virgin bride-to-be, Ursula. Positioned behind the dying martyr is a haunted Caravaggio, an eerie premonition of his own impending fate. The tumultuous history of the artist and the painting is documented in the free and highly informative tablet audioguide.

Caravaggio's masterpiece is one of around 120 works on display in the *palazzo*'s sumptuous rooms. Among the numerous standouts is Luca Giordano's robust *The Rape of Helen,* a graphic *Judith Beheads Holophernes* attributed to Louis Finson, Francesco Solimena's *Hagar and Ishmael in the Desert Confronted by the Angel* and a series of bronze and terracotta sculptures by Vincenzo Gemito. A fine collection of landscape paintings includes Gasper van Wittel's *View of Naples with Largo di Palazzo,* which offers a fascinating early 18th-century depiction of what is now Piazza del Plebiscito. The triple-arched fountain in the bottom right corner of the painting is the Fontana dell'immacolatella. Designed by Michelangelo Naccherini and Pietro Bernini in 1601, the fountain is now located at the corner of Via Partenope and Via Nazario Sauro, beside Borgo Marinaro. Gaspar van Wittel was the father of celebrated Neapolitan architect Luigi Vanvitelli.

Piazza Dante   PIAZZA
(Map p40; M Dante) On hot summer evenings, Piazza Dante turns into a communal living room, packed with entire families who stroll, eat, smoke, play cards, chase balloons and whinge about the in-laws.

Dominating the eastern flank of the square is the enormous facade of the **Convitto Nazionale**, the pièce de résistance of Luigi Vanvitelli's spectacular 18th-century square. Dedicated to the Bourbon king Charles VII, its protagonist is now a sand-blasted marble Dante looking out over Via Toledo. Below it all, the **Dante metro station** doubles as a contemporary-art space, with installations from some art-world heavyweights. As you head down on the escalator, look up and catch Joseph Kosuth's *Queste cose visibili* (These Visible Things) above you. Eye-squintingly huge and neon, it's an epic quotation from Dante's *Il Convivio*. Along the wall at the bottom of the escalator you'll find artist Jannis Kounellis's renegade train tracks running over abandoned shoes. Right behind you, above the second set of escalators, sits *Intermediterraneo*, Michelangelo Pistoletto's giant mirror map of the Mediterranean Sea.

Museo Nitsch   MUSEUM
(Map p40; 081 564 16 55; www.museonitsch.org; Vico Lungo Pontecorvo 29d; adult/reduced €10/5; 10am-7pm Mon-Fri, to 2pm Sat; M Dante) In 1974, experimental Austrian artist Hermann Nitsch was invited to perform one of his 'actions' (a bloody, ritualistic art performance) in Naples, leading to his immediate arrest and deportation from Italy. Not one for the squeamish or easily offended, this savvy museum and cultural centre documents the now revered artist's intriguing, symbolic, confronting works through photographs, video, painting and props.

Set in a converted power station with a superb panoramic view of Naples and Vesuvius from its rooftop, the centre also hosts regular cultural events.

La Pignasecca   MARKET
(Map p52; Via Pignasecca; 8am-1pm; M Toledo) Naples' oldest street market is a multisensory escapade into a world of wriggling seafood, fragrant delis and clued-up *casal-inghe* (homemakers) on the hunt for perfect produce. Fresh produce aside, the market's streetside stalls flog everything from discounted perfume and linen to Neapolitan hip-hop CDs and oh-so-snug *nonna* slippers.

Chiesa di Sant'Anna dei Lombardi   CHURCH
(Map p52; 081 551 33 33; Piazza Monteoliveto; 10am-1.30pm & 2-4pm Mon-Thu, to 6pm Fri & Sat May-Sep, to 4pm Mon-Sat rest of year; M Toledo) This magnificent church is testament to the close links that once existed between the Neapolitan Aragonese and the Florentine Medici dynasty. One particular highlight is Guido Mazzoni's spectacular *Pietà*. Dating to 1492, the terracotta ensemble is made up of eight life-size terracotta figures surrounding the lifeless body of Christ. Originally the figures were painted, but even without colour they still make quite an impression.

The **sacristy** is a work of art in itself. The walls are graced with gloriously inlaid wood panels by Giovanni da Verona, while the ceiling bursts with 16th-century frescoes by Giorgio Vasari depicting the Allegories and Symbols of Faith. Across Via Monteoliveto from the church is the 16th-century **Palazzo Gravina** (Via Monteoliveto 3), the seat of Naples University's architecture faculty.

Casa e Chiesa di Santa Maria Francesca delle Cinque Piaghe   CHURCH, HISTORIC SITE
(Map p52; 081 42 50 11; Vico Tre Re a Toledo 13; church 9.30am-12.30pm, apartment 9.30am-12.15pm, plus 4.30-7.30pm on the 6th of every month; M Toledo) The very essence of Naples' cultish brand of Catholicism, this holy sanctuary was once the stomping ground of stigmatic and mystic Santa Maria Francesca delle Cinque Piaghe, the city's only canonised woman. It is also home to her miraculous wooden chair: infertile believers come to be blessed while sitting on it in the hope of falling pregnant.

You'll find the holy furniture piece in the saint's meticulously preserved 18th-century **apartment**. Here, walls heave with modern baby trinkets and vivid 18th- and 19th-century paintings depicting fantastical holy healings – *ex voti* offered by those whose prayers have been answered. Other household objects include the stigmatic's blood-stained clothes, her bed and pillow, her self-flagellation cords and a rare, hand-painted *spinetta* (spinet or harpsichord) from 1682.

The apartment sits above a tiny **chapel** famed for its beautiful 18th-century Neapolitan liturgical art, including glass-eyed holy states. Particularly rare is the statue of the *Divina Pastora* (Divine Shepherdess) on the left side of the nave. The only sculpture of its kind in Naples, it features an unusual depiction of the Virgin Mary reclined and wearing a shepherdess' hat that has its roots in 18th-century Spain. To the left of the nave, a statue of Santa Maria Francesca contains the holy local's bones.

Galleria Umberto I   ARCHITECTURE
(Map p52; Via San Carlo; ☐R2 to Via San Carlo, ⓂMunicipio) Paging Milan's Galleria Vittorio Emanuele, Naples' most famous 19th-century arcade is a breathtaking pairing of richly adorned neo-Renaissance fronts and a delicate glass ceiling capped by a lofty 56m dome. Complete with a sumptuous marble floor, the *galleria* is at its most

THE ART OF THE NEAPOLITAN PRESEPE

Christmas nativity cribs may not be exclusive to Naples, but none match the artistic brilliance of the *presepe napoletano* (Neapolitan nativity crib). What sets the local version apart is its incredible attention to detail, from the life-like miniature *prosciutti* (hams) in the tavern to the lavishly costumed *pastori* (crib figurines or sculptures) adorning the newborn Christ.

While the origin of Christmas cribs stretches back to the early centuries of Christianity, Naples' homegrown *presepi* have their roots in 1535. It was in this year that a much-loved local priest by the name of Gaetano da Thiene ditched tradition, dressing his crib characters in Neapolitan garb instead of traditional biblical robes.

Da Thiene's crib makeover ignited a passion that would reach its zenith with the 18th-century *presepe del Settecento* (crib of the 1700s). This often-epic crib was quite a departure from its humbler DIY sibling, the *presepe popolare* (common crib). While the setting of the *presepe popolare* was often dark, gloomy and subterranean, with only the nativity brightly illuminated (symbolising the light of salvation), its baroque spin-off was set in bucolic, sunlit European landscapes, its hues reflecting the palettes of the era's great artists.

Despite their differing scale and composition, both versions shared the same rich symbolism, from the tavern as a representation of sin to the stream or fountain as a symbol of purification. In the *presepe del Settecento,* the nativity itself was often set among the ruins of a pagan temple, reflecting both Christianity's triumph over paganism and a fascination with the century's archaeological discoveries, among them Pompeii.

For the nobility and the bourgeoisie of 18th-century Naples, the *presepe* allowed a convenient marriage of faith and ego, the crib becoming as much a symbol of wealth and good taste as a meditation on the Christmas miracle. The finest sculptors were commissioned and the finest fabrics used. Even the royals got involved: Charles III of Bourbon consulted the esteemed *presepe* expert, Dominican monk Padre Rocco, on the creation of his 5000-*pastore* spectacular, still on show at the Palazzo Reale (p58). Yet even this pales in comparison to the epic crib showcased at the Certosa e Museo di San Martino (p63), considered the world's greatest.

Centuries on, the legacy continues, with presepe and pastore pedlars dotted across Naples. Sadly, many of these now sell mass-produced reproductions, with only a few workshops or studios completely handcrafting their pastori the old-fashioned way. Among the latter are Ars Neapolitana (p85) and La Scarabattola (p85), who share the honour with Sorrelle Corcione, Fratelli Sinno and, further out in suburban Torre del Greco, veteran *presepe* maestro Salvatore Giordano.

These artisans remain true to the *presepe's* golden age. Each *pastore's* bust is moulded from fine-grain clay on a damp wooden block called *il morto* (literally, 'the dead man'), commencing with the chest, then the neck and finally the head. After the basic bust is formed and aired for an hour, work begins on sculpting the details, from the neck muscles and nose to wrinkles. Tradition insists that the *pastore's* bodily features reflect those of the past, hence the prevalence of missing teeth, warts and goitres. Interestingly, some Neapolitans still wittily refer to the 'aesthetically challenged' as *'curiuso comm'a nu'pastore'* (as ugly as a crib figurine).

Once completed, the bust is fired in a kiln for eight hours before the character is given glass eyes and painted using either acrylic paint or traditional oil paint. The bust is then attached to the rest of the body (hemp thread wrapped around a metal skeleton) and – last but not least – adorned with an intricate, handmade costume.

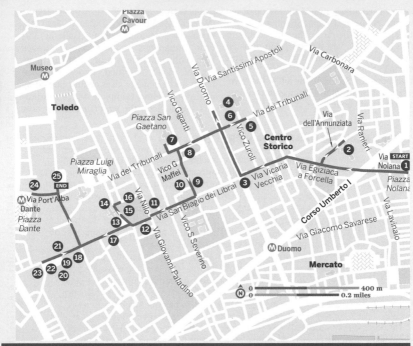

City Walk
Centro Storico: A World Heritage Wander

START PORTA NOLANA
END PIAZZA BELLINI
LENGTH 3KM; FOUR HOURS

Bustling for over 2000 years, Naples' *centro historico* (historic centre) is a rumbling mass of contradictions. Hyperactive streets sit atop silent ruins, crumbling facades mask mighty baroque interiors, and cultish shrines flank hedonistic bars. No other part of the city intrigues or intoxicates so intensely, and none offers such a density of artistic and architectural treasures.

Begin your walk at 15th-century city gate ❶ **Porta Nolana** (p51), its exterior wall featuring a marble relief of Ferdinand I, illegitimate son of Alfonso V of Aragon (who was also king of Naples from 1458 to 1494). On the other side of the gate is a 17th-century bust of San Gaetano. These days, Porta Nolana is

better known as the gateway to the Mercato di Porta Nolana.

After exploring the market, head west along Via Nolana. Cross Corso Umberto I, head right into Via Egiziaca a Forcella and then right again into Via dell'Annunziata. A little way down on your right you'll see the ❷ **Santissima Annunziata**, famous for its orphanage and *ruota*, the wooden wheel where babies were once abandoned. Head back to Via Egiziaca a Forcella and turn right into it. After crossing Via Pietro Colletta, follow the street as it veers left and merges into Via Vicaria Vecchia. Where it meets Via Duomo stands one of Naples' oldest churches, the ❸ **Basilica di San Giorgio Maggiore**. Built by St Severus in the 4th century but thoroughly restyled by Cosimo Fanzago in the mid-17th century, its original Palaeo-Christian apse is now part of the main entrance. Two blocks northwest up Via Duomo soars Naples' impressive cathedral, the ❹ **Duomo** (p45).

Double back down Via Duomo until you meet Via dei Tribunali. Known to the Romans as the *decumanus maior* (main road), this street runs parallel to the *decumanus inferior*, aka Spaccanapoli, aka Via San Biagio dei Librai. Before heading right into the heart of the *centro storico*, nip left to admire Caravaggio's masterpiece *Le Sette Opere di Misericordia* (The Seven Acts of Mercy) in the ❺ **Pio Monte della Misericordia** (p45). Soaring from the small square opposite is the ❻ **Guglia di San Gennaro** (p45).

After you've crossed Via Duomo make for Piazza San Gaetano, about 150m down on the right. The tiny square where the Roman forum once stood is now dominated by the imposing ❼ **Basilica di San Paolo Maggiore** (p48), whose sumptuous baroque sacristy is one of the city's hidden delights. Opposite the piazza is the ❽ **Complesso Monumentale di San Lorenzo Maggiore** (p48), its stark but beautiful Gothic basilica sitting atop evocative Roman *scavi* (excavations). Take a peek before heading down ❾ **Via San Gregorio Armeno** (p44) – in December people come from all over Italy to visit the *presepi* (nativity scene) shops that line this street. Also here is the rococo ❿ **Chiesa e Chiostro di San Gregorio Armeno** (p44).

At the end of the road you hit Via San Biagio dei Librai. Turn right and after about 250m you'll be on ⓫ **Piazzetta Nilo** (p43), home to the ancient Statua del Nilo and (less imposingly) the altar to footballer Maradona inside Bar Nilo. Further down on the left, the ⓬ **Chiesa di Sant'Angelo a Nilo** (p43) is home to an exquisite tomb.

From here it's only a few steps to handsome ⓭ **Piazza San Domenico Maggiore** (p43), location of the imposing ⓮ **Chiesa di San Domenico Maggiore** (p43). At No 9 stands the notorious ⓯ **Palazzo dei Di San-**gro** (p43), where composer Carlo Gesualdo brutally murdered his wife and her lover. Around the corner from the *palazzo* is Via Francesco de Sanctis, where you'll find the not-to-be-missed ⓰ **Cappella Sansevero** (p38), home to the mesmerising *Cristo velato* (Veiled Christ).

As you walk west on Via San Biagio dei Librai it becomes Via Benedetto Croce. On the left, at No 45, stands ⓱ **Palazzo Carafa della Spina**, designed by Domenico Fontana in the late 16th century and revamped in the first half of the 18th century. Its baroque *portone* (entrance) is one of Naples' finest. Further west is the ⓲ **Basilica di Santa Chiara** (p39), meticulously reconstructed after heavy bomb damage in WWII. Nearby ⓳ **Piazza del Gesù Nuovo** is home to nightly revelry and, at No 14, ⓴ **Libreria Dante & Descartes**, an erudite bookshop. Dominating the piazza's northern side is the glorious ㉑ **Chiesa del Gesù Nuovo** (p43), while at its centre is the ㉒ **Guglia dell'Immacolata** (p43), created between 1747 and 1750; the gilded copper statue of the Virgin Mary was added in 1753.

Cinephiles may recognise the central balcony of ㉓ **Palazzo Pandola**, at No 33, from the closing scene of Vittorio de Sica's *Matrimonio all'italiana* (Marriage, Italian Style), starring Sophia Loren and Marcello Mastroianni. Backtrack from the square, turning left into Via San Sebastiano. At the next intersection on your left, bookshop-lined Via Port'Alba leads down to ㉔ **Port'Alba** (p49), a city gate built in 1625 that leads into Piazza Dante.

Double back the way you came, turn left back into Via San Sebastiano, and a block ahead on your right is ㉕ **Piazza Bellini** (p49) and its restorative cafes.

spectacular at night, when it becomes a surreal setting for impromptu soccer games.

◉ Santa Lucia & Chiaia

At its southern end, Via Toledo spills into lavish Santa Lucia, whose grandiose residents include the sweeping Piazza del Plebiscito, art-slung Palazzo Reale, the velvety Teatro San Carlo and, further east, one-time Angevin stronghold Castel Nuovo (Maschio Angioino). Directly south of Castel Nuovo, hydrofoils for Capri, Ischia, Procida and Sorrento dock at Molo Beverello, while further southwest diners seated at candlelit tables tuck into seafood at harbourside Borgo Marinaro.

Soaring above Via Santa Lucia is Monte Echia and the Pizzofalcone district, inhabited since the 7th century BC, and a little-known warren of dark streets, macabre votive shrines and knockout views.

Further west, Chiaia is Naples' epicentre of the fashionable and the trendy, home to Vogue-endorsed Via Calabritto, former Rothschild address Villa Pignatelli and the city's hippest bars.

Castel Nuovo　　　　　　　　CASTLE, MUSEUM
(Map p40; ☑ 081 795 77 22; Piazza Municipio; admission €6; ⊙ 9am-7pm Mon-Sat, last entry 6pm; Ⓜ Municipio) Locals know this 13th-century castle as the Maschio Angioino (Angevin Keep) and its Cappella Palatina is home to fragments of frescoes by Renaissance maverick Giotto; they're on the splays of the Gothic windows. You'll find Roman ruins under the glass-floored Sala dell'Armeria (Armoury Hall), and a collection of mostly 17th- to early-20th-century Neapolitan paintings on the upper floors. The top floor houses the more interesting works, including landscape paintings by Luigi Crisconio and a watercolour drawing by architect Carlo Vanvitelli.

The history of the castle stretches back to Charles I of Anjou, who upon taking over Naples and the Swabians' Sicilian kingdom found himself in control not only of his new southern Italian acquisitions but also of possessions in Tuscany, northern Italy and Provence (France). It made sense to base the new dynasty in Naples, rather than Palermo in Sicily, and Charles launched an ambitious construction program to expand the port and city walls. His plans included converting a Franciscan convent into the castle that still stands in Piazza Municipio.

Christened the Castrum Novum (New Castle) to distinguish it from the older Castel dell'Ovo and Castel Capuano, it was completed in 1282, becoming a popular hang-out for the leading intellectuals and artists of the day – Giotto repaid his royal hosts by painting much of the interior. Of the original structure, however, only the Cappella Palatina remains; the rest is the result of Aragonese renovations two centuries later, as well as a meticulous restoration effort prior to WWII.

The two-storey Renaissance triumphal arch at the entrance – the **Torre della Guardia** – commemorates the victorious entry of Alfonso I of Aragon into Naples in 1443, while the stark stone **Sala dei Baroni** (Hall of the Barons) is named after the barons slaughtered here in 1486 for plotting against King Ferdinand I of Aragon. Its striking ribbed vault fuses ancient Roman and Spanish late-Gothic influences.

Palazzo Reale　　　　　　　　PALACE, MUSEUM
(Royal Palace; Map p60; ☑ 081 40 05 47; www.sbapsae.na.it/cms; Piazza del Plebiscito 1; adult/reduced €4/3; ⊙ 9am-8pm Thu-Tue; ☑ R2 to Via San Carlo, Ⓜ Municipio) Envisaged as a 16th-century monument to Spanish glory (Naples was under Spanish rule at the time), the magnificent Palazzo Reale is home to the **Museo del Palazzo Reale**, a rich and eclectic collection of baroque and neoclassical furnishings, porcelain, tapestries, sculpture and paintings, spread across the palace's royal apartments.

Among the many highlights is the Teatrino di Corte, a lavish private theatre created by Ferdinando Fuga in 1768 to celebrate the marriage of Ferdinand IV and Marie Caroline of Austria. Incredibly, Angelo Viva's statues of Apollo and the Muses set along the walls are made of papier mâché.

Snigger smugly in Sala (Room) XII, where the 16th-century canvas *Gli esattori delle imposte* (The Tax Collectors) by Dutch artist Marinus Claesz Van Raymerswaele confirms that attitudes to tax collectors have changed little in 500 years. Sala XIII used to be Joachim Murat's study in the 19th century but was used as a snack bar by Allied troops in WWII. Meanwhile, what looks like a waterwheel in Sala XXIII is actually a nifty rotating reading desk made for Marie Caroline by Giovanni Uldrich in the 18th century.

The Cappella Reale (Royal Chapel) houses an 18th-century *presepe napoletano* (Neapolitan nativity crib). Fastidiously detailed, its cast of *pastori* (crib figurines) were crafted by a series of celebrated Neapolitan artists, including Giuseppe Sanmartino, creator of the *Cristo velato* (Veiled Christ) sculpture in the Cappella Sansevero.

The palace is also home to the **Biblioteca Nazionale** (National Library; ☑ 081 781 91 11; www.bnnonline.it; ☺ 8.30am-7pm Mon-Fri, to 2pm Sat, papyri exhibition closes 2pm Mon-Sat), its own priceless treasures including at least 2000 papyri discovered at Herculaneum and fragments of a 5th-century Coptic Bible. The National Library's beautiful **Biblioteca Lucchesi Palli** (Lucchesi Palli Library; closed Saturday) – designed by some of Naples' most celebrated 19th-century craftspeople – is home to numerous fascinating artistic artefacts, including letters by composer Giuseppe Verdi. Bring photo ID to enter the Biblioteca Nazionale.

MeMus
MUSEUM

(Museum & Historical Archive of the Teatro San Carlo; Map p60; memus.squarespace.com; Palazzo Reale, Piazza del Plebiscito; adult/reduced €6/5, incl Palazzo Reale €10/5; ☺ 9.30am-5pm Mon, Tue & Thu-Sat, to 2pm Sun; ◻R2 to Via San Carlo, Ⓜ Municipio) Located inside the Palazzo Reale (purchase tickets at the palace ticket booth), modern museum MeMus documents the history of Europe's oldest working opera house, the Teatro San Carlo (p83). The collection includes costumes, sketches, instruments and memorabilia, displayed in annually changing themed exhibitions. One interactive, immersive exhibit allows visitors to enjoy the music of numerous celebrated composers with accompanying visuals by artists who have collaborated with the opera house, among them William Kentridge.

Upstairs, computers offer access to the Teatro San Carlo's rich archives, although all were out of order on our last visit.

Piazza del Plebiscito
PIAZZA

(Map p60; ◻R2 to Via San Carlo, Ⓜ Municipio) For Continental grandeur, it's hard to beat Piazza del Plebiscito. Whichever way you look, the view is show-stopping. To the northwest, vine-covered slopes lead up to Castel Sant'Elmo and the Certosa di San Martino; to the east, the pink-hued Palazzo Reale shows off its oldest facade. And to the west

stands Pietro Banchini's neoclassical facsimile of Rome's Pantheon, the **Chiesa di San Francesco di Paola** (☑ 346 2702576; Piazza del Plebiscito; ☺ 8.30am-noon & 4.30-7pm; ◻R2 to Piazza Trieste e Trento, Ⓜ Municipio).

A later addition to the columned colonnade of Joachim Murat's original 1809 piazza design, the church was commissioned by Ferdinand I in 1817 to celebrate the restoration of his kingdom after the Napoleonic interlude. Standing guard outside are Antonio Canova's statue of a galloping King Charles VII of the Bourbons and Antonio Calì's rendering of Charles' son Ferdinand I.

At its northern end, Piazza Plebiscito spills onto **Piazza Trieste e Trento**, the city's buzzing heart and home to its most glamorous cafe, Caffè Gambrinus (p81).

★ Tunnel Borbonico
HISTORIC SITE

(Map p60; ☑ 081 764 58 08, 366 2484151; www.tunnelborbonico.info; Vico del Grottone 4; 75min standard tour adult/reduced €10/5; ☺ standard tour 10am, noon, 3.30pm & 5.30pm Fri-Sun; ◻R2 to Via San Carlo) Traverse five centuries along Naples' engrossing Bourbon Tunnel. Conceived by Ferdinand II in 1853 to link the Palazzo Reale to the barracks and the sea, the never-completed escape route is part of the 17th-century Carmignano Aqueduct system, itself incorporating 16th-century cisterns. An air-raid shelter and military hospital during WWII, this underground labyrinth rekindles the past with evocative wartime artefacts. The standard tour doesn't require pre-booking, though the Adventure Tour (80 minutes; adult/reduced €15/10) and adults-only Speleo Tour (2½ hours; €30) do.

Tours also depart from Tunnel Borbonico's second entrance, reached through the Parcheggio Morelli (Via Domenico Morelli 40) parking complex in Chiaia.

Via Chiaia
STREET

(Map p60; ◻R2 to Via San Carlo, Ⓜ Municipio) Join the perma-tanned for a spot of window shopping on this popular pedestrianised strip. Linking Piazza Trieste e Trento with Piazza dei Martiri, it's a particular hit with evening *flâneurs,* not to mention home to 16th-century **Palazzo Cellamare** at No 149. Built as a summer residence for Giovan Francesco Carafa, it would go on to host numerous Bourbon royal guests, among them Goethe and Casanova.

Santa Lucia, Chiaia & Mergellina

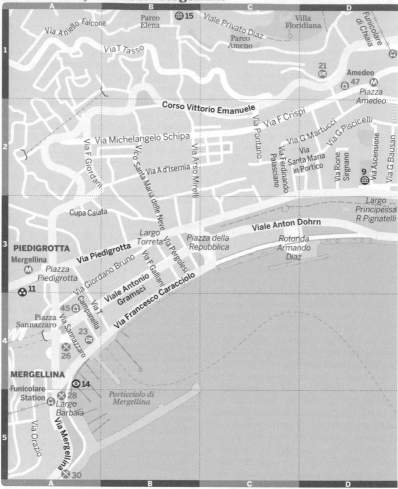

Towards the street's western end, what looks like a triumphal arch is in fact a bridge built in 1636 to connect the hills of Pizzofalcone and Mortella. Past the bridge, turn right into blue-ribbon Via Gaetano Filangieri and continue up to Via dei Mille, where sharply garbed locals and shops mix it with flouncy Stile Liberty (Italian art nouveau) architecture.

Piazza dei Martiri   PIAZZA
(Map p60; □ C24 to Piazza dei Martiri) If Chiaia is Naples' drawing room, then Piazza dei Martiri is its chaise longue. The square's centrepiece is Enrico Alvino's 19th-century monument to Neapolitan martyrs, with four lions representing the anti-Bourbon uprisings of 1799, 1820, 1848 and 1860. At No 30 is **Palazzo Calabritto**, designed by Luigi Vanvitelli, best known for creating Caserta's epic Palazzo Reale.

Great names of the fashion variety abound around the corner on exclusive Via Calabritto, among them legendary local tailor Finamore (p84). On the piazza itself is book and music store Feltrinelli (p87), where locals head to browse, cruise and guzzle espresso in the in-store basement cafe.

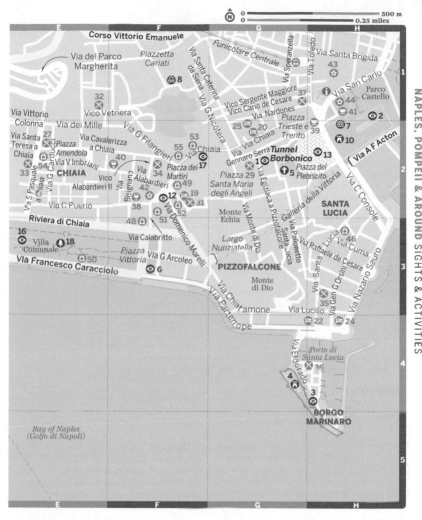

Castel dell'Ovo

CASTLE

(Map p60; 📞081 795 45 93; Borgo Marinaro; ⏰8am-6.45pm Mon-Sat, to 1.45pm Sun; 🚌128 to Via Santa Lucia) FREE Built by the Normans in the 12th century, Naples' oldest castle owes its name (Castle of the Egg) to Virgil. The Roman scribe reputedly buried an egg on the site where the castle now stands, warning that when the egg breaks, the castle (and Naples) will fall. Both are still standing, and walking up to the castle's ramparts will reward you with a breathtaking panorama.

Used by the Swabians, Angevins and Alfonso of Aragon, who modified it to suit his military needs, the castle sits on the rocky, restaurant-lined 'island' of **Borgo Marinaro**. According to legend, the heartbroken siren Partenope washed ashore here after failing to seduce Ulysses with her song. It's also where the Greeks first settled the city in the 7th century BC, calling the island Megaris. Its commanding position wasn't wasted on the Roman general Lucullus, either, who had his villa here long before the castle hit the skyline. Views aside, the castle is also the setting for temporary art exhibitions, special events, and no shortage of posing brides and grooms.

Santa Lucia, Chiaia & Mergellina

Lungomare   STREET, PARK
(Seafront; Map p60; Via Francesco Caracciolo; ⊞ 128 to Piazza Vittoria) When you need a break from Naples' hyperactive tendencies, take a deep breath on its pedestrianised seafront strip. Stretching 2.5km along Via Partenope and Via Francesco Carrociolo, its views are nothing short of exquisite, taking in the bay, Mt Vesuvius, two castles and Vomero's Liberty-style villas. It's particularly romantic at dusk, when Capri and the volcano take on a mellow orange hue.

Separating the Lungomare from Riviera di Chiaia is the **Villa Comunale** (Piazza Vittoria; ☉ 7am-midnight; ⊞ C25 to Riviera di Chiaia), a long, leafy park designed by Luigi Vanvitelli for private Bourbon frolicking. Its bountiful booty of fountains includes the Fontana delle Paperelle (Duck Fountain), which replaced the famous *Toro Farnese* after its transference to the Museo Archeologico Nazionale in 1825.

The park is also home to the **Stazione Zoologica** (Aquario; ☎ 081 583 32 18, 081 583 31 11; www.szn.it; Viale Aquario 1; adult/child €1.50/1; ☉ 9.30am-6.30pm Tue-Sun; ⊞ C25 to Riviera di Chiaia), Europe's oldest **aquarium**. Established by German Darwinist Anton Dohrn, it's housed in a stately neoclassical building designed by Adolf von Hildebrand. These days, the aquarium's tired-looking tanks are home to 200 species of marine flora and fauna from the city's bay. Arguably more impressive is the lovingly restored reading room upstairs, adorned with engaging 19th-century frescoes of Mediterranean life by German painter Hans von Marées and Hildebrand himself. Library visits must be pre-booked by phone.

Museo Pignatelli   MUSEUM
(Map p60; ☎ 081 761 23 56; http://museopignatelli.campaniabeniculturali.it; Riviera di Chiaia 200; adult/reduced €2/1; ☉ 8.30am-2pm Wed-

Mon; 🚌128 to Riviera di Chiaia) When Ferdinand Acton, a minister at the court of King Ferdinand IV (1759–1825), asked Pietro Valente to design Villa Pignatelli in 1826, Valente whipped up this striking Pompeiian facsimile. Now the Museo Pignatelli, its aristocratic hoard includes sumptuous furniture and decorative arts, as well as a beautiful collection of 19th- and 20th-century carriages in the adjoining Museo delle Carrozze.

Bought and extended by the Rothschilds in 1841, Villa Pignatelli became home to the Duke of Monteleone, Diego Aragona Pignatelli Cortes, in 1867, before his granddaughter Rosina Pignatelli donated it (and its treasures) to the state. Highlights of the permanent collection include a small yet fine array of local and foreign porcelain in the Salotto Verde (Green Room), and a leather-lined smoking room (known as the Biblioteca). The 1st floor hosts a handful of temporary exhibitions annually.

◉ Vomero

All roads might lead to Rome, but three Neapolitan funiculars lead to Vomero, a hilltop neighbourhood where quasi-anarchy is replaced with mild-mannered *professori*, Liberty villas and the stunning Certosa di San Martino. Panoramic bay and city views, not to mention one of Naples' best-loved public parks, make this neighbourhood an easily accessible antidote to the city centre's full-throttle intensity.

★Certosa e Museo di
San Martino   MONASTERY, MUSEUM
(Map p64; ☎081 229 45 68; www.polomusealenapoli.beniculturali.it; Largo San Martino 5; adult/reduced €6/3; ⊗8.30am-7.30pm Thu-Tue; Ⓜ Vanvitelli, 🚋 Montesanto to Morghen) The high point (quite literally) of the Neapolitan baroque, this charterhouse turned museum was founded as a Carthusian monastery in the 14th century. Centred on one of the most beautiful cloisters in Italy, it has been decorated, adorned and altered over the centuries by some of Italy's finest talent, most importantly Giovanni Antonio Dosio in the 16th century and baroque master Cosimo Fanzago a century later. Nowadays, it's a superb repository of Neapolitan artistry.

The monastery's church and the rooms that flank it contain a feast of frescoes and paintings by some of Naples' greatest 17th-century artists, among them Francesco Solimena, Massimo Stanzione, Giuseppe de Ribera and Battista Caracciolo. In the nave, Cosimo Fanzago's inlaid marblework is simply extraordinary.

Adjacent to the church, the Chiostro dei Procuratori is the smaller of the monastery's two cloisters. A grand corridor on the left leads to the larger Chiostro Grande (Great Cloister). Originally designed by Dosio in the late 16th century and added to by Fanzago, it's a sublime composition of Tuscan-Doric porticoes, marble statues and vibrant camellias. The skulls mounted on the balustrade were a light-hearted reminder to the monks of their own mortality.

Just off the Chiostro dei Procuratori, the small Sezione Navale documents the history of the Bourbon navy from 1734 to 1860, and features a small collection of beautiful royal barges. The Sezione Presepiale houses a whimsical collection of rare Neapolitan *presepi* (nativity scenes) from the 18th and 19th centuries, including the colossal 18th-century Cuciniello creation, which covers one wall of what used to be the monastery's kitchen. The Quarto del Priore in the southern wing houses the bulk of the picture collection, as well as one of the museum's most famous pieces, Pietro Bernini's tender *Madonna col Bambino e San Giovannino* (Madonna and Child with the Infant John the Baptist).

A pictorial history of Naples is told in Immagini e Memorie di Napoli (Images and Memories of Naples). Here you'll find portraits of historic characters; antique maps, including a 35-panel copper map of 18th-century Naples in Room 45; and rooms dedicated to major historical events such as the Revolt of the Masaniello (Room 36) and the plague (Room 37). Room 32 boasts the beautiful *Tavola Strozzi* (Strozzi Table); its fabled depiction of 15th-century maritime Naples is one of the city's most celebrated historical records.

You will need to book in advance to access the Certosa's imposing Sotterranei Gotici (Gothic basement), open to the public on Saturday and Sunday at 11.30am (with guided tour in Italian) and 4.30pm (without guided tour). The austere vaulted space is home to about 150 marble sculptures and epigraphs, including a statue of St Francis of Assisi by 18th-century master sculptor Giuseppe Sanmartino. To book a visit, email accoglienza.sanmartino@beniculturali.it at least two weeks in advance.

Vomero

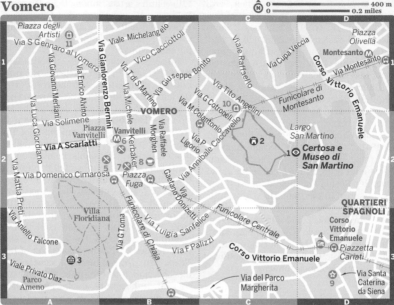

Castel Sant'Elmo CASTLE, MUSEUM
(Map p64; ☑081 558 77 08; www.coopculture.
it; Via Tito Angelini 22; adult/reduced €5/2.50;
⊙castle 8.30am-7.30pm Wed-Mon, museum
9am-7pm Wed-Mon; Ⓜ Vanvitelli, Ⓕ Montesanto to
Morghen) Star-shaped Castel Sant'Elmo was
originally a church dedicated to St Eras-
mus. Some 400 years later, in 1349, Robert of Anjou turned it into a castle before
Spanish viceroy Don Pedro de Toledo had it
further fortified in 1538. Used as a military
prison until the 1970s, it's now famed for its
jaw-dropping panorama, and for its **Museo
del Novecento**, dedicated to 20th-century
Neapolitan art.

The museum's collection of paintings,
sculpture and installations documents
major influences in the local art scene, including Futurism and the Nuclear Art movement. Standout works include Eugenio Viti's
sensual *La schiena* (The Back) in Room 7,
Raffaele Lippi's unnerving *Le quattro giornate di Napoli* (The Four Days of Naples)
in Room 9, and Giuseppe Desiato's mag-
nentic photograph *Monumento* in Room
18. In Room 17, Salvatore Cotugno's untitled
sculpture of a bound, wrapped, muted figure strangely recalls Giuseppe Sanmartino's
Cristo velato (Veiled Christ) in the Cappella
Sansevero (p38).

**Museo Nazionale della
Ceramica Duca di Martina** MUSEUM, GARDENS
(National Museum of Ceramics; Map p64; ☑081
578 84 18; www.polomusealenapoli.beniculturali.
it; Via Domenico Cimarosa 77; adult/reduced €2/1;
⊙museum 8.30am-2pm Wed-Mon, last entry
1.15pm, gardens 8.30am-1hr before sunset; Ⓜ Vanvitelli, Ⓕ Chiaia to Cimarosa, Centrale to Piazza
Fuga) The National Museum of Ceramics
houses a beautiful (albeit forlornly exhibited) collection of 6000 pieces, with priceless
Chinese Ming (1368–1644) ceramics and
Japanese Edo (1615–1867) vases on the lower floor, lively Renaissance majolica on the
midde floor, and more European ceramics
(including some sumptuous Meissen pieces)
on the top floor. You'll also find a smattering
of paintings from greats such as Francesco
Solimena, Francesco De Mura and Vincenzo Camuccini. The museum's home is the
stately **Villa Floridiana**, a not-so-modest
gift from King Ferdinand I to his second
wife, the Duchess of Floridia. Its lush, manicured gardens are worth the trip alone, with
dreamy bay and city views, and a pretty little
fountain sprinkled with tortoises.

**Museo del Tessile e dell'Abbigliamento
Elena Aldobrandini** MUSEUM
(Map p60; ☑081 497 61 04; www.fondazion-
emondragone.it; Fondazione Mondragone Napoli,

Vomero

Piazzetta Mondragone 18; admission €5;
⊙9.30am-3.30pm Mon-Fri; 🚋Centrale to Corso
Vittorio Emanuele) Despite the lack of information in English, this petite textile and
fashion museum is a good bet for those
after a lesser-known treat. Swoon over a
beautiful selection of mid-20th-century
gowns, including creations by late Neapolitan fashion great Emilio Schuberth, 'tailor of the stars' and mentor to Valentino.
The work of Campania's equally famous
Livio De Simone and Fausto Sarli is also
showcased, alongside vintage millinery,
gloves, and 18th-century ecclesiastical
garb. The museum is tucked away inside
the Fondazione Mondragone, established
as a 'retreat for noble matrons and virgins'
in the mid-17th century. To access it, head
through the gates and into the *palazzo's*
courtyard. Enter the building through the
glass door on your right and take the lift to
the 1st floor.

◎ Capodimonte & La Sanità

Rising to the north of the city centre is former royal hunting ground Capodimonte.
Here you'll find the sprawling green of Parco
di Capodimonte and its resident Palazzo di
Reale Capodimonte, a mammoth repository
of A-list art.

In stark contrast, the rough-and-tumble
Sanità district (squeezed between Via Foria
and Via Santa Teresa degli Scalzi directly
south of Capodimonte) delivers a one-of-
a-kind jumble of *bassi* (one-room, ground-
floor houses), baroque staircases and
ancient catacombs. To many, this is Naples
at its earthiest and most authentic, a fact not
lost on its growing number of resident artists and bohemians. It's also the birthplace
of Italian comic legend Totò (at Via Santa
Maria Antesaecula 109, to be precise!).

★**Palazzo Reale di Capodimonte** MUSEUM
(Map p66; ☑081 749 91 11; www.polomusealenapo
li.beniculturali.it; Via Miano 2; adult/reduced
€7.50/3.75; ⊙8.30am-7.30pm Thu-Tue; 🚌R4, 178
to Via Capodimonte) Originally designed as a
hunting lodge for Charles VII of Bourbon,
this monumental palace was begun in 1738
and took more than a century to complete.
It's now home to the **Museo Nazionale di
Capodimonte**, southern Italy's largest and
richest art gallery. Its vast collection – much
of which Charles inherited from his mother,
Elisabetta Farnese – was moved here in 1759
and ranges from exquisite 12th-century altarpieces to works by Botticelli, Caravaggio,
Titian and Andy Warhol.

The gallery is spread over three floors
and 160 rooms; for most people, a full morning or afternoon is enough for an abridged
best-of tour. The 1st floor includes works by
greats such as Michelangelo, Raphael and
Titian, with highlights including Masaccio's
Crocifissione (Crucifixion; Room 3), Botticelli's *Madonna col Bambino e due angeli*
(Madonna with Child and Angels; Room 6),
Bellini's *Trasfigurazione* (Transfiguration;
Room 8) and Parmigianino's *Antea* (Room
12). The floor is also home to the royal
apartments, a study in regal excess. The **Salottino di Porcellana** (Room 52) is an outrageous example of 18th-century chinoiserie,
its walls and ceiling dense with whimsically
themed porcelain 'stucco'. Originally created
between 1757 and 1759 for the Palazzo Reale
in Portici, it was transferred to Capodimonte in 1867. Upstairs, the 2nd-floor galleries
display work by Neapolitan artists from the
13th to the 19th centuries, including de Ribera, Giordano, Solimena and Stanzione. It's
also home to some spectacular 16th-century
Belgian tapestries. The piece that many
come to see, however, is Caravaggio's *Flagellazione* (Flagellation; 1607–10), which hangs
in reverential solitude in Room 78.

La Sanità & Capodimonte

If you have any energy left, the small gallery of modern art on the 3rd floor is worth a quick look, if for nothing else than Andy Warhol's poptastic *Mt Vesuvius*. The **Parco di Capodimonte** – the palace's 130-hectare estate – offers a breath of fresh air.

Catacomba di San Gennaro   CATACOMB
(Map p66; ☎ 081 744 37 14; www.catacombedi-napoli.it; Via Capodimonte 13; adult/reduced €8/5; ☺ 1hr tours every hour 10am-5pm Mon-Sat, to 1pm Sun; ☐ R4, 178 to Via Capodimonte) Naples' oldest and most sacred catacomb became a Christian pilgrimage site when San Gennaro's body was interred here in the 5th century. The carefully restored site allows visitors to experience an evocative otherworld of tombs, corridors and broad vestibules, its treasures including 2nd-century Christian frescoes, 5th-century mosaics and the oldest known portrait of San Gennaro.

The catacomb is home to three types of tomb, each corresponding to a specific social class. The wealthy opted for the open-room *cubiculum,* originally guarded by gates and adorned with colourful wall frescoes. One *cubiculum* to the left of the entrance features an especially beautiful funerary fresco of a mother, father and child: it's made up of three layers of fresco, one commissioned for each death. The smaller, rectangular wall niches, known as *loculum,* were the domain of the middle classes, while the *forme* (floor tombs) were reserved for the poor.

Further ahead you'll stumble upon the *basilica minore* (minor basilica), home to the tombs of San Gennaro and 5th-century archbishop of Naples Giovanni I. Sometime between 413 and 431, Giovanni I accompanied the martyr's remains from Pozzuoli to Naples, burying them here before Lombard prince Sico I of Benevento snatched them in the 9th century. The *basilica minore* also harbours fragments of a fresco depicting Naples' first bishop, Sant'Aspreno. The city's

La Sanità & Capodimonte

bishops were buried in this catacomb until the 11th century.

Close to the *basilica minore* is a 3rd-century tomb whose Pompeiian-hued artwork employs both Christian and pagan elements. In the image of three women building a castle, the figures represent the three virtues, while the castle symbolises the Church.

The lower level is even older, dating back to the 2nd century and speckled with typically pagan motifs like fruit and animals. The painting on the side of San Gennaro's tomb – depicting the saint with Mt Vesuvius and Mt Somma in the background – is the first known image of San Gennaro as the protector of Naples. Also on the lower level is the Basilica di Agrippino, named in honour of Sant'Agrippino. The sixth bishop of Naples, Agrippino was also the first Christian to be buried in the catacomb, back in the 3rd century. Tours of the catacomb are run by the **Cooperativa Sociale Onlus 'La Paranza'** (Map p66; ☑ 081 744 37 14; www.catacombedinapoli.it; Via Capodimonte 13; ☺10am-5pm Mon-Sat, to 1pm Sun; ☐ R4 to Via Capodimonte) , whose ticket office is to the left of the **Chiesa di Madre di Buon Consiglio** (☑ 081 741 00 06; ☺8am-12.30pm & 5-7pm Mon-Sat, 9am-1pm & 5-7pm Sun), a snack-sized replica of St Peter's in Rome completed in 1960. The co-operative runs a fascinating walking tour called Il Miglio Sacro (the Holy Mile), which explores the neighbouring Sanità district. It must be pre-booked.

THE CAPTAIN'S CURSE

Of the many macabre tales about the Cimitero delle Fontanelle (p72), none intrigues like that of *Il Capitano* (The Captain), the centre skull at the base of the cemetery's three Calvary crosses.

According to legend, a pious young woman from La Sanità adopted the skull, a common practice in Naples until the late 1960s. As incongruous as it seems, the Cimitero delle Fontanelle doubled as a lovers' lane for lovebirds with nowhere else to go. This was not lost on the woman's less-than-pious boyfriend, who convinced her to lose her virginity at the site.

Pensive and nervous, the young woman approached the Captain, asking the skull to bless their relationship and grant them a happy marriage. Not one for superstitious beliefs, the boyfriend began mocking her and the Captain, poking the skull's eye socket and daring it to turn up at their wedding. Adding insult to injury, he took his lover's virginity then and there.

Fast forward to the couple's wedding banquet, where a stranger enters wearing an eye patch and an old-fashioned officer's uniform. No less cocky than at the cemetery that fateful day, the young groom corners the guest as he is leaving, demanding to know who had invited him. The officer turns around, smiles, and replies, 'You did...at the Fontanelle', before opening his coat to reveal a full skeleton that immediately crumbles to the floor.

Not surprisingly, the shock killed both the groom and his bride, whose final resting place suitably remains a mystery. While some say that the couple's remains lie in the Cimitero delle Fontanelle, others believe that a funerary fresco of a couple in the Catacomba di San Gaudioso (p72) indicates their place of eternal regret.

LONELY PLANET/GETTY IMAGES ©

1. Parco Archeologico di Baia (p92), Campi Flegrei **2.** Ruins of Pompeii (p98) **3.** Tempio di Nettuno (p184), Paestum **4.** Ancient mosaic in Casa di Nettuno e Anfitrite (p96), Herculaneum

NEIL SETCHFIELD/GETTY IMAGES ©

MARTIN MOOS/GETTY IMAGES ©

Historical Riches

Few Italian regions can match Campania's historical legacy. Colonised by the ancient Greeks and loved by the Romans, it's a sun-drenched repository of A-list antiquities, from World Heritage wonders to lesser-known archaeological gems.

Paestum

Great Greek temples never go out of vogue and those at Paestum (p183) are among the greatest outside Greece itself. With the oldest structures stretching back to the 6th century BC, this place makes Rome's Colosseum feel positively modern.

Herculaneum

A bite-sized Pompeii, Herculaneum (p94) is even better preserved than its nearby rival. This is the place to delve into the details, from once-upon-a-time shop advertisements and furniture, to quirky mosaics and even an ancient security device.

Pompeii

Short of stepping into the Tardis, Pompeii (p98) is your best bet for a little time travel. Snap-locked in ash for centuries, its excavated streetscapes offer a tangible, 3D encounter with the ancients and their daily lives.

Subterranean Naples

Eerie aqueducts, mysterious burial crypts and ancient streetscapes: beneath Naples' hyperactive streets lies a wonderland of Graeco-Roman ruins. For a taste, head below the Complesso Monumentale di San Lorenzo Maggiore (p48) or follow the leader on a Napoli Sotterranea (p48) tour.

Campi Flegrei

The Phlegraean Fields simmer with ancient clues. Roam where emperors bathed at the Parco Archeologico di Baia (p92), sneak into a Roman engineering marvel at the Piscina Mirabilis, or spare a thought for doomed martyrs at the Anfiteatro Flavio.

The Baroque

Innately extravagant, effusive and loud, Naples found its soul mate in the baroque. As a booming metropolis, Naples was hungry for big, bold and bombastic – the baroque ensured it got it.

Cappella Sansevero

1 Incredibly, Francesco Maria Russo's vivid vault fresco has remained untouched since its debut in 1749. Then again, the di Sangro family chapel (p38) is not short of jaw-dropping revelations, among them Giuseppe Sanmartino's *Cristo velato* sculpture.

Reggia di Caserta

2 Four courtyards, 1000-plus rooms, two dozen state apartments, a library, theatre and one of Europe's most ambitious landscaped gardens: Caserta's Unesco-listed royal palace (p74) made sure the baroque went out with a very loud bang.

Cappella di San Gennaro

3 Every patron saint deserves a little attention, and Naples' San Gennaro gets plenty in the chapel (p46) that houses his liquefying blood. From Cosimo Fanzago's sculptures to Giovanni Lanfranco's 'Paradise' fresco, it's a spiritual tour de force.

Certosa di San Martino

4 The Carthusian monks at this charterhouse (p61) commissioned the baroque's finest to pimp their church. Their prayers were answered with luscious sculptures, canvases, and inlaid stone and wood.

Farmacia Storica dell'Ospedale degli Incurabili

5 Diva of Italian drugstores, the Farmacia Storica dell'Ospedale degli Incurabili (p49) is the country's most faithfully preserved 18th-century pharmacy, not to mention a high-inducing feast of walnut cabinets, majolica ceramics and brooding oil brushstrokes.

★ **Cimitero delle Fontanelle** CEMETERY
(Map p66; ☑ 081 1970 3197; www.cimiterofontanelle.com; Via Fontanelle 80; ☉ 9am-4pm; ⬚ C51 to Via Fontanelle) **FREE** Holding about eight million human bones, the ghoulish Fontanelle Cemetery was first used during the 1656 plague, before becoming Naples' main burial site during the 1837 cholera epidemic. At the end of the 19th century it became a hot spot for the *anime pezzentelle* (poor souls) cult, in which locals adopted skulls and prayed for their souls. Lack of information at the site makes joining a tour much more rewarding; reputable outfits include Co-operativa Sociale Onlus 'La Paranza' (p67). Avoid guides offering tours at the entrance.

Basilica Santa Maria della Sanità & Catacomba di San Gaudioso CHURCH, CATACOMB
(Map p66; ☑ 081 744 37 14; www.catacombedinapoli.it; Piazza Sanità 14; basilica free, catacomb adult/reduced €8/5; ☉ basilica 9am-1pm, 50min catacomb tours 10am, 11am, noon, 1pm; ⬚ C51 to Piazza Sanità, Ⓜ Piazza Cavour, Museo) While we love the baroque paintings by Andrea Vaccaro and Luca Giordano – not to mention the two contemporary sculptures by Riccardo Dalisi – it's the eerie, one-of-a-kind catacomb beneath this 17th-century basilica that makes the place so utterly unforgettable. Entered through the 5th-century *cripta* (crypt) below the high altar, its damp walls reveal a rather macabre method of medieval burial.

First, bodies would be stored in the arched wall niches, where the *schiattamorti* (literally 'corpse squashers') would poke them to release all blood and bodily fluids. Once dried out, the body would be buried, while the skull would be cemented to the wall and set over a fresco of the dearly departed. These frescoes are clearer than ever thanks to recent restoration work. The skull positioned above a frescoed body depicted with paintbrushes and a ruler belonged to 16th-century mannerist painter Giovanni Balducci. The Florentine artist had struck a deal with the Dominicans – in return for

---

RICCARDO DALISI & THE ART OF BENEVOLENCE

From his *Sette angeli di Paul Klee* (Seven Angels of Paul Klee) sculptures at Salvator Rosa metro station to his quirky light sculptures at La Stanza del Gusto, the art of Riccardo Dalisi (b 1931) has become iconic within Naples. Dubbing himself '*Il designer del opera buffa*' (the designer of humorous creations), Dalisi turns scrap metal and junk into lively, whimsical sculptures that radiate a fantastical, childlike sensibility – from 'dancing' cans with top hats to 'amorous' *caffettiere* (percolators). Indeed, the Neapolitan *caffettiera* – an elongated version of the standard Italian model – is one of Dalisi's trademark motifs, an obsession that began after Italian design company Alessi commissioned him to design one for its 1979 catalogue.

Despite a string of other famous commissions for the likes of Zanotta, Fiat and Bisazza, Dalisi has always eschewed diva demands, preferring humility, humanity and a social conscience. Graduating as an architect in 1957, he first achieved fame as a pioneer of Italy's anti-design movement in the 1960s, which decried consumerist thinking in design in favour of individuality, spontaneity and an acknowledgement of every person's creative potential. By the 1970s, the artist was running *design povero* (poor design) workshops for underprivileged Neapolitan youth, teaching them how to turn scrap metal into works of art. His more recent collaboration with locals from the rough-and-ready Sanità district reached fruition with the birth of the **Iron Angels** (www.ironangels.it), an artisan co-op based inside a deconsecrated neighbourhood church. Offering work and hope to youth otherwise vulnerable to a life of crime, the group's recycled creations adorn a number of locations, including the ancient Catacomba di San Gennaro (p66).

As you'd expect, a visit to Dalisi's own **studio** (Map p60; ☑ 081 68 14 05; studiodalisi@libero.it; Calata San Francesco 59; ☉ 9am-1pm Mon-Fri, call ahead; ⬚ 128 to Via Aniello Falcone) **FREE** is a wonderful experience, its collection of rooms packed to the rafters with charismatic prototypes, works in progress and roll upon roll of the artist's paintings and illustrations (the recycling theme continues here, with Dalisi using only pre-used paper, much of which comes from schools). The gentle *maestro* also offers free three-, four- or five-day workshops (book a week ahead), though note that he does not speak English. While all visitors are welcome, don't forget to call ahead and book a time with Dalisi's assistant, Carla Rabuffetti, first.

decorating their catacomb free of charge, they would allow him to be buried here (considered a privilege at the time).

Another fascinating feature is the so-called *Trionfo della croce* (Triumph of the Cross) mosaic. Created in the 5th or 6th century, its earthy tones and unusually large lambs suggest that the artist hailed from Africa. The African connection continues with the catacomb's namesake, San Gaudioso, a North African bishop who died in Naples in AD 452 and was buried on this site.

In the crypt itself, scan the walls for an intensely colourful 9th-century fresco of the Madonna and Child flanked by figures believed to be St Gregory and St Marciano. The image was discovered in the 1990s beneath a 19th-century fresco.

Laboratorio Oste   MUSEUM, GALLERY

(Map p66; ☑081 44 44 45; www.facebook.com/LaboratorioOste; Via dei Cristallini 138; ☺usually 9am-6pm Mon Fri; Ⓜ Piazza Cavour, Museo) The late Annibale Oste was one of Naples' most celebrated sculptors and designers and his workshop is now a small gallery-archive showcasing some of his works, including whimsical light sculptures, vases, and fantastical furniture pieces spanning 2001 to 2010. The venue, charming in itself, is now lovingly run by his artist children, Mariasole and Vincenzo, the latter's striking contemporary jewellery also on display (and for sale).

Deemed a visionary by his peers, Annibale Oste breathed a sense of energy and playfulness into materials as diverse as bronze, steel, wood, alabaster and glass. His use of fibreglass in the 1970s was lauded as pioneering, and his creations – which include a storage unit that evokes a deliciously giant chocolate block – are an extraordinary symphony of textures, shapes and colours. Interestingly, the building's courtyard was once used for staging plays, with the workshop's office used as a changing room by local actors. Among them was a young Totò, who would go on to become one of Italy's greatest comic film stars.

If you plan on visiting, it's always a good idea to email or call ahead to ensure that someone is there to let you in.

Palazzo dello Spagnuolo   ARCHITECTURE

(Map p66; Via dei Vergini 19; Ⓜ Piazza Cavour, Museo) In baroque-rich Naples, even staircases can be an event and the masterpiece gracing the courtyard of this *palazzo* is one of its most showstopping. Designed by Ferdi-nando Sanfelice and dating from 1738, its double-ramped, five-arched flights were put to good use in film classics like Luigi Zampa's *Processo alla città* (A City Stands Still) and Vittorio de Sica's *Giudizio universale* (Judgement Day). Believe it or not, horses once used the stairs, providing door-to-door service for lazy cavaliers.

If Sanfelice's sweeping architectural statement leaves you stair-crazy, a quick walk north will lead you to his debut effort inside the **Palazzo Sanfelice** (Via della Sanità 6; Ⓜ Cavour). Upon its completion in 1726 the double-ramped diva became the talk of the town, and from then on there was no stopping Sanfelice, who perfected his dramatic staircase design in various *palazzi* across the city.

Chiesa San Giovanni a Carbonara   CHURCH

(Map p66; ☑081 29 58 73; Via Carbonara 5; ☺9am-5.30pm Mon-Sat; Ⓜ Piazza Cavour, Museo) Sumptuous sculpture makes this Gothic church worth a detour. Andrea de Firenze, Tuscan sculptors and northern-Italian artists collaborated on the Gothic-Renaissance mausoleum of King Ladislas, soaring 18m behind the main altar. Behind it, the circular Cappella Caracciolo del Sole uplifts with its colourful 15th-century frescoes and Leonardo da Besozzo's tomb for Giovanni Caracciolo, the ambitious lover of King Ladislas' sister Queen Joan II of Naples. Caracciolo's increasing political power led the queen to plot his demise and in 1432 he was stabbed to death in the nearby Castel Capuano.

Other important works include the Cappella Caracciolo di Vico (renowned for showcasing early 16th-century Roman style in southern Italy), the *Monumento Miroballo* by Tommaso Malvito and Jacopo dell Pila and the colourful 14th-century Cappella Somma, complete with mannerist frescoes and an exquisite 16th-century altar executed by Annibale Caccarello and Giovan Domenico d'Auria. The 18th-century double-flight staircase leading up to the church itself is the work of baroque great Ferdinando Sanfelice. The church derives its name from its location, on the former site of an Angevin *carbonarius* (waste-disposal and incineration site).

◉ Mergellina & Posillipo

Located at the western end of the pedestrianised Lungomare (seafront), Mergellina exudes an air of faded grandeur with its Liberty *palazzi* and slightly scruffy seafront.

WORTH A TRIP

REGGIA DI CASERTA: THE ITALIAN VERSAILLES

The one compelling reason to stop at the otherwise nondescript town of Caserta, 30km north of Naples, is to gasp at the colossal, World Heritage–listed **Reggia di Caserta** (Palazzo Reale; ☑ 0823 27 71 11; www.reggiadicaserta.beniculturali.it; Viale Douhet 22; adult/reduced €12/6; ☺ palace 8.30am-7.30pm Wed-Mon, park 8.30am-1hr before sunset Wed-Mon, Giardino Inglese 8.30am-2hr before sunset Wed-Mon Jun-Aug, reduced hours rest of year; ℝ Caserta). With film credits including *Mission: Impossible 3* and the interior shots of Queen Amidala's palace in *Star Wars Episode 1: The Phantom Menace* and *Star Wars Episode 2: Attack of the Clones*, this former royal residence is Italy's monumental swan song to the baroque.

The complex began life in 1752 after Charles VII ordered a palace to rival Versailles. Neapolitan Luigi Vanvitelli was commissioned for the job and built a palace bigger than its French rival. With its 1200 rooms, 1790 windows, 34 staircases and 250m-long facade, it was reputedly the largest building in 18th-century Europe.

Vanvitelli's immense staircase leads up to the royal apartments, lavishly decorated with frescoes, art, tapestries, period furniture and crystal. The restored back rooms off the Sala di Astrea (Room of Astraea) house an extraordinary collection of historic wooden models of the Reggia, along with architectural drawings and early sketches of the building by Luigi Vanvitelli and his son, Carlo.

The apartments are also home to the Mostra Terrea Motus, an underrated collection of international modern art commissioned after the region's devastating earthquake in 1980. Among the contributors are US heavyweights Cy Twombly and Robert Mapplethorpe, as well as local luminaries Mimmo Paladino and Jannis Kounellis.

To clear your head afterwards, explore the elegant landscaped park, which stretches for some 3km to a waterfall and a fountain of Diana. Within the park is the famous **Giardino Inglese** (English Garden), a romantic oasis of intricate pathways, exotic flora, pools and cascades. Bicycle hire (€4) is available at the back of the palace building, as are pony-and-trap rides (€50 for 30 minutes, up to five people). Ignore the illegal souvenir hawkers roaming the palace grounds.

If you're feeling peckish, consider skipping the touristy palace cafeteria for local cafe **Martucci** (☑ 0823 32 08 03; Via Roma 9; pastries from €1.50, sandwiches from €3.50, salads €7.50; ☺ 5am-10.30pm Sun-Thu, to midnight Fri & Sat), located 250m east of the palace. Great coffee aside, the counters here heave with freshly made *panini* (sandwiches), salads, vegetable dishes, pastries and substantial cooked-to-order meals.

Regular trains connect Naples to Caserta (€3.90, 35 to 50 minutes) Monday to Saturday. Reduced services make Sunday an inconvenient day to visit. Caserta train station is located directly opposite the palace grounds. If you're driving, follow the signs for the Reggia.

Kitsch marina chalets sell gelato to loves-truck teens, while, close by, hydrofoils head out to the islands.

Further west, on the headland dividing the Bay of Naples from the Bay of Pozzuoli, Posillipo is a verdant, blue-ribbon neighbourhood of sprawling villas, secret swimming coves and the urban oasis of Parco Virgiliano.

Porticciolo
HARBOUR

(Map p60; Via Francesco Caracciolo; Ⓜ Mergellina) Once home to the area's fishing fleet, Mergellina's marina is now a crowd-pulling combo of anchored yachts and kitsch Neapolitan chalets, neon-lit seaside gelaterie and bars.

Pick up an ice-cream brioche at Chalet Ciro Mergellina (p80) and soak up the postcard view of the *castello* (castle) and volcano.

From here, opt for a lazy *passeggiata* (stroll) eastward along the car-free Lungomare (p62), or, if you don't mind the incline, head southwest along Via Mergellina, which becomes Via Posillipo, for enchanting vistas of the bay, the city and flouncy, salubrious villas.

Parco Vergiliano
ARCHAEOLOGICAL SITE, PARK

(Map p60; ☑ 081 66 93 90; Salita della Grotta 20; ☺ 9am-6pm; Ⓜ Mergellina) Head up the steep steps at this off-the-radar park and you'll find yourself peering into the world's longest

Roman tunnel. Designed by the architect Lucius Cocceius Auctus, the 700m-long engineering feat once linked Naples to Pozzuoli. At the top of the steps lies the tomb of Virgil, who died in Brindisi in 19 BC. Legend has it that the Roman poet's remains were carted to Naples and buried in this Augustan-era vault. Also buried in the park is the 19th-century poet Giacomo Leopardi.

Parco Virgiliano PARK

(Map p90; Viale Virgilio; ⊘ 7am-midnight May-Sep, to 9pm rest of year; 🚍 140 to Via Posillipo) Perched high above the shimmering sea on the westernmost tip of posh Posillipo hill, this much-loved park is the place to kick back on a terrace and soak up the views: Capri to the south; Nisida, Procida and Ischia to the southwest; and the Bay of Pozzuoli and Bagnoli to the west. Trendy Posillipo **market** takes place outside the main gates on Thursday between 9am and 2pm. History buffs may know that the tiny island of Nisida is where Brutus reputedly conspired against his overachieving nemesis Julius Caesar.

Kayak Napoli KAYAKING

(Map p90; ☑331 9874271; www.kayaknapoli.com; tours €20-30; 🚍140 to Via Posillipo) 🖋 Popular kayak tours along the Neapolitan coastline, gliding past often-inaccessible ruins, neoclassical villas and luscious gardens, as well as into secret sea grottoes. Tours cater to rookie and experienced paddlers, with day and night options. The meeting point is at Via Posillipo 68 (Baia delle Rocce Verdi) in the Posillipo neighbourhood. Tours are subject to weather and should be booked ahead.

⭐ Festivals & Events

Festa di San Gennaro RELIGIOUS

The faithful flock to the Duomo to witness the miraculous liquefaction of San Gennaro's blood on the Saturday before the first Sunday in May. Repeat performances take place on 19 September and 16 December.

Maggio dei Monumenti CULTURAL

(⊘May) A month-long cultural feast, with a bounty of concerts, performances, exhibitions, guided tours and events across Naples.

Wine & The City WINE

(www.wineandthecity.it; ⊘May) A two-week celebration of regional *vino,* with free wine tastings and events in palaces, museums, boutiques and eateries throughout the city.

Napoli Teatro Festival THEATRE

(www.napoliteatrofestival.it; ⊘ Jun) Three weeks of local and international theatre and performance art, staged in conventional and unconventional venues.

Madonna del Carmine RELIGIOUS

(⊘16 Jul) Pilgrims and fireworks on Piazza del Mercato, in honour of the Chiesa di Santa Maria del Carmine's miraculous Madonna.

Napoli Film Festival FILM

(www.napolifilmfestival.com; ⊘ Sep-Oct) Ten days of local and international flicks and celluloid chat.

✖ Eating

Naples is one of Italy's gastronomic darlings, and the bonus of a bayside setting makes for some seriously memorable meals. While white linen, candlelight and €50 bills are readily available, some of the best bites await in the city's spit-and-sawdust trattorias, where two courses and a salad can cost under €20. Even cheaper is Naples' plethora of top-notch pizzerias and *friggitorie* (fried-food kiosks). On the downside, many eateries close for two weeks in August, so call ahead if visiting then.

✖ Centro Storico & Mercato

⭐Pizzeria Gino Sorbillo PIZZA €

(Map p40; ☑081 44 66 43; www.accademiadellapizza.it; Via dei Tribunali 32; pizzas from €3.30; ⊘noon-3.30pm & 7pm-1am Mon-Sat; Ⓜ Dante) Day in, day out, this cult-status pizzeria is besieged by hungry hordes. While debate may rage over whether Gino Sorbillo's pizzas are the best in town, there's no doubt that his giant, wood-fired discs – made using organic flour and tomatoes – will have you licking finger tips and whiskers. Head in super early or prepare to queue.

⭐Salumeria BISTRO €

(Map p40; ☑081 1936 4649; www.salumeriaupnea.it; Via San Giovanni Maggiore Pignatelli 34/35; sandwiches from €3.70, charcuterie platters from €5.90; ⊘10am-midnight, closed Wed Sep-May; 🔊; Ⓜ Dante) The latest project for UpNea, a dynamic team known for hip arts events, this bistro-bar covers all bases, from coffee and house-baked morning muffins to soups, salads, charcuterie boards and insanely good *panini* (sandwiches) and hamburgers. The menu focuses on top-quality local produce;

WORTH A TRIP

BEACHSIDE DA GIONA

Slap bang on a sandy beach with views of Procida and Ischia, retro restaurant **Da Giona** (Map p90; ☑ 081 523 46 59; www.dagiona.it; Via Dragonara 6, Miseno; meals €35; ☺1-4pm Mon-Sun, plus 8-11pm Jun–mid-Sep; ☒ Cumana to Torregaveta, then EAV bus to Miseno) enjoys cult status among Neapolitans (book ahead on weekends). The seafood dishes are simple, fresh and lingering, from the *antipasto misto* (mixed antipasto, which might include fried zucchini and prawns, marinated carpaccio and octopus salad) to the unforgettable *spaghetti alle vongole* (spaghetti with clams). If the weather's on your side, request a table on the raffish deck (or right on the sand) and while away the hours with a local Falanghina. To get here from Naples, catch a Cumana train to Fusaro station, followed by an EAV bus to Miseno. Alternatively, take a taxi from Pozzuoli's Cumana or metro stations.

even the ketchup is made in-house using DOP Piennolo tomatoes from Vesuvius. Libations include Petragnola craft beers.

★Eccellenze Campane　　　NEAPOLITAN €
(☑ 081 20 36 57; www.eccellenzecampane.it; Via Benedetto Brin 49; pizzas from €6, meals €30; ☺7am-11pm Sun-Fri, to midnight Sat; ☐116, 192, 460, 472, 475) This is Naples' answer to Turin-based food emporium Eataly, an impressive, contemporary showcase for top-notch Campanian comestibles. The sprawling space is divided into various dining and shopping sections, offering everything from beautifully charred pizzas and light *fritture* (fried snacks) to finer-dining seafood, coveted Sal Da Riso pastries, craft beers and no shortage of take-home pantry treats. A must for gastronomes.

Tandem　　　NEAPOLITAN €
(Map p40; ☑ 081 1900 2468; Via G Paladino 51; meals €19; ☺noon-3.30pm & 7-11.30pm Thu-Tue; ☎; Ⓜ Duomo) *Ragù* might be a Sunday-lunch staple in Naples, but laid-back Tandem serves it up all week long. Whether you're tucking into *rigatoni al ragù* or a *ragù* fondue, expect rich, fragrant, warming goodness that could make your *nonna* weep. Complete with vegetarian options, it's a

small, simple spot with a cult following, so head in early or (on weekends) book.

La Campagnola　　　NEAPOLITAN €
(Map p40; ☑ 081 45 90 34; Via dei Tribunali 47; meals €18; ☺12.30-4pm & 7-11.30pm; ☎; Ⓜ Dante) Boisterous and affable, this spruced-up Neapolitan stalwart serves soul-coaxing classics. Daily specials include a killer *genovese* (pasta with a slow-cooked lamb, tomato and onion *ragù*) on Thursday, while week-round classics include hearty *salsiccia con friarielli* (pork sausage with Neapolitan bitter greens). If there's still room to move, conclude with the rum-soaked *babà*.

Jamón　　　DELI €
(Map p40; ☑ 335 7226405; Piazza San Domenico Maggiore 9; sandwiches €5, cheese & charcuterie tasting plates €5; ☺10am-midnight; Ⓜ Dante) Great for a piazza-side graze, this savvy little deli–wine bar sits at the top of sweeping Piazza San Domenico Maggiore. Offerings include niche and harder-to-find charcuterie and cheese; think organic, cinnamon-seasoned Tuscan mortadella and aged DOC San Daniele prosciutto. Savour them in a tasting plate, or sliced and freshly stuffed into a crusty *panino* (sandwich). Either way, wash down the goodness with an old-school tumbler or two of Italian or French wine.

★Gay-odin　　　SWEETS, GELATERIA €
(Map p40; ☑ 081 551 07 94; www.gay-odin.it; Via Benedetto Croce 61; gelato from €1.70; ☺9.30am-8.15pm Sun-Thu, to 11.30pm Fri & Sat; Ⓜ Dante) Not so much a chocolatier as an institution, Gay-odin concocts some of the city's finest cocoa creations, including oh-so-Neapolitan chocolate '*cozze*' (mussels). For a punch to the palate, try the chocolate-coated coffee beans or the fiery *peperoncino-cioccolato* (chilli-chocolate) combo. This branch also sells Gay-odin's sublime ice cream; it produces the city's best non-sorbet flavours.

La Masardona　　　NEAPOLITAN €
(Map p40; Via Capaccio Giulio Cesare 27; pizza fritta €4-5; ☺7am-3.30pm Tue-Fri, 7am-3.30pm & 6.30-11pm Sat, 7am-2pm Sun; ☎; Ⓜ Garibaldi) Naples' remarkably light *pizza fritta* – deep-fried pizza dough stuffed with pork *ciccioli* (dried lard cubes), salami, ham, smoked *provola* (provolone) cheese, ricotta and tomato – is best savoured at this legendary joint. Most regulars order it *senza ricotta* (without ricotta) and wash it down with sweet marsala wine. There's also an escarole, olive and

provola version. Snack-size *pizza fritta* is also available (€2 to €3). On Tuesday, owner Enzo serves his famous *tortaniello* (€3), a lip-smacking, oven-baked pie packed with *pecorino* cheese, salami, *cicoli* (pork lard) and hard-boiled egg.

Di Matteo
PIZZA, SNACKS €

(Map p40; ☑ 081 45 52 62; www.pizzeriadimatteo.com; Via dei Tribunali 94; snacks from €0.50, pizzas from €3; ☺ 9am-midnight Mon-Sat, to 3.30pm Sun; ☑ C55 to Via Duomo, Ⓜ Duomo) One of Naples' hardcore, low-frills pizzerias, Di Matteo is fronted by a popular streetfront stall that sells some of the city's best fried snacks, from *pizza fritta* (Neapolitan fried pizza) to nourishing *arancini* (fried rice balls). Inside, expect trademark sallow lighting, surly waiters and gorgeous pizzas.

Scaturchio
PASTRIES €

(Map p40; ☑ 081 551 70 31; Piazza San Domenico Maggiore 19; pastries from €1.50; ☺ 7.20am-8.30pm; Ⓜ Dante) In a city infamous for belt-busting temptations, this piazza-side *pasticceria* enjoys celebrity status. While you'll find all the local classics (including a particularly luscious *babà*), the star attraction is the *ministeriale*, a dark-chocolate medallion invented in the 19th century. The ingredients of its liqueur-laced ganache filling are a closely guarded secret.

Angelo Carbone
PASTRIES €

(Map p40; ☑ 081 45 78 21; Largo Regina Coeli 4-8; pastries from €1, sandwiches from €2.50; ☺ 7.20am-8pm Mon-Fri, 7am-5pm Sat & Sun; ☎ ; Ⓜ Piazza Cavour, Museo) Off the tourist trail, this chintzy bar-*pasticceria-rosticceria* makes one seriously buttery *sfogliatella* (sweet ricotta-filled pastry), not to mention a heavenly *pasticcino crema e amarena*

(short-pastry bun filled with cherries and custard). Savoury options include satisfying *panini*, not to mention warming *primi* (first-course dishes) for just €3 to €4. Don't miss the frescoed porticoes of the Chiesa Santa Maria Regina Coeli opposite.

Pizzeria Vesi
PIZZA €

(Map p40; ☑ 081 29 99 95; Via dei Tribunali 388; pizzas from €3; ☺ noon-5pm & 7pm-midnight Sun-Thu, to 1am Fri & Sat; Ⓜ Dante) If Gino Sorbillo is closed, this popular pizzeria makes for a handy back-up plan. The pizzas are more than decent and there's warm-weather alfresco seating for voyeuristic noshing.

Attanasio
BAKERY, PASTRIES €

(Map p40; ☑ 081 28 56 75; Vico Ferrovia 1-4; sfogliatelle €1.20; ☺ 6.30am-8pm Tue-Sun; Ⓜ Garibaldi) So you thought a *sfogliatella* from Pintauro was crispy perfection? Bite into the piping-hot ricotta filling at this retro pastry pedlar and prepare to reassess. But why stop there with so many trays of treats, from creamy *cannoli siciliani* to a runny, rummy *babà*? Savoury fiends shouldn't pass up the hearty *pasticcino rustico*, stuffed with *provola* cheese, ricotta and salami.

★ La Taverna di Santa Chiara
NEAPOLITAN €€

(Map p40; ☑ 339 8150346; Via Santa Chiara 6; meals €25; ☺ 12.30-3pm & 7-11pm Wed-Mon; ☎ ; Ⓜ Dante) Gragnano pasta, Agerola pork, Benevento *latte nobile:* this intimate, two-level eatery is healthily obsessed with small, local producers and Slow Food ingredients. The result is a beautiful, seasonal journey across Campania. For an inspiring overview, order the *antipasto misto* (mixed antipasto), then tuck into lesser-known classics like *zuppa di soffritto* (spicy meat stew) with a glass of smooth house *vino*.

A SCANDALOUS ADDRESS

Few buildings fire up the local gossipmongers like Posillipo's **Palazzo Donn'Anna** (Largo Donn'Anna 9; ☑ 140 to Via Posillipo). Incomplete, semiderelict yet hauntingly beautiful, it takes its name from Anna Carafa, for whom it was built as a wedding present from her husband, Ramiro Guzman, the Spanish viceroy of Naples. When Guzman hotfooted it back to Spain in 1644 he left his wife heartbroken in Naples. She died shortly afterwards and architectural whiz-kid Cosimo Fanzago gave up the project.

The grand-yet-forlorn heap sits on the site of an older villa, La Sirena (The Mermaid), reputed setting for Queen Joan's scandalous orgies and crimes of passion (rumour has it that fickle Joan dumped her lovers straight into the sea). Exactly which Queen Joan is up for debate. Some believe her royal nastiness was Joan I (1326–82), daughter of Charles, Duke of Calabria, whose list of alleged wicked deeds includes knocking off her husband. Others place their bets on Joan II (1373–1435), sister of King Ladislao, whose appetite for men remains the stuff of licentious legend. Palazzo Donn'Anna is not open to the public.

✖ Toledo & Quartieri Spagnoli

★ Pintauro
PASTRIES €

(Map p52; ☑ 348 7781645; Via Toledo 275; sfogliatelle €2; ⊙ 9am-8pm Mon-Sat, 9.30am-2pm Sun, closed mid-Jul–early Sep; ☑ R2 to Via San Carlo, Ⓜ Municipio) Of Neapolitan *dolci* (sweets), the cream of the crop is the *sfogliatella,* a shell of flaky pastry stuffed with creamy, scented ricotta. This local institution has been selling *sfogliatelle* since the early 1800s, when its founder supposedly brought them to Naples from their culinary birthplace on the Amalfi Coast.

Fantasia Gelati
GELATERIA €

(Map p52; ☑ 081 551 12 12; Via Toledo 381; gelato from €2.50; ⊙ 7am-1am Sun-Fri, to 2am Sat; Ⓜ Toledo) Many aficionados claim that when it comes to fruit flavours, no one comes close to this small gelateria, one of several Fantasia outposts across town. Make up your own mind with a serving of the sublime *cassata siciliana* flavour, made with sheep's-milk ricotta. The *gelato caldo* (hot gelato) flavours aren't actually warm – just creamier.

Trattoria San Ferdinando
NEAPOLITAN €€

(Map p60; ☑ 081 42 19 64; Via Nardones 117; meals €27; ⊙ noon-3pm Mon-Sat, 7.30-11pm Tue-Fri; ☑ R2 to Via San Carlo, Ⓜ Municipio) Hung with theatre posters, cosy San Ferdinando pulls in well-spoken theatre types and intellectuals. For a Neapolitan taste trip, ask for a rundown of the day's antipasti and choose your favourites for an *antipasto misto* (mixed antipasto). Seafood standouts include a delicate *seppia ripieno* (stuffed squid), while the homemade desserts make for a satisfying dénouement.

✖ Santa Lucia & Chiaia

★ Muu Muzzarella Lounge
NEAPOLITAN €

(Map p60; Vico II Alabardieri 7; dishes €7-14; ⊙ 12.30pm-1.30am Tue-Sat, 6.30am-1.30am Sun;

SECRET ARTISAN STUDIOS

Down dark streets, behind unmarked doors, in unsuspecting courtyards, artisan studios litter the *centro storico*. In these secret bolt-holes, some of Naples' most intriguing artists celebrate, reinterpret and sometimes subvert Neapolitan traditions – there's everything from meticulously crafted nativity statues to pop portraits of a scooter-riding Holy Family. Dive into the city's idiosyncratic arts scene at the following locations:

➜ **Lello Esposito** (Map p40; ☑ 335 5874189, 081 551 41 71; www.lelloesposito.com; Piazza San Domenico Maggiore 9; Ⓜ Dante) Dividing his time between Naples and New York, the infectiously charming Lello Esposito (who speaks very little English) is intrigued by Neapolitan cultural identity, symbolism and metamorphosis. It's a fascination that feeds large-scale sculptures and installations that explore and transform the city's folklore, from giant eggs with San Gennaro heads to bound Pulcinellas. According to Lello, modern Naples is no less baroque than its 18th-century self, a belief evident in the artist's thick, luscious, colour-saturated paintings. While you can always try your luck visiting unannounced – the studio is through the door to your right as you enter the *palazzo*'s main entrance – it's a good idea to call or email ahead (Lello's assistants can communicate in English).

➜ **Officina D'Arti Grafiche di Carmine Cervone** (Map p40; ☑ 081 29 54 83; carmine. cervone@libero.it; Via Anticaglia 12; ⊙ 9am-7.30pm Mon-Sat; Ⓜ Cavour, Museo) Lovers of print and typography shouldn't miss Carmine's one-of-a-kind printing workshop, crammed with rare vintage machinery, including a late 19th-century linotype machine. That Carmine speaks little English never detracts from the young gun's passion for his craft and his love of showing it off. Indeed, he often collaborates with artists, producing limited-edition prints, lithographs and books. He can even design and print business cards or invitations (allow two days) if you fancy your own take-home memento.

➜ **Zhao** (Map p40; ☑ 329 3469011; Via Atri 31; Ⓜ Dante) In a tiny studio opened with a giant 18th-century key, sculptor and painter Salvatore Vitagliano is known to use fragments of ancient terracotta figurines to create simple yet striking works that literally fuse old and new. This theme of 'temporal collision' extends to his Neapolitan playing cards, handpainted onto metro tickets. Call two days ahead to visit, though it's worth noting that Salvatore doesn't speak English.

☎; ☐C24 to Riviera di Chiaia) Pimped with milking-bucket lights and cow-hide patterned cushions, playful, contemporary Muu is all about super-fresh Campanian mozzarella, from cheese and charcuterie platters to creative dishes like buffalo bocconcini with creamy pesto and crunchy apple. Leave room for the chef's secret-recipe white-chocolate cheesecake, best paired with a glass of Guappa (buffalo-milk liqueur).

Antica Osteria Da Tonino   ITALIAN €
(Map p60; ☑ 081 42 15 33; Via Santa Teresa a Chiaia 47; meals €18; ☺ 1-4pm daily, plus 8pm-midnight Fri & Sat; Ⓜ Piazza Amedeo) Quick-witted octogenarian Tonino (nicknamed JR by his wife) is still going strong, just like his *osteria*. At the front, time-pressed *signore* pick up their takeaway orders, while at the few packed tables, Rubinacci suits, old-timers and the odd Nobel Prize winner (Dario Fo ate here) tuck into simple meals like *rigatoni ragù e ricottu* (rigatoni in a meat and ricotta sauce).

Moccia   PASTRIES, GELATERIA €
(Map p60; ☑ 081 41 13 48; Via San Pasquale a Chiaia 21-22; pastries from €0.70; ☺ 7am-8.30pm Wed-Mon; ☐ C24 to Riviera di Chiaia) With gleaming displays of dainty strawberry tartlets, liqueur-soaked *babà* and creamy gelato (try a watermelon and peach combo), no one is safe at this chichi *pasticceria* – blow-waved matriarchs, peckish professionals or waif-thin Chiaia princesses. The almond *caprese* is the best in town, and best washed down with a potent espresso.

★ L'Ebbrezza di Noè   NEAPOLITAN €€
(Map p60; ☑ 081 40 01 04; www.lebbrezzadinoe. com; Vico Vetriera 9; meals €37; ☺ 8.30pm-midnight Tue-Sun; Ⓜ Piazza Amedeo) A wine shop by day, 'Noah's Drunkenness' transforms into an intimate culinary hot spot by night. Slip inside for *vino* and conversation at the bar, or settle into one of the bottle-lined dining rooms for seductive, market-driven dishes like house special *paccheri fritti* (fried pasta stuffed with eggplant and served with fresh basil and a rich tomato sauce).

Topping it off are over 2000 wines, artfully selected by sommelier-owner Luca Di Leva. Book ahead.

★ Ristorantino dell'Avvocato   NEAPOLITAN €€
(Map p60; ☑ 081 032 00 47; www.ilristorantinodellavvocato.it; Via Santa Lucia 115-117; meals €40; ☺ noon-3pm & 7.30-11pm, lunch only Mon & Sun; ☎; ☐ 128 to Via Santa Lucia) This elegant yet welcoming restaurant has quickly won the respect of Neapolitan gastronomes. Apple of their eye is affable lawyer turned head chef Raffaele Cardillo, whose passion for Campania's culinary heritage merges with a knack for subtle, refreshing twists – think gnocchi with fresh mussels, clams, crumbed pistachio, lemon, ginger and garlic. The degustation menus (€40 to €45) are good value, as is the weekday 'three courses on a plate' lunch special (€12). Book ahead Thursday to Saturday.

Trattoria Castel dell'Ovo   SEAFOOD €€
(Map p60; ☑ 081 764 63 52; Via Luculliana 28; meals €25; ☺ 1-3.30pm & 8-11.30pm Fri-Wed, closed dinner Sun Nov-Apr; ☐ 128 to Via Santa Lucia) Many locals ditch the bigger, more touristy restaurants on Borgo Marinaro for this cheaper, friendlier bolt-hole. Sit beside bobbing boats and tuck into surf staples like *zuppa di pesce* (fish soup) and *insalata di polipo* (octopus salad with fresh tomato). Even if it's not on the menu, it's worth requesting the spaghetti with prawns, mussels, zucchini and Parmigiano. Cash only.

Da Ettore   NEAPOLITAN €€
(Map p60; ☑ 081 764 35 78; Via Gennaro Serra 39; meals €25; ☺ 12.30-3pm daily, 7.45-10.15pm Tue-Sat; ☐ R2 to Via San Carlo) This homely, eight table trattoria has an epic reputation. Scan the walls for famous fans like comedy great Totò, and a framed passage from crime writer Massimo Siviero, who mentions Ettore in one of his tales. Casting the spell are solid regional dishes like the signature *pasta patata e provola* (pasta with potato and cheese). Book two days ahead for Sunday lunch.

L'Altro Loco   ITALIAN €€€
(Map p60; ☑ 081 764 17 22; www.ristorantealtro loco.com; Vicoletto Cappella Vecchia 4/5; meals €55; ☺ 1-3.30pm Sat & Sun, 8-11.30pm Mon-Sat; ☐ C24 to Piazza dei Martiri) It might be a little overpriced, but few Neapolitan restaurants match the sophisticated ambience and service of this softly lit fine-diner, its booths peopled by well-tailored professionals and Loren lookalikes. The focus here is on freshness, lightness and subtlety, from the vibrant *insalatina di astici e gamberi* (lobster and shrimp salad) to a *millefoglie* paired with velvety Chantilly cream and strawberries.

The wine list is suitably compelling, with around 600 options, including unexpected New World standouts. Book ahead, especially on weekends.

✖ Vomero

Friggitoria Vomero
FAST FOOD €

(Map p64; ☑ 081 578 31 30; Via Domenico Cimarosa 44; snacks from €0.20; ⊗ 9.30am-2.30pm & 5-9.30pm Mon-Fri, to 11pm Sat; 🚋 Centrale to Piazza Fuga) The stuff of legend, this spartan snack bar makes some of the city's most scrumptious *fritture* (deep-fried snacks). Crunch away on tempura-style eggplant and spinach, *zeppole* (doughnuts), *frittatine di maccheroni* (fried pasta and egg) and *supplì di riso* (rice balls). Located opposite the funicular, it's a handy pit stop before legging it to the Certosa di San Martino.

Fantasia Gelati
GELATERIA €

(Map p64; ☑ 081 578 83 83; Piazza Vanvitelli 22; gelato from €2.50; ⊗ 7am-1am Mon-Fri, to 2am Sat, to 1.30am Sun; Ⓜ Vanvitelli) This branch of Naples' king of gelato serves fresh, seasonal, icy perfection to Vomero's middle-class gluttons. Do not deprive your taste buds!

Antica Cantina di Sica
NEAPOLITAN €€

(Map p64; ☑ 081 556 75 20; Via Gianlorenzo Bernini 17; meals €30; ⊗ noon-3.30pm Tue-Sun, 7-11.30pm Tue-Sat; Ⓜ Vanvitelli, 🚋 Chiaia to Cimarosa, Centrale to Piazza Fuga) This genteel gastronomic hideaway is true to classic regional fare made with salutary attention to detail. The generous antipasto is an inspiring introduction (think tender tripe in fragrant tomato sauce and buttery *parmigiana di melanzana*), while the *frittura mista* (mixed fried seafood) stays crispy to the last bite. The homemade desserts (try the velvety *cassata napoletana*) are equally inspired.

✖ Capodimonte & La Sanità

★ Pizzeria Starita
PIZZA €

(Map p66; ☑ 081 557 36 82; Via Materdei 28; pizzas from €3.50; ⊗ noon-4pm & 7pm-midnight Mon-Sat, 7pm-midnight Sun; Ⓜ Materdei) The giant fork and ladle hanging on the wall at this historic pizzeria were used by Sophia Loren in *L'Oro di Napoli*, and the kitchen made the *pizze fritte* sold by the actress in the film. While the 60-plus pizza varieties include a tasty *fiorilli e zucchine* (zucchini, zucchini flowers and *provola*), our allegiance remains to its classic marinara.

Cantina del Gallo
NEAPOLITAN €

(Map p66; ☑ 081 544 15 21; www.cantinadelgallo. com; Via Alessandro Telesino 21; pizzas from €4, meals €15; ⊗ 11am-4pm & 7pm-midnight Mon-Sat, noon-4pm Sun; 🐾; 🚌 C51 to Via Fontanelle) Neon-framed Catholic kitsch and a bucket of hot coals under the table to keep your tootsies toasty? No, you're not at *nonna's* house, just at one of La Sanità's best-loved locals. Tuck into *calzoncini* (stuffed wood-fired pizza dough) or the speciality *A'Cafona*, a garlicky wood-fired pizza topped with tomato, oregano, *peperoncino* (chili) and a combo of *pecorino*, Grana Padano and *parmigiano*. Staff are sweet but speak little English.

Tarallificio Esposito
BAKERY €

(Map p66; ☑ 081 45 49 06; Via Sanità 129; taralli from €0.50; ⊗ 8am-8.30pm Mon-Sat, to 2.30pm Sun; Ⓜ Piazza Cavour, Museo) Made with pepper, almonds and pork fat, oven-baked *taralli mandorlati* (savoury almond biscuits) are dangerously addictive and readily available at this heirloom Sanità bakery. But don't stop at the classic, with moreish variations including buttery *taralli* with *friarielli* (Neapolitan broccoli rabe), *olio* (olive oil) and lemon glaze. For a more substantial feed, fill up on the scrumptious focaccia.

✖ Mergellina & Posillipo

50 Kalò
PIZZA €

(Map p60; ☑ 081 192 04 66; www.50kalò.it; Piazza Sannazaro 201b; pizza from €5; ⊗ 12.30-4pm & 7.30pm-12.30am; 🐾; Ⓜ Mergellina) That this trendy pizzeria's name roughly translates as 'good dough' in Neapolitan is no coincidence. At the helm is third-generation *pizzaiolo* Ciro Salvo, whose obsessive research into Naples' most famous edible translates into wonderfully light, perfectly charred wood-fired pizzas. Quality is the key here: from the olive oil to the rustic pork salami, ingredients are sourced directly from local and artisanal producers.

Chalet Ciro Mergellina
GELATERIA €

(Map p60; ☑ 081 66 99 28; www.chaletciro.it; Via Mergellina 31; pastries from €2, gelato brioche €4; ⊗ 6.45am-2.30am Mon, Tue, Thu & Sun, to 3am Fri, to 4am Sat; Ⓜ Mergellina) This iconic seaside chalet sells everything from coffee and pastries to crêpes, but the reason to head here is for the *brioche con gelato*, a sweetened bun stuffed with delectable ice cream and topped with a dollop of *panna* (cream). Pay inside, choose your flavours at the streetside counter, and then kill the cals with a bayside saunter.

★ **Da Cicciotto**　　　　　SEAFOOD €€
(Map p90; ☑ 081 575 11 65; Calata Ponticello a
Marechiaro 32; meals €40; ☺ 1-4pm & 7pm-mid-
night; ☐ 140 to Via Posillipo) Perched on a cliff in
the fishing village of Marechiaro, low-key yet
elegant Cicciotto is a seasoned charmer. Edible highlights include a sublime *carpaccio
antipasto* (thin slices of raw seafood drizzled with lemon juice and olive oil), lightly
battered zucchini flowers stuffed with ricotta and a *pacchetti* pasta dish served with
local crab and cherry tomatoes.

Desserts such as *crostata* with lemon
cream, wild strawberries and Chantilly
cream are equally mesmerising. Book ahead.

Don Salvatore　　　　　NEAPOLITAN €€
(Map p60; ☑ 081 68 18 17; www.donsalvatore.it;
Via Mergellina 4a; meals €40; ☺ noon-4pm & 7.30-
11.30pm Thu-Tue; ☐ 140 to Via Mergellina) The
key to happiness? Balmy nights, sea breezes
and impeccable seafood. You're guaranteed
at least the last two at this stylish veteran,
with its *dolce vita* terrace and softly lit interior. Here, culinary clichés make way for
gems such as *cecinielle* (fried fish patties),
minestra in brodo (thick noodle broth) and
seppie con uva passa (baby squid with pine
nuts and raisins).

🍷 Drinking & Nightlife

Neapolitans aren't big drinkers, and in the
centro storico many people simply buy a
bottle of beer from the nearest bar and hang
out on the streets. Drinking hot spots here
include Piazza Bellini and Calata Trinità
Maggiore off Piazza del Gesù Nuovo, where
a high concentration of students, artists
and bohemians lend an energetic, live-and-
let-live vibe. Those after fashion-conscious
prosecco sessions should aim for Chiaia's
sleek bars, famed for their *aperitivo* spreads
(gourmet nibbles for the price of a drink,
nightly from around 6.30pm to 9.30pm).
Popular strips include Via Ferrigni, Via
Bisignano and Vico Belledonne a Chiaia.

Although Naples is no London, Milan
or Melbourne on the entertainment front,
it does offer some top after-dark options,
from opera and ballet to thought-provoking
theatre and cultured classical ensembles. To
see what's on, scan daily papers like *Corriere
del Mezzogiorno* or *La Repubblica* (Naples
edition), click onto www.napoliunplugged.
com, or ask at the tourist office. In smaller
venues you can usually buy your ticket at
the door; for bigger events try the box office inside **Feltrinelli** (Map p60; ☑ 081 032 23
62; www.azzurroservice.net; Feltrinelli Bookstore,
Piazza dei Martiri 23; ☺ 11am-2pm & 3-8pm Mon-
Sat; ☐ C24 to Piazza dei Martiri), or **Box Office**
(Map p60; ☑ 081 551 91 88; www.boxofficenapoli.
it; Galleria Umberto I 17; ☺ 9.30am-8pm Mon-Fri,
9.30am-1.30pm & 4.30-8pm Sat; ☐ R2 to Piazza
Trieste e Trento).

Spazio Nea　　　　　CAFE
(Map p40; ☑ 081 45 13 58; www.spazionea.it; Via
Constantinopoli 53; ☺ 9am-2am; 🛜; Ⓜ Dante)
Aptly skirting bohemian Piazza Bellini, this
whitewashed gallery features its own cafe-bar
speckled with books, flowers, cultured
crowds and alfresco seating at the bottom of a
baroque staircase. Eye up exhibitions of contemporary Italian and foreign art, then kick
back with a *caffè* or a Cynar *spritz*. Check
Nea's Facebook page for upcoming readings,
live music gigs or DJ sets. Satisfying bites include fresh, bountiful salads.

Intra Moenia　　　　　CAFE
(Map p40; ☑ 081 29 07 20; Piazza Bellini 70;
☺ 10am-2am; 🛜; Ⓜ Dante) Despite the sloppy
service, this ivy-clad literary cafe on Piazza
Bellini is a good spot for some square-side
downtime. Browse limited-edition books on
Neapolitan culture, pick up a vintage-style
postcard or simply sip a *prosecco* and
people-watch on the piazza. Wine costs from
€4 a glass and there's a range of *bruschette*,
salads and snacks to see off the munchies.

Caffè Gambrinus　　　　　CAFE
(Map p60; ☑ 081 41 75 82; www.grancaffegambri-
nus.com; Via Chiaia 12; ☺ 7am-1am Sun-Thu, to 2am
Fri, to 3am Sat; ☐ R2 to Via San Carlo, Ⓜ Municipio)
Grand, chandeliered Gambrinus is Naples'
oldest and most venerable cafe. Oscar Wilde
knocked back a few here and Mussolini had
some of the rooms shut to keep out left-wing
intellectuals. The prices may be steep, but
the *aperitivo* nibbles are decent and sipping
a *spritz* or a luscious *cioccolata calda* (hot
chocolate) in its belle époque rooms is something worth savouring.

Enoteca Belledonne　　　　　BAR
(Map p60; ☑ 081 40 31 62; www.enotecabelledonne.
com; Vico Belledonne a Chiaia 18; ☺ 10am-2pm &
4.30pm-2am Tue-Sat, 6.30pm-1am Mon & Sun; 🛜;
☐ C24 to Riviera di Chiaia) Exposed-brick walls,
ambient lighting and bottle-lined shelves
set a cosy scene at Chiaia's best-loved wine
bar – just look for the evening crowd spilling out onto the street. Swill, sniff and
eavesdrop over a list of well-chosen, mostly

Italian wines, including 30 by the glass. The decent grazing menu includes charcuterie and cheese (€16), crostini (from €6) and bruschetta (€7).

Cammarota Spritz   BAR

(Map p52; ☑ 320 2775687; Vico Lungo Teatro Nuovo 31; ◷ 4.30pm-midnight Mon, 11am-midnight Tue-Sat; ⓂToledo) Head to this threadbare Quartieri Spagnoli drinking hole for Naples' best bargain: €1 Aperol *spritz*, wine and beer. The place is a hit with local artists, students and eclectics, who guzzle and gossip under plastic grapes or perched on crates on the skinny street. Tip: if you're drinking wine, ask for the Fiano or Aglianico or you'll get the lesser-quality stuff.

Ba-Bar   BAR, CAFE

(Map p60; ☑ 081 764 35 25; www.ba-bar.it; Via Bisignano 20; ◷ 5pm-2am Sun-Fri, 11am-late Sat; ⓐ; ⓆC24 to Piazza dei Martiri) On a side street peppered with bars, vintage-pimped, candlelit Ba-Bar is a solid all-rounder, whether you're after a quick pre-dinner *spritz*, a lingering catch-up in the cosy back room, or a spirited foosball game in the basement. Expect a rotating list of interesting Italian wines, local and foreign beers, and a chilled, youthful vibe.

Mexico   CAFE

(Map p40; ☑ 081 551 52 99; Via Benedetto Croce 16; ◷ 7.30am-9pm Mon-Fri, to 1am Sat, to 11pm Sun; ⓂDante) Mexico may be a veteran of the local coffee scene, but its latest branch ditches old-school retro for new-school recycled timber, industrial detailing and Gen-Y baristas. Whether you opt for a stand-up espresso or a sit-down cappuccino, one thing remains unchanged: Mexico's velvety, aromatic brew. Decent sweet eats include plump *cornetti* (croissants), brownies and muffins.

Scaturchio   CAFE

(Map p60; Teatro San Carlo, Piazza Trieste e Trento; ◷ 8am-9pm; ⓆR2 to Via San Carlo, ⓂMunicipio) Cappuccinos come with complimentary arias at this sweeping, kitschy cafe, set inside the Teatro San Carlo. Settle into a chesterfield and sip away to Verdi, or kick back on the piazza and soak up the city's real-life opera scenes. While the cafe serves savouries such as *arancini*, stick to Scaturchio's trademark sweet treats, among them the celebrated *minestriale,* a decadent, dark-chocolate medallion.

Bar dell'Epoca   BAR

(Map p40; Via Santa Maria di Costantinopoli; ◷ 7am-2am Mon-Sat, to 2pm Sun; ⓐ; ⓂDante) You're not here for the lime walls or sallow lighting, you're here for Piazza Bellini's hottest bargains: €1.50 bottles of Peroni and €2 spritzes. These cut-priced libations draw no shortage of art- and music-school students and staffers, who spill out onto the street for fun, boisterous evening sessions. Banterous owner Peppe will even let you bring a pizza and eat it at his tables.

Libri e Caffè   CAFE

(Map p40; ☑ 081 1899 0753; www.facebook.com/LibriCaffeTeatroMercadante; Piazza Municipio 79; ◷ 9am-end of theatre show Mon-Sat, 4pm-end of theatre show Sun; ⓐ; ⓂMunicipio) ⌇ From the counter, tables and chairs to the bookshelves, much of this cafe-bookshop is made from recycled cardboard. Located inside the Teatro Mercadante, it's the brainchild of two local publishers, whose gusto for quality extends to the coffee and Italian wines. Edibles include organic *cornetti* and Slow Food Neapolitan dishes served in glass jars (€4; book ahead via email). Check the Facebook page for special events, which include occasional *aperitivo* DJ sessions, live music performances and book readings (in Italian).

Galleria 19   CLUB

(Map p40; www.galleria19.it; Via San Sebastiano 19; ◷ 11pm-5am Tue-Sat; ⓂDante) Set in a long, cavernous cellar scattered with chesterfields and industrial lamps, this popular *centro storico* club draws a uni crowd early in the week and twenty- and thirty-somethings on Friday and Saturday. Tunes span electronica, commercial and house. Check the website for upcoming events.

Fonoteca   CAFE, BAR

(Map p64; ☑ 081 556 03 38; www.fonoteca.net; Via Raffaele Morghen 31, C/F; ◷ noon-1am Mon-Thu, to 2am Fri & Sat, 6.30pm-1.30am Sun; ⓐ; ⓂVanvitelli, ⓆCentrale to Piazza Fuga) Groove away at this Vomero favourite, a hybrid music store/cafe/bar. Hunt for new and used vinyl and CDs spanning electronica and classic rock to jazz, blues and world, flick through art and music-themed tomes, or head straight to the slick back bar for *caffè*, cocktails and edibles like bruschetta and salads.

☆ Entertainment

Teatro San Carlo
OPERA, BALLET

(Map p60; ☎081 797 23 31; www.teatrosancarlo.it; Via San Carlo 98; ⊘box office 10am-5.30pm Mon-Sat, to 2pm Sun; 🚇R2 to Via San Carlo) One of Italy's top opera houses, the San Carlo stages opera, ballet and concerts. Bank on €50 for a place in the sixth tier, €100 for a seat in the stalls or – if you're under 30 and can prove it – €30 for a place in a side box. Ballet tickets range from €35 to €80, with €20 tickets for those under 30.

Be aware that not all shows take place on the main stage, with other venues including the smaller Teatrino di Corte in neighbouring Palazzo Reale.

Associazione Scarlatti
CLASSICAL MUSIC

(Map p60; ☎081 40 60 11; www.associazione scarlatti.it; Piazza dei Martiri 58; 🚇C24 to Piazza dei Martiri) Naples' premier classical music association organises an annual program of chamber-music concerts in venues including Castel Sant'Elmo and Palazzo Zevallos. Local talent mixes it with foreign guests, which have included the Amsterdam Baroque Orchestra, St Petersburg's Mariinsky Theatre Orchestra and Belgian composer Philippe Herreweghe. Tickets are normally available at the venue an hour before show time; expect to pay between €15 and €25 for a concert at Castel Sant'Elmo.

Centro di Musica Antica Pietà de' Turchini
CLASSICAL MUSIC

(Map p64; ☎081 40 23 95; www.turchini.it; Via Santa Caterina da Siena 38; 🚇Centrale to Corso Vittorio Emanuele) Classical-music buffs are in for a treat at this beautiful deconsecrated church, an evocative setting for concerts of mostly 17th- to 19th-century Neapolitan works. Tickets usually cost €10 (reduced €7), and upcoming concerts are listed on the venue's website.

Lanificio 25
LIVE MUSIC

(Map p40; www.lanificio25.it; Piazza Enrico De Nicola 46; admission €5-10; ⊘9pm-late Fri & Sat; MGaribaldi) This Bourbon-era wool factory and 15th-century cloister is now a burgeoning party and culture hub, strung with coloured lights and awash with video projections. Live music (usually from 10pm) is the mainstay, with mostly Italian outfits playing indie, rock, world music, electronica and more to an easy, arty, cosmopolitan crowd. Check the website or Facebook page for upcoming events.

Galleria Toledo
THEATRE

(Map p52; ☎081 42 50 37; www.galleriatoledo.org; Via Concezione a Montecalvario 34; ⊘box office 6-7.30pm Tue-Sat; MToledo) If it's cutting edge, independent or experimental, chances are it's playing at this cult-status theatre, tucked away in the Quartieri Spagnoli. Gigs span local and global plays and live music, with the odd offbeat arthouse flick thrown in for good measure. Phone bookings are taken (including at weekends), with ticket pick-up at the box office 30 minutes prior to the performance.

★Stadio San Paolo
FOOTBALL

(Map p90; Piazzale Vincenzo Tecchio; MNapoli Campi Flegrei) Naples' football team, Napoli, is the third most supported in Italy after Juventus and Milan, and watching it play in the country's third-largest stadium is a rush. The season runs from late August to late May; seats cost €20 to €100. Tickets are available from selected tobacconists, the agency inside Feltrinelli (p81), or Box Office (p81); bring photo ID.

On match days, tickets are also available at the stadium itself.

Teatro Palapartenope
LIVE MUSIC

(Map p90; ☎081 570 00 08; www.palapartenope it; Via Dai Bagallo 115; ⊘box office 9am-1pm & 2-5.30pm Mon-Fri, 9am-12.45pm Sat; 🚇Cumana to Edenlandia) Located in suburban Fuorigrotta, west of central Naples, the architecturally uninspiring Palapartenope is the biggest indoor concert venue in town. A 6000-plus seating capacity sets the scene for big-name Italian and international acts, which have included late local crooner Pino Daniele, Lou Reed and Spandau Ballet.

🔒 Shopping

Shopping in Naples is a highly idiosyncratic experience, dominated by specialist, family-heirloom businesses. For Neapolitan tailors and high-end labels, hit Chiaia's Via Calabritto, Via dei Mille and Via Gaetano Filangieri. For antiques, explore Via Domenico Morelli in Chiaia and Via Costantinopoli in the *centro storico*. Also in the *centro storico*, walk down Vico San Domenico Maggiore for a handful of interesting little shops selling everything from designer homewares to organic soaps. For the ultimate Neapolitan shopping experience, however, hit the markets, which peddle everything from dirt-cheap kinky knickers, frocks and shoes, to pots and pans. Many shops close for two weeks in August.

🏠 Centro Storico & Mercato

Kiphy   BEAUTY
(Map p40; ☑ 340 2849691; www.kiphy.it; Vico San Domenico Maggiore 3; ⊙10.30am-2pm & 4-7.30pm Mon-Fri Jun-Sep, 10.30am-2pm & 4-6.30pm Tue-Sat rest of year; Ⓜ Dante) ✦ In her heavenly-scented workshop, Pina Malin-

conico crafts handmade slabs of soap that look as beautiful as they smell. Lined up under low-slung lights, varieties include a refreshing orange-and-cinnamon blend. The freshly made shampoos, creams and oils use organic, fair-trade ingredients and can be personally tailored. Best of all, products are gorgeously packaged, reasonably priced and made with love.

Opening times are subject to change, so call before making a dedicated trip.

SARTORIAL NAPLES

Milan may be the international face of Italian style, but Naples is its heart and soul. The city's bespoke tailors are legendary and once drew the likes of early 20th-century Italian king Emmanuel III to their needles and threads.

The key to this success is traditional, handmade production, superlative fabrics and minute attention to detail and form. Suitwise, the look is more brat pack than power broker – slim-fit flexible cut, natural and unengineered shoulders (great for gesticulating), high-set armholes and the signature *barchetta* (little boat) breast pocket. A classic Neapolitan shirt will often feature fine Italian, Swiss or Irish cottons, hand-stitched collar, yoke and sleeve, hand-sewn buttonholes and gathered pleating at the shoulder.

While most of the boutiques offer prêt-à-porter threads and accessories (including ready-made suits), creating a shirt or suit from scratch will usually involve a couple of fittings and anything from three to eight weeks. Finished items can be shipped overseas.

Credit card at the ready, hit these needle-savvy icons for a Neapolitan revamp:

Anna Matuozzo (Map p60; ☑ 081 66 38 74; www.annamatuozzo.it; Viale Antonio Gramsci 26; Ⓜ Mergellina) The softly spoken Signora Matuozzo is a seasoned and respected *maestra* in the world of bespoke shirt-making. With a starting price of €400, her creations are well known for their exceptional fabrics, unique style and vintage hand-stitching. Silk ties complete the elegant look. Fittings must be booked.

Cilento (Map p40; ☑ 081 551 33 63; www.cilento1780.com; Via Medina 61-63; Ⓜ Municipio) In business since 1780, Cilento is as much a heritage site as it is a gentlemen's atelier, with 18th- and 19th-century family garments on display, and its own charming little textile museum next door (open on request). Bespoke suits aside, its seven-fold silk ties are also highly prized. Other temptations include handsome handmade shoes, ready-to-wear Cilento polo shirts, men's and women's bags, hard-to-find fragrances, and scarves.

Finamore (Map p60; ☑ 081 246 18 27; www.finamore.it; Via Calabritto 16; ⊙10am-1.30pm & 4-8pm Mon-Sat; ⧉ C24 to Piazza dei Martiri, C25 to Riviera di Chiaia) Trading since 1925, Finamore's strength is ready-to-wear and bespoke hand-sewn shirts for men. Pair with elegant sweaters and cardigans, or scan the racks for suit jackets and trousers. Irresistible accessories include scarves, handkerchiefs, and harder-to-find fragrances. There's a small selection of women's shirts.

Mariano Rubinacci (Map p60; ☑ 081 40 39 08; www.marianorubinacci.net; Via Chiaia 149E; ⊙10am-1.30pm & 4.30-8pm Mon-Sat; ⧉ C24 to Piazza dei Martiri) Beautiful, lightweight and precisely fitting suits from the granddaddy of Neapolitan tailoring, with prices to match. Former clients include Neapolitan film director Vittorio de Sica.

E. Marinella (Map p60; ☑ 081 764 42 14; www.marinellanapoli.it; Via Riviera di Chiaia 287; ⊙8am-8pm Mon-Sat, 9am-1pm Sun; ⧉ C25 to Riviera di Chiaia, C24 to Piazza dei Martiri) One-time favourite of Luchino Visconti and Aristotle Onassis, this pocket-sized, vintage boutique is *the* place for prêt-à-porter and made-to-measure silk ties in striking patterns and hues. Match them with an irresistible selection of luxury accessories, including shoes, vintage colognes and scarves for female style queens.

Scriptura ACCESSORIES
(Map p40; ☎081 29 92 26; Via San Sebastiano 22; ⏰3-8pm Mon, 10.30am-8pm Tue-Sat; Ⓜ Dante) Family-run Scriptura crafts beautiful, soft leather goods using top-shelf Tuscan leather. Its range includes handbags, satchels, wallets, belts and leather-bound notebooks, with styles and colours covering both the classic and the contemporary. Best of all, prices are reasonable, with bags starting at €38 and wallets at €35.

La Scarabattola CRAFTS
(Map p40; ☎081 29 17 35; www.lascarabattola.it; Via dei Tribunali 50; ⏰10.30am-2pm & 3.30-7.30pm Mon-Fri, 10am-6pm Sat; 🚌C55 to Via Duomo) Not only do La Scarabattola's handmade sculptures of *magi* (wise men), devils and Neapolitan folk figures constitute Jerusalem's official Christmas crèche, the artisan studio's fans include fashion designer Stefano Gabbana and Spanish royalty. Figurines aside, sleek ceramic creations (think Pulcinella-inspired place-card holders) inject Neapolitan folklore with refreshing contemporary style.

Colonnese ARTS, BOOKS
(Map p40; ☎081 45 98 58; www.colonnese.it; Via San Pietro a Maiella 32-33; ⏰9am-1.30pm & 4-7pm Mon-Sat; Ⓜ Dante) Neighbouring one of Italy's most esteemed music conservatories, this erudite bookshop fills with the sound of practising musicians. While most of its new and vintage-edition titles are in Italian, you'll also find quality original and reproduction Neapolitan prints from the 18th and 19th centuries. Look out for the collectable postcards dating back to the late 19th and early 20th centuries. The store occasionally opens on Sunday from 10am to 2pm.

Ars Neapolitana ARTS, CRAFTS
(Map p40; ☎392 537 71 16; Via dei Tribunali 303; ⏰10am-6.30pm Mon-Fri, to 3pm Sat, plus 10am-6.30pm Sat & Sun late Oct-early Jan; 🚌C55 to Via Duomo) Guglielmo Muoio sold his first *pastore* (nativity-scene figurine) at age 13. A decade on, the talented artisan has even exhibited at the European Parliament in Strasbourg. Drop into his little workshop-showroom and you'll probably find him sculpting or painting one of his impressively detailed terracotta saints, angels or 18th-century folkloric characters.

SerenDPT VINTAGE
(Map p40; ☎081 1899 5400; Via Santa Chiara 36/37; ⏰10.30am-8pm Mon-Sat; Ⓜ Università) Hankering for a '60s miniskirt? A 1920s cocktail frock? Gold lamé boots? Chances are you'll find them at this unisex repository of vintage cool. The shop also stocks one-off creations by local designers, including owners Amalia and Oriana, known for transforming anything from denim and curtains into cool wearables and accessories with cute detailing.

Interestingly, the shop runs a barter system: bring in your old clothes (in good nick and of the season) and receive credits that can be used to pay for up to 80% of an item's value. The shop also does small repairs.

Charcuterie Esposito FOOD & DRINK
(Map p40; ☎081 551 69 81; Via Benedetto Croce 43; ⏰9am-8pm Mon-Sat, to 2.30pm Sun; Ⓜ Dante) Even the doors heave with gourmet grub at this jam-packed little deli. Fill your bags with everything from pasta, macaroons and grappa (Italian pomace brandy) to lemon-flavoured olive oil and chocolate-coated figs.

Limonè FOOD & DRINK
(Map p40; ☎081 29 94 29; www.limoncellodinapoli.it; Piazza San Gaetano 72; ⏰10.40am-8.15pm; 🚌C55 to Via Duomo) For a taste of Napoli long after you've gone home, stock up on a few bottles of Limonè's homemade *limoncello* (lemon liqueur), made with organic lemons from the Campi Flegrei. Ask nicely and you might get a sip for free. Other take home treats include lemon pasta and risotto, lemon-infused grappa and *torrone* (nougat), and a refreshing *crema di melone* (melon liqueur).

Toledo & Quartieri Spagnoli

Talarico ACCESSORIES
(Map p52; ☎081 40 77 23; www.mariotalarico.it; Vico Due Porte a Toledo 4b; ⏰8am-8pm Mon-Sat; Ⓜ Toledo) Mario Talarico and his nephews have turned the humble umbrella into a work of art. Sought after by heads of state, each piece is a one-off, with mother-of-pearl buttons, a horn tip and a handle made from a single tree branch. While top-of-the-range pieces can fetch €300, there are more affordable options that will keep the budget-conscious singing in the rain.

Santa Lucia & Chiaia

Bowinkel ANTIQUES
(Map p60; ☎081 764 07 39; www.bowinkel.it; Via Santa Lucia 25; ⏰10am-1.30pm & 4-7.30pm Mon-Fri, to 1.30pm Sat; 🚌128 to Via Santa Lucia) The

city's finest vintage prints, photographs, paintings and frames. If you can't find what you're looking for here, check out its sister branch (☑081 764 43 44; Piazza dei Martiri), where you're just as likely to stumble across a Liberty-era fan or a model of a long-gone tram. Perfect if shopping for someone who has it all. Staff can arrange shipments.

Tramontano
ACCESSORIES
(Map p60; ☑081 41 48 37; www.tramontano.it; Via Chiaia 143-144; ⊙10am-1.30pm & 4-8pm Mon-Sat; ☑C24 to Piazza dei Martiri) Tramontano has a solid rep for its exquisitely crafted Neapolitan leather goods, from glam handbags and preppy-chic satchels to duffels and totes. Each year, a new bag is added to the Rock Ladies' Collection, inspired by a classic song, whether it's Patti Smith's 'Kimberley' or Creedence Clearwater Revival's 'Proud Mary'.

Contemporastudio
JEWELLERY
(Map p60; ☑081 247 99 37; www.asadventrella. it; Via Francesco Crispi 50; ⊙10am-1.30pm & 4-7.30pm Mon-Fri, 10am-1.30pm Sat; Ⓜ Piazza Amedeo) Concrete-clad Contemporastudio stocks funky, experimental jewellery by Neapolitan Asad Ventrella. From pasta-shaped necklaces made of solid silver to fat double-faced rings inspired by mythical sirens, Ventrella's creations burst with whimsy, confidence and an undeniable sense of place.

Livio De Simone
FASHION
(Map p60; ☑081 764 38 27; www.lds-fabrics.com; Via Domenico Morelli 17; ⊙10am-1.30pm & 4.30-8pm Mon-Sat; ☑C24 to Piazza dei Martiri) The late Livio De Simone put Capri on the catwalk, dressing Audrey Hepburn and Jackie O in his bold, colourful creations. Inspired by the island, summer and the sea, his daughter, Benedetta, keeps the vision alive with the label's distinctive hand- and block-printed *robe chemesiers* (shirt dresses), frocks, suits, coats, and matching bags, purses, luggage tags, cushion covers and bowls.

January and February sales serve up some fantastic savings.

TO MARKET, TO MARKET

Porta Nolana and La Pignasecca are only two of Naples' loud and legendary markets. Stock up on cheap shoes, cut-price kitchenware and the odd vintage gem at the following favourites:

Mercatino dell'Umberto (Map p60; Via Imbriani; ⊙7am-3pm Mon-Sat, closed Aug; ☑C25 to Riviera di Chiaia) Hit the stalls on Via Imbriani for hip bags, jewellery, shoes, threads, even the odd sarong. In the colder months you'll find a decent selection of scarves. Don't haggle. This is Chiaia, *bella*.

Fiera Antiquaria Napoletana (Map p60; Villa Comunale; ⊙usually 8am-2pm 3rd Sun of month, closed Aug; ☑C25 to Riviera di Chiaia) Suspended temporarily on our last visit, this waterfront antiques market usually peddles vintage silverware, jewellery, furniture, paintings, prints and wonderful, overpriced junk. A perfect spot for weekend ambling and hunting. Contact the tourist office for updates.

Mercatino di Antignano (Map p64; Piazza degli Artisti; ⊙8am-2pm Mon-Fri; Ⓜ Medaglie D'Oro) Up high in mild-mannered Vomero, this place is popular for bags, jewellery, linen, kitchenware, shoes, and new and end-of-season clothing. Hawk-eyed shoppers will usually find a decent deal.

Mercatino di Posillipo (Map p90; Parco Virgiliano; ⊙9am-2pm Thu; ☑140 to Via Posillipo) Located outside the main gates of Parco Virgiliano, this isn't the cheapest market, but it's the best for quality goods. Top buys include genuine designer clothing, women's swimwear, underwear, boots, linen, and cut-price jewellery and cosmetics. It's only the African vendors who don't mind a haggle.

Mercato Caramanico a Poggioreale (Via Marino di Caramanico; ⊙7am-1pm Fri-Mon, closed Aug; ☑1 or 2 to Via Nuova Poggioreale) Also known as the Mercatino delle Scarpe (Shoe Market), Naples' largest open-air market is famous for its kicks, from designer overstock to no-frills everyday brands. Located 2.5km northeast of Stazione Centrale (catch a tram to the market from the west side of Piazza Garibaldi), the place has over 550 stalls, with other good buys including handbags, casual wear, suits, colourful rolls of fabric,, and kitchenware.

Feltrinelli
BOOKS, MUSIC

(Map p60; ☑199 151173; www.lafeltrinelli.it; Piazza dei Martiri 23; ☺10am-9pm Mon-Fri, to 10pm Sat, 10am-2pm & 4-10pm Sun; ☑C24 to Piazza dei Martiri) Pick up anything from Italian music CDs and DVDs to novels and coffee-table tomes at this three-level book and music megastore, complete with cafe for a leisurely sip and browse. There's a fair-sized English-language section in the basement.

🅐 Vomero, Capodimonte & La Sanità

De Paola Cameos
JEWELLERY

(Map p64; ☑081 1916 8284; Via Annibale Caccavello 69; ☺9.30am-8pm Mon-Sat, to 1.30pm Sun, reduced hours winter; ☑Centrale to Piazza Fuga) Head here for a beautiful range of finely carved, made-on-site cameos as well as classic coral necklaces, earrings, pendants and bracelets. The workshop also sells Naples' renowned Capodimonte porcelain.

ℹ️ Information

Emergencies

For an ambulance, call ☑118.

Loreto-Mare Hospital (Ospedale Loreto Mare; ☑081 254 27 01, emergency room 081 254 27 43; Via A Vespucci 26; ☑154, ☑1, 2, 4) Central-city hospital with an emergency department.

Police Station (Questura; ☑081 794 11 11; Via Medina 75; ☑Università) Has an office for foreigners. To report a stolen car, call ☑081 79 41 43.

Tourist Information

Tourist Information Office (Map p40; ☑081 551 27 01; Piazza del Gesù Nuovo 7; ☺9am-5pm Mon-Sat, to 1pm Sun; ☑Dante) In the *centro storico*.

Tourist Information Office (Map p40; ☑081 26 87 79; Stazione Centrale; ☺8.30am-7.30pm; ☑Garibaldi) Inside Stazione Centrale (Central Station).

Tourist Information Office (Map p60; ☑081 40 23 94; Via San Carlo 9; ☺9am-5pm Mon-Sat, to 1pm Sun; ☑R2 to Via San Carlo, ☑Municipio) At Galleria Umberto I, directly opposite the Teatro San Carlo.

ℹ️ Getting There & Away

Air

Capodichino (p267), 7km northeast of the city centre, is southern Italy's main airport, linking Naples with most Italian and several other European cities, as well as New York. Budget carrier EasyJet operates several routes to/from Capodichino, including London, Paris, Brussels and Berlin.

Boat

Fast ferries and hydrofoils for Capri, Ischia, Procida and Sorrento depart from Molo Beverello in front of Castel Nuovo; hydrofoils for Capri, Ischia and Procida also sail from Mergellina.

Ferries for Sicily, the Aeolian Islands and Sardinia sail from Molo Angioino (right beside Molo Beverello) and neighbouring Calata Porta di Massa.

Bus

Most national and international buses now leave from **Terminal Bus MetroPark** (Map p40; ☑800 650006; Corso Arnaldo Lucci; ☑Garibaldi), located on the southern side of Stazione Centrale. The bus station is home to **Biglietteria Vecchione** (☑081 563 03 20; ☺6.30am-7.30pm Mon-Sat), a ticket agency selling national and international bus tickets.

Terminal Bus MetroPark serves numerous bus companies offering regional services, the most useful of which is **SITA** (☑089 40 51 45; www.sitasudtrasporti.it). Connections from Naples include Amalfi, Positano and Salerno.

In mid-2015, CLP and CTP buses were departing directly in front of Stazione Centrale on Piazza Garibaldi. This may change as construction work on the piazza nears completion; always check the departure point with your bus company as the area is in a state of flux.

Car & Motorcycle

Naples is on the north–south Autostrada del Sole, the A1 (north to Rome and Milan) and the A3 (south to Salerno and Reggio di Calabria).

Train

Naples is southern Italy's rail hub and on the main Milan–Palermo line, with good connections to other Italian cities and towns.

National rail company Trenitalia (p268) runs regular services to Rome (2nd class €11.80 to €43, 70 minutes to 2¾ hours, up to 49 daily). High-speed private rail company **Italo** (☑06 07 08; www.italotreno.it) also runs daily services to Rome (2nd class €15 to €39, 70 minutes, up to 15 daily). Not all Italo services stop at Roma Termini, with many stopping at Roma Tiburtina instead.

ℹ️ Getting Around

Non-resident vehicles are banned in much of central Naples, though there is no need for a car as a visitor. The city centre is relatively compact and best explored on foot. Furthermore, Naples is generally well served by buses, metro and suburban trains, trams and funiculars.

TIC (Ticket Integrato Campani) tickets – available at kiosks, tobacconists and vending machines – are valid on all city metro, bus, tram and funicular services, including Circumvesuviana and Cumana trains within the Naples city zone. The TIC *biglietto integrato urbano* (€1.50, 90 minutes) allows for only one trip on each mode of transport (except buses) within 90 minutes of validation. The TIC *biglietto giornaliero integrato urbano* (€4.50, daily), valid until midnight from validation, allows for unlimited travel on all city buses, trams, metro trains and funiculars.

The city's various transport companies offer their own tickets, for use on their services only. For example, ANM – which runs city buses, the four funiculars, and metro lines 1 and 6 – offers a €1 single-use ticket. State railway company FS (Ferrovie dello Stato) runs metro line 2, offering a €1.20 single-use ticket for use on that metro line.

Prices listed here are for integrated TIC tickets (*biglietto orario*).

Boat

Hydrofoils and ferries connect Naples to the islands of Capri, Ischia and Procida, as well as to Sorrento, year-round.

City Buses

A much cheaper alternative to a taxi, airport shuttle Alibus (p267) connects the airport to Piazza Garibaldi (Stazione Centrale) and Molo Beverello (€3 from selected tobacconists, €4 on board; 45 minutes; every 20 to 30 minutes).

ANM (p269) buses serve the city and its periphery. Many routes pass through Piazza Garibaldi.

City Funiculars

Three services connect central Naples to Vomero, while a fourth connects Mergellina to Posillipo.

City Trains

Metro Line 1 (Linea 1; www.anm.it) Runs from Garibaldi (Stazione Centrale) to Vomero and the northern suburbs via the city centre. Useful stops include Duomo and Università (southern edge of the *centro storico*), Municipio (hydrofoil and ferry terminals), Toledo (Via Toledo and Quartieri Spagnoli), Dante (western edge of the *centro storico*) and Museo (National Archaeological Museum).

Metro Line 2 (Linea 2; www.trenitalia.com) Runs from Gianturco to Garibaldi (Stazione Centrale) and on to Pozzuoli. Useful stops include Piazza Cavour (La Sanità and northern edge of *centro storico*), Piazza Amedeo (Chiaia) and Mergellina (Mergellina ferry terminal).

Change between lines 1 and 2 at Garibaldi or Piazza Cavour (known as Museo on Line 1).

Metro Line 6 (Linea 6; www.anm.it) A light-rail service running between Mergellina and Mostra.

City Trams

The most useful route is Line 1, which connects Poggioreale Market to Piazza Garibaldi (Stazione Centrale), the ferry and hydrofoil terminals, and Piazza Vittoria in Chiaia.

Taxi

Official fares from the airport are as follows: €23 to a seafront hotel or to Mergellina hydrofoil terminal; €19 to Piazza del Municipio or Molo Beverello ferry terminal; and €16 to Stazione Centrale.

Book a taxi by calling any of the following companies:

Consortaxi ☑ 081 22 22

Consorzio Taxi Napoli ☑ 081 88 88

Radio Taxi La Partenope ☑ 081 01 01

CAMPI FLEGREI

Stretching west of Posillipo Hill to the Tyrrhenian Sea, the oft-overlooked Campi Flegrei (Phlegrean Fields) counterbalances its ugly urban sprawl with steamy active craters, lush volcanic hillsides and priceless ancient ruins. While its Greek settlements are Italy's oldest, its Monte Nuovo is Europe's youngest mountain. Gateway to the region is the port town of Pozzuoli, home to archaeological must-sees and handy for ferries to Ischia and Procida.

❶ Getting There & Away

Metro Line 2 runs frequently from Naples to Bagnoli (€1.50) and Pozzuoli (€2.50) in the Campi Flegrei. Ferrovia Cumana commuter trains also run frequently between Naples, Bagnoli and Pozzuoli. In Naples, Cumana trains depart Stazione Cumana di Montesanto on Piazza Montesanto, 500m southwest of Piazza Dante. The Cumana line is also handy for Lucrino (€2.50, 29 minutes) and Fusaro (€3.20, 33 minutes).

EAV (☑ 800 211388; www.eavsrl.it) runs bus services throughout the Campi Flegrei, connecting Cumana trains to Bacoli and Cuma. That said, connections are often inconvenient and services unreliable. Beyond Pozzuoli, the easiest way to explore the Campi Flegrei is with a reputable local tour outfit such as **Yellow Sudmarine** (☑ 329 1010328, 334 1047036; www.yellowsudmarine.com; 2hr Pompeii guided tours €110).

Pozzuoli & Around

Founded around 530 BC by political exiles from the Aegean island of Samos, Pozzuoli (ancient Dikaiarchia) came into its own under the Romans, who in 194 BC colonised it, renamed it Puteoli (Little Wells) and turned it into a major port. It was here that St Paul is said to have landed in AD 61, that San Gennaro was beheaded and that screen goddess Sophia Loren spent her childhood. A bout of bradyseism (the slow upward and downward movement of the earth's crust) saw Pozzuoli's seabed rise 1.85m between 1982 and 1984, rendering its harbour too shallow for large vessels.

Indeed, geological curiosities surround the town, from the scorching Solfatara Crater 1.2km to the east to novice mountain Monte Nuovo 3km to the west.

◉ Sights

Anfiteatro Flavio RUIN
(Map p90; ✆848 80 02 88; Via Nicola Terracciano 75; adult/reduced €4/2; ⊙9am-1hr before sunset Wed-Mon; Ⓜ Pozzuoli, Ⓡ Cumana to Pozzuoli) Back in its ancient heyday, Italy's third-largest amphitheatre – desired by Nero, and completed by Vespasian from AD 69 to 79 – could hold over 20,000 spectators and was occasionally flooded for mock naval battles. Its best-preserved remains lie under the main arena. Wander among the fallen columns and get your head around the complex mechanics involved in hoisting caged wild beasts up to their waiting victims through the overhead 'skylights'.

Rione Terra HISTORIC SITE, RUIN
(Map p90; ✆848 80 02 88; www.cattedralepozzuoli.it; Largo Sedile di Porto; ⊙Duomo 10am-noon & 5.30-6.30pm Sat, 10-11.30am & 5.30-8pm Sun; Ⓜ Pozzuoli, Ⓡ Cumana to Pozzuoli) Rione Terra is Pozzuoli's oldest quarter and its ancient acropolis. The original 2nd-century-BC temple to Jupiter, Juno and Minerva was replaced by a temple to Augustus in the 1st century. The latter's marble columns now form part of the 17th-century Duomo, home to 13 paintings by 17th-century greats including Artemisia Gentileschi, Giovanni Lanfranco and Jusepe De Ribera. Below the current cluster of buildings is a trove of an ancient ruins, expected to reopen to the public in the near future.

Dating back to when Pozzuoli was the ancient port of Puteoli, the ruins include the *decumanus maximus* (main street), flanked by ancient taverns, millers' shops (complete with intact grindstones) and graffiti written by the poet Catallus in a slaves' cell. Archaeologists made the startling find after volcanic activity in the 1970s forced a mass evacuation of the quarter. Guided tours of the Duomo (€5) are run by cultural association Nemea and can be conducted in English if organised in advance by emailing info@associazionenemea.it. Contact Nemea for updates on the expected reopening of the ruins.

Solfatara Crater VOLCANO
(Map p90; ✆081 526 23 41; www.solfatara.it; Via Solfatara 161; adult/reduced €7/5; ⊙8.30am-7pm Apr-Oct, to 4.30pm rest of year; Ⓜ Pozzuoli) Some 2km up Via Rosini, which becomes Via Solfatara (about 900m north of the metro), the surreal Solfatara crater was known to the Romans as the Forum Vulcani (home of the god of fire). At the far end of the steaming, malodorous crater are the Stufe, in which two ancient grottoes were excavated at the end of the 19th century to create two brick *sudatoria* (sweat rooms). Guided 2½-hour evening visits (adult/reduced €15/6) also run regularly; see the website for dates.

Tempio di Serapide RUIN
(Map p90; Via Serapide; Ⓜ Pozzuoli, Ⓡ Cumana to Pozzuoli) Just east of the port, sunken in a

---

ℹ BEFORE YOU EXPLORE

Before exploring the Campi Flegrei, it's worth stopping at the helpful **tourist office** (Map p90; ✆081 526 14 81; www.infocampiflegrei.it; Largo Matteotti 1a; ⊙9am-3pm Mon-Fri; Ⓜ Pozzuoli, Ⓡ Cumana to Pozzuoli) in Pozzuoli to pick up tourist information and maps of the area. An easy five-minute walk downhill from the metro station, the tourist office also sells the good-value €4 cumulative ticket, which covers the Museo Archeologico dei Campi Flegrei, the Parco Archeologico di Baia, the Anfiteatro Flavio and the Scavi Archeologici di Cuma.

Also useful is bookshop **Libreria Lanovecento** (Map p90; ✆081 526 13 63; Via Carmine 2c/d; ⊙5-8pm Mon, 9am-1pm & 5-8pm Tue-Sat; Ⓜ Pozzuoli, Ⓡ Cumana to Pozzuoli), which stocks great books and information on the area and has internet access.

Campi Flegrei

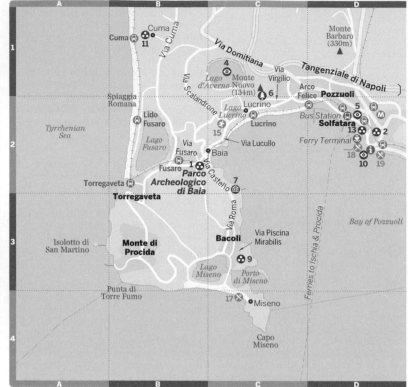

leafy piazza, sits the Tempio di Serapide. Despite its name, it wasn't a temple at all but an ancient *macellum* (town market) – the site is named after a statue of the Egyptian god Serapis found here in 1750. Its toilets (at either side of the eastern apse) are considered works of ancient ingenuity.

Mercato del Pesce di Pozzuoli — MARKET
(Pozzuoli Fish Market; Map p90; Via Nicola Fasano; ⊙7.30am-1.30pm Tue-Sun; M Pozzuoli, ℝ Cumana to Pozzuoli) Pozzuoli's atmospheric fish market is just the spot for an appetising morning stroll, though the best bargains are had at closing on Sunday. Good weather brings in the best catches, with local staples including *pesce azzurro* (mackerel), *pesce bandiera* (sailfish), *seppie* (squid), *polipi* (octopus), *alici* (anchovies) and *gamberoni* (giant prawns). The second of the two aisles is a mouth-watering spectacle of robust salami and *salsiccie* (sausages), plump cheeses,

local fruits and vegetables, and crunchy *casareccio* (home-style) bread.

Peckish? Stock up for an impromptu picnic on nearby Monte Nuovo. The market is an easy 300m walk northwest of the ancient market ruins of the Tempio di Serapide.

Monte Nuovo — PARK
(New Mountain; Map p90; ☑081 804 14 62; Via Virgilio; ⊙9am-1hr before sunset Mon-Sun, to 1pm Sun; ℝ Cumana to Arco Felice) At 8pm on 29 September 1538, a crack appeared in the earth near the ancient Roman settlement of Tripergole, violently spewing out a concoction of pumice, fire and smoke over six days. By the end of the week, Pozzuoli had a new 134m-tall neighbour. Today, Europe's newest mountain is a lush and peaceful nature reserve, its shady sea-view slopes the perfect spot for a picnic.

The mountain's 'conception' actually goes back to the early 1530s, when an unusual level of seismic activity began rattling the

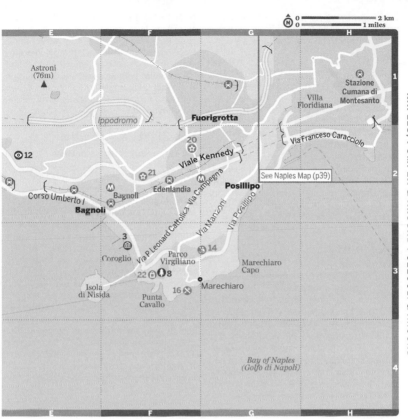

Campi Flegrei

◉ **Top Sights**

1 Parco Archeologico di Baia B2

◉ **Sights**

2 Anfiteatro Flavio.................................... D2
3 Città della Scienza F3
4 Lago d'Averno C1
5 Mercato del Pesce di Pozzuoli D2
6 Monte Nuovo C1
7 Museo Archeologico dei Campi
   Flegrei C2
8 Parco Virgiliano.................................... F3
9 Piscina Mirabilis C3
10 Rione Terra... D2
11 Scavi Archeologici di Cuma................. B1
12 Solfatara Crater E2
13 Tempio di Serapide D2

◉ **Activities, Courses & Tours**

14 Kayak Napoli..G3
15 Terme Stufe di Nerone C2

◉ **Eating**

16 Da Cicciotto... F3
17 Da Giona C4
18 Exytus Caffè... D2
19 Pizzaló.. D2

◉ **Entertainment**

20 Stadio San Paolo F2
21 Teatro Palapartenope F2

◉ **Shopping**

Libreria Lanovecento.................... (see 2)
22 Mercatino di Posillipo F3

area. It was at this time that locals also noticed a dramatic uplift of the land between Lago d'Averno, Monte Barbaro and the sea, a shift that displaced the coast by several hundred metres. Little did they know that under them a Monte Nuovo was preparing for its unforgettable entrance.

Città della Scienza
MUSEUM

(Science City; Map p90; ☑081 735 24 24; www. cittadellascienza.it; Via Coroglio 104; adult/reduced €8/5.50; ☺9am-3pm Mon-Sat, 10am-5pm Sun; ☒Cumana to Bagnoli, then C1 or R7 bus to Via Coroglio) Still rebuilding after a devastating fire in 2013, the interactive City of Science is part of a long-term redevelopment of the Bagnoli steelworks area, 5km southeast of central Pozzuoli. The hands-on museum is a particular hit with kids, who can explore everything from physics and constellations to volcanoes and healthy eating through a series of fun, engaging exhibitions.

Eating

Exytus Caffè
CAFE €

(Map p90; ☑081 526 70 90; Corso della Repubblica 126, Pozzuoli; cornetti €0.80; ☺7.30am-2am; ☒Pozzuoli, ☒Cumana to Pozzuoli) It might just be a tiny hole-in-the-wall (OK, technically, there are two holes in the wall), but Exytus is a street cafe with a big reputation. Join the kerbside crowd for espresso with perfect *schiuma zuccherata* (sugared froth), best enjoyed with a scrumptious *cornetto* (croissant); we have a major crush on the *crema e amarena* (custard and cherry) combo.

Pizzaló
PIZZA, NEAPOLITAN €€

(Map p90; ☑081 658 75 66; Corso Umberto I 17/19, Pozzuoli; meals €30; ☺noon-3.30pm & 7pm-midnight; ☏; ☒Pozzuoli, ☒Cumana to Pozzuoli) Facing Pozzuoli's popular esplanade, upbeat restaurant-pizzeria Pizzaló serves decent pizzas, as well as Neapolitan dishes with unexpected twists: *parmigiana di melanzane* (eggplant parmigiana) made with squid, or *paccheri alla genovese* (tube-shaped pasta with slow-cooked onion) laced with seafood. From extended families to local Kardashian wannabes, the outdoor tables are highly coveted on sunny days.

Lucrino, Baia & Bacoli

This string of towns spreads west from Pozzuoli along a built-up and inspiring coastal road. First up is Lucrino, where you'll find peaceful Lago d'Averno (the mythical entrance to hell) and a famous thermal spa centre. A further 3km southwest, Baia takes its name from Baios, a shipmate of Ulysses'

who died and was buried here. A glamorous Roman holiday resort with a sordid reputation, the ancient town is now mostly under water (bradyseism again), though evocative ruins and a recently expanded archaeological museum help kickstart the imagination. A further 4km south is the sleepy fishing town of Bacoli, home to the magical Piscina Mirabilis.

◉ Sights & Activities

★ Parco Archeologico di Baia
RUIN

(Map p90; ☑081 868 75 92; www.coopculture.it; Via Sella di Baia; Sat & Sun adult/reduced, €4/2 Tue-Fri free; ☺9am-3pm Tue-Sun Oct, Nov, Jan & Feb, to 4pm Tue-Sun Mar & Apr, to 6pm Tue-Sun May-Aug, to 5pm Tue-Sun Sep, to 2.45pm Tue-Sun Dec; ☒EAV to Baia, ☒Cumana to Fusaro) In Roman times, these 1st-century-BC ruins were part of a sprawling palace and spa complex. Emperors would entertain themselves and their guests in a series of lavishly decorated thermal baths that descended to the sea. Among the surviving snippets are exquisite floor mosaics, a beautifully stuccoed *balneum* (bathroom), an outdoor theatre and the impressive Tempio di Mercurio, its oculus-punctured dome predating Rome's Pantheon. The dome once covered a *frigidarium* (cold-water pool), located approximately 7m below the current water level.

On our last visit, weekend visitors were required to pre-purchase their tickets at the Museo Archeologico dei Campi Flegrei (p92). Note that if you have already purchased the cumulative ticket (p89) in Pozzuoli, you will avoid the hassle of trudging uphill to the Museo Archeologico dei Campi Flegrei for the sake of getting into the Parco Archeologico di Baia.

To get here on public transport, catch the Cumana train to Fusaro station and walk 150m north to Via Fusaro. From here, the site is a 900m walk east along Via Fusaro. Alternatively, from Via Fusaro, you can catch a Monte di Procida–bound EAV bus to the site (services run roughly every 20 minutes Monday to Saturday and every hour on Sunday). This bus can also be caught in central Naples, at Piazza Municipio or Piazza Vittoria.

Museo Archeologico dei Campi Flegrei
MUSEUM, CASTLE

(Archaeological Museum of the Campi Flegrei; Map p90; ☑081 523 37 97; cir.campania.beniculturali. it/museoarcheologicocampiflegrei; Via Castello 39; Sat & Sun €4, Tue-Fri free; ☺9am-2pm Tue-Sun, last entry 1pm; 🚌 EAV to Baia) This usually crowd-free museum occupies the Castello di Baia, built in the late 15th century by the Aragonese as a defence against possible French invasion. Later enlarged by Spanish viceroy Don Pedro de Toledo, it served as a military orphanage for most of the 20th century. Today, it's home to an interesting collection of local archaeological treasures. Among the highlights is a bewitching nymphaeum, dredged up from underwater Baiae and skilfully reassembled.

Other highlights include a bronze equestrian statue of the Emperor Domitian (altered to resemble his more popular successor Nerva upon his deposition) as well as finds from Rione Terra. Due to funding and management issues, opening times and access to various parts of the collection are notoriously changeable; on our last visit, both the nymphaeum and the statue of Domitian were off-limits to visitors. Contact the museum for updates.

Piscina Mirabilis   RUIN

(Marvellous Pool; Map p90; 📞 333 6853278; Via Piscina Mirabilis; donation appreciated; ⊙ hours vary, closed Mon; 🚆 Cumana to Fusaro, then EAV bus to Bacoli) You'll need to book (by phone) at least two hours ahead to visit the world's largest Roman cistern, but it's well worth the effort to stand in this underrated ancient wonder. Bathed in an eerie light and featuring 48 soaring pillars and a barrel-vaulted ceiling, the Marvellous Pool is more 'subterranean cathedral' than 'giant water tank'. While there is no entrance fee, a small tip (around €3 per person) is appropriate.

The cistern was an Augustan-era creation, its 12,600-cubic-metre water supply serving the military fleet at nearby Miseno. Fresh water flowed into the cistern from the Serino river aqueduct, which was then raised up to the terrace with hydraulic engines, exiting through doors in the central nave. Engineers still marvel at its technical sophistication.

Lago d'Averno   LAKE, RUIN

(Lake Averno; Map p90; Via Lucrino Averno; 🚆 Cumana to Lucrino) In Virgil's *Aeneid*, it is from Lago d'Averno that Aeneas descends into the underworld. It's hard to imagine hell in such a bucolic setting, where old vineyards and citrus groves fringe the ancient crater. A popular walking track now circles the perimeter of the lake, located an easy 1km walk north of Lucrino train station.

The lake's name stems from the Greek word άορνος, meaning 'without birds': according to legend, birds who flew over the lake would fall out of the sky. A likely explanation for this phenomenon was the release of poisonous volcanic gases from the lake's fumaroles. While it may have been unlucky for feathered critters, Lago d'Averno proved useful to Roman general Marcus Vipsanius Agrippa, who in 37 BC linked it to nearby Lago Lucrino and the sea, turning hell's portal into a strategic naval dockyard. The battleships may have gone, but the lakeside ruins of the **Tempio di Apollo** (Temple of Apollo) remain. Built during the reign of Hadrian in the 2nd century AD, this thermal complex once sported a domed roof almost the size of the Pantheon's in Rome. Alas, only four great arched windows survive.

Terme Stufe di Nerone   SPA

(Map p90; 📞 081 868 80 06; www.termestufe dinerone.it; Via Stufe di Nerone 45; day admission €30, 40min massage €35; ⊙ 8am-8pm daily Jun-Aug, 8am-8pm Mon, Wed & Sat, to 11pm Tue, Thu & Fri, to 6pm Sun rest of year; 🚆 Cumana to Lucrino) Your body will thank you after a trip to this verdant thermal-spa complex. Built on the site of an ancient Roman prototype (spot the remnants in the bar), its steamy grottoes, mineral baths and pools are a soothing antidote to Naples' muscle-tensing energy. Day passes must be booked via the website, where you can also book beauty treatments and massages.

Book treatments at least two days in advance. Swimming caps are obligatory for use of the pools and can be purchased (along with a towel) for €8. Flip-flops are also available for €3. From Lucrino train station, walk 500m southwest along Via Miliscola before turning right into Via Stufe di Nerone. The entrance is 200m ahead. If you have your own wheels, on-site parking costs €2.50.

Cuma

Founded in the 8th century BC by Greek colonists from the island of Euboea, Cumae exerted a powerful sway on the ancient imagination. Today its ruins are among the region's most evocative, overlooking lush Mediterranean flora and the Tyrrhenian Sea.

Scavi Archeologici di Cuma   RUIN

(Map p90; 📞 081 854 30 60; Via Montecuma; admission €4; ⊙ 9am-3pm Jan, Feb, Oct & Nov, to

NAPLES, POMPEII & AROUND CUMA

2.45pm Dec, to 4pm Mar & Apr, to 6pm May-Aug, to 5pm Sep; 🚆 Cumana to Fusaro, then EAV bus to Cuma) Dating back to the 8th century BC, Cuma was the first Greek settlement on the Italian mainland. Its ruins are shrouded in ancient mythology: the Antro della Sibilla Cumana (Cave of the Cumaean Sibyl) – closed indefinitely in 2014 after the partial collapse of a wall – is where the oracle reputedly passed on messages from Apollo.

The poet Virgil, probably inspired by a visit to the cave himself, writes of Aeneas coming here to seek the sibyl, who directs him to Hades (the underworld), entered from nearby Lago d'Averno. More prosaic are recent studies that maintain that the 130m-long trapezoidal tunnel was actually built as part of Cuma's defence system.

Even more fantastical is the **Tempio di Apollo** (Temple of Apollo), built on the site where Daedalus is said to have flown in Italy. According to Greek mythology, Daedalus and his son Icarus took to the skies to escape King Minos in Crete. En route Icarus flew too close to the sun and plunged to his death as his wax-and-feather wings melted from the heat. At the top of the ancient acropolis stand the ruins of the Tempio di Giove (Temple of Jupiter). Dating back to the 5th century BC, it was later converted into a Christian basilica, of which the remains of the altar and the circular baptismal font are visible.

From the Fusaro Cumana station, walk 150m north to Via Fusaro, from where Cuma-bound EAV buses run roughly every 30 minutes Monday to Saturday and every hour on Sunday.

BAY OF NAPLES

Buried for centuries beneath metres of volcanic debris, Naples' archaeological sites are among the best-preserved and most spectacular Roman ruins in existence. And it's here, in the dense urban sprawl stretching from Naples to Castellammare, that you'll find Italy's blockbuster finest: Pompeii and Herculaneum, as well as a host of lesser-known jewels, from salubrious ancient villas to the country's largest vintage-clothes market.

While Pompeii, Herculaneum and Oplontis are within easy walking distance of stations on the Naples–Sorrento Circumvesuviana train line, Stabiae and Boscoreale both require a bit more searching around.

As for Mt Vesuvius, it's an easy shuttle-bus trip from Ercolano or Pompeii.

Herculaneum (Ercolano)

Ercolano is an uninspiring Neapolitan suburb that's home to one of Italy's best-preserved ancient sites: Herculaneum. A superbly conserved fishing town, the site is smaller and less daunting than Pompeii, allowing you to visit without the nagging feeling that you're bound to miss something.

◎ Sights

★ Ruins of Herculaneum
ARCHAEOLOGICAL SITE

(📱 081 732 43 27; www.pompeiisites.org; Corso Resina 187; adult/reduced €11/5.50, incl Pompeii €20/10; ⊙ 8.30am-7.30pm summer, to 5pm winter; 🚆 Circumvesuviana to Ercolano-Scavi) Upstaged by its larger rival, Pompeii, Herculaneum harbours a wealth of archaeological finds, from ancient advertisements and stylish mosaics to carbonised furniture and terror-struck skeletons. Indeed, this superbly conserved Roman fishing town of 4000 inhabitants is easier to navigate than Pompeii, and can be explored with a map and audioguide (€6.50).

From the site's main gateway on Corso Resina, head down the walkway to the ticket office (at the bottom on your left). Ticket purchased, follow the walkway to the actual entrance to the ruins.

Herculaneum's fate runs parallel to that of Pompeii. Destroyed by an earthquake in AD 62, the AD 79 eruption of Mt Vesuvius saw it submerged in a 16m-thick sea of mud that essentially fossilised the city. This meant that even delicate items, such as furniture and clothing, were discovered remarkably well preserved. Tragically, the inhabitants didn't fare so well; thousands of people tried to escape by boat but were suffocated by the volcano's poisonous gases. Indeed, what appears to be a moat around the town is in fact the ancient shoreline. It was here in 1980 that archaeologists discovered some 300 skeletons, the remains of a crowd that had fled to the beach only to be overcome by the terrible heat of clouds surging down from Vesuvius.

The town itself was rediscovered in 1709 and amateur excavations were carried out intermittently until 1874, with many finds carted off to Naples to decorate the houses of the well-to-do or ending up in museums. Serious archaeological work began again

Herculaneum

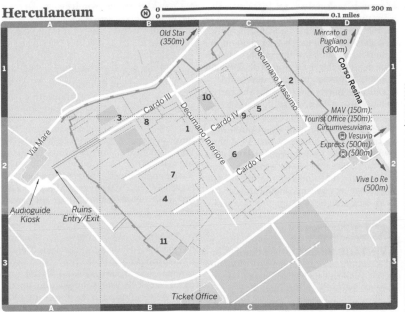

in 1927 and continues to this day, although with much of the ancient site buried beneath modern Ercolano it's slow going. Indeed, note that at any given time some houses will invariably be shut for restoration.

➡ Casa d'Argo

(Argus House) This noble house would originally have opened onto Cardo II (as yet unearthed). Onto its porticoed, palm-treed garden opens a *triclinium* (dining room) and other residential rooms.

➡ Casa dello Scheletro

(House of the Skeleton) The modest Casa dello Scheletro features five styles of mosaic flooring, including a design of white arrows at the entrance to guide the most disorientated of guests. In the internal courtyard, don't miss the skylight, complete with the remnants of an ancient security grill. Of the house's mythically themed wall mosaics, only the faded ones are originals; the others now reside in Naples' Museo Archeologico Nazionale (p51).

➡ Terme Maschili

(Men's Baths) The Terme Maschili were the men's section of the **Terme del Foro** (Forum Baths). Note the ancient latrine to the left of the entrance before you step into the *apodyterium* (changing room), complete with a

Herculaneum

◎ Sights

bench for waiting patrons and a nifty wall shelf for sandal and toga storage.

While those after a bracing soak would pop into the *frigidarium* (cold bath) to the left, the less stoic headed straight into the *tepadarium* (tepid bath) to the right. The sunken mosaic floor here is testament to the seismic activity preceding Mt Vesuvius' catastrophic eruption. Beyond this room lies the *caldarium* (hot bath), as well as an exercise area.

➡ Decumano Massimo

Herculaneum's ancient high street is lined with shops, and fragments of advertisements – listing everything from the weight of goods to their price – still adorn the walls. Note the one to the right of the Casa del Salone Nero. Further east along the street, a crucifix found in an upstairs room of the Casa del Bicentenario (Bicentenary House) provides possible evidence of a Christian presence in pre-Vesuvius Herculaneum.

⮞ Casa del Bel Cortile

(House of the Beautiful Courtyard) Inside the Casa del Bel Cortile lie three of the 300 skeletons discovered on the ancient shore by archaeologists in 1980. Almost two millennia later, it's still poignant to see the forms of what are understood to be a mother, father and young child huddled together in the last, terrifying moments of their lives.

⮞ Casa di Nettuno e Anfitrite

(House of Neptune & Amphitrite) This aristocratic pad takes its name from the extraordinary mosaic in the *nymphaeum* (fountain and bath). The warm colours in which the sea god and his nymph bride are depicted hint at how lavish the original interior must have been.

⮞ Casa del Tramezzo di Legno

(House of the Wooden Partition) Unusually, this house features two atria, which likely belonged to two separate dwellings that were merged in the 1st century AD. The most famous relic here is a wonderfully well-preserved wooden screen, separating the atrium from the *tablinum*, where the owner

---

WORTH A TRIP

VINTAGE VILLAS

Buried beneath the unappealing streets of Torre Annunziata, **Oplontis** (Via dei Sepolcri, Torre Annunziata; ⬚ Circumvesuviana to Torre Annunziata) was once a blue-ribbon seafront suburb under the administrative control of Pompeii. First discovered in the 18th century, only two of its houses have been unearthed, and only one, Villa Poppaea, is open to the public. This villa is a magnificent example of an *otium* villa (a residential building used for rest and recreation), thought to have belonged to Sabina Poppaea, Nero's second wife. Particularly outstanding are the richly coloured 1st-century wall paintings in the *triclinium* (dining room) and *caldarium* (hot bathroom) in the west wing. Marking the villa's eastern border is a garden with an envy-inducing swimming pool (17m by 61m). The villa is a straightforward 300m walk south from Torre Annunziata Circumvesuviana train station along Via Sepolcri.

South of Oplontis, **Stabiae** (Via Passeggiata Archeologica, Castellammare di Stabia; ⬚ Circumvesuviana to Via Nocera) stood on the slopes of the Varano hill overlooking what was then the sea and is now modern Castellammare di Stabia. Here at Stabiae you can visit two villas: the 1st-century-BC Villa Arianna and the larger Villa San Marco, said to measure more than 11,000 sq metres. Neither is in mint condition, but the frescoes in Villa Arianna suggest that it must once have been quite something. Stabiae is a 1.7km walk northeast of Via Nocera Circumvesuviana station. Alternatively, catch bus 074 or 077 from the station.

Some 3km north of Pompeii, the archaeological site of **Boscoreale** (Via Settetermini, Boscoreale; ⬚ Circumvesuviana to Pompeii-Scavi-Villa dei Misteri) consists of a rustic country villa dating back to the 1st century BC, and a fascinating antiquarium showcasing artefacts from Pompeii, Herculaneum and the surrounding region. Among the more unusual items on display are shreds of Roman fabric, eggshells from Pompeii and a carbonised loaf of bread. Closed for restoration on our last visit, the villa was due to reopen sometime in mid-2016; check www.pompeiisites.org or contact the Pompeii tourist office for updates. To reach the site on public transport, take the Circumvesuviana train to Torre Annunziata station and change to a Poggiomarino-bound train; Boscoreale station is two stops away. From the station, it's a 1.5km walk south to the ruins – head south (right) along Via M del Corte (which becomes Via Pompeii), then turn right into Via Settembrini (follow the signs for Antiquarium Boscoreale).

Opening times across the sites are standard: 8.30am to 7.30pm (last entry 6pm) April to October, 8.30am to 5pm (last entry 3.30pm) November to March. All three sites are covered by a single ticket (adult/reduced €5.50/2.75). The sites are also covered by a five-sites cumulative ticket (adult/reduced €20/10), which also includes Pompeii and Herculaneum.

talked business with his clients. The second room off the left side of the atrium features the remains of an ancient bed.

➡ Casa dell'Atrio a Mosaico

(House of the Mosaic Atrium) An ancient mansion (closed for restoration), the House of the Mosaic Atrium harbours extensive floor tile-work, although time and nature have left the floor buckled and uneven. Particularly noteworthy is the black-and-white chessboard mosaic in the atrium.

➡ Casa del Gran Portale

(House of the Large Portal) Named after the elegant brick Corinthian columns that flank its main entrance, the House of the Large Portal is home to some well-preserved paintings.

➡ Casa dei Cervi

(House of the Stags) Closed indefinitely on our last visit, the Casa dei Cervi is an imposing example of a Roman noble family's house that, before the volcanic mudslide, boasted a seafront address. Constructed around a central courtyard, the two-storey villa contains murals and some beautiful still-life paintings. Waiting for you in the courtyard is a diminutive pair of marble deer assailed by dogs, and an engaging statue of a drunken, peeing Hercules.

➡ Terme Suburbane

(Suburban Baths) Marking Herculaneum's southernmost tip is the 1st-century-AD Terme Suburbane (closed for restoration), one of the best-preserved Roman bath complexes in existence, with deep pools, stucco friezes and bas-reliefs looking down upon marble seats and floors. This is also one of the best places to observe the soaring volcanic deposits that smothered the ancient coastline.

| MAV | MUSEUM |

(Museo Archeologico Virtuale; ☑081 1980 6511; www.museomav.com; Via IV Novembre 44; adult/reduced €7.50/6, optional 3D documentary €4; ☺9am-5.30pm daily Mar-Sep, reduced hours rest of year, ☒Circumvesuviana to Ercolano-Scavi) Using high-tech holograms and computer-generated recreations, this 'virtual archaeological museum' brings ruins like Pompeii's forum and Capri's Villa Jovis back to virtual life. Especially fun for kids, it's a useful place to comprehend just how impressive those crumbling columns once were.

| Mercato di Pugliano | MARKET |

(Via Pugliano; ☺9am-1pm Mon-Sat; ☒Circumvesuviana to Ercolano-Scavi) Straddling Via Pugliano in the heart of Ercolano, Italy's largest pre-loved clothing market sells everything from stock-standard junk to fabulous offbeat finds (killer cocktail dresses, vinyl-LP handbags and the odd military jacket). One of the best shops is Old Star (Via Pugliano 60; ☺8am-1pm Mon-Sun); ask politely to check out the rare stock upstairs, often borrowed by international designers for study and inspiration.

Look out for the vintage Moschino and Fendi, ornate 1970s Indian fashion, and top-quality cashmere sweaters. From the Circumvesuviana Ercolano-Scavi station, walk downhill 400m to Prima Traversa Mercato. Turn right into it and you'll stumble onto Via Pugliano 200m later.

✖ Eating

★ Viva Lo Re — NEAPOLITAN €€

(☑081 739 02 07; www.vivalore.it; Corso Resina 261; meals €35; ☺noon-4pm & 8.30pm-late Tue-Sat, noon-4pm Sun; ☒Circumvesuviana to Ercolano-Scavi) Located 500m southeast of the ruins of Herculaneum on Corso Resina – dubbed the Miglio d'oro (Golden Mile) for its once-glorious stretch of 18th-century villas – Viva Lo Re is a stylish, inviting osteria, where vintage prints and bookshelves meet a superb wine list, gracious staff and gorgeous, revamped regional cooking. Start on a high note with the artful antipasto, whose row of 'tastings' may include a polpettina di baccalà (salted-cod patty), crocchetta di taleggio con porcino (taleggio and porcini croquette) or a ricotta-filled zucchini flower. Topping it all off are some delectable desserts, like a heavenly strawberry tartlet.

ℹ Information

Tourist Office (Via IV Novembre 44; ☺9am-5.30pm Mon-Sat; ☒Circumvesuviana to Ercolano-Scavi) Ercolano's new tourist office is located in the same building as MAV (p97), between the Circumvesuviana Ercolano-Scavi train station and the Herculaneum scavi (ruins).

ℹ Getting There & Away

If travelling by Circumvesuviana train (€2.50 from Naples or Sorrento), get off at Ercolano-Scavi station and walk 500m downhill to the ruins – follow the signs for the scavi down the main street, Via IV Novembre.

NAPLES, POMPEII & AROUND HERCULANEUM (ERCOLANO)

If driving from Naples, the A3 runs southeast along the Bay of Naples. To reach the ruins of Herculaneum, exit at Ercolano Portico and follow the signs to car parks near the site. From Sorrento, head north along the SS145, which spills onto the A3.

From late May to October, tourist train Campania Express runs three times daily between Naples (Porta Nolana and Piazza Garibaldi Circumvesuviana stations) and Sorrento, stopping at Ercolano-Scavi and Pompei Scavi-Villa dei Misteri only. One-day return tickets (€15; €10 for Artecard holders) can be purchased at the stations, online at www.eavsrl.it or www.campaniartecard/grandtour, or call ☑ 800 600601.

VESUVIUS

Rising formidably beside the Bay of Naples, Mt Vesuvius forms part of the Campanian volcanic arch, a string of active, dormant and extinct volcanoes that include the Campi Flegrei's Solfatara and Monte Nuovo, and Ischia's Monte Epomeo. Infamous for its explosive Plinian eruptions and surrounding urban sprawl, it's also one of the world's most carefully monitored volcanoes. Another full-scale eruption would be catastrophic. Over half a million people live in the so-called 'red zone', the area most vulnerable to pyroclastic flows and crushing pyroclastic deposits in a major eruption. Yet, despite government incentives to relocate, few residents are willing to leave.

◉ Sights

Mt Vesuvius VOLCANO
(☑081 239 56 53; adult/reduced €10/8; ⊗9am-6pm Jul & Aug, to 5pm Apr-Jun & Sep, to 4pm Mar & Oct, to 3pm Nov-Feb, ticket office closes 1hr before the crater) Since exploding into history in AD 79, Vesuvius has blown its top more than 30 times. What redeems this slumbering menace is the spectacular panorama from its crater, which takes in Naples, its world-famous bay, and part of the Apennine mountains. Vesuvius is the focal point of the **Parco Nazionale del Vesuvio** (www.epnv.it), with nine nature walks around the volcano – download a simple map from the park's website. **Naples Trips & Tours** (☑349 7155270; www.naplestripsandtours.com; guided tour €50) also runs a daily horse-riding tour (€50, three to four hours).

The mountain is widely believed to have been higher than it currently stands, claiming a single summit rising to about 3000m rather than the 1281m of today. Its violent outburst in AD 79 not only drowned Pompeii in pumice and pushed the coastline back several kilometres but also destroyed much of the mountain top, creating a huge caldera and two new peaks. The most destructive explosion after that of AD 79 was in 1631, while the most recent was in 1944.

❶ Getting There & Away

Vesuvius can be reached by bus from Ercolano and Pompeii.

From Piazzale Stazione Circumvesuviana, outside Ercolano-Scavi train station, **Vesuvio Express** (☑081 739 36 66; www.vesuvioexpress.it; return incl admission to summit €20; ⊗every 40min, 9.30am to 4pm) runs buses to the summit car park. From here, an 860m path (best tackled in trainers and with sweater in tow) leads up to the crater (roughly a 25-minute climb).

Shuttle buses (☑340 9352616; www.busviadelvesuvio.com; Via Villa dei Misteri, Pompeii; return incl entry to summit adult/reduced €22/7; ⊗9am-4pm) depart hourly from outside Pompei Scavi-Villa dei Misteri Circumvesuviana train station, travelling to Boscoreale Terminal Interchange. From here, it's a 25-minute journey up the national park in a 4WD-style bus. Bookings are not required.

When the weather is bad the summit path is shut and bus departures are suspended.

If travelling by car, exit the A3 at Ercolano Portico and follow signs for the Parco Nazionale del Vesuvio.

POMPEII

Modern-day Pompeii (Pompei in Italian) may feel like a nondescript satellite of Naples, but it's here that you'll find Europe's most compelling archaeological site: the ruins of Pompeii. Sprawling and haunting, the site is a stark reminder of the malign forces that lie deep inside Vesuvius.

◉ Sights

★**Ruins of Pompeii** ARCHAEOLOGICAL SITE
(☑081 857 53 47; www.pompeiisites.org; entrances at Porta Marina, Piazza Esedra & Piazza Anfiteatro; adult/reduced €11/5.50, incl Herculaneum €20/10; ⊗8.30am-7.30pm summer, to 5pm winter) The ghostly ruins of ancient Pompeii make for one of the world's most engrossing archaeological experiences. Much of the site's value lies in the fact that the town wasn't simply blown away by Vesuvius in AD 79 but buried under a layer of *lapilli* (burning fragments of pumice stone). The result is a remarkably

well-preserved slice of ancient life, where visitors can walk down Roman streets and snoop around millennia-old houses, temples, shops, cafes, amphitheatres, and even a brothel.

The origins of Pompeii are uncertain, but it seems likely that it was founded in the 7th century BC by the Campanian Oscans. Over the next seven centuries the city fell to the Greeks and the Samnites before becoming a Roman colony in 80 BC. In AD 62, a mere 17 years before Vesuvius erupted, the city was struck by a major earthquake. Damage was widespread and much of the city's 20,000-strong population was evacuated. Fortunately, many had not returned by the time Vesuvius blew, but 2000 men, women and children perished nevertheless.

After its catastrophic demise, Pompeii receded from the public eye until 1594, when the architect Domenico Fontana stumbled across the ruins while digging a canal. Exploration proper, however, didn't begin until 1748. Of Pompeii's original 66 hectares, 44 have now been excavated. Of course that doesn't mean you'll have unhindered access to every inch of the Unesco-listed site – expect to come across areas cordoned off for no apparent reason, a noticeable lack of clear signs, and the odd stray dog. Audioguides are a sensible investment (€6.50, cash only) and a good guidebook will also help – try *Pompeii*, published by Electa Napoli.

In recent years, the site has suffered a number of high-profile incidents due to bad weather. Most recently, heavy rain caused the wall of an ancient shop to collapse in March 2014. Maintenance work is ongoing, but progress is beset by political, financial and bureaucratic problems.

➡ Terme Suburbane

Just outside ancient Pompeii's city walls, this 1st-century-BC bathhouse is famous for several erotic frescoes that scandalised the Vatican when they were revealed in 2001. The panels decorate what was once the *apodyterium* (changing room). The room leading to the colourfully frescoed *frigidarium* (cold bath) features fragments of stuccowork, as well as one of the few original roofs to survive at Pompeii. Beyond the *tepadarium* (tepid bath) and *caldarium* (hot bath) rooms are the remains of a heated outdoor swimming pool.

➡ Porta Marina

The ruins of Pompeii's main entrance is at Porta Marina, the most impressive of the seven gates that punctuated the ancient town walls. A busy passageway now, as it was then, it originally connected the town with the nearby harbour, hence the gateway's name. Immediately on the right as you enter the gate is the 1st-century-BC **Tempio di Venere** (Temple of Venus), formerly one of the town's most opulent temples.

➡ Foro

(Forum) A huge grassy rectangle flanked by limestone columns, the *foro* was ancient Pompeii's main piazza, as well as the site of gladiatoral battles before the Anfiteatro was constructed. The buildings surrounding the forum are testament to its role as the city's hub of civic, commercial, political and religious activity.

➡ Basilica

The basilica was the 2nd-century-BC seat of Pompeii's law courts and exchange. Their semicircular apses would later influence the design of early Christian churches.

➡ Tempio di Apollo

(Temple of Apollo) The oldest and most important of Pompeii's religious buildings, the Tempio di Apollo largely dates to the 2nd century BC, including the striking columned portico. Fragments remain of an earlier version dating to the 6th century BC.

➡ Tempio di Giove

(Temple of Jupiter) One of the two flanking triumphal arches of the Tempio di Giove still remains.

ⓘ PREPARING FOR POMPEII

If visiting Pompeii's ruins in summer, bring a hat, sunblock and plenty of water. If you've got small children, try to visit in the early morning or late afternoon, when the sun's not too hot. Unfortunately, there's not much you can do about the uneven surfaces, which are a challenge for strollers. To do justice to the place, allow at least three or four hours, longer if you want to go into detail. And don't forget to bring a passport or ID card to claim discounts or hire an audioguide.

Pompeii

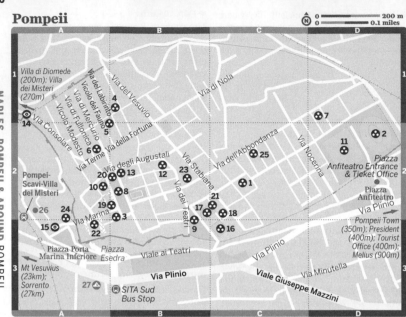

Pompeii

◉ Sights

◉ Activities, Courses & Tours

◉ Sleeping

➡ **Granai del Foro**

(Forum Granary) The Granai del Foro is now used to store hundreds of amphorae and a number of body casts that were made in the late 19th century by pouring plaster into the hollows left by disintegrated bodies. Among these casts is a pregnant slave; the belt around her waist would have displayed the name of her owner.

➡ **Macellum**

The *macellum* was the city's main produce market. The circular area in the centre was the *tholos*, a covered space in which fish and seafood were sold. Surviving market frescoes reveal some of the goods for sale, including prawns.

➡ **Lupanare**

Ancient Pompeii's only dedicated brothel, Lupanare is a tiny two-storey building with five rooms on each floor. Its collection of raunchy frescoes was a menu of sorts for clients. The walls in the rooms are carved with graffiti – including declarations of love and hope written by the brothel workers.

➡ **Foro Triangolare**

The verdant Foro Triangolare would originally have overlooked the sea.

➡ Teatro Grande

The 2nd-century-BC Teatro Grande was a huge 5000-seat theatre carved into the lava mass on which Pompeii was originally built.

➡ Quadriportico dei Teatri

Behind the Teatro Grande's stage, the porticoed Quadriportico dei Teatri was initially used for the audience to stroll between acts and later as a barracks for gladiators.

➡ Teatro Piccolo

Also known as the Odeion, the Teatro Piccolo was once an indoor theatre renowned for its acoustics.

➡ Tempio di Iside

(Temple of Isis) The pre-Roman Tempio di Iside was a popular place of cult worship.

➡ Casa del Menandro

Better preserved than the larger Casa del Fauno, luxurious Casa del Menandro has an outstanding, elegant peristyle (a colonnade-framed courtyard) beyond its beautifully frescoed atrium. On the peristyle's far right side a doorway leads to a private bathhouse, lavished with exquisite frescoes and mosaics. The central room off the far end of the peristyle features a striking mosaic of the ancient Greek dramatist Menander, after which the rediscovered villa was named.

➡ Via dell'Abbondanza

(Street of Abundance) The Via dell'Abbondanza was ancient Pompeii's Main Street. The elevated stepping stones allowed people to cross the street without stepping into the waste that washed down the thoroughfare.

➡ Terme Stabiane

At this typical 2nd-century-BC bath complex, bathers would enter from the vestibule, stop off in the vaulted *apodyterium* (changing room), and then pass through to the *tepidarium* (warm room) and *caldarium* (hot room). Particularly impressive is the stuccoed vault in the men's changing room, complete with whimsical images of *putti* (winged babies) and nymphs.

➡ Casa della Venere in Conchiglia

(House of the Venus Marina) Casa della Venere in Conchiglia harbours a lovely peristyle looking onto a small, manicured garden. Here in the garden you'll find the striking Venus fresco after which the house is named.

➡ Anfiteatro

(Amphitheatre) Gladiatorial battles thrilled up to 20,000 spectators at the grassy *anfiteatro*. Built in 70 BC, it's the oldest known Roman amphitheatre in existence.

➡ Grande Palestra

Lithe ancients kept fit at the Grande Palestra, an athletics field with an impressive portico dating to the Augustan period. At its centre, and closed off to public access, lie the remains of a swimming pool.

➡ Casa del Fauno

(House of the Faun) Covering an entire *insula* (city block) and boasting two atria at its front end (humbler homes had one), Pompeii's largest private house is named after the delicate bronze statue in the *impluvium* (rain tank). It was here that early excavators found Pompeii's greatest mosaics, most of which are now in Naples' Museo Archeologico Nazionale (p51). Survivors include a beautiful, geometrically patterned marble floor.

➡ Casa del Poeta Tragico

(House of the Tragic Poet) Hidden behind scaffolding when we visited, the Casa del Poeta Tragico features the world's first known 'beware of the dog' – *cave canem* – warnings.

➡ Casa dei Vettii

The Casa dei Vettii is home to a famous depiction of Priapus with his gigantic phallus balanced on a pair of scales...much to the anxiety of many a male observer.

➡ Villa dei Misteri

This recently restored, 90-room villa is one of the most complete structures left standing in Pompeii. The **dionysiac frieze**, the most important fresco still on site, spans the walls of the large dining room. One of the biggest and most arresting paintings from the ancient world, it depicts the initiation of a bride-to-be into the cult of Dionysus, the Greek god of wine. A farm for much of its life, the villa's *vino*-making area is still visible at the northern end. Follow Via Consolare out of the town through **Porta Ercolano**. Continue past **Villa di Diomede**, turn right, and you'll come to Villa dei Misteri.

POMPEII TOURS

You'll almost certainly be approached by a guide outside the ticket office. Authorised guides wear identification tags. Reputable tour operators include:

➡ **Yellow Sudmarine** (p88)

➡ **Walks of Italy** (www.walksofitaly.com; 2½hr Pompeii guided tour per person €52)

For more information, contact the town's tourist office (p104).

Tragedy in Pompeii

24 AUGUST AD 79

8am Buildings including the **Terme Suburbane** ❶ and the **foro** ❷ are still undergoing repair after an earthquake in AD 63 caused significant damage to the city. Despite violent earth tremors overnight, residents have little idea of the catastrophe that lies ahead.

Midday Peckish locals pour into the **Thermopolium di Vetutius Placidus** ❸. The lustful slip into the **Lupanare** ❹, and gladiators practise for the evening's planned games at the **anfiteatro** ❺. A massive boom heralds the eruption. Shocked onlookers witness a dark cloud of volcanic matter shoot some 14km above the crater.

3pm–5pm Lapilli (burning pumice stone) rains down on Pompeii. Terrified locals begin to flee; others take shelter. Within two hours, the plume is 25km high and the sky has darkened. Roofs collapse under the weight of the debris, burying those inside.

25 AUGUST AD 79

Midnight Mudflows bury the town of Herculaneum. Lapilli and ash continue to rain down on Pompeii, bursting through buildings and suffocating those taking refuge within.

4am–8am Ash and gas avalanches hit Herculaneum. Subsequent surges smother Pompeii, killing all remaining residents, including those in the **Orto dei Fuggiaschi** ❻. The volcanic 'blanket' will safeguard frescoed treasures like the **Casa del Menandro** ❼ and **Villa dei Misteri** ❽ for almost two millennia.

TOP TIPS

» Visit in the afternoon
» Allow three hours
» Wear comfortable shoes and a hat
» Bring drinking water
» Don't use flash photography

Terme Suburbane
The *laconicum* (sauna), *caldarium* (hot bath) and large, heated swimming pool weren't the only sources of heat here; scan the walls of this suburban bathhouse for some of the city's raunchiest frescoes.

Villa di Diomede

Casa del Poeta Tragico

Porta Ercolano

Casa del Fauno

Tempio di Apollo

Basilica

Porta Marina

Terme del Foro

Macellum

Teatro Grande

Quadriportico dei Teatri

Porta di Stabia

Teatro Piccolo

Foro
An ancient Times Square of sorts, the forum sits at the intersection of Pompeii's main streets and was closed to traffic in the 1st century AD. The plinths on the southern edge featured statues of the imperial family.

Villa dei Misteri

Home to the world-famous *Dionysiac Frieze* fresco. Other highlights at this villa include *trompe l'oeil* wall decorations in the *cubiculum* (bedroom) and Egyptian-themed artwork in the *tablinum* (reception).

Lupanare

The prostitutes at this brothel were often slaves of Greek or Asian origin. Mattresses once covered the stone beds and the names engraved in the walls are possibly those of the workers and their clients.

Thermopolium di Vetutius Placidus

The counter at this ancient snack bar once held urns filled with hot food. The *lararium* (household shrine) on the back wall depicts Dionysus (the god of wine) and Mercury (the god of profit and commerce).

Casa dei Vettii

Porta del Vesuvio

EYEWITNESS ACCOUNT

Pliny the Younger (AD 61–c 112) gives a gripping, first-hand account of the catastrophe in his letters to Tacitus (AD 56–117).

Porta di Nola

Casa della Venere in Conchiglia

Porta di Sarno

③

⑦

Tempio di Iside

⑥

Grande Palestra

⑤

Casa del Menandro

This dwelling most likely belonged to the family of Poppaea Sabina, Nero's second wife. A room to the left of the atrium features Trojan War paintings and a polychrome mosaic of pygmies rowing down the Nile.

Orto dei Fuggiaschi

The Garden of the Fugitives showcases the plaster moulds of 13 locals seeking refuge during Vesuvius' eruption – the largest number of victims found in any one area. The huddled bodies make for a moving scene.

Anfiteatro

Magistrates, local senators and the games' sponsors and organisers enjoyed front-row seating at this veteran amphitheatre, home to gladiatorial battles and the odd riot. The parapet circling the stadium featured paintings of combat, victory celebrations and hunting scenes.

✖ Eating

You'll find an on-site cafeteria at the ruins, and no shortage of touristy, mediocre eateries directly outside the site. The modern town is home to a few better-quality options.

Melius DELI €
(☑081 850 25 98; Via Lepanto 156-160; ⊙8am-3pm & 4.30-8pm Mon-Fri, 8am-2pm & 4.30-8pm Sat, 8am-2pm Sun; ℝFS to Pompei, Circumvesuviana to Pompei Scavi-Villa dei Misteri) Beef up the larder (or picnic hamper) at this luscious gourmet deli, where local delicacies include fresh *mozzarella di bufala,* Graniano pasta, *sopressata Cilentana* (smoked salami from Cilento), citrusy Amalfi Coast marmalades and *liquore alla mela annurca,* a liqueur made using Annurca apples.

For a self-catered treat, pick up some fragrant bread, a bottle of local Falanghina and some ready edibles; the peppery marinated eggplant and *pizza di scarole* (escarole pie) are equally divine.

★President CAMPANIAN €€
(☑081 850 72 45; www.ristorantepresident.it; Piazza Schettini 12; meals €35; ⊙noon-4pm & 7pm-midnight, closed Mon Oct-Apr; ℝFS to Pompei, ℝCircumvesuviana to Pompei Scavi-Villa dei Misteri) With its dripping chandeliers and gracious service, the Michelin-starred President feels like a private dining room in an Audrey Hepburn film. At the helm is charming owner-chef Paolo Gramaglia, whose passion for local produce, history and culinary creativity translates into bread made to ancient Roman recipes, slow-cooked snapper paired with tomato purée and sweet-onion gelato, and deconstructed *pastiera* (sweet Neapolitan tart). The menu is creative and visual brilliance is matched by sommelier Eulalia Buondonno's swoon-inducing wine list, which features around 600 drops from esteemed and lesser-known Italian winemakers; best of all, the staff are happy to serve any bottle to the value of €100 by the glass.

A word of warning: if you plan on catching a *treno regionale* (regional train) back to Naples from nearby Pompei station (more convenient than the Pompei Scavi – Villa dei Misteri station on the Circumvesuviana train line), check train times first as the last service from Pompei can depart as early as 9.40pm.

ℹ Information

Tourist Office (☑081 850 72 55; Via Sacra 1; ⊙8.30am-3.30pm Mon-Fri) Located in the centre of the modern town.

ℹ Getting There & Away

To reach the *scavi* (ruins) by Circumvesuviana train (€3.20 from Naples, €2.80 from Sorrento), alight at Pompei Scavi-Villa dei Misteri station, located beside the main entrance at Porta Marina. Regional trains (www.trenitalia. com) stop at Pompei station in the centre of the modern town.

If driving from Naples, head southeast on the A3, using the Pompei exit and following the signs to Pompei Scavi. Car parks (about €5 all day) are clearly marked and vigorously touted. Among them is **Camping Spartacus** (☑081 862 40 78; Via Plinio 127), conveniently located opposite the ruins. From Sorrento, head north along the SS145, which connects to the A3 and Pompeii.

From late May to October, tourist train Campania Express runs three times daily between Naples (Porta Nolana and Piazza Garibaldi Circumvesuviana stations) and Sorrento, stopping at Ercolano-Scavi and Pompei-Scavi-Villa dei Misteri only. One-day return tickets (€15; €10 for Artecard holders) can be purchased at the stations or online.

The Islands

Best Places to Eat

➜ È Divino (p115)

➜ Il Focolare (p135)

➜ Il Geranio (p117)

➜ Caracalè (p138)

Best Places to Stay

➜ Hotel Villa Eva (p202)

➜ Mezzatorre Resort & Spa (p203)

➜ Hotel Semiramis (p203)

➜ Hotel La Vigna (p204)

Why Go?

Tossed like colourful dice into the beautiful blue Bay of Naples, the islands of the Amalfi Coast are justifiably famous and sought out. They are tantalisingly diverse as well. Procida, Ischia and Capri vary not just in ambience and landscape but also in their sights, activities and size. Picturesque Procida is the smallest of the trio; tiny, tranquil and unspoiled, and possible to explore in just a few hours. The fashionable flipside is Capri, with its celebrity circuit of experiences, sights and shops; plan your day (and your footwear) with care, especially if you're hoping to hike. Ischia is the largest island, with natural spas, botanical gardens, hidden coves and exceptional dining. If that all sounds too challenging, make a beeline for the beaches – they are the Bay of Naples' best.

When to Go

➜ The Bay of Naples' islands follow the climatic footsteps of the rest of Campania.

➜ Avoid August, which is when most Italians take their annual holiday, adding significantly to the swell of other nationalities who descend on the islands in midsummer. July is also busy, particularly on Ischia and Capri.

➜ The best months are April to May and September to October, which all enjoy generally clear skies and mild to warm temperatures.

➜ Easter can also be crowded, although the processions on Procida are an unmissable spectacle.

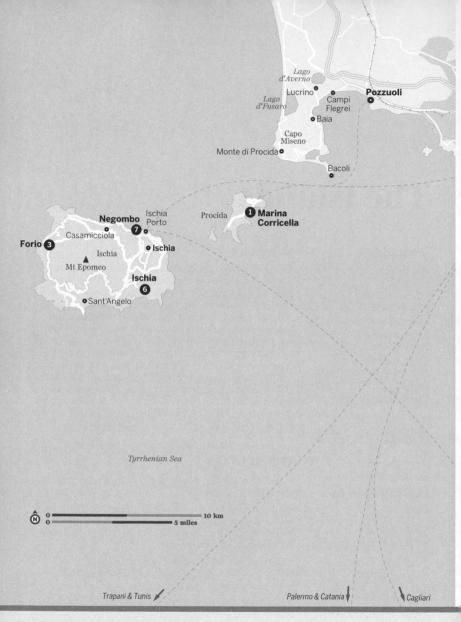

The Islands Highlights

1 Enjoying a lazy lunch at a seafood restaurant in the pastel-hued fishing village of **Marina Corricella** (p137).

2 Cruising the turquoise waters around Capri in a **hired boat** (p114).

3 Exploring the lush garden paradise of **La Mortella** (p132) in Forio.

4 Taking the chairlift to the top of **Monte Solaro** (p111), the highest point on Capri.

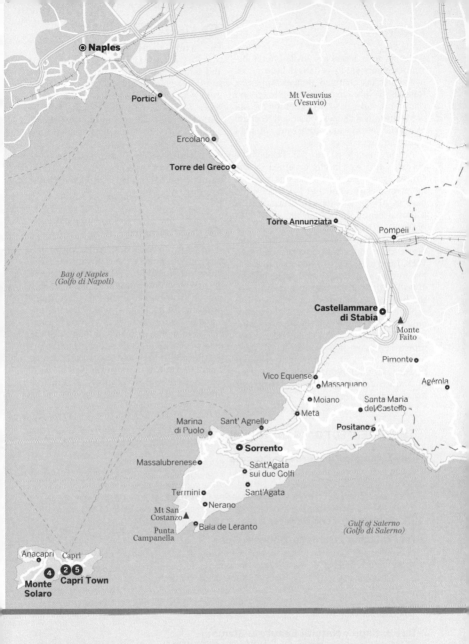

Naples

Portici

Mt Vesuvius
(Vesuvio)

Ercolano

Torre del Greco

Torre Annunziata

Pompeii

*Bay of Naples
(Golfo di Napoli)*

**Castellammare
di Stabia**

Monte
Faito

Pimonte

Agérola

Vico Equense

Massaquano

Moiano

Santa Maria
del Castello

Meta

Positano

Marina
di Puolo

Sant' Agnello

Sorrento

Massalubrense

Sant'Agata
sui due Golfi

Termini

Sant'Agata

*Gulf of Salerno
(Golfo di Salerno)*

Nerano

Mt San
Costanzo

Punta
Campanella

Baia de Leranto

Anacapri

Capri

4 **2 5**

**Monte
Solaro**

Capri Town

5 Strolling from Capri Town
to a **Roman villa** (p109) and a
natural rock arch.

6 Relaxing on one of the
pristine sandy stretches in
Ischia (p134).

7 Indulging in a soothing
dip and massage at spa park
Negombo (p131).

CAPRI

POP 12,200

Welcome to a legendary idyll: Capri's beguiling combination of fabled beauty and hedonism has charmed Roman emperors, Russian revolutionaries and Hollywood stars for decades. It's the perfect microcosm of Mediterranean appeal – a smooth cocktail of chichi piazzas and cool cafes, Roman ruins and rugged seascapes.

Already inhabited in the Palaeolithic period, Capri was briefly occupied by the Greeks before Emperor Augustus made it his private playground and Tiberius retired here in AD 27. Its modern incarnation as a tourist centre dates from the early 20th century.

It's also a hugely popular day-trip destination and a summer favourite of holidaying VIPs. Inevitably, the two main centres, Capri Town and its uphill rival Anacapri, are almost entirely given over to tourism, with the high prices that predictably follow. But explore beyond the swish cafes and designer boutiques and you'll find that Capri retains an unspoilt charm, with grand villas, overgrown vegetable plots, sun-bleached, peeling stucco and banks of brilliantly coloured bougainvillea. All of this overlooks the deep blue water that laps into secluded coves and mysterious grottoes.

◉ Sights & Activities

The name Capri comes, appropriately, from the ancient Greek *kaprie* (wild goat) and some would say that you need to be as sure-footed and nimble as a goat to explore the island properly. If time (or your pair of shoes) is tight, the island's sights may be visited by funicular, bus and/or taxi. The island has three distinct areas: sophisticated and downright good-looking Capri Town; more rural, low-key Anacapri; and bustling Marina Grande, which – unless you travel by helicopter – is likely to be your point of entry.

◉ Capri Town

With its whitewashed stone buildings and tiny, car-free streets, Capri Town feels more film set than real life. A diminutive model of upmarket Mediterranean chic, it's a pristine mix of luxury hotels, expensive bars, fancy restaurants and designer boutiques. In summer the centre swells with crowds of camera-wielding day trippers and gangs of the glossy rich, but don't be put off from exploring the atmospheric and ancient side streets, where the crowds quickly thin. And the walk west out of town to Villa Jovis shouldn't be missed.

THREE PERFECT DAYS ON THE ISLANDS

Day 1: Simple Pleasures on Procida

Escape the clamour and crowds of Naples and enjoy a day of tranquillity a short ferry hop away on this picturesque, unspoilt island. After a gentle stroll in the *centro storico* (historic centre), pull up a chair at lovely **Marina Corricella** (p137) for a simple meal of fresh seafood overlooking the fishing boats. Take an afternoon **boat trip** (p138) around the island's evocative hidden coves.

Day 2: Ischia's Gardens, Shops & Spas

Plan on an early arrival in Ischia, then head for the botanical gardens of **La Mortella** (p132) for a wander along the shady, cool pathways surrounded by exotic plants. Spend lunch near the beach at scenic **Sant'Angelo** (p135). In the afternoon, catch a water taxi to **Terme Cavascura** (p135), the island's oldest natural spa, for an afternoon of restorative self-pampering. Round off the day poking around the eclectic mix of **shops** (p129) on Via Roma, within walking distance of the ferry pier.

Day 3: Capri's Natural Beauty & Glamour

Turn up before the day trippers descend and join the local who's-who brigade at the emblematic square **La Piazzetta (Piazza Umberto I)**. Leave the surrounding sophisticated strut of shops behind as you head towards the nearby **Giardini di Augusto** (p111), with flower-filled terraces and some of the best views in Capri. Pick a restaurant overlooking the water, then enjoy the beauty of the island's **trails** (p114), with either a country amble or a more demanding hike.

Piazza Umberto I   PIAZZA

(Map p112; La Piazzetta) Located beneath the clock tower and framed by see-and-be-seen cafes, this showy, open-air salon is central to your Capri experience, especially in the evening when the main activity in these parts is dressing up and hanging out. Be prepared for the cost of these front-row seats – the moment you sit down for a drink, you're going to pay handsomely for the grandstand views (around €6 for a coffee and €16 for a couple of glasses of white wine).

★ **Villa Jovis**   RUIN

(Jupiter's Villa; Map p110; Via A Maiuri; admission €2; ⊙11am-3pm, closed Tue 1st-15th of month, closed Sun rest of month) A 45-minute walk east of Capri along Via Tiberio, Villa Jovis was the largest and most sumptuous of the island's 12 Roman villas and Tiberius' main Capri residence. A vast pleasure complex, now reduced to ruins, it famously pandered to the emperor's debauched tastes, and included imperial quarters and extensive bathing areas set in dense gardens and woodland.

The villa's spectacular location posed major headaches for Tiberius' architects. The main problem was how to collect and store enough water to supply the villa's baths and 3000-sq-metre gardens. The solution they eventually hit upon was to build a complex canal system to transport rainwater to four giant storage tanks, whose remains you can still see today.

The stairway behind the villa leads to the 330m-high **Salto di Tiberio** (Tiberius' Leap), a sheer cliff from where, as the story goes, Tiberius had out-of-favour subjects hurled into the sea. True or not, the stunning views are real enough; if you suffer from vertigo, tread carefully.

A shortish but steep walk from the villa, down Via Tiberio and Via Matermània, is the **Arco Naturale** (Map p110) – a huge rock arch formed by the pounding sea; you can time this walk to take in lunch at cave restaurant Le Grotelle (p115).

Chiesa di Santo Stefano   CHURCH

(Map p112; Piazza Umberto I; ⊙8am-8pm) Overlooking Piazza Umberto I, this baroque 17th-century church boasts a well-preserved marble floor (taken from Villa Jovis) and a statue of San Costanzo, Capri's patron saint. Note the pair of languidly reclining patricians in the chapel to the south of the main altar, who seem to mirror some of the mildly

GETTING YOUR BEARINGS

All hydrofoils and ferries arrive at Marina Grande, the island's transport hub. From here, the quickest way up to Capri Town is by funicular, but there are also buses and more costly taxis. On foot, it's a tough 2.3km climb along Via Marina Grande. At the top, turn left (east) at the junction with Via Roma for the centre of town or right (west) for Via Provinciale Anacapri, which eventually becomes Via Giuseppe Orlandi as it leads up to Anacapri.

Pint-sized Piazza Umberto I is the focal point of Capri Town. A short hop to the east, Via Vittorio Emanuele leads down to the main shopping street, Via Camerelle.

Up the hill in Anacapri, buses and taxis drop you off in Piazza Vittoria, from where Via Giuseppe Orlandi, the main strip, runs southwest and Via Capodimonte heads up to Villa San Michele di Axel Munthe.

debauched folk in the cafes outside. Beside the northern chapel is a reliquary with a saintly bone that reputedly saved Capri from the plague in the 19th century.

Certosa di San Giacomo   MONASTERY

(Map p112; ☑081 837 62 18; Viale Certosa 40; admission €4; ⊙9am-2pm Tue-Sun, plus 5 8pm summer) Founded in 1363, this picturesque monastery is generally considered to be the finest remaining example of Caprese architecture and today houses a school, a library, a temporary exhibition space and a museum with some evocative 17th-century paintings. Be sure to look at the two cloisters, which have a real sense of faded glory (the smaller is 14th century, the larger 16th century).

To get here take Via Vittorio Emanuele, east of Piazza Umberto I, which meanders down to the monastery.

The monastery's history is a harrowing one: it became the stronghold of the island's powerful Carthusian fraternity and was viciously attacked during Saracen pirate raids in the 16th century. A century later, monks retreated here to avoid the plague and were rewarded by an irate public (whom they should have been tending), who tossed corpses over the walls. There are some soothing 17th-century frescoes in the church, which will hopefully serve as an antidote as you contemplate the monastery's dark past.

Capri

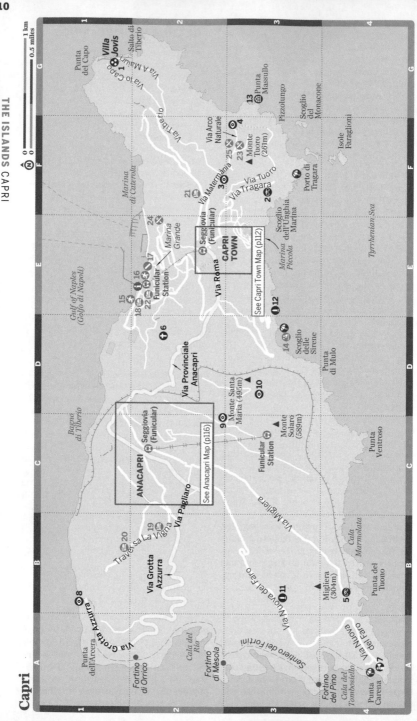

Capri

Giardini di Augusto　　　　GARDENS
(Gardens of Augustus; Map p112; admission €1; ⊙9am-1hr before sunset) Escape the crowds by seeking out these colourful gardens near the Certosa di San Giacomo. Founded by Emperor Augustus, they rise in a series of flowered terraces to a lookout point offering breathtaking views over to the Isole Faraglioni, a group of three limestone stacks that rise out of the sea.

Measuring 109m, 81m and 104m respectively, the *isole* are home to a rare blue lizard that was once thought to be unique to the Faraglioni but has since been found on the Sicilian coast.

From the gardens, pretty and hairpin Via Krupp winds down to Marina Piccola and past a bust of Lenin overlooking the road from a nearby platform; no one seems to know who placed it here, or why.

⊙ Anacapri & Around

Traditionally Capri Town's more subdued neighbour, Anacapri is no stranger to tourism. The focus is largely limited to Villa San Michele di Axel Munthe and the souvenir stores on the main streets. Delve further, though, and you'll discover that Anacapri is still, at heart, the laid-back, rural village that it's always been.

Villa San Michele di Axel Munthe　　　MUSEUM, GARDENS
(Map p116; ☑081 837 14 01; www.villasanmichele.eu; Via Axel Munthe 34; admission €7; ⊙9am-6pm summer, reduced hours rest of year) The former home of Swedish doctor, psychiatrist and animal-rights advocate Axel Munthe, San Michele di Axel Munthe should be included on every visitor's itinerary. Built on the site of the ruins of a Roman villa, the gardens make a beautiful setting for a tranquil stroll, with pathways flanked by immaculate flowerbeds. There are also superb views from here, plus some fine photo props in the form of Roman sculptures.

If you are here between July and September, you may be able to catch one of the classical concerts that take place in the gardens. Check the Axel Munthe Foundation website (www.sanmichele.org) for the current program and reservation information.

★ **Seggiovia del Monte Solaro**　　CABLE CAR
(Map p116; ☑081 837 14 38; www.capriseggiovia.it; single/return €7.50/10; ⊙9.30am-5pm summer, to 3.30pm winter) A fast and painless way to reach Capri's highest peak, Anacapri's Seggiovia del Monte Solaro chairlift whisks you to the top of the mountain in a tranquil, beautiful ride of just 12 minutes. The views from the top are outstanding – on a clear day, you can see the entire Bay of Naples, the Amalfi Coast and the islands of Ischia and Procida.

If all that camera clicking has worked up an appetite, there's a cafeteria here that serves snacks, drinks and ice creams.

Casa Rossa　　　MUSEUM
(Map p116; ☑081 838 21 93; Via Giuseppe Orlandi 78; admission €3.50; ⊙10am-1.30pm & 5.30-8pm) The striking Moroccan-style 'Red House' was built by American colonel John Clay MacKown in 1876. Constructed around a 16th-century defensive tower, the building houses an eclectic collection of 19th-century

Capri Town

THE ISLANDS CAPRI

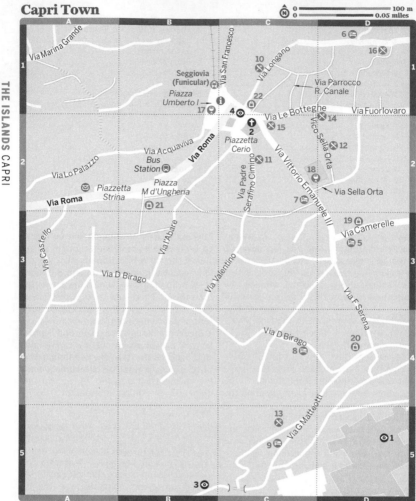

paintings, including some evocative scenes of Capri by Gonsalvo Carelli (1818–1900), and by French painter Eduard Alexandre Sain, who ably captures the island's spirit in works such as *Wedding in Capri*. Also here is a colossal 1st-century Roman statue discovered during excavations of the Grotta Azzurra in the early 19th century.

Chiesa di San Michele
CHURCH

(Map p116; Piazza San Nicola; adult/reduced €2/ free; ⊙ 9.30am-7pm) If you appreciate the colours, intricate patterns and historical tradition of antique majolica tiles, check out this stunning church. The glorious octagonal 18th-century tiled floor vividly depicts Adam and Eve, along with a bizarre menagerie including a unicorn, a bull, several goats and an elephant.

Faro
LIGHTHOUSE

(Map p110; Punta Carena) Rising above Punta Carena, Capri's rugged southwesterly point, is the *faro,* Italy's second-tallest and most powerful lighthouse. The rocks nearby are a great place to swim in summer, with lots of rocks to dive (safely) from and clear turquoise water. To take the plunge, hop on the

Capri Town

bus that runs from the centre of Anacapri every 20 minutes to the *faro* in summer (if you're a real chill seeker, it runs every 40 minutes in winter).

⊙ Marina Grande

Capri's main port is a shabbily attractive place and very Italian, with little evidence of the cosmopolitan glitz that awaits up the hill. For those desperate for a swim, there's an attractive 200m-long pebble beach to the west of the port.

Chiesa di San Costanzo   CHURCH
(Map p110; Via Marina Grande) This is the island's oldest church and the only real sight around the marina. Dating from the 5th century, this whitewashed *chiesa* is dedicated to the island's patron saint, who settled on Capri after escaping a vicious storm en route from Constantinople to Rome. Its original incarnation was built over an earlier Roman construction, although the Byzantine version you see today is the result of a 10th-century makeover. Inside, the sign of the building's great antiquity is its charterfully patched and mismatched columns.

DON'T MISS

GROTTA AZZURRA

Grotta Azzurra (Blue Grotto; Map p110; admission €13; ⊙9am-1hr before sunset) Capri's single most famous attraction is the Grotta Azzurra, a stunning sea cave illuminated by an other-worldly blue light. The easiest way to visit is to take a **tour** (☑081 837 56 46; www.motoscafisticapri.com; Private Pier 0, Marina Grande; online €12, in person €14) from Marina Grande; tickets include the return boat trip and a rowing boat into the cave, but the admission fee is paid separately. Allow a good hour.

The grotto had long been known to local fishermen when it was rediscovered by two Germans – writer Augustus Kopisch and painter Ernst Fries – in 1826. Subsequent research, however, revealed that Emperor Tiberius had built a quay in the cave around AD 30, complete with a *nymphaeum* (shrine to the water nymph). Remarkably, you can still see the carved Roman landing stage towards the rear of the cave.

Measuring 54m by 30m and rising to a height of 15m, the grotto is said to have sunk by up to 20m in prehistoric times, blocking every opening except the 1.3m-high entrance. And this is the key to the magical blue light. Sunlight enters through a small underwater aperture and is refracted through the water; this, combined with the reflection of the light off the white sandy seafloor, produces the vivid blue effect to which the cave owes its name.

The grotto is closed if the sea is too choppy and swimming in it is forbidden, although you can swim outside the entrance – get a bus to Grotta Azzurra, take the stairs down to the right and dive off the small concrete platform. When visiting, keep in mind that the singing 'captains' are included in the price, so don't feel any obligation if they push for a tip.

FOUR GREAT CAPRI WALKS

Surprisingly for such a small place, Capri offers some memorable hiking. A network of well-maintained paths weaves its way across the island, leading through areas that even in the height of summer are all but deserted. The following are four of the most popular and best-known walks; the tourist offices can provide you with maps.

Arco Naturale to Punta dell'Arcera

➜ **Length** 1.2km; 1¼ hours

This fine walk starts east of Capri Town at the **Arco Naturale** (p109), a curious eroded-limestone arch that was part of a large grotto. At the end of Via Matermània, backtrack to Le Grottelle restaurant and take the nearby set of stairs. About halfway down you'll pass the **Grotta di Matermània** (Map p110), a giant natural cave used by the Romans as a *nymphaeum* (shrine to the water nymph). You can still see traces of the mosaic wall decorated with shells. At the bottom, continue down the path as it follows the rocky coastline south. The striking flat-roofed red villa you eventually see on your left, on the Punta Massullo promontory, is **Villa Malaparte** (Map p110), the former holiday home of Tuscan writer Curzio Malaparte (1898–1957). Carrying on, the sea views become increasingly impressive as the path continues westward around the lower wooded slopes of **Monte Tuoro**. A few hundred metres further along you will arrive at a staircase on your right, which leads up to the **Belvedere di Tragara** (Map p110) and some stunning views of the Isole Faraglioni.

Anacapri to Monte Solaro

➜ **Length** 2km; two hours

Rising 589m above Anacapri, **Monte Solaro** (p111) is Capri's highest point. To get to the top you can either take the *seggiovia* (chairlift) from Piazza Vittoria or you can walk. To do

★ **Banana Sport** BOATING
(Map p110; ☎ 081 837 51 88; Marina Grande; 2hr/day rental €90/200; ⊙May-Sep) Located on the eastern edge of the waterfront, Banana Sport hires out five-person motorised dinghies, allowing you to explore secluded coves and grottoes. You can also visit the popular swimming spot **Bagno di Tiberio** (€10), a small inlet west of Marina Grande; it's said that Tiberius once swam here.

★ **Capri Whales** BOATING
(Map p110; ☎081 837 58 33; www.capriwhales. it; Marina Grande 17; 2hr rental €90, 3hr tour €200; ⊙May-Oct; ⊕) These dinghies are well equipped for families, with coolers, snorkelling gear, floats and water toys. They run tours around the island and to the mainland.

Sercomar DIVING
(Map p110; ☎ 081 837 87 81; www.capriseaservice. com; Via Colombo 64, Marina Grande; ⊙Apr-Oct; ⊕) Sercomar offers various diving packages costing from €100 for a single dive (maximum of three people) to €150 for an individual dive and €350 for a four-session beginner's course. It also organises children's snorkelling classes from €35 for 30 minutes (12 years and over).

◉ **Marina Piccola**

Little more than a series of private bathing facilities, Marina Piccola is on the southern side of the island, directly south of Marina Grande. A short bus ride from Capri Town, or a downhill 15-minute walk, it has a 50m-long public pebble beach hemmed in by the **Scoglio delle Sirene** (Rock of the Sirens) at the western end and the **Torre Saracena** (Saracen Tower; Map p110) at the other. The swimming's not great, but the two rocks rising out of the water about 10m offshore make excellent **diving** boards.

Bagni Lo Scoglio delle Sirene CANOEING
(Map p110; ☎081 837 02 21; Via Mulo 77; ⊙Jun-Sep) This reliable outfit charges around €15 per hour for a double canoe or €8 for a single.

✖ **Eating**

Traditional Italian food served in traditional Italian trattorias is what you'll find on Capri. Prices are high but drop noticeably the further you get from Capri Town.

The island's culinary gift to the world is *insalata caprese*, a salad of fresh tomatoes, basil and silky mozzarella drizzled with olive the latter, take Via Axel Munthe and turn right up Via Salita per il Solaro. Follow the steep trail until you come to the pass known as **La Crocetta** (Map p110), marked by a distinctive iron crucifix. Here the path divides: turn right for the summit and its spectacular views over the Bay of Naples and the Amalfi Coast, or take a left for the valley of Cetrella and the picturesque hermitage of **Santa Maria a Cetrella** (Map p110) (generally open on Saturday afternoon until sunset).

Anacapri to Belvedere di Migliera

➡ **Length** 2km; 45 minutes

A lovely, relaxing walk, this leads out to the **Belvedere di Migliera** (Map p110), a panoramic platform with spectacular sea views.

The route couldn't be simpler: from Piazza Vittoria take Via Caposcuro and carry on straight along its continuation, Via Migliera. Along the way you'll pass orchards, vineyards and small patches of woodland. Once at the Belvedere you can return to Anacapri via the **Torre di Materita** (Map p110) or, if you've still got the legs, continue up Monte Solaro – but note that this tough walk is graded medium-difficult by the Club Alpino Italiano (CAI; Italian Alpine Club).

Punta Carena to Punta dell'Arcera (the Sentiero dei Fortini)

➡ **Length** 5.2km; three hours

Snaking its way along the island's oft-overlooked western coast, the **Sentiero dei Fortini** (Path of the Small Forts) is a wonderful if somewhat arduous walk that takes you from Punta Carena, at the island's southwestern tip, up to Punta dell'Arcera near the **Grotta Azzurra** (p113) in the north. Named after the three coastal forts (Pino, Mèsola and Orrico) along the way, it passes through some of Capri's most unspoilt countryside.

---

oil. Look out for *caprese* cheese, a cross between mozzarella and ricotta, and *ravioli caprese*, ravioli stuffed with *caprese* cheese and herbs. Many restaurants, like the hotels, close over winter and only reopen at Easter.

✕ Capri Town & Around

★ È Divino   ITALIAN €

(Map p112; ☑ 081 837 83 64; Vico Sella Orta; meals €20; ⏱ 1-3pm & 7.30pm-midnight Tue-Sun) Look hard for the sign: this Slow Food restaurant is a well-kept secret. Step inside and you find yourself in what resembles a traditional sitting room; the only hints that this is a restaurant are the tantalising aromas and the distant tinkle of glasses. The menu changes daily, according to whatever is fresh from the garden or market.

Some tables are outside in the tiled courtyard amid lemon trees, while other seating is spread throughout a couple of more homey rooms, decorated with antiques, family pics and a fireplace.

★ Raffaele Buonacore   FAST FOOD €

(Map p112; ☑ 081 837 78 26; Via Vittorio Emanuele III 35; snacks €1-6; ⏱ 6am-5pm Mar-Oct; 🐕) Ideal for a quick fill-up, this popular and down-to-earth snack bar does a roaring trade in savoury and sweet treats, including frittatas, *panini* (sandwiches), pastries, waffles and legendary ice cream. Hard to beat, though, are the delicious *sfogliatelle* (cinnamon-infused ricotta in a puff-pastry shell, €1) and the feather-light speciality *caprilu al limone* (lemon and almond cakes).

Le Grottelle   ITALIAN €€

(Map p110; ☑ 081 837 57 19; Via Arco Naturale 13; meals around €28; ⏱ noon-2.30pm & 7-11pm Jul & Aug, noon-2.30pm & 7-11pm Fri-Wed Jun & Sep, noon-2.30pm Fri-Wed Apr, May & Oct) This is a great place to impress someone – not so much for the food, which is decent enough (simple pasta dishes followed by grilled fish, chicken or rabbit), but for the dramatic setting. About 150m from the Arco Naturale, it's got two dining areas: one set in a cave, the other on a terrace above a steep wooded hillside.

La Palette   ITALIAN €€

(Map p110; ☑ 081 837 72 83; Via Matermània 36; meals €30; ⏱ 11am-midnight) Among all the long-established Capri restaurants, it's fun to see a new venture with a rosy future. East

Anacapri

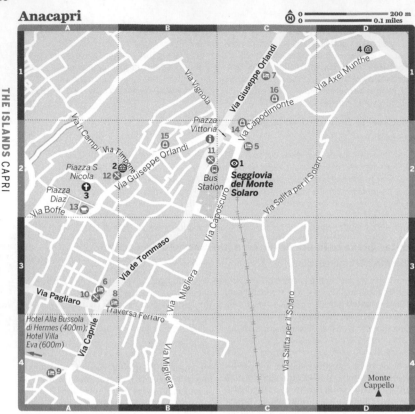

of Capri Town and with swooningly romantic bay views framed by umbrella pines, La Palette efficiently serves up local dishes such as *ravioli caprese* with a modern twist and elegant presentation.

Al Grottino
NEAPOLITAN €€

(Map p112; ☑ 081 837 05 84; www.ristorantealgrottino.net; Via Longano 27; meals from €30; ⊙ 11.45am-3.30pm & 6.30pm-midnight Apr-Oct) Expect a queue here. Dating from 1937, Al Grottino was a VIP spot in the '50s and '60s (check out the photos in the window), and it continues to lure locals and visitors with traditional Neapolitan dishes like *ravioli al ragù* (ravioli in meat and garlic sauce) and specials like *cocotte* (handmade pasta with mixed seafood served in a paella-like pan).

The small dining space is reassuringly traditional, right down to the decorative chianti bottles.

L'Approdo
ITALIAN €€

(Map p110; ☑ 081 837 89 90; www.approdocapri.com; Piazzetta Ferraro 8, Marina Grande; pizzas from €4, meals €25; ⊙ 11am-midnight) If you've arrived on the ferry with an appetite, head here, a three-minute walk to the left from where you disembark. You can easily fill up on the superb antipasti spread (€15) and the pizzas are tasty and varied – try the *sfilatino* with ricotta, ham and mozzarella. Seafood is pricier but as fresh as the day's catch.

There are picturesque views of the colourful fishing boats and nets from the sprawling outdoor terrace, with little to remind you of Capri's fabled glitz up the hill.

Scialapopola
TRATTORIA €€

(Map p112; ☑ 081 837 90 54; www.scialapopologastronomia.com; Via Gradoni Sopramonte 6-8; meals from €25; ⊙ noon-2.30pm & 7-11pm) Tucked up a side street, this is a welcoming place jauntily decorated with strings of peppers and tambourines: the name is a reference to lo-

Anacapri

cal folk musicians. The menu includes such homespun classics as *pasta e ceci con noci* (pasta with chickpeas and nuts) as well as international surprises like vegetable couscous. A bustling takeaway counter dishes up pizza.

Donna Rachele   TRATTORIA €€
(Map p112; ☑081 837 53 87; www.donnarachele. com; Via Padre Serafino Cimmino 2; pizzas from €7, meals €25; ⊙11am-3.30pm & 6pm-midnight) Tucked away in a corner, this place has a traditional trattoria atmosphere, with small rooms, decorative tiles and walls lined with bottles. Vegetarians will do well, with such antipasti choices as grilled artichokes, sautéed spinach, and white beans, while seafood lovers will enjoy specialities on the main menu like *moscardini* (octopus baked in a pizza-like crust) and traditional Neapolitan fish soup.

There are a couple of tables on the outside terraces.

★ **Il Geranio**   SEAFOOD €€€
(Map p112; ☑081 837 06 16; www.geraniocapri. com; Via G Matteotti 8; meals €50; ⊙noon-3pm & 7-11.30pm Apr-Oct) Time to pop the question, celebrate an anniversary or quell those pre-departure blues? The terrace here has stunning views over the pine trees to the sea and beyond to the extraordinary Isole Faraglioni rocks. Seafood is the house speciality, particularly the salt-baked fish. Other good choices include octopus salad and linguine with saffron and mussels. Dress to impress.

La Capannina   TRATTORIA €€€
(Map p112; ☑081 837 07 32; www.capanninacapri. com; Via le Botteghe 12; meals €50; ⊙noon-3pm & 7-11.30pm mid-Mar–Oct) Dating back to 1931, this is the island's most famous traditional trattoria and a long-time favourite on the celebrity circuit. Set up to look like a Hollywood version of a rustic eatery – pink tablecloths, pink roses, hanging copper pots and carved wooden chairs – it serves a classic island menu of comfort food.

Popular dishes include high-quality seafood pasta, *ravioli caprese*, grilled meat and fresh fish, as well as the speciality, *linguine al sugo di scorfano* (flat ribbons of pasta with scorpion fish). Reservations are recommended.

🍴 **Anacapri & Around**

Trattoria Il Solitario   TRATTORIA €
(Map p116; ☑081 837 13 82; Via Giuseppe Orlandi 96; pizzas from €5, meals around €20; ⊙11am-midnight Mon & Wed-Sun Apr-Oct; 🖫) Eating here is a bit like being invited to someone's home: tables are set in a small backyard with lemon trees and children's toys in the corner, and the ambience is one of unhurried holiday time. The menu lists the usual island fare – pasta, seafood, grilled meat, pizzas – but the helpings are large and the quality high.

The pizzas include a vast pizza *bianche* selection, which is handy if you're tiring of tomatoes.

La Rondinella   ITALIAN €€
(Map p116; ☑081 837 12 23; www.ristorantepizzeri alarondinella.com; Via Giuseppe Orlandi 295; meals €30; ⊙noon-2.30pm & 7-11.30pm Fri-Mon) La Rondinella has a relaxed, rural feel and remains one of Anacapri's better restaurants; apparently Graham Greene had a favourite corner table here. The menu features a number of Italian classics such as *saltimbocca alla romana* (veal slices with ham and sage).

For something different, try chef Michele's *linguine alla ciammura*, a delicious pasta dish with a creamy white sauce of anchovies, garlic and parsley. Top it all off with *torta di mandorle* (chocolate and almond tart).

Le Arcate   CAMPANIAN, PIZZA €€
(Map p116; ☑081 837 35 88; Via de Tommaso 24; pizzas €7-11, meals €30; ◷noon-3pm & 7pm-midnight) This is the restaurant that the locals recommend – and frequent. An unpretentious place with hanging baskets of ivy, sunny yellow tablecloths and well-aged terracotta tiles, it specialises in delicious *primi* (first courses) and pizzas. A real show-stopper is the *risotto con polpa di granchio, rughetta e scaglie di parmigiano* (risotto with crab meat, rocket and shavings of Parmesan).

🍷 Drinking & Nightlife

Capri's nightlife is a showy business. The main activity is dressing up and hanging out, ideally at one of the cafes on La Piazzetta (Piazza Umberto I). Aside from the cafes, the nightlife here is fairly staid, with surprisingly few clubs given the penchant the locals have for glamming up.

Pulalli   WINE BAR
(Map p112; ☑081 837 41 08; Piazza Umberto I, Capri Town; ◷noon-3pm & 7pm-11.30pm daily Aug, closed Tue Sep-Jul) Climb the clock-tower steps to the right of the tourist office and your reward is this lofty local hang-out where fabulous wine meets a discerning selection of cheese, charcuterie and more substantial fare such as *risotto al limone* (lemon risotto). Try for a seat on the terrace or, best of all, the coveted table on its own balcony. Meals are €35 to €40.

Taverna Anema e Core   CLUB
(Map p112; ☑081 837 64 61; www.anemaecore. com; Vico Sella Orta 39E, Capri Town; ◷noon-11pm Apr-Oct) Lying beyond a humble exterior is one of the island's most famous nightspots, run by the charismatic Guido Lembo. This smooth and sophisticated bar-club attracts an appealing mix of super-chic and casually dressed punters, here for the relaxed atmosphere and regular live music, including unwaveringly authentic Neapolitan guitar strumming and singing.

CELEBRITY ISLAND

A byword for Mediterranean chic, Capri has long enjoyed a reputation as a haunt for the famous, as evidenced in umpteen photos of spaghetti-eating celebs proudly plastered in the windows of local restaurants.

The first big name to decamp here was Emperor Tiberius in AD 27. A man of sadistic sexual perversions, at least if the Roman author Suetonius is to be believed, he had 12 villas built on the island, including the vast Villa Jovis. He also left deep scars and, until modern times, his name was equated with evil by the islanders. When the Swedish doctor Axel Munthe first began picking about the Roman ruins on the island in the early 20th century and built his villa on the site of a Tiberian palace, locals would observe that it was all 'roba di Tiberio' – Tiberius' stuff.

But more than Tiberius' capers, it was the discovery of the Grotta Azzurra in 1826 that paved the way for Capri's celebrity invasion. As news of the spectacular cave spread, artists such as John Singer Sargent, musicians including Debussy, intellectuals, industrialists and writers began to visit, attracted by the island's isolated beauty and, in some cases, the availability of the local lads. An early habitué, Alfred Krupp, the German industrialist and arms manufacturer, was involved in a gay scandal, while author Norman Douglas and French count Jacques Fersen set all manner of tongues wagging.

The island also proved an escape for Russian revolutionaries. In 1905 the author Maxim Gorky moved to Capri after failing to topple the Russian tsar, and five years later Lenin stopped by for a visit. In the course of the early 20th century Chilean poet Pablo Neruda and German author Thomas Mann visited regularly, British writers Compton Mackenzie and Graham Greene lived here for extended periods, and Britain's wartime singer Gracie Fields retired here.

More recently, singer Mariah Carey bought a holiday villa here, Leonardo DiCaprio was spotted sipping a coffee at a pavement cafe and Rihanna partied on a boat moored under the Capri cliffs. Stars like this help keep Capri's reputation for frivolity alive – and its overworked paparazzi in business.

Caffè Michelangelo — CAFE

(Map p116; Via Giuseppe Orlandi 138, Anacapri; ⊗8am-1am) It's not that flashy, but the position of the delightful Caffè Michelangelo, on a street flanked by tasteful shops and near two lovely piazzas, makes it a perfect spot for indulging in a little people-watching-and-cocktail-sipping time. Large, cushioned chairs and a raised terrace add to the kick-back appeal.

🛍 Shopping

Boasting more designer boutiques per square metre than almost anywhere else on earth, Capri's shopping scene is conservative and expensive. Along the town's two main strips, Via Vittorio Emanuele III and Via Camerelle, you'll find most of the fashion big guns as well as a number of jewellery and shoe shops. If you are looking for souvenirs or gourmet goodies, lemons reign supreme, pictured on everything from T-shirts to tea towels. The island is famous for its perfume and *limoncello*. (lemon liqueur) The former smells like lemons and the latter tastes like sweet lemon vodka.

La Parisienne — FASHION

(Map p112; ☑081 837 02 83; www.laparisienne-capri.it; Piazza Umberto I 7, Capri Town; ⊗9am-10pm) First opened in 1906 (yes, that is not a misprint!), and best known for introducing Capri pants in the 1960s, famously worn by Audrey Hepburn, who bought them here, La Parisienne can run you up a made-to-measure pair within a day. It also sells off-the-rack Capri pants (from €250).

Jackie O was a customer, and Clark Gable apparently favoured the fashions here, particularly the Bermuda shorts, which (believe it or not) were considered quite raffish in their day.

Limoncello di Capri — DRINK

(Map p116; ☑081 837 29 27; www.limoncello.com; Via Capodimonte 27, Anacapri; ⊗9am-7.30pm) Don't be put off by the gaudy yellow display; this historic shop stocks some of the island's best *limoncello*. In fact, it was here that the drink was first concocted (or at least that is the claim...). Apparently, the grandmother of current owner Vivica made the tot as an after-dinner treat for the guests in her small guesthouse. Nowadays, the shop produces some 70,000 bottles each year, as well as lemon and orange chocolates, lemon marmalade and lemon honey. It also sells a tasty lemon sorbet (€2), which is 2% alcohol.

Carthusia I Profumi di Capri — BEAUTY

(Map p112; ☑081 837 53 35; www.carthusia.it; Via F Serena 28, Capri Town; ⊗9am-6pm) Allegedly, Capri's famous floral perfume was discovered in 1380 by the prior of the Certosa di San Giacomo. Caught unawares by a royal visit, he displayed the island's most beautiful flowers for the queen. Changing the water in the vase, he discovered a floral scent. This became the base of the perfume now sold at this smart laboratory outlet.

Capri Naturale — FASHION

(Map p116; ☑081 837 47 19; Via Capodimonte 15, Anacapri; ⊗9am-8pm Apr-Oct) One of the better shops along touristy Via Capodimonte, Capri Naturale sells a limited range of women's fashions. Expect whisper-thin linen frocks in delphinium blue or dip-dyed lavender and a small selection of handmade sandals. Everything is made locally and prices are reasonable, all things considered.

Da Costanzo — SHOES

(Map p112; ☑081 837 80 77; Via Roma 49, Capri Town; ⊗9am-8.30pm Mar-Nov) In 1959 Clarke Gable stopped off at this tiny, unpretentious shoe shop to get a pair of handmade leather sandals, and the shop still sells a range of colourful styles to passers-by and shoe aficionados. Prices start at around €90, a small investment for a piece of Hollywood history.

Capri Watch — ACCESSORIES

(Map p112; ☑081 837 71 48; www.capricapri.com; Via Camerelle 21, Capri Town; ⊗9am-5pm Mon-Sat) The flashy selection of watches here is made by local watchmaker Silvio Staiano. Prices start surprisingly low, around €50 for a relatively straightforward timepiece, spiralling up to several zeros worth of precious and semi-precious jewel-encrusted numbers.

Elegantia — FASHION

(Map p116; Via Giuseppe Orlandi 75, Anacapri; ⊗9am-8pm Mon-Sat) Always fancied yourself flouncing around in one of those sherbet-yellow, baby-pink or powder-blue floppy hats? Then this is the place to pick one up (€15). The owner can also run up copies of clothing and do alterations and repairs.

ℹ Information

Tourist Office (Map p116; ☑081 837 15 24; www.capritourism.com; Via Giuseppe Orlandi 59, Anacapri; ⊗9am-3pm) Capri Town (Map p112; ☑081 837 06 86; www.capritourism.com; Piazza

(Continued on page 122)

1. Picturesque Procida (p135)
Pastel-painted doorway in a colourful Procida fishing village.

2. Marina Corricella (p137), Procida
The multihued waterfront village of Marina Corricella is a riot of colours overlooking a boat-filled habour and marina.

3. La Mortella (p132), Ischia
Maypop flower in La Mortella, one of Italy's finest botanical gardens with more than 1000 rare and exotic plants.

4. Monte Solaro (p111), Capri
View from atop Monte Solaro, Capri's highest peak. It's easily reached via a chairlift.

(Continued from page 119)

Umberto I; ⊙9am-1pm & 3-6.15pm Mon-Sat, 9am-1pm Sun) Marina Grande (Map p110; ☑081 837 06 34; www.capritourism.com; Banchina del Porto, Marina Grande) Can provide a map of the island (€1) with town plans of Capri and Anacapri. For hotel listings and other useful information, ask for a free copy of *Capri è*.

ℹ Getting There & Away

Unless you're prepared to pay €1300 for a **helicopter transfer** (☑0828 35 41 55; www.capri-helicopters.com) from Naples' Capodichino Airport (20 minutes), you'll arrive in Capri by boat.

BOAT

The two major ferry routes to Capri are from Naples and (more seasonally) Sorrento, although there are also connections with Ischia and the Amalfi Coast (Amalfi, Positano and Salerno).

Caremar (☑081 837 07 00; www.caremar. it) Ferries to/from Naples and Capri (€11.20, 1¼ hours, seven daily) and hydrofoils to/from Sorrento (€13.20, 25 minutes, four daily).

Gescab (☑081 807 18 12; www.gescab.it) Hydrofoils to/from Sorrento and Capri (€16.80, 20 minutes, 18 daily).

Navigazione Libera del Golfo (p269) Hydrofoils to/from Naples and Capri (€19.75, 45 minutes, nine daily).

SNAV (☑081 428 55 55; www.snav.it) Hydrofoils to/from Naples and Capri (€20.10, 45 minutes, up to 13 daily).

ℹ Getting Around

BUS

Sippic (☑081 837 04 20; Bus Station, Via Roma, Capri Town; tickets €1.80) Regular buses

---

ℹ FERRY FACTS

Ferries are the most likely way of getting to the islands. Note that ferries departing from Positano and Amalfi operate solely from Easter to September. At other times of the year, you will have to catch services from Naples or Sorrento. Ferries leave from both the Molo Beverello and adjacent Mergellina ports in Naples; there is a strip of booths with the times, berth numbers and costs clearly displayed. Generally, there is no need to book: just turn up around 35 minutes before departure in case there's a queue.

---

to/from Marina Grande, Anacapri and Marina Piccola.

Staiano Autotrasporti (☑081 837 24 22; www.staianotourcapri.com; Bus Station, Via Tommaso, Anacapri; tickets €1.80, day tickets €8.60) Buses serve the Grotta Azzurra and Punta Carena *faro* (lighthouse).

FUNICULAR

Funicular (tickets €1.80; ⊙6.30am-12.30am) The first challenge facing visitors is how to get from Marina Grande to Capri Town. The most enjoyable option is the funicular, if only for the evocative en-route views over the lemon groves and surrounding countryside.

SCOOTER

Ciro dei Motorini (☑081 837 80 18; www.capriscooter.com; Via Marina Grande 55, Marina Grande; per 2/24hr €30/65) If you're looking to hire a scooter at Marina Grande, stop here.

Rent A Scooter (☑081 837 38 88; Piazza Barile 20, Anacapri; per hour/day €15/65).

ISCHIA

POP 62,200

The volcanic outcrop of Ischia is the most developed and largest of the islands in the Bay of Naples. It is an intriguing concoction of sprawling spa towns, abundant gardens, buried necropolises and spectacular scenery, with forests, vineyards and picturesque small towns. Ischia only attracts a fraction of the day trippers that head for Capri from Naples in summer. Perhaps someone should tell them that the beaches are a lot better here.

Most visitors head straight for the north-coast towns of Ischia Porto, Ischia Ponte, Casamicciola Terme, Forio and Lacco Ameno. Of these, Ischia Porto boasts the best bars, Casamicciola the worst traffic and Ischia Ponte and Lacco Ameno the most appeal.

On the calmer south coast, the car-free perfection of Sant'Angelo offers a languid blend of a cosy harbour, sunbathing cats and nearby bubbling beaches. In between the coasts lies a less-trodden landscape of dense chestnut forests, loomed over by Monte Epomeo, Ischia's highest peak.

A narrow coastal band of development rings the thickly forested and mainly vertiginous slopes of the island's heartland. This is not a place of verdant open meadows and rambling walks, although there are excellent guided geological hikes. Land is at a premium in Ischia and the main circular highway can get clogged with traffic in the height of summer. This, combined with the penchant the local youth have for overtaking on blind corners and the environmental impact of just too many cars, means that you may want to consider riding the excellent network of buses or hopping in a taxi to get around. The distance between attractions and the lack of pavements on the busy roads makes walking unappealing.

Eating is one of the island's great pleasures; while seafood is an obvious speciality, Ischia is also famed for its rabbit, bred on inland farms. Another local speciality is *rucolino*, a green, liquorice-flavoured liqueur made from *rucola* (rocket) leaves.

The island was an important stop on the trade route from Greece to northern Italy in the 8th century but has since seen its fair share of disaster. The 1301 eruption of the now extinct (and unfortunately named) Monte Arso forced the locals to flee to the mainland, where they remained for four years. Five centuries later, in 1883, an earthquake killed more than 1700 people and razed the burgeoning spa town of Casamicciola. To this day, the town's name signifies 'total destruction' in the Italian vernacular.

ℹ️ Information

Tourist Office (Map p128; ☑ 081 507 42 11; www.infoischiaprocida.it; Corso Sogliuzzo 72, Ischia Porto; ⊙ 9am-2pm & 3-8pm Mon-Sat) A slim selection of maps and brochures.

ℹ️ Getting There & Away

Caremar (☑ 081 837 07 00; www.caremar.it) Operates up to seven daily hydrofoils to/from Naples and Ischia (€19, 45 minutes).

Alilauro (☑ 081 837 69 95; www.alilauro.it) Hydrofoils to/from Naples and Ischia (€17.60, 50 minutes, 10 daily).

SNAV (☑ 081 837 75 77; www.snav.it) Hydrofoils to/from Naples and Ischia (€18.60, one hour, four daily).

ℹ️ Getting Around

Ferries and hydrofoils reach Casamicciola Terme and Ischia Porto. The latter is Ischia's major

CASTELLO ARAGONESE

Castello Aragonese (Aragon Castle; Map p124; ☑ 081 991 959, 081 992 834; Rocca del Castello, Ischia Ponte; adult/reduced €10/6; ⊙ 9am-90min before sunset) The elegant 15th-century Ponte Aragonese connects Ischia Ponte to Castello Aragonese, a sprawling, magnificent castle perched high and mighty on a rocky islet. While Syracusan tyrant Gerone I built the site's first fortress in 474 BC, the bulk of the current structure dates from the 1400s, when King Alfonso of Aragon gave the older Angevin fortress a thorough makeover, building the fortified bastions, current causeway and access ramp cut into the rock.

At the base of the complex you pay the entrance fee and then ascend via a lift or a series of paths that take you on a looping route through the buildings and lush gardens. Further up lie the sunbaked, stuccoed ruins of the 14th-century Cattedrale dell'Assunta, which collapsed under British cannon fire in 1809. The 11th-century crypt below features snippets of 14th-century frescoes inspired by Giotto. Better preserved is the 18th-century Chiesa dell'Immacolata, with its Greek-cross plan and dome studded with curved tympanum windows. Commissioned by the adjoining Convento delle Clarisse (convent for Clarisse nuns), it was left in its minimalist state after building funds ran out. When the nuns' own lives expired, they were left to decompose sitting upright on stone chairs in the macabre Cimitero delle Monache Clarisse as a grim reminder of mortality; the now empty chairs remain on view.

Carry on until you reach the elegant, hexagonal Chiesa di San Pietro a Pantaniello and sombre Carcere Borbonico, the one-time prison for leading figures of the Risorgimento (the 19th-century Italian unification movement), such as Poerio, Pironti, Nisco and Settembrini. There's a small and grisly Museo delle Torture, with a collection of medieval torture instruments and impressive armour and weaponry. While you are strolling around, you may want to counteract all that darkness surrounding the building's history with a touch of fairy-tale romance: in the 1500s, the castle was home to Vittoria Colonna, a poet-princess who married Ferrante d'Avalos here before becoming closely linked with Michelangelo. The great artist wrote romantic poetry dedicated to Vittoria and sent her a painting, the *Crucifixion*, for her private chapel.

The complex includes a couple of attractive terrace cafes and a hotel (p203).

gateway and tourist hub. The island's main bus station is a one-minute walk west of the pier, with buses servicing all other parts of the island. East of the pier, shopping strip Via Roma eventually becomes Corso Vittoria Colonna and heads southeast to Ischia Ponte.

BUS

The island's main bus station is located in Ischia Porto. There are two principal lines: the CS (Circolo Sinistro, or Left Circle), which circles the island anticlockwise, and the CD line (Circolo Destro, or Right Circle), which travels in a clock-

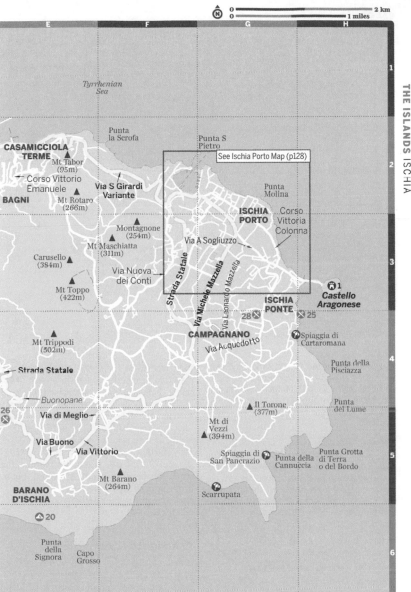

0 —— 2 km
0 —— 1 miles

Tyrrhenian Sea

Punta la Scrofa

Punta S Pietro

CASAMICCIOLA TERME
Mt Tabor (95m)
Corso Vittorio Emanuele
BAGNI
Mt Rotaro (266m)

Via S Girardi Variante

See Ischia Porto Map (p128)

Punta Molina

ISCHIA PORTO
Corso Vittoria Colonna

Montagnone (254m)
Mt Maschiatta (311m)

Via A Sogliuzzo

Carusello (384m)

Via Nuova dei Conti

Mt Toppo (422m)

Strada Statale

Via Michele Mazzella

Via Leonardo Mazzella

Castello Aragonese ☺1

ISCHIA PONTE
28 ☒ ☒ 25

Mt Trippodi (502m)

CAMPAGNANO
Via Acquedotto

Spiaggia di Cartaromana

Punta della Pisciazza

Strada Statale

Buonopane

Il Torone (377m)

Punta del Lume

26 ☒

Via di Meglio

Mt di Vezzi (394m)

Via Buono
Via Vittorio

Spiaggia di San Pancrazio
Punta della Cannuccia
Punta Grotta di Terra o del Bordo

Mt Barano (264m)

BARANO D'ISCHIA

Scarrupata

☖20

Punta della Signora
Capo Grosso

wise direction, passing through each town and departing every 30 minutes. Buses pass near all hotels and campsites. A single ticket, valid for 90 minutes, costs €1.90, an all-day, multi-use ticket €6, a two-day ticket €10, a three-day ticket €13 and a weekly ticket €26. Taxis and micro-taxis (scooter-engined three-wheelers) are also available.

CAR & SCOOTER

You can do this small island a favour by not bringing your car. If you want to hire a car or a scooter for a day, there are plenty of hire

Ischia

companies. **Balestrieri** (☑ 081 98 56 91; www. autonoleggiobalestrieri.it; Via Iasolino 35, Ischia Porto; per day/week €20/140) hires out cars and scooters, and it also has mountain bikes (€15 per day). You can't take a hired vehicle off the island.

Parking

If you're hiring a car in high season, parking is going to be a headache. Go for a smart car if you can, which takes up minimal space. There's a small car park at the entrance to Sant'Angelo (two hours €3) and Ischia Porto and Ischia Ponte both have signposted central car parks (€1.50 per hour).

Ischia Porto & Ischia Ponte

Although technically two separate towns, Ischia Porto and Ischia Ponte are bookends to one long, sinuous sprawl of pastel-coloured buildings, terrace bars and restaurants, and palm-fringed shops and hotels, all of which makes for relaxed and enjoyable wandering.

The ferry port itself was a crater lake, opened up to sea at the request of Spanish king Ferdinand II in 1854. While the story goes that he couldn't stand the stench of the lake, his request was more likely inspired by the prospect of increasing shipping-tax revenue. Whatever the reason, it was a great idea, and now the harbour is fringed by a string of restaurants serving fresh seafood. Head further east and you'll hit the Spiaggia dei Pescatori, where the compelling scene of brightly painted fishing boats, bronzed flesh and lurid beach umbrellas is backed by the pyramid silhouette of the Castello Aragonese.

⊙ Sights & Activities

Chiesa di Santa Maria delle Grazie CHURCH
(Map p128; cnr Corso Vittoria Colonna & Via G Gigante, Ischia Porto; ⊙ 8am-12.30pm & 4-7.30pm) Check out this church's 18th-century baroque extravaganza, with its fetching peach-coloured facade, semicircular chapels and elevated terrace popular with flirty teens and gossipy *signore* (women). Grab an ice cream from the nearest gelateria and absorb the *dolce vita* atmosphere on the terrace.

Santa Maria Assunta CHURCH
(Map p128; Via Luigi Mazzella, Ischia Ponte; ⊙8am-12.30pm & 4.30-8pm) A striking 15th-century watchtower, Torre del Mare, now serves as the bell tower to Ischia's cathedral. The current church, designed by Antonio Massinetti and completed in 1751, stands on the site of two older churches, one 13th century and the other 17th century. Step inside its fanciful baroque interior and you'll find an ancient baptismal font salvaged from the nearby castle and propped up by marble statues of the virtues, and a sombre Romanesque wooden crucifix.

Museo del Mare MUSEUM
(Map p128; ☑081 98 11 24; Via San Giovanni da Procida 2, Ischia Ponte; adult/reduced €2.50/free; ⊙10.30am-12.30pm & 4-7pm Mar-Jan; 🔂) If you are an old salt at heart (or have a penchant for model ships), don't miss Ischia's maritime museum with its lovingly documented exhibits. Objects include cult ex-votos (offerings to the saints) from sailors, ancient urns, beautifully crafted model ships and revealing photographs of island life in the 20th century, including the arrival of Ischia's very first American car in 1958 – you can just imagine what a celebratory occasion that must have been.

Orizzonti Blu DIVING
(Map p128; ☑340 4259162; www.orizzontiblu.net; Via Iasolino 86, Ischia Porto) If diving takes your fancy, this reputable outfit organises open-water dives and courses, including a six-lesson dive-master course (€800).

Ischia Diving DIVING
(Map p128; ☑081 98 18 52; www.ischiadiving.net; Via Iasolino 106, Ischia Porto; single dive €40) This well-established diving outfit offers some attractively priced dive packages, like five dives including equipment for €185.

🍴 Eating

Bar de Maio GELATERIA €
(Map p128; ☑081 99 18 70; Piazza Antica Reggia 9, Ischia Porto; ice cream from €1.50; ⊙24hr) This bar has been raising the locals' cholesterol levels since 1930 with a delicious selection of ultracreamy ice creams, as well as coffee, cocktails and snacks. Take a seat in the square with your cone; this central piazza is a prime people-watching spot. According to residents, it's the best ice-cream parlour on the island.

Gran Caffè Vittoria CAFE €
(Map p128; ☑081 199 16 49; Corso Vittoria Colonna 110, Ischia Porto; pastries €2; ⊙8am-11pm) At the smarter end of the port, this elegant, wood-panelled cafe has been spoiling customers and waistlines for more than 100 years with its irresistible cakes, pastries, coffees and cocktails, all served by old-school, bow-tied waiters. The outdoor terrace sits on the other side of the road.

Da Ciccio CAFE €
(Map p128; ☑081 199 13 14; www.bardaciccio.it; Via Porto 1, Ischia Porto; snacks from €1; ⊙8am-midnight) Just the spot for ferry-weary arrivals, this much-loved bar does light meals, luscious pastries and dangerously good gelati, including organic strawberry – fabulous! Eat in or take away savoury treats like the *calzone* (pizza folded over to form a pie) stuffed with spinach, pine nuts and raisins (€2). At the very least, cool down with an orange and mint *granita*.

DON'T MISS

CASA MUSEO

Casa Museo (House Museum; Map p124; ☑349 7198879; SS 270, Serrara Fontana; ⊙10am-7pm) The good news is that this museum is well signposted and has a car park. The bad news is that it's on a perilous corner on Ischia's mountain road between Buonopane and Fontana. Double back if you can because beguiling Casa Museo is far more interesting than its name suggests. Tunnelled into the rock face, every room contains extraordinary sculptures and carvings made out of stone, wood and pebbles, the latter including such quirky exhibits as a life-size pig.

Other wonderful pieces include a stone head of Neptune, fanciful pebble reptiles, wooden furniture carved out of gnarled tree trunks and intricately patterned pebble mosaics covering the walls, even in the bathroom... check out the *Alice in Wonderland*–style tunnels that lead here, there – and absolutely nowhere! The museum is free, although a donation is appreciated.

Ischia Porto

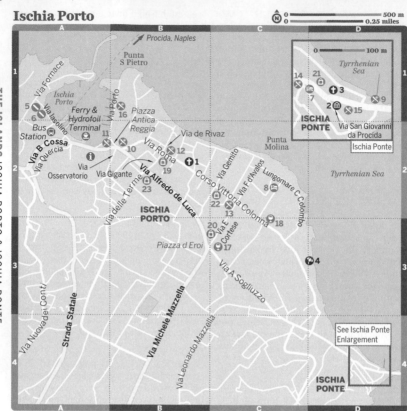

Al Pontile
ITALIAN €

(Map p128; ☎ 081 98 34 92; Via Luigi Mazzella 15, Ischia Ponte; mains from €9; ⏰ noon-3pm & 7pm-midnight Mar-Oct) Sit outside, front or back, with the castle as an evocative backdrop to the shopping street or sea. The reassuringly brief menu includes pasta mainstays like *puttanesca* with capers, tomatoes and olives, and reliable meat and fish mains. Smile sweetly and the owner will bring a bottle of *limoncello* along with the bill, allowing you your fill of lemony top-ups.

Ristorante Aglio, Olio & Pomodoro
ITALIAN €

(Map p128; www.aglioolioepomodoro.com; Via Luigi Mazzella 84, Ischia Ponte; meals €20; ⏰ noon-4pm & 7pm-midnight) Warmly welcoming traditional restaurant serving local dishes such as rabbit, plus excellent pizzas and – of course – seafood. It's not the most elegant option in town, but it's reasonably priced and great fun.

Ristorante Nascondiglio dell'Amore
ITALIAN €

(Map p124; www.nascondigliodellamore.it; Via Serbatoio, Ischia Ponte; meals €22; ⏰ noon-11.30pm Mon, noon-midnight Tue-Sun) Homely and friendly hilltop restaurant with sea and castle vistas, serving an acclaimed *coniglio all'ischitana* (rabbit cooked in wine and herbs). It also dishes up pizza at moderate prices – it's a good option if you want to steer clear of the swisher Ischian joints. All this plus carafes of the restaurant's own wine.

★ Gardenia Mare
MEDITERRANEAN €€

(Map p124; ☎ 081 99 11 07; www.gardeniamare.it; Via Nuova Cartaromana 66, Ischia Ponte; meals €34; ⏰ 9am-6pm & 8.30-11.30pm) With bamboo furniture, surrounding greenery and wonderful views of the Castello Aragonese, this makes for a fantastically romantic sunset dinner spot. It's a beach-club restaurant, so you can

Ischia Porto

work up your appetite for the seafood dishes with a swim first.

Ristorante La Pantera Rosa   ITALIAN €€
(Map p128; ☑ 081 99 24 83; Via Porto 53, Ischia Porto; meals €28; ⊙noon-2.30pm & 7-11.30pm) There are some good choices and good prices for those suffering from black-tie burnout at this laid-back restaurant on the port's suppertime strip. The menu has all the traditional pasta and pizza choices, plus specialities like *risotto alla pescatora* (seafood risotto), which comes warmly recommended. Owner Amedeo is something of a linguist and speaks fluent English and French.

Da Raffaele   ITALIAN €€
(Map p128; ☑ 081 99 12 03; www.daraffaele.it; Via Roma 29, Ischia Porto; meals €28; ⊙noon-3pm & 6.30-11.30pm Mar-Nov; 🖫) Handily situated in the middle of Via Roma, this brightly lit,

welcoming place has few surprises on the menu but prepares everything well. Try the *frittura di pesce all'ischitana* (mixed fried fish) or *melanzane a funghetti* (fried eggplant with tomatoes, mushrooms, garlic and basil) and grab a table out front for the best people-watching potential on this pedestrian shopping street.

★ Ristorante da Ciccio   ITALIAN €€
(Map p128; ☑ 081 99 16 86; Via Luigi Mazzella 32, Ischia Ponte; meals €25; ⊙noon-3.30pm & 7.30-11.30pm, closed Tue Dec-Feb) Sublime seafood and charming host Carlo make this atmospheric place a winner. Highlights include *tubattone* pasta with clams and pecorino cheese, a zesty mussel soup topped with fried bread and *peperoncino* (chilli), and a delicious chocolate and almond cake. Tables spill out onto the pavement in summer, from where there are fabulous castle views.

🍷 Drinking & Nightlife

Ischia is not Ibiza. That said, the area around Ischia Porto has the best buzz, with a handful of bars and clubs that stay open way past cocoa time.

Bar Calise   BAR
(Map p128; ☑ 081 99 12 70; www.barcalise.com; Piazza degli Eroi 69, Ischia Porto; ⊙11am-4pm & 6pm-2am Thu-Sun) One of the oldest bars on the island, founded in 1925 and located near the harbour. The atmosphere here is one of languid gentility: waistcoated waiters serve cocktails and coffees to a background of live Latin, swing and folk music. The *pasticceria* is a great place to pick up *sfogliatelle*.

Valentino Ischia   CLUB
(Map p128; ☑ 081 98 25 69; www.valentinoischia.eu; Corso Vittoria Colonna 97, Ischia Porto; ⊙10pm-5am Wed-Sun) A surprisingly lively club playing international house music, and with the aesthetic bonus of some pretty, traditional majolica tilework.

🛍 Shopping

Ischia's shopping is centred on Via Roma and the web of narrow streets leading to Ischia Ponte. From floss-thin bikinis to decadent jars of *babà* (rum-soaked sponge cake), there's enough shopping on these cobbled streets to shift your credit card into overdrive. For a more low-key experience, explore the tiny boutiques and art galleries in Sant'Angelo and Forio.

LOCAL KNOWLEDGE

ISCHIA ON A FORK

Ischian restaurateur Carlo Buono of Da Ciccio (p127) gives the low-down on his cherished classic island cuisine:

'Fresh, seasonal ingredients are the cornerstone of Ischian cooking, from silky olive oil to plump *pomodorini* (cherry tomatoes). Like Neapolitan cooking, the emphasis is on simple, uncomplicated home cooking. Traditionally, there are two types of Ischian cuisine: coastal and mountain. For centuries, fishermen would barter with farmers, who'd offer wine, vegetables, pork and rabbit in exchange for the catch.

'Rabbit is a typical Ischian meat and we're seeing a revival of the traditional *fossa* (pit) breeding method, where rabbits are bred naturally in deep *fosse* instead of in cages. The result is a more tender, flavoursome meat. Leading this renaissance is local Slow Food advocate Riccardo D'Ambra, whose famous trattoria Il Focolare (p135) is well known for its rabbit and rustic mountain dishes. Definitely worth eating on the island is a popular Sunday dish called *coniglio all'ischitana* (Ischia-style rabbit), prepared with olive oil, unpeeled garlic, chilli, tomato, basil, thyme and white wine.

'Typical local fish include *pesce bandiera* (sailfish), the flat *castagna, lampuga* and *palamide* (a small tuna). A popular way of cooking it is in *acqua pazza* (crazy water). Traditionally prepared on the fishing boats, it's a delicate sauce made with *pomodorini*, garlic and parsley. Fried fish is also very typical; a fresh serve of *frittura di mare* (mixed fried seafood) drizzled with lemon juice is just superb. May to September is *totano* (squid) season and a great time to try *totani imbotti* (squid stuffed with olives, capers and breadcrumbs, and stewed in wine).

'Equally wonderful is fresh, wood-fired *casareccio* bread – it's perfect for doing the *scarpetta* (wiping your plate clean) or for filling with salami or *parmigiano* cheese. If you have any room left, track down a slice of *torta caprese,* a moist chocolate and almond cake. *Buon appetito.*'

★**Antica Macelleria di Francesco Esposito** FOOD
(Map p128; ☑081 98 10 11; Via delle Terme 2, Ischia Porto; ☺8am-1.30pm & 4.30-10pm) This century-old deli is gourmet foodie heaven. Drop in from 8am for fresh mozzarella and wood-fired *casareccio* bread, plus a lip-smacking choice of cheese, prosciutto, homemade *peperoncino* salami and marinated peppers. In fact, it's got everything you need for a picnic on the beach, including the obligatory bottle of Falanghina (dry white wine).

Atelier delle Dolcezze FOOD
(Cioccolateria e Gelateria d'Arte; Map p128; Via Edgardo Cortese; ☺9am-1.30pm & 4.30-8.30pm Tue-Sun) Fabulous modern chocolatier, combining ranks of sweet chocolate treats with sumptuous artisanal ice cream. The pretty boxes of goodies make an enticing gift.

Filippo Cianciarelli CERAMICS
(Artigianato Ischitano; Map p128; www.ceramichecianciarelli.it; Via Luigi Mazzella 113, Ischia Ponte; ☺9am-1pm & 4-8pm Mon-Sat) Filippo is a highly original artist who creates vividly patterned pieces, including striking tall pyramid-shaped vases, tiled pictures with abstract themes and smaller, easy-to-pack plates, mugs and the like. Displays of his work are combined with more traditional ceramic pieces.

Judith Major FASHION
(Map p128; ☑081 98 32 95; Corso Vittoria Colonna 174, Ischia Porte; ☺9.30am-1.30pm & 4-8pm) Despite the headmistressy name, this boutique is the exclusive stockist of Italian label Brunello Cucinelli. The look is Polo Ralph Lauren with a sexy Italian twist: cashmere sweaters, suave shirts, blazers and chic womenswear. Shoes include Prada, Barrett and Alberto Guardiani for men and Stuart Weitzman and Pedro Garcia for women. There's everything you'll need for a jaunt on the yacht.

Scaglione Renato JEWELLERY
(Map p128; ☑081 98 45 03; Via Alfredo de Luca 109, Ischia Porto) This little shop has a small but sparkling range of exquisite jewellery, incorporating turquoise, amethyst, amber and coral. Prices are slightly lower than the glitzier options on nearby Via Roma.

Lacco Ameno

In the 1950s and 1960s, French starlets and European royalty came to play at the legendary Terme Regina Isabella spa resort. The stars may have gone, but one local icon remains, sprouting out of the sea: the iconic Il Fungo (The Mushroom) is a 10m volcanic rock formation spat out by Monte Epomeo thousands of years ago.

According to legend, the body of the martyr Restituta was washed ashore on nearby San Montano Beach in the 4th century on a boat steered from Tunisia by a seaworthy angel. Her subsequent cult spread from North Africa to Italy and is historically associated with the expulsion of Catholics from North Africa by the king of the Vandals, Genseric.

Every May, residents re-enact her arrival on the beach.

◎ Sights & Activities

Area Archeologica di Santa Restituta   ARCHAEOLOGICAL SITE
(Map p124; ☑ 081 98 05 38; Piazza Restituta; admission €3; ⊘ 9.30am-12.30pm & 5-7pm Mon-Sat, 9.30am-12.30pm Sun) Beneath the pretty-in-pink Chiesa di Santa Restituta, rebuilt after the 1883 earthquake, be sure to visit the Area Archeologica. Excavations undertaken between 1951 and 1974 have uncovered parts of an ancient Greek kiln, a Roman temple and street, 4th-century burial amphorae and an early Christian basilica. Rows of cabinets display other ancient objects, from Roman bracelets and votive gifts to a 3300-year-old stove from Procida.

The ground-floor collection features exquisite 17th-century *pastori* (nativity-scene figurines), colourful 18th-century ceramics, high-camp clerical garb and the 18th-century wooden statue of Santa Restituta still used in the annual procession in the Bay of San Montano. You can borrow an informative, handwritten guide to the excavations from the ticket desk.

Museo Archeologico di Pithecusae   MUSEUM
(Map p124; ☑ 081 99 61 83; www.pithecusae.it; Corso Angelo Rizzoli 210; admission incl Museo Angelo Rizzoli €5; ⊘ 9.30am-1pm & 3-6.30pm Tue-Sun) Housed in the elegant Villa Arbusto, former home of local celeb Angelo Rizzoli, the Museo Archeologico di Pithecusae enjoys a heady historical location overlooking Monte Vico, site of the ancient settlement and acropolis of Pithecusae. The museum has a fascinating collection of important finds from the island's Hellenic settlement, ranging from imported earthenware to parts of the acropolis itself. A highlight is the legendary 7th-century-BC Nestor's Cup in Sala (Room) II, bearing one of the oldest-known Greek inscriptions – which, appropriately, celebrates the wine of Ischia. The space also encompasses the Museo Angelo Rizzoli.

Museo Angelo Rizzoli   MUSEUM
(Map p124; ☑ 081 99 61 83; www.museoangelorizzoli.it; Corso Angelo Rizzoli 210; admission incl Museo Archeologico di Pithecusae €5; ⊘ 9.30am-1pm & 3-6.30pm Tue-Sun; 🐾) This small, entertaining museum pays homage to the man who turned humble little Lacco into a celebrity hot spot in the 1950s. Cool paparazzi shots and clippings of a Hitchcock-esque Rizzoli and his famous pals decorate rooms that once played host to the likes of Gina Lollabrigida, Grace Kelly and Federico Fellini. Equally striking are the villa's gardens, complete with lemon trees, fountain, a children's playground and star-worthy views towards the Campi Flegrei.

★ Negombo   SPA
(Map p124; ☑ 081 98 61 52; www.negombo.it; Baia di San Montano; admission all day €32, from 2pm €20; ⊘ 8.30am-7pm late Apr-Oct) This is the place to come for a dose of pampering. Part spa resort, part botanical wonderland, with more than 500 exotic plant species, Negom-

---

MONTE EPOMEO
Lace up those hiking boots and set out on a roughly 2.5km (50-minute) uphill walk from the village of Fontana, which will bring you to the top of Ischia's Monte Epomeo (Map p124) (788m). Formed by an underwater eruption, it boasts superlative views of the Bay of Naples.

The little church near the top is the 15th-century Cappella di San Nicola di Bari (Map p124), where you can check out the pretty majolica floor. The adjoining hermitage was built in the 18th century by an island governor who, after narrowly escaping death, swapped politics for poverty and spent the rest of his days here in saintly solitude. Have a peek inside, then head back down the hill, thankful that your saintliness doesn't exclude good wining and dining, Ischia style.

bo's combination of Zen-like thermal pools, hammam, contemporary sculpture and private beach on the Baia di San Montano tends to draw a younger crowd than many other Ischian spa spots. There's a Japanese labyrinth pool for weary feet, a decent *tavola calda* (snack bar), and a full range of massage and beauty treatments. Those arriving by car or scooter can park all day on-site (car €4, scooter €2.50). For a free dip in the bay, follow the signs to the *spiaggia* (beach) out the front of Negombo.

✖ Eating

La Cantina del Mare ITALIAN €€
(Map p124; ☑081 333 03 22; Corso Angelo Rizzoli 20; meals €25; ⏰noon-2.30pm & 7pm-midnight) Tired of sand in your sandwiches? This friendly place is just across the road from the beach and serves excellent dishes to locals and wised-up tourists; seafood is the speciality. Sit on the pretty terrace or in the moodily lit interior lined with shelves of wine. The bread is pretty special too: made in the island's oldest bread oven and delivered daily.

🛍 Shopping

Stella di Mare CLOTHING
(Map p124; ☑081 199 43 96; Corso Angelo Rizzoli 150; ⏰9.30am-1pm & 5-10pm) Gorgeous womenswear: silk and linen skirts and kaftans to keep you cool in every sense, plus sandals, brogues and tassled and beaded bags.

Forio & the West Coast

The largest town on the island, and apparently the favoured destination of Tennessee Williams and Truman Capote in the 1950s, Forio is home to some of the best restaurants on Ischia, as well as good beaches and a couple of stunning botanical gardens.

⦿ Sights & Activities

Chiesa di Santa Maria del Soccorso CHURCH
(Map p124; Via Soccorso 1, Forio; ⏰10am-sunset) This dazzling white church located on the western edge of town was originally part of a 14th-century Augustinian monastery; its side chapel and dome were added in 1791 and 1854 respectively, the latter rebuilt after the 1883 earthquake. The 18th-century mismatched majolica tiles adorning the

semicircular staircase out the front are truly beautiful; from here, the views are heavenly.

Giardini Ravino GARDENS
(Map p124; ☑081 99 77 83; www.ravino.it; SS 270, Forio; adult/reduced €9/4; ⏰9am-sunset Wed & Fri-Mon Mar–mid-Nov) The vision of local botanist Giuseppe D'Ambra, who has collected plants since the 1960s, this 6000-sq-metre garden pays homage to the not-so-humble cactus. There is a diverse collection here, as well as other succulent plants, many of which are said to have homeopathic qualities. You can join a guided walk every Sunday at 11am; at other times, reserve in advance.

The gardens are also the site of concerts and art and craft exhibitions, and there are self-catering apartments to rent.

★ La Mortella GARDENS
(Place of the Myrtles; Map p124; ☑081 98 62 20; www.lamortella.it; Via F Calese 39, Forio; adult/reduced €12/7; ⏰9am-7pm Tue, Thu, Sat & Sun Apr-early Nov) Designed by Russell Page and inspired by the Moorish gardens of Spain's Alhambra, La Mortella is recognised as one of Italy's finest botanical gardens and is well worth a couple of hours of your time. Stroll among terraces, pools, palms, fountains and more than 1000 rare and exotic plants from all over the world. The lower section of the garden is humid and tropical, while the upper level features Mediterranean plants.

This veritable Eden was established by the late British composer Sir William Walton and his Argentine wife, Susana (who died in March 2010, aged 83), who made it their home in 1949, entertaining such venerable house guests as Sir Laurence Olivier, Maria Callas and Charlie Chaplin. Walton's life is commemorated in a small museum and his music wafts over the loudspeakers at the elegant cafe. There are classical-music concerts here in spring and autumn.

La Colombia BUILDING
(Museo Luchino Visconti; Map p124; ☑081 333 21 47; www.fondazionelacolombaia.it; Via F Calise 130, Forio; admission €5; ⏰10am-1pm & 4pm-sunset Tue-Sun) One of the joys of coming to Ischia is experiencing its untamed rural character, a feeling exemplified by handsome neo-Renaissance villa La Colombaia. It's little wonder, perhaps, as this is the former bachelor pad of flamboyant Italian film director Luchino Visconti.

Born into one of Milan's wealthiest families in 1906, Visconti received an Academy

Award nomination for best screenplay for his 1969 film *The Damned*, about a wealthy German family that turns fascist. His aesthetically restored home now houses an arts foundation, which includes a documentary library focusing on Visconti and cinema history, as well as costumes, set pieces and stills from his films. It's also a venue for the Ischia Film Festival (p136) and regularly holds edgy and interesting exhibitions.

★ **Giardini Poseidon** SPA
(Poseidon Gardens; Map p124; ✆ 081 908 71 11; www.giardiniposeidonterme.com; Via Mazzella, Spiaggia di Citara; passes per day €32, half-day €27, evening €5; ⏱ 9am-7pm Apr-Oct) South of Forio, spa lovers can enjoy sprawling Giardini Poseidon. There is a wide choice of treatments and facilities, including massages, saunas, Jacuzzis, various health treatments and terraced pools spilling down the volcanic cliffside. If it's all too stressful, settle for the dazzling private beach below.

Geo-Ausfluge HIKING
(✆ English spoken 081 90 30 58; www.eurogeopark.com; walks €17-26) Unlike Capri and Procida, Ischia is not easily accessible to hikers. If you're interested in exploring the hinterland, Italian geologist Aniello Di Lorio conducts a selection of walks throughout the island ranging from three to five hours, including lunch, with various collection points in Ischia; pickup in Casamicciola and

---

WILLIAM & SUSANA WALTON & THE PLACE OF THE MYRTLES

The first meeting between William Walton, renowned 46-year-old British composer, and Susana Gil, a 22-year-old Argentine secretary working for the British Council, has become legend. Spotting Susana at a cocktail party in Buenos Aires, Walton told Benjamin Britten that he intended to marry her. He proposed to Susana, repeating the question every day for two weeks until, to the dismay of her parents, she capitulated – they were married in 1948. It was not to be a fairy tale: Walton had umpteen affairs and made Susana have a dangerous backstreet abortion when she was carrying their child. But from then until the end of her life, her husband, and his music, came first for Susana.

Walton was at the height of his fame at the time of their marriage: he had been knighted in 1951, the same year that the full score of *Façade* was published. This, his most famous work, came about as a collaboration with his patron Edith Sitwell; a setting to music of her surrealistic poems written in 1922, it was greeted as a major contribution to modernism. An innovative viola concerto (1929) was followed by the dazzling and ambitious *First Symphony* in 1935. And, in 1944, Walton wrote the music – by turns masterfully nuanced and clarion-like – for Laurence Olivier's film of *Henry V*.

Despite the composer's acclaim, money was tight, and the couple moved from London to the wilds of volcanic Ischia. Their new home, bought despite concerns voiced by their friend Laurence Olivier, was a barren quarry with myrtles *(mortelle)* growing from the rocks. In 1956 Susana and designer Russell Page began to work on La Mortella, transforming the rocky landscape into a layered and theatrical tropical paradise full of rare and exotic plants, such as the huge water lily *Victoria amazonica*, with flowers that turn from white to crimson. As the fame and beauty of the garden increased so Walton's star faded, eclipsed by the progress of Britten: his work came to be seen as old-fashioned, an exercise in orchestral nostalgia.

But the garden was a cherished refuge for the couple, where they were visited by stars such as Laurence Olivier and Vivien Leigh, Maria Callas, Charlie Chaplin and the British dramatist Terence Rattigan.

When Walton died in 1983, Susana encased his ashes in a pyramidal rock at La Mortella, and created the William Walton Trust and Foundation in his memory. She built a recital hall in the garden, featuring busts of the Sitwells, a bronze of Walton himself, and John Piper's design for the ballet version of *Façade*.

Susana's spirited presence in jewel-coloured clothes lit up the garden for visitors into her old age. She died in 2010 aged 83, and the garden is now run by the trust. Visitors to this wonderful place have a double pleasure in store: as well as losing themselves among the lush plants, they will hear Walton's irresistibly bright and sensual music. And they will see Susana's own memorial, which touchingly recalls a woman who 'loved tenderly, worked with passion and believed in immortality'.

Panza costs a further €9 return. Note that the walks are primarily conducted in German and Italian but can be provided in English with advance notice. Even if you don't understand all the explanations, you'll still have the opportunity to explore some beautiful parts of Ischia that would be difficult to access solo.

Westcoast   BOATING

(Map p124; ✆ 081 90 86 04; www.westcoastischia.it; Porto di Forio; boat hire from €100) Westcoast provides full-day hire of motorised boats and dinghies (with or without a sailor). This is a particularly good idea in August, when the more popular beaches are crowded and you are desperate to find a quiet sandy cove.

✗ Eating

Zi Carmela   ITALIAN €

(Map p124; ✆ 081 99 84 23; Via Schioppa 27, Forio; meals €20, 4-course set menu €28; ⊙ noon-3pm & 7pm-midnight Apr-Oct; 🖤) Dating back decades, this restaurant has a lovely terrace decorated with copper pans, ceramic mugs and strings of garlic and chillies. Locals come for seafood dishes such as the *fritturina e pezzogne* (white fish baked in the pizza oven) or *tartare di palamito al profumo d'arancia* (tartar of fish with citrus).

Ristorante Pietratorcia   ITALIAN €€

(Map p124; ✆ 081 90 72 32; www.ristorantepietratorcia.it; Via Provinciale Panza 267, Forio; set menu from €28; ⊙ 11am-11pm Tue-Sun Apr-Oct) Enjoying a bucolic setting among tumbling vines, wild fig trees and rosemary bushes, this A-list winery is a foodie's nirvana. Tour the old stone cellars, sip a local drop and eye up the delectable degustation menu. Offerings

include fragrant bruschetta and cheeses, hearty Campanian sausages and spicy *salumi* (charcuterie).

★ Montecorvo   ITALIAN €€

(Map p124; ✆ 081 99 80 29; www.montecorvo.it; Via Montecorvo 33, Forio; meals €30; ⊙ 12.30-3.30pm & 7.30pm-1am, closed lunch Jul & Aug) At this extraordinary place part of the dining room is tunnelled into a cave and the terrace looks as though it belongs in a jungle. Owner Giovanni prides himself on the special dishes he makes daily, with an emphasis on grilled meat and fish, and the menu also includes a good range of pasta and vegetable antipasti.

You will need more than a good compass to find this spot, hidden amid lush foliage outside Forio and fronted by lofty pines, a tumbling waterfall and steep steps. Fortunately, it is well signposted. Prepare yourself for an exuberant welcome from Giovanni – he's that kind of guy.

Umberto a Mare   ITALIAN €€€

(Map p124; ✆ 081 99 71 71; Via Soccorso 2, Forio; meals €46; ⊙ noon-3pm & 7-11pm Mar-Dec) By the Spanish mission–style Soccorso church, this waterside restaurant dating from 1936 has the choice of a low-key cafe-bar for light snacks or the more formal seasonal restaurant. Restaurant highlights include penne with lobster and asparagus, and a delicate *al profumo di mare* (lightly grilled freshly caught fish).

Sant'Angelo & the South Coast

Tiny Sant'Angelo attracts a voguish crowd with its chic boutiques, seafront restaurants

---

ISCHIA'S BEST BEACHES

Spiaggia dei Maronti (Map p124) Long, sandy and very popular; the sand here is warmed by natural steam geysers. Reach the beach by bus from Barano, by water taxi from Sant'Angelo (€5 one-way) or on foot along the path leading east from Sant'Angelo.

Baia di Sorgeto (p135) Catch a water taxi from Sant'Angelo (€7 one-way) or reach the beach on foot from the town of Panza. Waiting at the bottom is an intimate cove complete with bubbling thermal spring. Perfect for a winter dip.

Spiaggia dei Pescatori (Map p128) Between Ischia Porto and Ischia Ponte, Fishermen's Beach is the island's most down to earth and popular seaside strip; it's perfect for families.

Baia di San Montano (Map p124) Due west of Lacco Ameno, this gorgeous bay is the place for warm, shallow, crystal-clear waters. You'll also find the Negombo (p131) spa park here.

Punta Caruso (Map p124) Located on Ischia's northwestern tip, this secluded rocky spot is perfect for a swim in clear, deep water. To get here, follow the walking path that leads off Via Guardiola down to the beach. Not suitable for children or when seas are rough.

and great beaches. Quiet lanes spill down the hill to fashionable Piazzetta Ottorino Troia, where tanned locals sip Campari and soda and take in late-night summer music concerts. Keeping an eye on it all is the great hulking *scoglio* (rock), joined to the village by a sandbar sprinkled with fishing boats, beach umbrellas and *bagnini* (lifeguards).

Catch a brightly painted water taxi from the pier to the sandy Spiaggia dei Maronti or the intimate cove of Baia di Sorgeto.

◎ Sights & Activities

Baia di Sorgeto   BEACH
(Map p124; Via Sorgeto; ☺Apr-Oct) Your knees may suffer descending the 300 or so steps to this secluded beach (signposted – though poorly – from the village of Panza), but a wallow in the warm thermal waters should revive them. The water naturally emerges at high temperatures, and then is ameliorated by the waves. There's a toilet here, and a summertime cafe.

The beach can also be reached by water taxi from Sant'Angelo (€7 one-way).

Terme Cavascura   SPA
(Map p124; ☑081 90 55 64, 081 99 92 42; www.cavascura.it; Via Cavascura 1, Spiaggia dei Maronti, Sant'Angelo; basic thermal bath €12, mud & thermal bath €27; ☺8.30am-6pm mid-Apr–mid-Oct) Experience an earthy spa by catching a water taxi to Cavascura (one-way €3.50) and following signs 300m down a gorge to Terme Cavascura. Wedged between soaring cliffs, this historic no-frills outdoor spa is Ischia's oldest. Soak in Roman baths hewn into the cliff or sweat it out in a grotto.

For an extra fee, have a mud mask and face massage (€24), manicure (€15) or anti-stress massage (€30). The sulphurous waters are beneficial for rheumatic, bronchial and skin conditions.

Parco Termale Aphrodite Apollon   SPA
(Map p124; ☑081 99 92 19; www.aphroditeapollon.it; Via Petrelle, Sant'Angelo; per day/half-day €35/25; ☺8am-6pm mid-Apr–Oct) A spectacular, partly strenuous 2km walk above the coast from Sant'Angelo brings you to this luxurious spa, now part of the Miramare Sea Resort. Beyond its ivy-draped entrance is a marble-clad complex of gyms, saunas, lush terraced gardens and 12 differently heated pools, including one for hydro-cycling. The spa offers an extensive range of beauty treatments and therapies.

✖ Eating

★Il Focolare   ITALIAN €€
(Map p124; ☑081 90 29 44; www.trattoriailfocolare.it; Via Creajo al Crocefisso 3, Barano d'Ischia; meals €30; ☺12.30-2.45pm & 7.30-11.30pm Jun-Oct, 12.30-2.45pm Wed, 7.30-11.30pm Sat & Sun Nov-May) A good choice for those seeking a little turf instead of surf, this is one of the island's best-loved restaurants. Family run, homey and rustic, it has a solidly traditional meat-based menu with steaks, lamb cutlets and specialities including *coniglio all'ischitana* (typical local rabbit dish with tomatoes, garlic and herbs) and *tagliatelle al ragù di cinghiale* (ribbon-shaped pasta with wild-boar ragout). On the sweet front, the desserts are homemade and exquisite. Owner Riccardo D'Ambra (who runs the restaurant together with his son, Agostino) is a leading local advocate of the Slow Food movement. If you want seafood, coffee or soft drinks, you'll have to go elsewhere; they're not on the menu here.

🛍 Shopping

L'Isoletto   FOOD
(Map p124; ☑081 99 93 74; Via Chiaia delle Rose 36, Sant'Angelo; ☺9am-9pm Mon-Sat) Stock up on a mouth-watering selection of local produce, from spicy *peperoncino*, rum-soaked *babà* and lemon-cream *cannoncelli* (pastry filled with lemon cream) to Ischian *vino* and the ubiquitous *limoncello*. Less tasteful – but deliciously kitsch – is the collection of tourist souvenirs, from seashell placemats to 3D souvenir wall plates.

PROCIDA

POP 10,800

The Bay of Naples' smallest island is also its best-kept secret. Dig out your paintbox: this soulful blend of lemon groves and pastel-hued houses is memorably picturesque. Mercifully off the mass-tourist radar, Procida is like the Portofino prototype and is refreshingly real. August aside – when beach-bound mainlanders flock to its shores – its narrow, sun-bleached streets are the domain of the locals: young boys clutch fishing rods, mothers push prams and old seamen swap yarns. Here, the hotels are smaller, fewer waiters speak broken German and the island's welcome is untainted by too much tourism.

If you have the time, Procida is an ideal place to explore on foot. The most compelling areas (and where you will also find most of the hotels, bars and restaurants) are Marina Grande, Marina Corricella and Marina di Chiaiolella. Beaches are not plentiful here, apart from the Lido di Procida, where, aside from August, you shouldn't have any trouble finding some towel space.

Prime waterfront dining needn't equal overpriced disappointment, with portside trattorias serving fresh classic fare. Several inland trattorias use home-grown produce and game in their cooking: try zesty local dish *insalata al limone,* a lemon salad infused with chilli oil.

ℹ Information

Pro Loco (☑ 081 810 19 68; www.prolocoprocida.it; Via Roma, Stazione Marittima, Marina Grande; ⊙ 9.30am-6pm) Located at the Ferry & Hydrofoil Ticket Office, this modest office has sparse printed information but should be able to advise on activities and the like.

ℹ Getting There & Away

BOAT

Caremar (☑ 081 837 07 00; www.caremar.it) operates up to eight daily hydrofoils to/from Naples and Procida (€14.90, 25 minutes).

SNAV (www.snav.it) operates four daily hydrofoils to/from Naples and Procida (€18. 60, 25 minutes).

ℹ Getting Around

The island measures a mere 3.8 square kilometres and can be walked. Apparently, it has been deduced (by an extremely bored person) that no matter where you want to get to on the island, it will take you a maximum of 6000 steps.

BUS

There is a limited bus service (€1), with four lines radiating from Marina Grande. Bus L1 connects the port and Via Marina di Chiaiolella.

Marina Grande

At Marina Grande, tumbledown buildings in hues of pinks, whites and yellow crowd the waterfront as an evocative first introduction to the island. Fishermen mend their nets under laundry hung out to dry and drink at earthy local bars, while waiters serve the catch of the day in well-worn restaurants. Narrow streets curve uphill to the wind-beaten complex of buildings culminating in a rambling ancient abbey: the distinctive surrounding houses feature wide arches and external staircases typical of the island.

⊙ Sights & Activities

★ **Abbazia di San Michele Arcangelo** CHURCH, MUSEUM
(☑ 334 8514028, 334 8514252; associazionemillennium@virgilio.it; Via Terra Murata 89, Terra Murata; admission €3; ⊙10am-1pm & 3-6pm) Soak in the dizzying bay views at the belvedere be-

---

ISLAND FESTIVALS

Capri Tango Festival (www.capritourism.com; ⊙ Jun) A skirt-swirling combo of music, dancing, exhibitions and tango classes.

Festa di Sant'Anna (www.infoischiaprocida.it; Ischia; ⊙26 Jul) The allegorical 'burning of the Castello Aragonese' on the feast day of St Anne; hypnotic procession of boats and fireworks.

Grape harvest It's a moveable feast, dependent on weather and conditions, but September sees the grape harvest celebrated on the islands; it's a picturesque time to be here.

Settembrata Anacaprese (www.capritourism.com; Capri; ⊙1-15 Sep) Annual celebration of the grape harvest with gastronomic events and markets.

Ischia Film Festival (www.ischiafilmfestival.it; ⊙Jun/Jul) Serving up free flicks and exhibitions in star locations, including Castello Aragonese, Villa Arbusto and La Colombaia.

Ischia Jazz Festival (www.ischiajazz.com; ⊙ usually Sep) Ischia's annual jazz festival pumps out five days of Italian sax with a dash of foreign acts.

Procession of the Misteri Good Friday sees a colourful procession when a wooden statue of Christ and the Madonna Addolorata, along with life-size plaster and papier-mâché tableaux illustrating events leading to Christ's crucifixion, are carted across the island. Men dress in blue tunics with white hoods, while many of the young girls dress as the Madonna.

fore exploring the adjoining Abbazia di San Michele Arcangelo. Built in the 11th century and remodelled between the 17th and 19th centuries, this one-time Benedictine abbey houses a small museum with some arresting pictures done in gratitude by shipwrecked sailors, plus a church with a spectacular coffered ceiling and an ancient Greek alabaster basin converted into a font, and a maze of catacombs that leads to a tiny secret chapel.

Blue Dream Yacht
Charter Boating BOATING
(☑ 339 5720874, 081 896 05 79; www.bluedream-charter.com; Via Vittorio Emanuele 14; per week from €1500) If you have 'Champagne on the deck' aspirations, you can always charter your very own yacht from here. Sleeps six.

Barobe & Gommoni BICYCLE RENTAL
(☑ 339 7163303; Via Roma 134; per day €10; 🚖) The bicycles for hire here are one of the best ways to explore the island. Small, open micro-taxis can also be hired for two to three hours for around €35, depending on your bargaining prowess.

✗ Eating

Bar Cavaliere PASTRIES €
(☑ 081 810 10 74; Via Roma 42; pastries from €1; ☺ 7am-midnight) Procida's prime pastry shop has a delicious range of cakes, pastries and sweets. A local treat is *lingua di bue* (ox tongue), a flaky pastry shaped like a tongue and filled with *crema pasticcera* (custard). The place doubles as a cocktail bar if all that sugar builds up a thirst.

Da Giorgio TRATTORIA €
(☑ 081 896 79 10; Via Roma 36; meals €18; ☺ noon-3pm & 7-11.30pm Mar-Oct; 🚖) These folks try hard to please, with a reasonably priced menu, welcoming window boxes and inexpensive beer. The menu holds few surprises, but the ingredients are fresh; try the *antipasto di mare* (€10) or *gnocchi alla sorrentina* (gnocchi in a tomato, basil and *pecorino* cheese sauce).

Fammivento SEAFOOD €€
(☑ 081 896 90 20; Via Roma 39; meals €25; ☺ noon-12.30am Tue-Sat, noon-3pm Sun Apr-Oct) Get things going with the *frittura di calamari* (fried squid), then try the *fusilli carciofi e calamari* (pasta with artichokes and calamari). For a splurge, go for the house speciality of *zuppa di crostaci e moluschi* (crustacean and mollusc soup).

🛍 Shopping

Low-key Procida isn't a shopping heavyweight. Good buys include wine and flouncy beach wear.

Enoteca Borgo Antico DRINK
(☑ 081 896 96 38; Via Vittorio Emanuele 13; ☺ 9am-9pm) This slick little bottle shop stocks the best of Campanian *vino* and a smattering of other Italian drops. The friendly owner will advise you (in Italian) of the best local wines and the best deals. *Limoncello* and a wide choice of traditional and more modern flavoured grappas are also available.

Maricella ACCESSORIES
(☑ 081 896 05 61; www.maricella.it; Via Roma 161; ☺ 9am-8.30pm) A sweet little boutique selling brightly coloured accessories, including jewellery that looks good enough to eat: necklaces strung with what resemble M&Ms, brilliant sherbet-yellow earrings, gobstopper-sized rings, as well as pretty sandals, raffia bags and totes for the beach.

Mediterraneo FASHION
(☑ 081 196 69 09; Via Roma 32; ☺ 9.30am-9pm) The fashions here are made from wispy fine cotton, perfect for those sizzling summer days. Floaty dresses patterned with wild flowers, long light-as-a-feather skirts, snowdrift-white transparent shirts, shopping bags in bold prints and some dressier wear with colourful designs.

Marina Corricella

From panoramic Piazza dei Martiri, the village of Marina Corricella tumbles down to its marina in a waterfall of pastel colours: pinks, yellows and whites. Fishing boats complete the rainbow of colours, docked alongside piles of fishing nets, sleek cats and, in the summer, a sprawl of terrace cafes and restaurants. The international hit film *Il Postino* was partly filmed here; it really *is* a magical spot – don't miss it.

Further south, off Via Pizzaco, a steep flight of steps leads down to sand brushed **Spiaggia di Chiaia**, one of the island's most beautiful beaches and home to several good seafood restaurants.

🧭 Tours

Cesare Boat Trips BOAT TOUR
(per 2½hr €26; ☺ May-Oct) On the harbour at Marina Corricella, ask for friendly Cesare

Procida

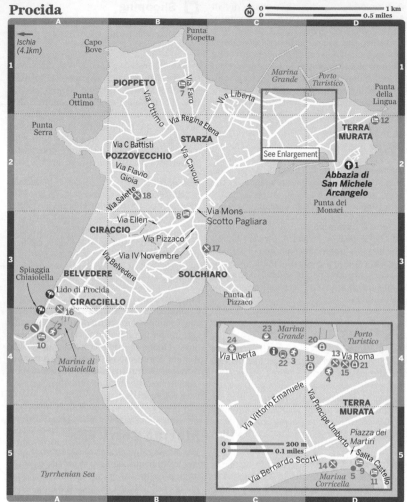

in your best Italian. Look for the colourful boats with his name emblazoned across the side or check at one of the beach bars – he won't be far away. Cesare runs some great boat trips as well as half-day trips in a traditional galleon for €100.

✗ Eating

Caracalè   SEAFOOD €€
(📞081 896 91 92; Via Marina Corricella 6, Marina Corricella; meals €28; ⏱12.30-3.30pm & 7-11pm, closed Tue Mar-Jun & Sep–mid-Nov) Along this unpretentious marina, with its old fishing boats, piles of fishing nets and meandering

cats, any restaurant will provide you with a memorable dining experience. This place, tucked away to the left as you face the sea, is one of the best. Go for a simple fresh seafood dish, like soup with mussels or grilled swordfish. Delicious.

La Lampara   SEAFOOD €€
(📞081 896 75 75; Hotel La Corricella, Marina Corricella; meals €25; ⏱noon-2.30pm & 7-11pm May-Oct) Enjoy the view of the picturesque marina from the restaurant terrace here. The dishes of choice are centred on seafood, based on the freshest catch of the day. Get

Procida

your feet wet with the marinated seafood antipasti before taking the plunge with a hearty plate of *ravioli a'sapore di mare* (seafood ravioli).

Marina di Chiaiolella

All pink, white and blue, crescent-shaped Marina di Chiaiolella was once the crater of a volcano. Today it features a yacht-stocked marina, old-school eateries and a laid-back charm. From the pier, you can catch a brightly painted water taxi to reach several superb beaches in the area (from €8). The crystal-clear waters around here are perfect for diving too.

◉ Sights & Activities

Procida Diving Centre   DIVING
(☑081 896 83 85; www.vacanzeaprocida.it; Via Cristoforo Colombo 6; ☺Jun-Sep; ☗) Conveniently located right on the marina, this well-established outfit organises dives and courses, and hires out equipment. There are four diving sites in Procida: Punta Pizzaco (intermediate to experienced), Secca delle Formiche (beginner to intermediate), Capo Bove (beginner) and Punta Solchiaro (intermediate). The price ranges from €45 for a single dive to €130 for a snorkelling course, with more advanced open-water diving and rescue courses.

Barcheggiando   BOATING
(☑081 810 19 34; Marina Chiaiolella) This outfit hires out motor boats and *gommoni* (wooden boats) from €100 per day.

✖ Eating

★Da Mariano   ITALIAN €
(☑081 896 73 50; Marina di Chiaiolella; meals €22; ☺noon-3pm & 7pm-midnight) Hugely popular with locals for its simple but perfectly executed local dishes such as stuffed calamari and *spaghetti alle vongole*. The fish, including swordfish, is jumping fresh, and you eat looking out at the bay. Round off lunch or dinner with peaches cooked in wine.

La Conchiglia   SEAFOOD €€
(☑081 896 76 02; www.laconchigliaristorante.com; Via Pizzaco 10, Solchiaro; meals €25; ☺1-3.30pm & 8-9.30pm summer) Views from this beachfront place are magical: turquoise water below, with the pastel jumble of Marina di Corricella in the distance. More elegant than most Procida restaurants, with gems such as *spiedini di mazzancolle* (prawn kebabs) and superb *spaghetti alla povera* (with *peperoncino* and green capsicum). Take the steep steps down from Via Pizzaco or book a boat from Corricella.

Ristorante Scarabeo   ITALIAN €€
(☑081 896 99 18; Via Salette 10; meals €28) Behind a jungle of lemon trees and located near the centre of the island is this venerable kitchen, where they whip up classics such as *fritelle di basilico* (fried patties of bread, egg, Parmesan and basil), and homemade aubergine and *provola* ravioli (€10). They breed their own rabbits, make Falanghina wine and it's yours to devour under a pergola.

The Amalfi Coast

Best Places to Eat

➡ Donna Rosa (p161)

➡ Next2 (p161)

➡ Marina Grande (p168)

➡ L'Antica Trattoria (p147)

Best Places to Stay

➡ Pensione Maria Luisa (p208)

➡ Ulisse (p205)

➡ Hotel Caruso (p211)

➡ Hotel Lidomare (p210)

Why Go?

Deemed by Unesco to be an outstanding example of a Mediterranean landscape, the Amalfi Coast is a beguiling combination of great beauty and gripping drama: coastal mountains plunge into the sea in a stunning vertical scene of precipitous crags, picturesque towns and lush forests.

Among the glittering string of coastal gems, legendary Positano and Amalfi sparkle the brightest, while mountain-top Ravello has the glossy fame of its grandiose villas and Wagnerian connection. Amalfi Coast gateway Sorrento is a handsome and venerable cliff-top resort that has miraculously survived the onslaught of package tourism.

Aside from its sheer beauty, the region is home to some superb restaurants and hotels. It is also one of Italy's top spots for hiking, with well-marked trails providing a great means of getting away from the coastal clamour.

When to Go

➡ The Amalfi Coast is strictly seasonal, with the majority of hotels, restaurants and bars pulling down their shutters from late October to Easter.

➡ April to June and September to October are less-crowded periods.

➡ Neapolitans descend en masse in August, especially at weekends, when restaurants and sunbeds fill up fast.

➡ The best time for hiking is spring, when wildflowers are a colourful bonus and the weather is pleasantly temperate, albeit occasionally wet.

SORRENTO

POP 16,500

An unashamed resort, Sorrento is nonetheless a civilised and beautiful town. Even the souvenirs are a cut above the norm, with plenty of fine old shops selling the ceramics, lacework and *intarsio* (marquetry items) that are famously produced here. The main drawback is the lack of a proper beach: the town straddles the cliffs overlooking the water to Naples and Mt Vesuvius.

Sorrento makes a good base for exploring the region's highlights: to the south is the best of the peninsula's unspoilt countryside, to the east is the Amalfi Coast, to the north lie Pompeii and other archaeological sites, and offshore is the fabled island of Capri.

◉ Sights

The centre is compact: all the main sights are within walking distance of Piazza Tasso. Sorrento is a glorious town for an evening *passeggiata* (stroll), the lively streets punctuated with jaw-dropping cliff-top spots to take in the sunset.

Museo Correale   MUSEUM

(☏081 878 18 46; www.museocorreale.it; Via Correale 50; admission €7; ⊗9.30am-6.30pm Tue-Sat, to 1.30pm Sun) East of the city centre, this museum is well worth a visit whether you're a clock collector, an archaeological egghead or into embroidery. In addition to the rich assortment of 17th- to 19th-century Neapolitan art and crafts, there are Japanese, Chinese and European ceramics, clocks, furniture and, on the ground floor, Greek and Roman artefacts. The bulk of the collection, along with the 18th-century villa housing it, was donated to the city in the 1920s by aristocratic counts Alfredo and Pompeo Correale. Be sure to wander around the gardens, with their breathtaking coastal views and rare plants and flowers.

Marina Grande   HARBOUR

(Via Marina Grande) The closest thing to a *spiaggia* (beach) is this pleasant sandy stretch at Marina Grande harbour; if you want to just loll in the sun, nearby jetties sport umbrellas and deckchairs. While it's far smaller than the island of Procida in the Bay of Naples, this former fishing district has a glimmer of similarity, with its pastel-coloured houses, brightly painted boats and fishermen mending nets. There are some earthy seafood restaurants serving fish from the morning's catch.

Sedile Dominava   HISTORIC BUILDING

(Via San Cesareo) Incongruously wedged between racks of lemon-themed souvenir merchandise, this 15th-century domed *palazzo* (mansion) has exquisite, albeit faded, original frescoes. Crowned by a cupola, the terrace, open to the street on two sides, was originally a meeting point for the town's medieval aristocracy; today it houses a working men's club where local pensioners sit around playing cards.

Centro Storico   AREA

(Corso Italia) The bustling *centro storico* (historic centre) ranges along Corso Italia, a major hub for shops, restaurants and bars. Duck into the side streets and you'll find narrow lanes flanked by traditional green-shuttered buildings, interspersed with the occasional *palazzo*, piazza or church. Souvenir shops, trattorias and some fine old buildings also jostle for space in this tangle of cobbled backstreets.

Duomo   CATHEDRAL

(Corso Italia; ⊗8am-12.30pm & 4.30-9pm) To get a feel for Sorrento's history, stroll down Via Pietà from Piazza Tasso and past two medieval palaces en route to the cathedral, with its striking exterior fresco, triple-tiered bell tower, four classical columns and elegant majolica clock. Take note of the striking marble bishop's throne (1573) and the beautiful wooden choir stalls decorated in the local *intarsio* style. The cathedral's original structure dates from the 15th century, but the building has been altered several times, most recently in the early 20th century when the current facade was added.

Museo Bottega della
Tarsia Lignea   MUSEUM

(☏081 877 19 42; www.museomuta.it; Via San Nicola 28; adult/reduced €8/5; ⊗10am-6.30pm Apr-Oct, to 5pm Nov-Mar) Since the 18th century, Sorrento has been famous for its *intarsio* furniture, made with elaborately designed inlaid wood. Some wonderful

---

BEST AMALFI COAST BEACHES
••••••••••••••••••••••••••••••••

Baia de Ieranto (p156)

Spiaggia di Fornillo (p159)

Marina di Praia (p163)

Bagni Regina Giovanna (p146)

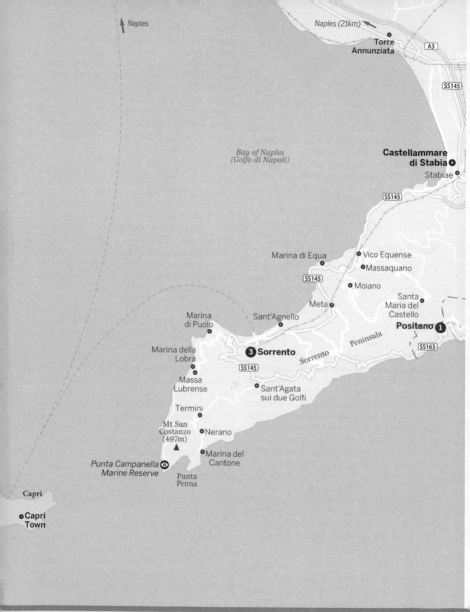

Map labels:
- ↑ Naples
- Naples (21km) →
- Torre Annunziata
- A3
- SS145
- Castellammare di Stabia ●
- Stabiae ●
- SS145
- Bay of Naples
  (Golfo di Napoli)
- Marina di Equa ●
- Vico Equense ●
- Massaquano ●
- SS145
- Moiano ●
- Meta ●
- Santa Maria del Castello ●
- Positano 1
- Marina di Puolo ●
- Sant'Agnello ●
- Peninsula
- SS163
- Marina della Lobra ●
- 3 Sorrento
- Sorrento
- Massa Lubrense ●
- Sant'Agata sui due Golfi ●
- Termini ●
- Mt San Costanzo (497m) ▲
- ● Nerano
- Marina del Cantone ●
- Punta Campanella Marine Reserve ◎
- Punta Penna
- Capri
- Capri Town ●

The Amalfi Coast Highlights

❶ Mixing with the beautiful people on the designer-lined streets of vertiginous **Positano** (p157).

❷ Sitting down to super-fresh seafood at the pastel-painted harbour of **Cetara** (p174).

❸ Going shopping in **Sorrento** (p150) for traditional marquetry artworks.

❹ Dancing at one of the most stunningly situated nightclubs in Italy in **Praiano** (p164).

❺ Pottering round **Atrani** (p164), with its ancient piazza, pavement cafes and pretty cove beach.

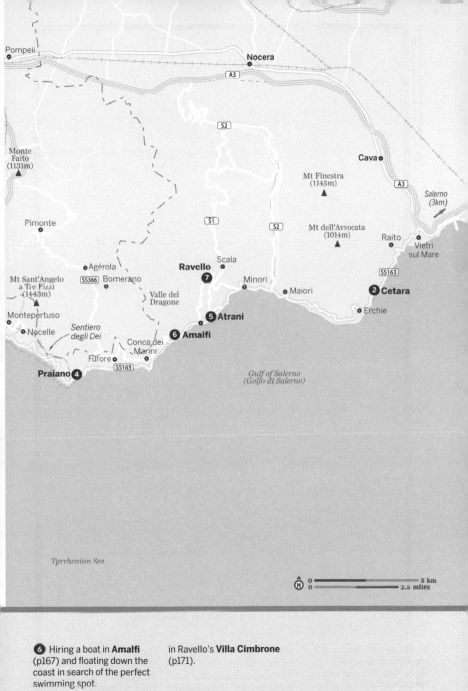

6 Hiring a boat in **Amalfi** (p167) and floating down the coast in search of the perfect swimming spot.

in Ravello's **Villa Cimbrone** (p171).

7 Swooning at the views from the Belvedere of Infinity

THE AMALFI COAST SORRENTO

Sorrento

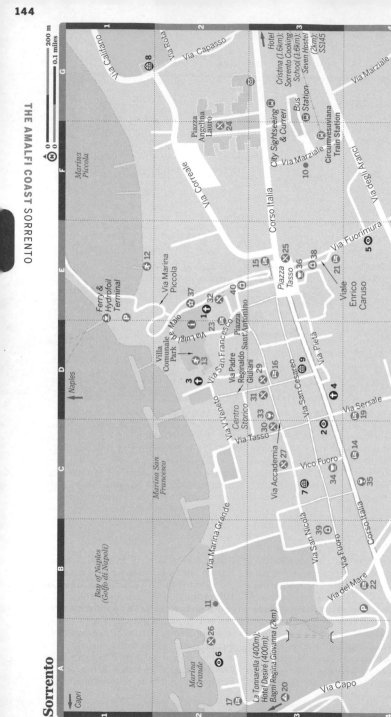

Sorrento

examples can be found in this museum, housed in an 18th-century palace, complete with beautiful frescoes. There's also an interesting collection of paintings, prints and photographs depicting the town and surrounding area in the 19th century.

If you're interested in purchasing a new *intarsio* piece, visit Gargiulo & Jannuzzi (p150), one of the longest-established specialist shops in town; they are happy to ship purchases.

Chiesa di San Francesco　　CHURCH
(Via San Francesco; ⊙8am-1pm & 2-8pm) Located next to the Villa Comunale Park, this is one of Sorrento's most beautiful churches. Surrounded by bougainvillea and birdsong, the evocative cloisters have an Arabic portico and interlaced arches supported by octagonal pillars. The church is most famous, however, for its summer program of concerts featuring world-class performers from the classical school. If this strikes a chord, check out the schedule at the tourist office. There are also regular art exhibitions.

Il Vallone dei Mulino　　HISTORIC SITE
(Valley of the Mills; Via Fuorimura) ⚑ Just behind Piazza Tasso, a stunning natural phenomenon is on view from Via Fuorimura. Il Vallone dei Mulino is a deep mountain cleft that dates from a volcanic eruption 35,000 years ago. Sorrento was once bounded by three gorges, but today this is the only one that remains. The valley is named after the ancient wheat mills that were once located here, the ruins of which are still clearly visible.

Basilica di Sant'Antonino　　CHURCH
(Piazza Sant'Antonino; ⊙9am-noon & 5-7pm) Named after the patron saint of Sorrento, the oldest church in town dates from the 11th century. A few Roman artefacts have ended up here, as well as some dark medieval paintings and the oddity of two whale ribs. Apparently, the much-loved saint performed numerous miracles, including one in which he rescued a child from a whale's stomach. The saint's bones lie beneath the baroque interior in an 18th-century crypt.

🤾 Activities

Hiring a boat is an excellent way to explore this rugged coastline.

★ Sic Sic
BOATING

(☑ 081 807 22 83; www.nauticasicsic.com; Marina Piccola; ☉ May-Oct) Seek out the best beaches by rented boat, with or without a skipper. This outfit rents a variety of motor boats, starting at around €40 per hour or €100 per day. It also organises boat excursions, wedding shoots and similar.

Bagni Regina Giovanna
SWIMMING

Sorrento lacks a decent beach, so consider heading to Bagni Regina Giovanna, a rocky beach with clear, clean water about 2km west of town, set among the ruins of the Roman Villa Pollio Felix. It's possible to walk here (follow Via Capo), although you'll save your strength if you get the SITA bus headed for Massa Lubrense.

Villa Comunale Park
OUTDOORS

(☉ 8am-midnight summer, to 10.30pm winter) This landscaped park commands stunning views across the water to Mt Vesuvius. A popular green space to while away the sunset hours, it's a lively spot, with benches, operatic buskers and a small bar.

MAKE YOUR OWN GELATI

Impress your dinner-party pals with homemade Italian gelato by taking a course at **Gelateria David** (☑ 081 807 36 49; www.gelateriadavidsorrento.it; Via Marziale 19), a cream-of-the-crop gelateria run by the third generation in the ice-cream business. Classes (€19) last around an hour and culminate in your very own certificate. Times vary according to demand, so call or drop by to organise; they speak excellent English.

Specialities include the delicious *profumo de Sorrento*, an orange, lemon and tangerine sorbet, and *babà* (rum-soaked sponge cake). Aside from mango, the gelateria uses only fresh fruit, which means that choices vary throughout the season. It also makes all the traditional, more commercial flavours, which are wonderfully creamy and bear little resemblance to that supermarket tub back home.

🍷 Courses

Sorrento Cooking School
COOKING COURSE

(☑ 081 878 35 55; www.sorrentocookingschool.com; Viale dei Pini 52, Sant'Agnello; ☉ Apr-Oct) You can opt for a serious culinary vacation here or one of the popular three-hour classes (€60), learning to make such Italian staples as pizza, ravioli and tiramisu (OK, more a sin than a staple) in a beautiful spot surrounded by lemon trees. The class ends with a meal of the goodies prepared, accompanied by local wine.

Sant'Anna Institute
LANGUAGE COURSE

(Sorrento Lingue; ☑ 081 807 55 99; www.sorrentolingue.com; Via Marina Grande 16) There is something very appealing about rattling off your shopping list in faultless Italian. This is one of the longest-established language schools on the Amalfi Coast, attracting students from all over the globe. Prices start at €198 for a week of tuition, plus a €60 enrollment fee. It also runs language/cooking and language/history courses.

🎉 Festivals & Events

Sorrento Festival
MUSIC

World-class classical concerts are held in the cloisters of the Chiesa di San Francesco between July and September.

Sant'Antonino
RELIGIOUS

(☉ 14 Feb) The city's patron saint, Sant'Antonino, is remembered annually with processions and huge markets. The saint is credited with having saved Sorrento during WWII when Salerno and Naples were heavily bombed.

Settimana Santa
RELIGIOUS

(Holy Week) Famed throughout Italy; the first procession takes place at midnight on the Thursday preceding Good Friday, with robed and hooded penitents in white; the second occurs on Good Friday, when participants wear black robes and hoods to commemorate the death of Christ.

Sagra della Salsiccia e Ceppone
FOOD

(☉ 13 Dec) Sausage lovers can salivate at this annual festival, when hundreds of kilos of sausages are barbecued over a giant bonfire, accompanied by hearty local wine.

🍴 Eating

The centre of town heaves with bars, cafes, trattorias, restaurants and even the odd

THREE PERFECT DAYS ON THE AMALFI COAST

Day 1: Take to the Seas

Wake up in picturesque **Positano** (p157) and head for the Spiaggia Grande to sip a cappuccino overlooking the bodies beautiful and bobbing fishing boats. Peruse the fashions, duck into the church and stroll around the cliff to low-key **Fornillo** (p159) for lunch. Catch a ferry to pretty **Amalfi** (p164) and explore the extraordinary cathedral, the museums, the medieval backstreets and the *pasticcerie* (pastry shops). Have dinner in lovely, atmospheric Atrani, a short stroll away.

Day 2: Hike Amid Stunning Scenery

Hiking trails wend their way through compelling coastal routes and countryside. Energetic souls can stride out on the poetically named **Sentiero degli Dei** (p166), high up in the hills. It takes six hours, so it's breathtaking in all senses of the word. If this sounds a little daunting, there are some delightful shorter walks available – as well as more challenging and less busy routes; tourist offices and bookshops can provide maps.

Day 3: Head for the Wild West

Rent a car from Sorrento and take in the fabulous mountains and seascapes in this little-known western corner. Leave town on the minor coastal road, winding through groves of olive and lemon trees. Dip down to the beach at Marina di Puolo, admire the view of Capri from the lookout in **Massa Lubrense** (p152) and head for dramatic Punta Campanella for more killer views. Continue to Nerano, and walk to **Baia di Ieranto beach** (p149) – the walk takes about an hour – before carrying on to tranquil **Sant'Agata sui due Golfi** (p153) and doubling back to Sorrento.

kebab takeaway shop. Many places, particularly those with waistcoated waiters stationed outside (or the ones displaying sun-bleached photos of the dishes), are unashamed tourist traps serving bland food at inflated prices. But not all are and it's perfectly possible to eat well. If you've got your own wheels there are some superb restaurants dotted around the nearby countryside, including one of Italy's top restaurants in Sant'Agata sui due Golfi (p153).

★**Da Emilia**   TRATTORIA €
(☑081 807 27 20; Via Marina Grande 62; meals €20; ☉noon-2.30pm & 7pm-midnight; ⊞) Founded in 1947 and still run by the same family, this is a homely yet atmospheric joint overlooking the fishing boats in Marina Grande. There's a large informal dining room, complete with youthful photos of former patron Sophia Loren, a scruffily romantic terrace and a menu of straightforward, no-fail dishes like mussels with lemon, and spaghetti with clams.

Angelina Lauro   ITALIAN €
(☑081 807 40 97; Piazza Angelina Lauro 39-40; self-service meals €15; ☉10am 11pm Wed Mon; ⊞) Rafael is your congenial host at this brightly lit, roomy place that has a passing resemblance to a college canteen and has been

family run since 1980. It hits the spot for a filling, inexpensive self-service lunch: grab a tray and choose from the selection of pastas, meats and vegetable side dishes. The owners produce their own wine and olive oil.

★**L'Antica Trattoria**   ITALIAN €€
(☑081 807 10 82; www.lanticatrattoria.com; Via Padre Reginaldo Giuliani 33; mains €21-25, 4 courses €60; ☉noon-11pm) Head to the upstairs terrace with its traditional tiles and trailing grape vines and you seem miles away from the alleyways outside. With a deserved reputation as the finest restaurant in town, it has a mainly traditional menu, with homemade pasta and a daily fish special. There are vegetarian and gluten-free menus, plus a resident mandolin player.

Aurora Light   ITALIAN €€
(☑081 877 26 31; www.auroralight.it; Piazza Tasso 3 4; mains €15; ☉noon-midnight) At first glance the menu here looks more Californian than Campanian, with such imaginative salads as spicy chickpea and spinach, and fennel with beetroot and orange. The enthusiastic young owner has tapped into traditional dishes and given them an innovative twist: white-bean soup with baby squid, aubergine *parmigiana* with swordfish sauce, stuffed-pepper roulade and so on.

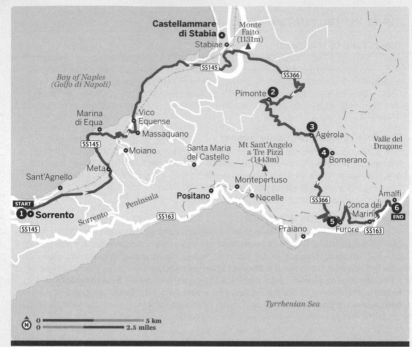

Bay of Naples (Golfo di Napoli)

Tyrrhenian Sea

0 — 5 km
0 — 2.5 miles

🏃 Driving Tour
Sorrento to Amalfi: The 'Green Ribbon' Route

START SORRENTO
END AMALFI
LENGTH 51KM; TWO HOURS

This drive is an alternative to the famous Amalfi Coast road (p156) and passes through some stunning mountain scenery. From ❶ **Sorrento**, hug the coast following signs to Naples on the SS145. Just before Castellammare di Stabia, exit onto the SS366 and head to ❷ **Pimonte**. This is a small rural town with tractors trundling through the streets. Stop at the main piazza for the delicious almond-based speciality *torta palummo*. Expect curious stares; tourists are a rarity here. Continue along the SS366, enjoying forests of beech trees and a backdrop of mountains thickly quilted with pines. You are now in the depths of the verdant Parco Regionale dei Monte Lattari.

Next stop is the pretty dairy-producing village of ❸ **Agérola**. Step into one of the numerous delis for local cheeses like *fior di latte* (cow-milk mozzarella) and *caciocavallo*

(gourd-shaped traditional curd cheese), produced on the fertile slopes around town. You can also find top-quality local salamis and sausages. The road continues to ❹ **Bomerano** (37km), a familiar name to hikers embarking on the Walk of the Gods. Duck into the 16th-century Chiesa San Matteo Apostolo to check out the ceiling frieze, consider the nostalgic treat of poached eggs on toast at Albergo Gentile (geared towards northern European hikers), then stop by Fusco at Via Principe di Piemonte 3 for a tub of homemade yoghurt.

The road winds dramatically down to the sea – lookouts allow you to gaze at the view with Conca dei Marini twinkling in the distance. At ❺ **Furore** there's handy parking next to the picturesque Maria SS delle Grazie church, with its adjacent terraced restaurant and small deli. Follow the road round the magnificent Furore fjord, which slices through the mountains all the way to the sea. At 49.7km the road divides and you can turn off to Positano (16km) or continue the remaining kilometre or so to ❻ **Amalfi**.

The setting on Piazza Tasso is one of the best for people-watching, though one of the worst for exhaust fumes.

Inn Bufalito
ITALIAN €€

(☑ 081 365 69 75; www.innbufalito.it; Vico Fuoro 21; meals €25; ⊙ 11am-midnight; 🐾🎵) 🐾 Owner Franco Coppola (no relation to the movie man) exudes a real passion for showcasing local produce – the restaurant is a member of the Slow Food movement. A mozzarella bar as well as a restaurant, this effortlessly stylish place boasts a menu including delights such as Sorrento-style cheese fondue and buffalo-meat *carpaccio*.

Cheese tastings are a regular event, along with photography and art exhibitions, and occasional live music.

O'Murzill
NEAPOLITAN €€

(☑ 081 020 23 71; Via Accademia 17; meals from €20; ⊙ 11.30am-1.30am Mon-Sat) With just six gingham-clothed tables in what resembles a homey front room with the kitchen beyond, this restaurant looks as though it belongs in a small village rather than in the heart of Sorrento. The reassuringly brief menu concentrates on traditional Neapolitan dishes like pasta with lobster and no-fuss antipasti such as grilled mushrooms.

There's no complimentary *limoncello* (lemon liqueur) or tomato-topped bruschetta, just well-priced and honest home-style cooking.

Refood
ITALIAN €€

(☑ 081 878 14 80; www.refoods.it; Via Accademia 10; meals €35; ⊙ 5.30pm-midnight) The postmodern decor, with its imaginative lighting, exposed steel pipes and jujube-coloured seating, is a far cry from that of Sorrento's traditional trattorias. Go for one of the specialities like large tube pasta in a fish stew or a classic Châteaubriand.

La Fenice
ITALIAN €€

(☑ 081 878 16 52; www.ristorantelafenicesorrento.com; Via degli Aranci 11; meals €24; ⊙ noon-2.45pm & 7-11.30pm Tue-Sun) It's too large and bright for a romantic dinner for two, but locals continue to recommend this place for its down-to-earth, well-prepared dishes, particularly the seafood, such as mussels with garlic and parsley, and grilled squid.

Ristorante il Buco
ITALIAN €€€

(☑ 081 878 23 54; www.ilbucoristorante.it; Rampa Marina Piccola 5; meals €60; ⊙ 12.30-2.30pm & 7.30-11pm Thu-Tue Feb-Dec) Housed in a former monks' wine cellar, this dress-up restaurant offers far-from-monastic cuisine. The emphasis is on innovative regional cooking, so expect modern combos such as pasta with rockfish sauce, or *treccia* (local cheese) and prawns served on capers with tomato and olive sauce. In summer there's outdoor seating near one of the city's ancient gates. Reservations recommended.

🍸 Drinking & Nightlife

You can do the whole drinking trip in Sorrento: down pints of lager while watching Sky Sports on a big screen, quaff local wines in wood panelled dens, and sip cocktails in swish bars.

Cafè Latino
CAFE, BAR

(☑ 081 878 37 18; Vico Fuoro 4a; ⊙ 10am-1am summer) Think locked-eyes-over-cocktails time. This is the place to impress your date with cocktails (from €7) on the terrace, surround-

---

HIKING THE PENINSULA

Forming a giant horseshoe between **Punta Campanella** and **Punta Penna**, the beautiful **Baia di Ieranto** is generally regarded as the top swimming spot on the Sorrento Peninsula. To get there you have two alternatives: get a boat, or walk from the village of Nerano, the steep descent forming part of a longer 6.5km hike from nearby Termini.

This picturesque path is just one of 20 (for a total of 110km) that cover the area. These range from tough all-day treks such as the 14.1km **Alta Via dei Monti Lattari** from the Fontanelle hills near Positano down to the Punta Campanella, to shorter walks suitable for all the family.

Tourist offices throughout the area can provide maps detailing the colour-coded routes. With the exception of the Alta Via dei Monti Lattari, which is marked in red and white, long routes are shown in red on the map; coast-to-coast trails in blue; paths connecting villages in green; and circular routes in yellow. On the ground, trails are fairly well marked, although you may find that some signs have faded to near-indecipherable levels.

ed by orange and lemon trees. Sip a Mary Pickford (rum, pineapple, *grenadino* and maraschino) or a glass of chilled white wine. If you can't drag yourselves away, you can also eat here (meals around €30).

Bollicine   WINE BAR
(☑081 878 46 16; Via Accademia 9; ☻7.30pm-2am) The wine list at this unpretentious bar with a dark, woody interior includes all the big Italian names and a selection of interesting local labels. If you can't decide what to go for, the amiable bar staff will advise you. There's also a small menu of *panini* (sandwiches), bruschettas and one or two pasta dishes.

English Inn   PUB
(☑081 807 43 57; www.englishinn.it; Corso Italia 55; ☻9am-2am) The vast upstairs garden terrace, with its orange trees and dazzle of bougainvillea, is a delight and attracts a primarily expat crowd, who head here for the disco beats and karaoke nights, accompanied by Guinness on tap. The party atmosphere continues late into the night, while the bacon-and-eggs breakfast is a suitable reviver.

Fauno Bar   CAFE
(☑081 878 11 35; Piazza Tasso; ☻7am-midnight mid-Mar–mid-Jan) On Piazza Tasso, this elegant cafe with besuited waiters covers half the square and offers the best people-watching in town. It serves stiff drinks at stiff prices: cocktails start around €8.50. Snacks and sandwiches are also available (from €7).

UNICO COSTIERA

If you plan to do much travelling by SITA bus and/or Circumvesuviana train, then it saves money and hassle to invest in a Unico Costiera (www.unicocampania.it) card, available for durations of 45 minutes (€2.50), 90 minutes (€3.80), 24 hours (€7.60) or 72 hours (€18). Aside from the SITA buses, the 24- and 72-hour tickets also allow you to hop on the City Sightseeing tourist bus, which travels between Amalfi and Ravello and Amalfi and Maiori. Several tickets can be bought at one time for repeat trips. Note that the ticket-use time begins when the ticket is punched on entering the bus or train, not when the ticket is purchased.

☆ Entertainment

Teatro Tasso   THEATRE
(☑081 807 55 25; www.teatrotasso.it; Piazza Sant'Antonino; incl a cocktail €25; ☻Sorrento Musical 9.30pm summer) The southern-Italian equivalent of a London old-time music hall, Teatro Tasso is home to the *Sorrento Musical,* a sentimental 75-minute revue of Neapolitan classics such as 'O Sole Mio' and 'Trona a Sorrent'.

🛍 Shopping

The pedestrian-only *centro storico* is the place to shop. Look out for inlaid wood, Murano glass jewellery, and embroidery (including smocked children's dresses).

Gargiulo & Jannuzzi   ARTS, CRAFTS
(☑081 878 10 41; www.gargiulo-jannuzzi.it; Viale Enrico Caruso 1; ☻8am-8pm May-Oct, 9am-7pm Nov, Dec & Mar-Apr) Dating from 1863, this old-fashioned warehouse-shop is a classic. Knowledgable assistants guide you through the three floors of locally made goods, ranging from ceramic crockery to *intarsio* wooden pieces, embroidered lace and pottery. The prices are as good as you will get anywhere in town and the choice is certainly superior. Shipping is free for purchases over €220.

La Rapida   SHOES
(☑338 877705; Via Fuoro 67; ☻9am-8pm) There are numerous shops selling leather sandals in the *centro storico,* but head to the far end of Via Fuoro and you'll find this tiny cobbler. An old-fashioned shop, it doesn't have a huge range, but the quality's as good as anywhere else and the prices (from €30) are generally better. It also does repairs.

Stinga   ARTS, CRAFTS
(☑081 878 11 30; www.stingatarsia.com; Via Luigi de Maio 16; ☻9am-8.30pm) Well worth seeking out, this place sells distinctive inlaid-wood items made in Sorrento by the same family of craftsmen (and women) for three generations. The pieces are highly original, especially in their use of colour and design, which is often mosaic or geometric. Fine jewellery, including coral pieces, is also on display, made by family member Amulè.

ℹ Information

Main Tourist Office (☑081 807 40 33; www.sorrentotourism.com; Via Luigi de Maio 35; ☻8.30am-8pm Mon-Sat, 9am-1pm Sun Jul-Sep) In the Circolo dei Forestieri (Foreigners' Club). Ask for the useful publication *Surrentum*.

ℹ Getting There & Away

BOAT

Sorrento is the main jumping-off point for Capri and also has excellent ferry connections to Ischia, Naples and Amalfi coastal resorts during the summer months.

Caremar (☎ 081 807 30 77; www.caremar.it) Runs hydrofoils to Capri (€14.70, 25 minutes, four daily).

Gescab (☎ 081 807 18 12; www.gescab.it) Runs hydrofoils to Naples (€16.80, 20 minutes, 18 daily) and to Capri (€16.80, 20 minutes, 18 daily), Ischia (€19, one hour, two daily), Positano (€14.50, 30 minutes, one daily) and Amalfi (€14.50, 50 minutes, one daily).

BUS

SITA (☎ 199 730749; www.sitabus.it) buses serve Naples, the Amalfi Coast and Sant'Agata, leaving from the bus stop across from the entrance to the Circumvesuviana train station. Buy tickets at the station or from shops bearing the blue SITA sign.

CAR & MOTORCYCLE

Coming from Naples and the north, take the A3 autostrada until Castellammare di Stabia; exit there and follow the SS145 south.

ℹ Getting Around

TO/FROM THE AIRPORT

Naples' Capodichino Airport (p267) is the closest airport to Sorrento and the Amalfi Coast.

Bus

Curreri (p267) runs eight daily services to Sorrento from Naples Capodichino airport. Buses depart from outside the arrivals hall and arrive in Piazza Angelina Lauro. Buy tickets (€10) for the 75-minute journey on the bus.

Taxi

A taxi from the airport to Sorrento costs €85.

CAR & MOTORCYCLE

The big international care-hire operators, as well as some local outfits, are based in Sorrento.

Autoservizi De Martino (☎ 081 878 28 01; www.autoservizidemartino.com; Via Parsano 8) Has cars from €54 a day, €280 per week, plus 50cc scooters from €23 for four hours.

Avis (☎ 081 878 24 59; www.avisautonoleggio.it; Corso Italia 322)

Hertz (☎ 081 807 16 46; www.hertz.it; Via Capo 8)

COASTAL TRAVEL

Consider well-connected Sorrento your base and luxuriate in ferry travel, which connects the major resorts from April to September. Bicycles and scooters can also be useful for exploring inland, as can your own two legs: there are numerous walking trails in the area. The Circumvesuviana train runs from Naples' Piazza Garibaldi to Sorrento, from where there is a regular and efficient bus service to Positano, Amalfi and Salerno.

You can hire a car in Sorrento and drive the umpteen wiggles of the famous Amalfi Coast road, but note that – although distances between the resorts and towns are not great – congestion in the summer months means car travel can be slow and stressful.

Parking

In midsummer, finding a parking spot can be a frustrating business, particularly as much of the parking on the side streets is for residents only and the city centre is closed to traffic for most of the day. There are well-signposted car parks near the ferry terminal, on the corner of Via degli Aranci and Via Renato, and heading west out of town near Via Capo (€2 per hour).

TRAIN

Sorrento is the last stop on the Circumvesuviana (p272) line from Naples. Trains run every half-hour for Naples (70 minutes, €4.50), via Pompeii (30 minutes, €2.80) and Ercolano (50 minutes, €3.40). Invest in a Unico Costiera (p150) card.

WEST OF SORRENTO

If you are here in midsummer, consider escaping the crowds by heading to the green hills around Sorrento. Known as the land of the sirens, in honour of the mythical maiden-monsters who were said to live on Li Galli (a tiny archipelago off the peninsula's southern coast), the area to the west of Massa Lubrense is among the least developed and most beautiful in the country.

Tortuous roads wind their way through hills covered in olive trees and lemon groves, passing through sleepy villages and tiny fishing ports. There are magnificent views at every turn, the best from the high points overlooking Punta Campanella, the westernmost point of the Sorrento Peninsula. Offshore, Capri looks tantalisingly close.

Massa Lubrense

The first town you come to following the coast west from Sorrento is Massa Lubrense. Situated 120m above sea level, it's a disjointed place, comprising a small town centre and 17 *frazioni* (fractions or hamlets) joined by an intricate network of paths and mule tracks. For those without a donkey, there are good road connections and SITA buses regularly run between them.

◎ Sights & Activities

Chiesa di Santa Maria della Grazia CHURCH
(Largo Vescovado; ⊙ 7am-noon & 4.30-8pm) The town's former cathedral, the 16th-century Chiesa di Santa Maria della Grazia, is worth a quick look for its bright majolica-tiled floor, which would look *so* good in your kitchen here. The church stands on the northern flank of the central Largo Vescovado. Don't forget your camera, as there are fabulous views over Capri from here.

Marina della Lobra HARBOUR
From central Largo Vescovado it's a 2km descent to this pretty little marina backed by ramshackle houses and verdant slopes – or, rather, it's a 40-minute downhill walk and a wheezing hour-long ascent. The marina is a good place to rent a boat, the best way of reaching the otherwise difficult-to-get-to bays and inlets along the coast.

Coop Marina della Lobra BOATING
(☑ 081 808 93 80; www.marinalobra.com; Marina della Lobra; per hour from €30) A reliable boat-hire outfit, operating out of a kiosk by the car park. It also runs tours of Capri (€45).

✗ Eating

★ La Torre SEAFOOD €€
(☑ 081 80 89 56; www.latorreonefire.it; Piazzetta Annunziata 7, Annunziata; meals €42; ⊙ 9am-midnight Mon & Wed-Thu, 9am-1am Fri-Sun Apr-Feb)
🥐 This delightful, laid-back Slow Food restaurant on a tranquil square serves mouthwatering traditional cuisine with an emphasis on seafood. The menu changes seasonally, but you can usually depend on classics like *tonani con patate* (tuna with potatoes). Consider the cholesterol-overdose indulgence of a nine-cheese taster (€6), ranging from fresh *caciottina* from Massa Lubrense to *provolone del Monaco* (seasoned semi-hard cheese).

Eat alfresco on the terrace, then stroll down to the belvedere for a rare wide-angle shot of Capri, Ischia, Procida, Naples and Vesuvius.

Funiculi Funiculá SEAFOOD €€
(Via Fontanelle 16, Marina della Lobra; meals €32; ⊙ noon-3pm Tue-Sun, plus 7-11.30pm Sat & Sun Apr-Oct; 🖭) This great bar-restaurant on the seafront at Marina della Lobra has views of Ischia, Capri and Vesuvius. Unsurprisingly, the menu is dominated by seafood, but there are also family-friendly meal-in-one salads and the usual array of grilled-meat dishes. Have a fresh fruit salad for dessert, or pop next door to the cafe for a chocolate-filled crêpe or ice cream.

ℹ Information

Tourist Office (☑ 081 533 90 21; www.massalubrense.it; Viale Filangieri 11; ⊙ 9.30am-1pm daily, plus 4.30-8pm Mon, Tue & Thu-Sat) Can provide bus timetables and maps.

CELEB-STYLE SEAFOOD

The only one of the marina's restaurants directly accessible from the sea, **Lo Scoglio** (☑ 081 808 10 26; www.hotelloscoglio.com; Piazza delle Sirene 15, Massa Lubrense; meals €60; ⊙ 12.30-5pm & 7.30-11pm) attracts a steady ripple of visiting celebs. Johnny Depp, Stephen Spielberg and Sienna Miller are all recent diners, while Elton John, Rod Stewart and Michael Caine have posed for pics (on display) in the past.

The locale is certainly memorable – a glass pavilion on a wooden jetty built around a kitsch fountain spurting into a pond full of fish – and the food is top notch (and priced accordingly). Although you can eat *ravioli alla caprese* and steak here, you'd be sorry to miss the superb seafood. Sample such saltwater specialities as a €30 antipasto of raw seafood on ice, followed by the local classic: *spaghetti al riccio* (spaghetti with sea urchins). Despite the whiff of glamour surrounding the clientele, this is an unpretentious, family-run place, complete with grandma keeping a watchful eye on the till.

ℹ Getting There & Around

BUS

SITA (☑ 199 73 07 49; www.sitabus.it) runs buses (hourly 7am to 9pm) departing from the Circumvesuviana train station in Sorrento.

CAR

Massa Lubrense is an easy 20-minute drive from Sorrento.

Parking

A matter of trawling the streets; there are some meters in the centre (€2 per hour).

Sant'Agata sui due Golfi

Perched high in the hills above Sorrento, Sant'Agata sui due Golfi is the most famous of Massa Lubrense's 17 *frazioni*. Boasting spectacular views of the Bay of Naples on one side and the Gulf of Salerno on the other (hence its name, 'St Agatha on the two Gulfs'), it's a tranquil place that manages to retain its rustic charm despite a fairly heavy hotel presence.

For hikers, this area offers around 22 marked and well-maintained trails, stretching a total length of some 110km (66 miles). The tourist office can provide details. If you fancy a relatively easy stroll that doesn't require a compass or hiking boots, there's a picturesque 3km trail between Sorrento and Sant'Agata. From Piazza Tasso in Sorrento, venture south along Viale Caruso and Via Fuorimura to pick up the Circumpiso footpath, marked in green on the walking maps available from tourist offices. The walk should take approximately one hour.

◉ Sights

Chiesa di Sant'Agata   CHURCH
(Piazza Sant'Agata; ☺ 8am-1pm & 5-7pm) Located in the centre of the village, the cool decorative interior of this 17th-century parish church is famed for its polychrome marble altar, an exquisite work of inlaid marble, mother-of-pearl, lapis lazuli and malachite.

Convento del Deserto   MONASTERY, VIEWPOINT
(☑ 081 878 01 99; Via Deserto; ☺ gardens 8am-7pm, lookout 10am-noon & 5-7pm summer, 10am-noon & 3-5pm winter) This Carmelite convent is located 1.5km uphill from the village centre, so read on carefully before striding out. It was founded in the 17th century and is still home to a closed community of Benedictine nuns. While the convent is of only moderate interest (unless you are one of the nuns), the 360-degree views really make the knee-wearying hike worthwhile.

✕ Eating

For such a small place, Sant'Agata has a surprisingly sophisticated culinary repertoire.

Lo Stuzzichino   NEAPOLITAN €
(☑ 081 533 00 10; www.ristorantelostuzzichino.it; Via Deserto 1a; tasting menu €40, meals €18, pizzas from €5; ☺ Feb-Dec) ✈ This Slow Food Movement–affiliated restaurant has a gregarious host in owner Paolo de Gregorio. Try the specialities: fish rolls stuffed with smoked cheese or seafood stew with seasonal vegetables. The rare *gamberetti di Crapolla* (prawns) taste a whole lot better than they sound.

★ Ristorante Don
Alfonso 1890   MEDITERRANEAN €€€
(☑ 081 533 02 26; www.donalfonso.com; Corso Sant'Agata 11; meals €115-125; ☺ closed Mon & Tue, except Tue night Jun-Sep, closed Jan-early Mar, Nov & Dec; ℗) This two-Michelin-star restaurant is generally regarded as one of Italy's finest. Prepared with produce from the chef's own 6-hectare farm, the seasonally changing menu includes such hallmark dishes as lightly seared tuna in red-pepper sauce and pasta with clams and zucchini. The international wine list is one of the country's most extensive and best. Reservations are essential. The restaurant is part of the hotel of the same name and also organises cooking courses.

ℹ Information

Tourist Office (☑ 081 533 01 35; www.santagatasuiduegolfi.it; Corso Sant'Agata 25; ☺ 9am-1pm & 5.30-9pm) For information on the village and surrounding countryside, stop by this small office on the main square.

ℹ Getting There & Around

BUS

SITA (☑ 199 730749; www.sitabus.it) buses depart hourly from Sorrento's Circumvesuviana train station.

CAR

Follow the SS145 west from Sorrento for about 7km until you see signs off to the right.

Parking

There is generally street parking available, although August can be busy, especially in the evening.

2

JAN JKAB2/GETTY IMAGES ©

3

SLOW IMAGES/GETTY IMAGES ©

1. Sorrento (p141), Amalfi Coast
The vibrant resort town of Sorrento is a good base for exploring the riches of the Amalfi Coast.

2. Villa Rufolo (p171), Ravello
Created in 1853, Villa Rufolo is famed for its beautiful, cascading gardens.

3. Positano (p157), Amalfi Coast
The Amalfi Coast's most picturesque town, Positano is also a popular summer beach destination.

Marina del Cantone

Round the coast from Massa Lubrense, a beautiful hiking trail leads down from **Nerano** to the stunning **Baia de Ieranto** and Marina del Cantone. This unassuming village with its small pebble beach is not only a lovely, tranquil place to stay but also one of the area's prime dining spots: VIPs regularly boat over from Capri to eat here.

🏃 Activities

A popular diving destination, the protected waters here are part of an 11-sq-km reserve called the **Punta Campanella**; it supports a healthy marine ecosystem, with flora and fauna flourishing in underwater grottoes.

Nettuno Diving   DIVING
(☑081 808 10 51; www.sorrentodiving.com; Via Vespucci 39; 🚗) Dive the depths of this marine reserve with a PADI-certified outfit that runs underwater activities for all ages and abilities. These include snorkelling excursions, beginner's courses, cave dives and immersions off Capri and the Li Galli islands. Costs start at €25 (children €15) for a day-long outing to the Baia de Ieranto. It can also organise reasonably priced accommodation.

ℹ Getting There & Away

SITA (☑199 730749; www.sitabus.it) Regular buses between Sorrento and Marina del Cantone from the Circumvesuviana train station in Sorrento.

EAST OF SORRENTO

More developed and less appealing than the coast west of Sorrento, the area to the east of town is not totally without interest. There's the district's longest sandy beach, Spiaggia di Alimuri, at Meta di Sorrento and the Roman villas at Castellammare di Stabia, 12km further on.

Rising above Castellammare and accessible by an eight-minute **cable-car ride** (adult/reduced €7/3.50; ⊙ about 30 daily Apr-Oct) from the town's Circumvesuviana train station is Monte Faito (1131m), one of the highest peaks in the Lattari mountains. Covered in thick beech forests, the summit offers some fine walks with sensational views.

Vico Equense

Known to the Romans as Aequa, Vico Equense (Vico) is a small cliff-top town about 10km east of Sorrento and just five stops away via the Circumvesuviana train. Largely bypassed by international tourists, it's a laid-back, authentic place worth a

---

THE BLUE RIBBON DRIVE

Stretching from Vietri sul Mare to Sant'Agata sui due Golfi, near Sorrento, the **SS163**, nicknamed the Nastro Azzurro (Blue Ribbon), remains one of Italy's most stunning and dramatic roads. Commissioned by Bourbon king Ferdinand II and completed in 1853, it wends its way along the Amalfi Coast's entire length, snaking round impossibly tight curves, over deep ravines and through tunnels gouged out of sheer rock. It's a magnificent feat of civil engineering, although, as John Steinbeck pointed out in his 1953 essay, *My Positano*, the road is also 'carefully designed to be a little narrower than two cars side by side...'.

In short, it is a severe test of driving skill and courage, a white-knuckle 50km ride that will pit you against the extraordinary ability of the local bus drivers. The price for those sublime views is numerous switchbacks and plunging drops to the sea, frequently with only waist-high barriers between you and oblivion.

Originally designed for horse-drawn carriages, the road tends to become even narrower on hairpin bends. To avoid blocking oncoming buses, check the circular mirrors on the roadside and listen for the sound of klaxons – if you hear one, slow right down as it will invariably be followed by a coach. Avoid peak season (July and August) and morning, lunchtime and evening rush hours. The trick to driving the coast is to stay calm, even when your toddler throws up all over the back seat or your partner tells you to look at the view while you're inching around a blind corner.

Never fear: if you're (understandably) not up for getting behind the wheel yourself, you can easily hop on one of the SITA buses that follow this route daily.

HISTORIC HAMLETS

Dotted around Vico's surrounding hills are a number of ancient hamlets, known as *casali*. Untouched by mass tourism, they offer a glimpse into a rural way of life that has changed little over the centuries. You will, however, need wheels to get to them. From Vico, take Via Roma and follow Via Rafaelle Bosco, which passes through the *casali* before circling back to town. Highlights include **Massaquano** and the Capella di Santa Lucia (open on request), famous for its 14th-century frescoes from the school of Giotto di Bondone (recognised as the forerunner of modern Western painting). **Moiano** is also worth checking out; an ancient path from here leads to the summit of Monte Faito. And then there is **Santa Maria del Castello**, with its fabulous views towards the southeast.

Three kilometres to the west of Vico, **Marina di Equa** stands on the site of the Roman settlement of Aequa. Among the bars and restaurants lining the popular pebble beaches are the remains of the 1st-century-AD Villa Pezzolo, as well as a defensive tower, the Torre di Caporivo, and the Gothic ruins of a medieval limestone quarry.

---

quick stopover, if only to sample some of the famous pizza by the metre.

◉ Sights

Chiesa dell'Annunziata   CHURCH
(Via Vescovado; ⊙10am-noon Sun) Vico's clifftop former cathedral is the only Gothic church on the Sorrento Peninsula. Little remains of the original 14th-century structure other than the lateral windows near the main altar and a few arches in the aisles. In fact, most of what you see today, including the chipped pink-and-white facade, is 17th-century baroque.

In the sacristy, check out the portraits of Vico's bishops, all of whom are represented here except for the last one, Michele Natale, who was executed for supporting the ill-fated 1799 Parthenopean Republic. His place is taken by an angel with its finger to its lips, an admonishment to the bishop to keep his liberal thoughts to himself.

✖ Eating

Ristorante & Pizzeria da Gigino   PIZZA
(☑081 879 83 09; www.pizzametro.it; Via Nicotera 15; pizza per metre €12-26; ⊙noon-1am; ☝) Run by the five sons of pizza king Gigino Dell'Amura, who was the very first to introduce pizza by the metre to the world, this barnlike pizzeria produces kilometres of pizza each day in three huge ovens to the right of the entrance. There's a large selection of toppings and the quality is a crust above the norm. Although it seats around 200, you may still have to wait for a table. No reservations are taken.

ⓘ Information

Tourist Office (☑081 801 57 52; www.vicoturismo.it; Piazza Umberto I; ⊙9am-2pm & 3-8pm Mon-Sat, 9.30am-1.30pm Sun) General information on the area's attractions is available from this helpful office on the main square.

AMALFI COAST TOWNS

Positano

POP 3900

Positano is the coast's most picturesque and photogenic town, with vertiginous houses tumbling down to the sea in a cascade of sun-bleached peach, pink and terracotta colours. No less colourful are its steep streets and steps lined with wisteria-draped hotels, smart restaurants and fashionable boutiques.

Look beyond the facades and the fashion, however, and you will find reassuring signs of everyday reality: crumbling stucco, streaked paintwork and even, on occasion, a faint whiff of drains. There's still a southern-Italian holiday feel about the place, with sunbathers eating pizza on the beach, kids pestering parents for gelati and chic women from Milan checking out the boutiques. The fashionista history runs deep. *moda Positano* was born here in the '60s and the town was the first in Italy to import bikinis from France.

John Steinbeck visited in 1953 and wrote in an article for *Harper's Bazaar:* 'Positano bites deep. It is a dream place that isn't quite real when you are there and becomes beckoningly real after you have gone'.

Positano

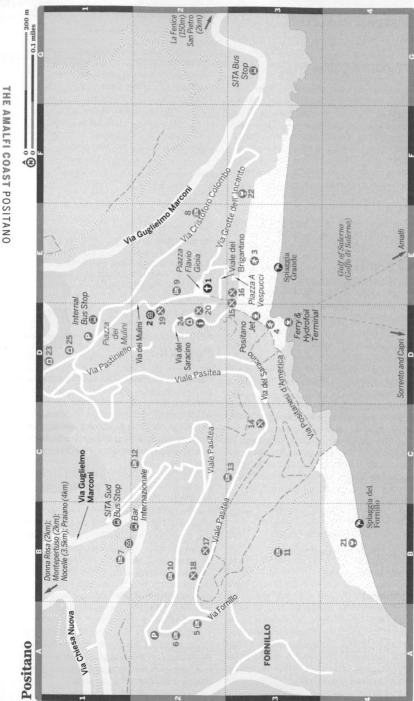

There certainly is something special about the place and this is reflected, predictably, in the prices, which tend to be higher here than elsewhere on the coast.

◉ Sights & Activities

Positano's most memorable sight is its pyramidal townscape, with pastel-coloured houses arranged down the slope to **Spiaggia Grande**, the main beach. Although it isn't anyone's dream beach, with greyish sand covered by legions of bright umbrellas, the water's clean and the setting is memorable. Hiring a chair and umbrella on the fenced-off areas costs around €18 per person per day, but the crowded public areas are free.

Getting around town is largely a matter of walking. If your knees can take the slopes, there are dozens of narrow alleys and stairways that make walking relatively easy and joyously traffic free. The easy option is to take the local bus to the top of the town for the best views, and wind your way down on foot, via steps and slopes, enjoying the memorable vistas en route.

Chiesa di Santa Maria Assunta   CHURCH
(Piazza Flavio Gioia; ☺8am-noon & 4-9pm) This church, with its colourful majolica-tiled dome, is the most famous and – let's face it – pretty much the only sight in Positano. If you are visiting at a weekend you will probably have the added perk of seeing a wedding; it's one of the most popular churches in the area for exchanging vows.

Step inside to see a delightful classical interior, with pillars topped with gilded Ionic

---

DON'T MISS

A WALK TO FORNILLO

This gentle walk, with (hooray!) an acceptable number of steps, leads from Positano's main Spiaggia Grande to Spiaggia di Fornillo. Toss off the stilettos and don the trainers: Fornillo is more laid-back than its swanky *spiaggia* (beach) neighbour and is also home to a handful of summer beach bars, which can get quite spirited after sunset.

To reach here, head for the western end of Spiaggia Grande, by the ferry harbour, and climb the steps. Walk past the Torre Trasita, one of the coast's many medieval watchtowers built to warn inhabitants of pirate raids and now a private residence. Continue on as the path passes dramatic rock formations, tiny inlets of turquoise water and bobbing boats until you reach the appealing Fornillo beach in time to enjoy a long, cold drink or multiscoop ice cream.

---

capitals and winged cherubs pecking from above every arch. Above the main altar is a 13th-century Byzantine Black Madonna and Child. During restoration works of the square and the crypt, a Roman villa was discovered; still under excavation, it is closed to the public.

Franco Senesi   GALLERY
(☎089 87 52 57; www.francosenesifineart.com; Via dei Mulini 16; ☺10am-midnight Apr-Nov) Nestled between the colourful boutiques and

---

Positano

LOCAL KNOWLEDGE

ZIA LUCY, HIKING GUIDE

Zia Lucy (www.zialucy.it) was born and raised in Positano and organises hikes throughout the region. She is an expert on the local history, flora and wildlife.

Which is your favourite hike on the Amalfi Coast? There are so many wonderful hikes around here, but I have to say that the Walk of the Gods is still the one I love the most. It has everything: fabulous scenery, beautiful flowers like wild orchids, and is accessible to many, as it is not a tough walk.

What about routes for people who want to get off the beaten track? I really enjoy going to Le Ferriere, above Amalfi. It's a place full of history and nature and you can walk from the village of Pontone to Pogerola, or to Amalfi. Here you'll see the ruins of ancient paper mills that once produced luxury paper made with cotton. Another favourite hike is from Ravello to Minori, though the hamlet of Sanbuco.

What is your favourite time of year for a hike? I love hiking during spring, when lots of beautiful flowers are blooming: my favourite are the *Orchis italica* and the rock roses.

Any advice for hikers? It sounds obvious, but many people still wear open sandals when they're hiking, which is unsafe not just because they can slip but also because there are occasionally snakes.

Favourite local restaurant? I really like eating at the Wine Dark House on the beach in Positano; my favourite dish is pasta with meat cooked in red wine. Another restaurant is Donna Rosa in Montepertuso. I go there for special occasions.

lemon-themed ceramics shops, Franco Senesi is a light and airy exhibition space with several rooms showcasing over 20 Italian modern artists and sculptors. You can walk around here without being hassled, admiring (and buying?) artworks that are sufficiently varied to suit most tastes, spanning exquisite life drawings, colourful surrealistic landscapes and edgy abstract sculptures. Shipping can be arranged.

Palazzo Murat   PALACE
(☑089 875 51 77; www.palazzomurat.it; Via dei Mulini 23) Just west of the Chiesa di Santa Maria Assunta church, this *palazzo* is now a luxury hotel. It may be beyond your budget to stay, but you can still visit the stunning flower-filled courtyard, have a drink in the vine-draped patio and contemplate the short, tragic life of flamboyant Joachim Murat, the 18th-century French king of Naples who had the palace built as a summer residence for himself and his wife, Caroline Bonaparte.

★**Blue Star**   BOATING
(☑089 81 18 88; www.bluestarpositano.it; Spiaggia Grande; ☺8.30am-9pm) Operating out of a kiosk on Spiaggia Grande, Blue Star hires out small motor boats for €60 per hour (€200 for four hours). Consider heading for the archipelago of Li Galli, the four small islands where, according to Homer, the sirens lived. The company also organises popular

and fun yacht excursions to Capri and the Grotta dello Smeraldo (€60).

At Gullo Lungo you will spy a magnificent villa; the former home of Rudolf Nureyev, it's still privately owned.

L'Uomo e il Mare   BOATING
(☑089 81 16 13; www.gennaroesalvatore.it; ☺9am-8pm) An Italian-English couple offers a range of tours, including Capri and Amalfi day trips (from €55), out of a kiosk near the ferry terminal. They also run a romantic sunset cruise to Li Galli, complete with champagne (€30).

✗ Eating

Take note that, overall, the nearer you get to the seafront, the more expensive everything becomes. Many places close over winter, making a brief reappearance for Christmas and New Year.

La Brezza   CAFE €
(☑089 87 58 11; www.labrezzapositano.it; Via Regina Giovanna 2; snacks around €6; ☺9am-1am; 🛜) With a steely grey-and-white interior, free internet and wi-fi, and a terrace with views over the sea and quay, this is the best beachfront place for *panini* or snacks. There are regular art exhibitions and a daily 'happy hour' (6pm to 8pm), with drinks accompanied by complimentary light eats.

★**Donna Rosa**   ITALIAN €€

(☑089 81 18 06; www.drpositano.com; Via Montepertuso 97-99, Montepertuso; meals from €40; ⊗noon-2.30pm & 7-11.30pm Mon, Tue & Thu-Sun Apr-Dec, closed lunch Aug) This is one of the Amalfi Coast's most reputable restaurants, located in mountainside Montepertuso, above Positano. Once a humble trattoria and now run by Rosa's daughter Raffaella, the lineage is set to continue with Raffaella's daughter Erika, who studied with Jamie Oliver in London. The celebrity chef dined here on his honeymoon and declared it one of his favourite restaurants.

The menu changes frequently, but you can be guaranteed some of the best food – and views – on the coast. Don't miss the hot chocolate soufflé and be sure to book ahead. It also runs excellent cooking courses.

★**Next2**   RISTORANTE €€

(☑089 812 35 16; www.next2.it; Viale Pasitea 242; meals €45; ⊗6.30-11.30pm) Understated elegance meets creative cuisine at this contemporary set-up. Local and organic ingredients are put to impressive use in beautifully presented dishes such as ravioli stuffed with aubergine and prawns or sea bass with tomatoes and lemon-scented peas. Desserts are wickedly delicious, and the alfresco sea-facing terrace is summer perfection.

La Cambusa   SEAFOOD €€

(☑089 81 20 51; www.lacambusapositano.com; Piazza A Vespucci 4; meals €40; ⊗noon-midnight Mar-Nov) This restaurant, run by amiable Luigi, is on the front line, which, given the number of cash-rich tourists in these parts, could equal high prices for less-than-average food. Happily, that is not the case here. The locals still rate La Cambusa as a top place for seafood.

Go for simple spaghetti with clams, oven-baked sea bass or splash out with the Mediterranean lobster. There is a good selection of side dishes, like roasted artichokes, and the position is Positano at its best.

Da Vincenzo   ITALIAN €€

(☑089 87 51 28; www.davincenzo.it; Viale Pasitea 172-178; meals €40; ⊗noon-2.30pm & 6-11pm Wed-Mon, 6.30-11pm Tue) Superbly prepared dishes are served here by the third generation of restaurateurs. The emphasis is on fish dishes, which range from the adventurous, like grilled octopus tentacles skewered with deep-fried artichokes, to seasonal pasta dishes such as spaghetti with broad beans and fresh ricotta. Be sure to try co-owner Marcella's legendary desserts, considered the best in town. Reservations recommended.

You can also enjoy twanging Neapolitan guitarists during the summer months.

Wine Dark House   ITALIAN €€

(☑089 81 19 25; Via del Saracino 6/8; meals €28; ⊗noon-3pm & 7pm-midnight) This terracotta-coloured restaurant features a lovely enclosed terrace: it's a small, low-key spot where the emphasis is on tasty standards and charming service.

Ristorante il Saraceno d'Oro   ITALIAN €€

(☑089 81 20 50; www.saracenodoro.it; Viale Pasitea 254; pizzas from €5, meals €28; ⊗12.30-3pm & 6.30-11pm Mar-Oct) There is something so typically Italian about the set-up of this restaurant, where waiters have to dash to and fro across the road with their dishes. But in the evening the traffic is light and the wacky layout will only add to the delight of eating here. The pizza and pasta choices are good; the *contorni* (vegetables) excellent.

Splurge on the legendary profiteroles in chocolate sauce for dessert.

Ristorante Max   ITALIAN €€

(☑089 87 50 56; www.ristorantemax.it; Via dei Mulini 22; meals €40; ⊗9am-11pm Mar-Nov) Here you can peruse the gorgeously cluttered artwork (in lieu of a sea view) while choosing your dish. This upmarket restaurant and wine bar serves such dishes as sautéed clams and mussels, and zucchini flowers stuffed with ricotta and salmon. Cooking courses are available in summer.

🍷 Drinking & Nightlife

Unless the idea of parading up and down town with a cashmere sweater draped over your shoulders turns you on, Positano's nightlife, overall, is not going to do much for you. More piano bar than warehouse, with a handful of exceptions, it's genteel, sophisticated and safe.

La Zagara   CAFE

(☑089 812 28 92; www.lazagara.com; Via dei Mulini 8; cakes €3, panini €5; ⊗8am-midnight) Dating back to 1950, this is the quintessential Italian terrace, draped with foliage and flowers, with an offshoot bar and superb *pasticceria* (pastry shop), elderly red-vested waiters, Neapolitan background music and some great Positano poseur-watching potential. Enjoy sumptuous creamy cakes as well as savoury snacks. There's live music in summer.

Music on the Rocks   CLUB
(☎089 87 58 74; www.musicontherocks.it; Via Grotte dell'Incanto 51; cover €10-30; ☺10pm-late) This is one of the town's few genuine nightspots and one of the best clubs on the coast. Music on the Rocks is dramatically carved into the tower at the eastern end of Spiaggia Grande. Join the flirty, good-looking crowd and some of the region's top DJs spinning mainstream house and reliable disco.

Da Ferdinando   BAR
(☎089 87 53 65; Spiaggia dei Fornillo; ☺10am-3am May-Oct) This summer-only beach bar rents out sun loungers and serves drinks and light snacks. The music is designed to make sure you shift into suitable party mood after sunset.

🛍 Shopping

You can't miss Positano's colourful boutiques – everywhere you look, shop displays scream out at you in a riot of exuberant colour. The humble lemon also enjoys star status; it's not just in *limoncello* and lemon-infused candles but emblazoned on tea towels, aprons and pottery.

La Bottego di Brunella   FASHION
(☎089 87 52 28; www.brunella.it; Viale Pasitea 72; ☺9am-9pm) This shop is one of the reasons local women always look so effortlessly chic. It is one of just a handful of boutiques where the clothes are designed and made in Positano (most boutiques import despite the sometimes-deceptive labelling). The gar-

ments here are made from pure linen and silks, the colours earthy shades of cream, ochre, brown and yellow.

There are two other branches in town, including a smaller boutique opposite Palazzo Murat.

La Botteguccia de Giovanni   SHOES
(☎089 81 18 24; www.labottegucciapositano.it; Via Regina Giovanni 19; ☺9.30am-9pm May-Oct) Come here for handmade leather sandals by craftsman Giovanni in his small workroom at the back of the shop. Choose the colour and any decorative bits and pieces you want (shells are particularly well suited to Positano somehow...), tell him your size and then nip round the corner for a cappuccino while he makes the shoes. Prices start at around €50.

Umberto Carro   CERAMICS
(☎089 87 53 52; Viale Pasitea 30; ☺9.30am-8.30pm May-Oct) On offer here is a sumptuous display of locally produced ceramics to stress you – and your hand luggage – at check-in time; a better bet is to go for the shipping option. The colours and designs are subtle and classy, and there's a wide range of pieces, from magnificent urns to minute eggcups and quirky, brightly coloured animals and ornaments.

ℹ Information

Tourist Office (☎089 87 50 67; Via del Saracino 4; ☺9am-7pm Mon-Sat, to 2pm Sun summer, 9am-4pm Mon-Sat winter) Can provide lots of information; expect to pay for walking maps and similar.

ℹ Getting There & Away

BOAT
Positano has excellent ferry connections to the coastal towns and islands from April to October.
Positano Jet (☎089 87 50 32) Operates hydrofoils to Capri (€17, 45 minutes, three daily).

BUS
About 16km west of Amalfi and 18km from Sorrento, Positano is on the main SS163 coastal road. There are two main bus stops: coming from Sorrento and the west, the first stop you come to is SITA Sud, opposite Bar Internazionale; arriving from Amalfi and the east, the first stop is the SITA stop at the top of Via Cristoforo Colombo. To get into town from the former, follow Viale Pasitea; from the latter (a far shorter route), take Via Cristoforo Colombo. When de-

---

AT A SNAIL'S PACE

Positano is one of around 55 towns in Italy to have gained Slow City status (an extension of the Slow Food movement, established in northern Italy in 1986). In order to be considered, certain criteria must be met: towns need to have fewer than 55,000 inhabitants, no fast-food outlets or neon-lit hoardings, plenty of cycling and walking paths, and neighbourhood restaurants serving traditional cuisine with locally sourced ingredients. For more information, check www.cittaslow.org.

parting, buy bus tickets at Bar Internazionale or, if headed east, from the *tabaccheria* (tobacconist) at the bottom of Via Cristoforo Colombo.

SITA (☑ 199 73 07 49; www.sitabus.it) Runs frequent buses to/from Amalfi and Sorrento.

Flavia Gioia (☑ 089 81 18 95; www.flaviogioia. com; Via Cristoforo Colombo 49) These local buses follow the lower ring road every half-hour. Stops are clearly marked and you can buy your ticket (€1.20) on board. The Flavia Gioia buses pass by both SITA bus stops. There are also 17 daily buses up to Montepertuso and Nocelle.

CAR & MOTORCYCLE

Take the A3 autostrada to Vietri sul Mare and then follow the SS163 coastal road. To hire a scooter, try **Positano Rent a Scooter** (☑ 089 812 20 77; www.positanorentascooter.it; Viale Pasitea 99; per day from €60). Don't forget that you will need to produce a driving licence and passport.

Parking

Parking here is no fun in summer. There are some blue-zone parking areas (€3 per hour) and a handful of expensive private car parks. **Parcheggio da Anna** (Viale Pasitea 173; per day €18) is located just before the Pensione Maria Luisa, at the top of town. Nearer the beach and town centre, **Di Gennaro** (Via Pasitea 1; per day €23) is near the bottom of Via Cristoforo Colombo.

Praiano

POP 1900

An ancient fishing village, a low-key summer resort and, increasingly, a popular centre for the arts, Praiano is a delight. With no centre as such, its whitewashed houses pepper the verdant ridge of Monte Sant'Angelo as it slopes towards Capo Sottile. Formerly an important silk-production centre, it was a favourite of the Amalfi doges (dukes), who made it their summer residence.

◉ Sights & Activities

Praiano is 120m above sea level, and exploring involves lots of steps. There are also several trails that start from town, including a scenic walk – particularly stunning at sunset – that leaves from beside the San Gennaro church, descending due west to the **Spiaggia della Gavitelli** beach (via 300 steps), and carrying on to the medieval defensive Torre di Grado. The town is also a starting point for the Sentiero degli Dei.

WORTH A TRIP

NOCELLE

A tiny, still relatively isolated mountain village, located beyond Montepertuso, Nocelle (450m) commands some of the most spectacular views on the entire coast. A world apart from touristy Positano, it's a sleepy, silent place where not much ever happens and where the few residents are happy to keep it that way.

If you want to stay, consider delightful **Villa della Quercia** (☑ 089 812 34 97; www.villadellaquercia.com; Via Nocelle 5; r €70-80; ☉ Apr-Oct; ☎), a former monastery with spectacular views. For food, **Trattoria Santa Croce** (www.ristorantesantacrocepositano.com; Via Nocelle 19; ☉ noon-2.30pm & 7-11pm Apr-Oct) is a reliable low-key restaurant in the main part of the village.

The easiest way to get to Nocelle is by local bus from Positano (€1.20, 30 minutes, 17 daily). If you're driving, follow the signs from Positano. Hikers tackling the Sentiero degli Dei might want to stop off as they pass through.

Marina di Praia HARBOUR

Located a couple of kilometres east of the centre, this charming small beach and harbour are why most people stop off here. From the SS163 (next to the Hotel Onda Verde), a steep path leads down the cliffs to a tiny inlet with a small stretch of coarse sand and very tempting water; the best water is actually off the rocks, just before you get to the bottom. You can also rent boats here. In what were once fishermen's houses, there are now four restaurants, including an excellent place for seafood.

Chiesa di San Luca CHURCH

(Via Oratorio 1) In the upper village, the 16th-century Chiesa di San Luca features a richly colourful majolica floor, paintings by the 16th-century artist Giovanni Bernardo Lama and a late-17th-century bust of St Luke the Evangelist.

Centro Sub Costiera Amalfitana DIVING

(☑ 089 81 21 48; www.centrosub.it; Via Marina di Praia; dives from €80; ☎) This well-respected local dive outfit offers lessons for adults and children over eight years, as well as night dives and full diving days with snacks on board.

DON'T MISS

ART IN A TOWER

Torre a Mare (🖉 339 4401008; www.paolosandulli.com; Torre a Mare; ☺ 9am-1pm & 3.30-7pm) Defensive towers sit all along the Amalfi Coast; ironically, they are generally known as Saracen towers, named after the very invaders they were erected to thwart. Although most lie empty, some are privately owned. At Marina di Praia you can combine a visit to one such tower, all while enjoying the original sculptures and artwork of Paolo Sandulli. Most distinctive are his 'heads' with the colourful sea-sponge hairdos. A spiral staircase leads to more works upstairs, including paintings.

Paolo's work is on display throughout the Amalfi Coast, including at Positano's prestigious Palazzo Murat.

✕ Eating

Da Armandino   SEAFOOD €€
(🖉 089 87 40 87; www.trattoriadaarmandino.it; Via Praia 1, Marina di Praia; meals €35; ☺ 1-4pm & 7pm-midnight Apr-Nov; 🖷) Seafood lovers should head for this widely acclaimed, no-frills restaurant located in a former boatyard on the beach at Marina di Praia. Da Armandino is great for fish fresh off the boat. There's no menu; just opt for the dish of the day – it's all excellent.

The holiday atmosphere and appealing setting – at the foot of sheer cliffs towering up to the main road – round things off nicely.

Onda Verde   ITALIAN €€
(🖉 089 87 41 43; www.hotelondaverde.it; Via Terramare 3; meals €38; ☺ 1-2.30pm & 7.30-9.30pm Apr-Nov) Part of a hotel of the same name, this restaurant is located halfway down the steep steps leading to the marina (just beyond the defensive tower). Sit outside for the best views of the bay. The food here reflects an innovative take on traditional cuisine and includes a plentiful salad choice – just the thing on a sizzling summer's day.

La Brace   ITALIAN €€
(🖉 089 87 42 26; www.labracepraiano.com; Via G Capriglione; pizzas from €5, meals €25; ☺ 12.30-3pm & 6.30-10.30pm Mon, Tue & Thu-Sun) Located on the main street in town, this long-established restaurant has a decent reputation for seafood and pizzas. The dining room has sweeping views over the rooftops to the sea, and owner Gianni greets everyone like an old friend – in Italian, naturally; it's a favourite haunt of locals.

🍷 Drinking & Nightlife

★ **Africana**   CLUB
(🖉 089 81 11 71; www.africanafamousclub.com; ☺ 7.30pm-3am May-Sep) This club near Marina di Praia makes for a memorable boogie – though beware the pricey drinks. Africana has been going since the '50s, when Jackie Kennedy was just one of the famous VIP guests. It has an extraordinary cave setting, complete with natural blowholes and a glass dance floor so you can see fish swimming under your feet.

Shuttle buses run regularly from Positano, Amalfi and Maiori during summer. You can also catch a water taxi (€10) with **Positano Boats** (🖉 339 2539207; www.positanoboats.info).

Furore

Marina di Furore, a tiny fishing village, was once a busy little commercial centre, although it's difficult to believe that today. In medieval times its unique natural position freed it from the threat of foreign raids and provided a ready source of water for its flour and paper mills.

Originally founded by Romans fleeing barbarian incursions, it sits at the bottom of what's known as the fjord of Furore, a giant cleft that cuts through the Lattari mountains. The main village, however, stands 300m above, in the upper Vallone del Furore. A one-horse place that sees few tourists at any time of the year, it exudes a distinctly rural air despite the colourful murals and unlikely modern sculpture.

To get to upper Furore by car, follow the SS163 and then the SS366 signposts to Agerola. Otherwise, regular SITA buses depart from the bus terminus in Amalfi (€1.60, 30 minutes, 17 daily).

Amalfi

POP 5428

It is hard to grasp that pretty little Amalfi, with its sun-filled piazzas and small beach, was once a maritime superpower with a population of more than 70,000. For one thing, it's not a big place – you can easily walk from one end to the other in about

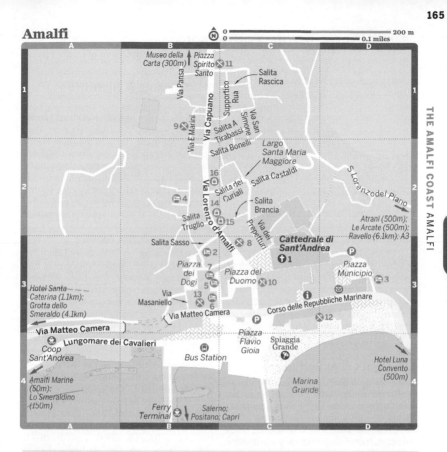

Amalfi

◎ Top Sights
1 Cattedrale di Sant'Andrea C3

◎ Sights
Chiostro del Paradiso .... (see 1)

◎ Sleeping
2 Albergo Sant'Andrea B3
3 DieciSedici D3
4 Hotel Amalfi B2
5 Hotel Centrale B3
6 Hotel Lidomare B3
7 Residenza del Duca B3

◎ Eating
8 Da Maria C3
9 Il Teatro B1
10 La Pansa C3
11 La Taverna del Duca D1
12 Marina Grande D3
13 Ristorante La Caravella B3

◎ Shopping
14 Anastasio Nicola Sas B2
15 Il Ninfeo C2
16 L'Arco Antico B2

20 minutes. For another, there are very few historical buildings of note. The explanation is chilling: most of the old city, and its populace, simply slid into the sea during an earthquake in 1343.

Today, although the permanent population is a fairly modest 5000 or so, the numbers swell significantly during summer, when day trippers pour in by the coachload.

Just around the headland, neighbouring **Atrani** is a picturesque tangle of whitewashed alleys and arches centred on a lively, lived-in piazza and popular beach; don't miss it.

SENTIERO DEGLI DEI (WALK OF THE GODS)

By far the best-known walk on the Amalfi Coast is the three-hour, 12km Sentiero degli Dei, which follows the high ridge linking Praiano to Positano. The walk commences in the heart of **Praiano**, where a thigh-challenging 1000-step start takes you up to the path itself. An easier alternative is to opt for the bus to **Bomerano**, near Agerola in the mountains between Sorrento and Amalfi: take the SITA bus to the Agerola turn-off, then another bus to Agerola. Bomerano is located immediately south of Agerola. Do consider the stepped route, though, which winds through well-tended gardens and makes for a charming start.

The route proper is not advised for vertigo sufferers: it's a spectacular, meandering trail along the top of the mountains, with caves and terraces set dramatically in the cliffs and deep valleys framed by the brilliant blue of the sea. It can sometimes be cloudy in the dizzy heights, but that somehow adds to the drama, with the cypresses rising through the mist like dark, shimmering sword blades and shepherds herding their goats through fog-wreathed foliage. Buy a picnic at the deli in Praiano to eat at the top (take a penknife for cheese and so on, as they don't make up rolls). Bring a rucksack and plenty of water and wear proper walking shoes, as the going is rough and the descents are steep. You may want to pack swimming gear too, and end the walk with a refreshing plunge into the sea.

The **Praiano tourist office** (☑ 089 87 45 57; www.praiano.org; Via G Capriglione 116b; ⊙ 9am-1pm & 4-8pm) can provide maps and guidance. Just downhill and on the same side is **Alimentari Rispoli** (☑ 089 87 40 18; 82 Via Nazionale), where you can buy *panini*, cheeses, meat, drinks and fruit for the hike. The steps out of town begin at Via Degli Ulivi, which leads off the main road almost opposite Hotel Smereldo. Brace yourself for the long climb to come, and be sure to follow the brown arrows placed at regular intervals along the flower-edged paths. After around 45 minutes you'll emerge at **Fontanella**, at Chiesa

◉ Sights & Activities

First stop is Piazza del Duomo, the town's focal-point square, with its majestic cathedral. To glean a sense of the town's medieval history, be sure to explore the narrow alleys parallel to the main street, with their steep stairways, covered porticoes and historic shrine niches.

Amalfi also has a beautiful seaside setting; it's the perfect spot for long, lingering lunches. If you're intent on going for a swim, you're better off hiring a boat and heading out to sea. You'll find a number of operators along Lungomare dei Cavalieri.

★ **Cattedrale di Sant'Andrea**   CATHEDRAL
(☑ 089 87 10 59; Piazza del Duomo; ⊙ 7.30am-7.45pm) A melange of architectural styles, Amalfi's cathedral, one of the few relics of the town's past as an 11th-century maritime superpower, makes a striking impression at the top of its sweeping flight of stairs. Between 10am and 5pm entrance is through the adjacent Chiostro del Paradiso, a 13th-century cloister.

The cathedral dates in part from the early 10th century and its stripy facade has been rebuilt twice, most recently at the end of the 19th century. Although the building is a hybrid, the Sicilian Arabic-Norman style predominates, particularly in the two-tone masonry and the 13th-century bell tower. The huge bronze doors also merit a look – the first of their type in Italy, they were commissioned by a local noble and made in Syria before being shipped to Amalfi. Less impressive is the baroque interior, although the altar features some fine statues and there are some interesting 12th- and 13th-century mosaics.

Chiostro del Paradiso   CHURCH
(☑ 089 87 13 24; Piazza del Duomo; adult/reduced €3/1; ⊙ 9am-7pm) To the left of Amalfi's cathedral porch, these magnificent Moorish-style cloisters were built in 1266 to house the tombs of Amalfi's prominent citizens; 120 marble columns support a series of tall, slender Arabic arches around a central garden. From the cloisters, go through to the **Basilica del Crocefisso**, where you'll find various religious artefacts displayed in glass cabinets and some fading 14th-century frescoes. Beneath lies the 1206 crypt containing the remains of Sant'Andrea.

Grotta dello Smeraldo   CAVE
(admission €5; ⊙ 9.30am-4pm) Four kilometres west of Amalfi, this grotto is named after the eerie emerald colour that emanates from

di Santa Maria a Castro, a lovely whitewashed chapel with a 15th-century fresco of the Madonna. You can also explore the spare chambers of the Convento San Domenico.

Just beyond you'll see a natural rock arch over the path to the right; don't go through it but continue uphill, where after around 20 minutes of steep terrain and craggy rock steps you'll come to the path proper, where you should take the turning to the left signed 'Positano Nocelle'. It's a long, delightful, gentle descent from here to Nocelle: if there's cloud cover the combination of this and the glimpses of dizzying views is unforgettable. The route is marked by red and white stripes daubed on rocks and trees and is easy to follow.

You eventually emerge at tiny **Nocelle**, where cold drinks and coffee are served at a charming terraced kiosk with fresh flowers on the tables. Or head a little further through the village to Piazza Santa Croce, where a stall dispenses fantastic freshly squeezed orange and lemon juice.

Continue down through the village and a series of steps will take you through the olive groves and deposit you on the road just east of Positano. A nicer though longer option – especially if you're weary of steps at this point – is to continue on the path that leads west out of Nocelle towards **Montepertuso**. Don't miss the huge hole in the centre of the cliff at Montepertuso, where it looks as though some irate giant has punched through the slab of limestone. From here the route winds its way to the northern fringes of **Positano**. From here you can dip down through town to the beachfront bars and balmy sea.

Hiking maps can be downloaded at www.amalficoastweb.com. Another reliable regional hiking map is the Club Alpino Italiano (CAI; Italian Alpine Club) *Monti Lattari, Peninsola Sorrentina, Costiera Amalfitana: Carta dei Sentieri* (€9) at 1:30,000. If you prefer a guided hike, there are a number of reliable local guides, including American Frank Carpegna (www.positanofrankcarpegna.com), a longtime resident here, and Zia Lucy (www.zialucy.it).

the water. Stalactites hang down from the 24m-high ceiling, while stalagmites grow up to 10m tall. Buses regularly pass the car park above the cave entrance (from where you take a lift or stairs down to the rowing boats). Alternatively, **Coop Sant'Andrea** (☑ 089 87 29 50; www.coopsantandrea.com; Lungomare dei Cavalieri 1) runs boats from Amalfi (€10 return, plus cave admission. Allow 1½ hours for the return trip.

Each year, on 24 December and 6 January, skin divers from all over Italy make their traditional pilgrimage to the ceramic *presepe* (nativity scene) submerged beneath the water.

★ **Museo della Carta**   MUSEUM
(☑ 089 830 45 61; www.museodellacarta.it; Via delle Cartiere 23; admission €4; ☺ 10am-6.30pm daily Mar-Oct, 10am-3.30pm Tue, Wed & Fri-Sun Nov-Feb) Amalfi's paper museum is housed in a rugged, cavelike 13th-century paper mill (the oldest in Europe). It lovingly preserves the original paper presses, which are still in full working order, as you'll see during the 15-minute guided tour (in English), which explains the original cotton-based paper production and the later wood-pulp manufacturing. Afterwards you may well be inspired to pick up some of the stationery sold

in the gift shop, alongside calligraphy sets and paper pressed with flowers.

Amalfi Marine   BOATING
(☑ 329 2149811; www.amalfiboats.it; Spiaggia del Porto, Lungomare dei Cavalieri) Run by American local resident Rebecca Brooks, Amalfi Marine hires out boats (without a skipper from €250 per day, per boat; maximum six passengers). It also organises day-long excursions along the coast and to the islands (from €45 per person).

🍴 Eating & Drinking

Inevitably, most of the restaurants in and around Amalfi's centre cater to the tourist trade. Standards are generally high, however, and it's rare to eat badly. Most places serve pizza and a range of pasta, grilled meat and seafood. The Amalfi drinking scene is fairly subdued, revolving around streetside cafes and bars. It gets a tad more boisterous in Atrani but is hardly hard-core.

La Pansa   CAFE €
(☑ 089 87 10 65; www.pasticceriapansa.it; Piazza del Duomo 40; cornetti & pastries from €1.50; ☺ 8am-10pm Wed-Mon) A marbled and mirrored 1830 cafe on Piazza del Duomo where

black-bow-tied waiters serve a great Italian breakfast: freshly made *cornetti* (croissants) and deliciously frothy cappuccino.

Il Teatro
TRATTORIA €€

(☑089 87 24 73; Via E Marini 19; meals €25; ⊙11.30am-3pm & 6.30-11pm, closed Wed; ☂) Superb no-fuss trattoria tucked away in the atmospheric backstreets of the *centro storico* (Via E Marini is reached via Salita delgi Orafi). Seafood specialities include *pesce spada il teatro* (swordfish in a tomato, caper and olive-oil sauce), plus there are good vegetarian options, including *scialatielli al teatro* (pasta with tomatoes and aubergines).

The old-fashioned interior has a series of arches and walls decorated with black-and-white photos and assorted bric-a-brac.

La Taverna del Duca
SEAFOOD €€

(☑089 87 27 55; www.amalfilatavernadelduca. it; Piazza Spirito Santo 26; pizzas from €7, meals €35; ⊙noon-3pm & 7-11.30pm Fri-Wed) Grab a chair on the square at this popular restaurant with its fishy reputation. Specials vary according to the catch of the day but might include *carpaccio di baccalà* (thin strips of raw salted cod) or linguine with scampi. Or go for a pasta dish like *pasta fagioli e cozze* (with mussels and beans).

There's an excellent and generous antipasti spread and the interior is elegant, with candles on the tables and tasteful oil paintings on the walls.

Da Maria
ITALIAN €€

(☑089 87 18 80; www.amalfitrattoriadamaria. com; Via Lorenzo d'Amalfi 16; pizzas around €6, meals €25; ⊙noon-3pm & 7-11pm Dec-Oct; ☂) Just off Piazza del Duomo, at the beginning of the main pedestrian thoroughfare, this cavernous place attracts a dedicated crowd ranging from off-the-yacht Neapolitans to coachloads of tourists. But don't be put off, as the wood-fired pizzas are excellent, the atmosphere is jolly, and the pastas and main courses are solidly reliable, if a tad overpriced.

Lo Smeraldino
SEAFOOD €€

(☑089 87 10 70; www.ristorantelosmeraldino.it; Piazzale dei Protontini 1, Lungomare dei Cavalieri; pizzas around €9, meals €30; ⊙11.45am-3pm & 6.45-11.15pm daily Jul & Aug, closed Tue Sep-Jun) Situated west of the centre, on the waterfront overlooking the fishing boats, this inviting blue-and-white beachside restaurant was founded in 1949. As well as crisp-based pizzas, this is a good place for fancy risottos, like smoked salmon and caviar, or simple classics like grilled or poached local fish.

Despite the location, this is not a place where you come wrapped in a sarong and wearing flip-flops; the atmosphere is one of understated elegance. Book ahead.

Le Arcate
ITALIAN €€

(☑089 87 13 67; www.learcate.net; Largo Orlando Buonocore, Atrani; pizzas from €6, meals €25; ⊙12.30-3pm & 7.30-11.30pm Tue-Sun Sep-Jun, daily Jul & Aug; ☀) On a sunny day, it's hard to beat the dreamy location: at the far eastern point of the harbour overlooking the beach, with Atrani's ancient rooftops and church tower behind you. Huge white parasols shade the sprawl of tables, while the dining room is a stone-walled natural cave. Pizzas are served at night; daytime fare includes risotto with seafood and grilled swordfish.

The food is good, but it's a step down from the setting.

★ Marina Grande
SEAFOOD €€€

(☑089 87 11 29; www.ristorantemarinagrande. com; Viale Delle Regioni 4; tasting menu lunch/ dinner €25/60, meals €45; ⊙noon-3pm & 6.30-11pm Tue-Sun Mar-Oct) ☘ Run by the third generation of the same family, this beachfront restaurant serves fish so fresh it's almost flapping. It prides itself on its use of locally sourced organic produce, which, in Amalfi, means high-quality seafood.

Ristorante La Caravella
ITALIAN €€€

(☑089 87 10 29; www.ristorantelacaravella.it; Via Matteo Camera 12; tasting menus €50-120; ⊙noon-2.30pm & 7.30-11pm Wed-Mon; ☀) The regional food here recently earned the restaurant a Michelin star, with dishes that

---

HIGH-DIVING CHAMPIONSHIP

Every July Furore hosts a high-diving competition: the **Mediterranean Cup** (www.comunefurore.it), when fearless – or foolhardy – high divers arrive from all over the world to swan dive off the famous bridge traversing the Furore fjord. The plummeting distance is some 28m and the typical speed around 100km/h. Generally held on a Sunday towards the beginning of the month, it's a highlight not to be missed. It's especially spectacular viewed from a boat.

offer *nouvelle* zap, like black ravioli with cuttlefish ink, scampi and ricotta, or that are unabashedly simple, like the catch of the day served grilled on lemon leaves. Wine aficionados are likely to find something to try on the 15,000-label list. Reservations are essential. This is one of the few places in Amalfi where you pay for the food rather than the location, which in this case is far from spectacular, sandwiched between the rushing traffic of the road and the old arsenal. But that doesn't worry the discreet, knowledgable crowd who eat here.

🛍 Shopping

You'll have no difficulty loading up on souvenirs here – Via Lorenzo d'Amalfi is lined with garish shops selling local ceramic work, artisanal paper gifts and *limoncello*. Prices are set for tourists, so don't expect many bargains.

Il Ninfeo   CERAMICS
(☑089 873 63 53; www.amalficoastceramics. com; Via Lorenzo d'Amalfi 28; ☺9am-9pm) Unabashedly tourist-geared, Il Ninfeo has a vast showroom displaying an excellent selection of ceramics, ranging from giant urns to fridge magnets. If they're not too busy, ask whether you can see the fascinating remains of a Roman villa under the showroom. It makes you realise just how much is hidden under this town.

Anastasio Nicola Sas   FOOD, BEAUTY
(☑089 87 10 07; Via Lorenzo d'Amalfi 32; ☺9am-8.30pm) Unless you're flying long haul, gourmet goodies can make excellent gifts. In this upscale supermarket, among the hanging hams, you'll find a full selection, ranging from local cheese and preserves to coffee, chocolate, *limoncello* and every imaginable shape of pasta. There's also a collection of fruit-scented soaps and natural shampoos, perfumes and moisturisers.

L'Arco Antico   SOUVENIRS
(☑089 873 63 54; Via Capuano 4; ☺9.30am-8.30pm) Amalfi's connection with paper making dates back to the 12th century, when the first mills were set up to supply the republic's small army of bureaucrats. Although little is made here now, you can still buy it and the quality is still good. This attractive shop sells a range of products, including beautiful writing paper, leather-bound notebooks and huge photo albums.

BEST COASTAL FOOD FESTIVALS
·······························
Sagra della Salsiccia e Ceppone (p146) Sorrento

Gustaminori (p173) Minori

Sagra del Tonno (p174) Cetara

ℹ Information

Tourist Office (☑089 87 11 07; www.amalfitouristoffice.it; Corso delle Repubbliche Marinare 33; ☺9am-1pm & 2-6pm Mon-Sat)

ℹ Getting There & Away

BOAT
Caremar (Map p40; ☑02 577 65 871; www. caremar.it) Runs hydrofoils from Sorrento to Capri (€18.30, 17 daily) and daily hydrofoils/ ferries from Capri to Positano (€17.40), Amalfi (€19.50) and Salerno (€21.50).

BUS
SITA (☑199 730749; www.sitabus.it) Located in Piazza Flavio Gioia, SITA runs at least 12 buses a day from the piazza to Sorrento (via Positano), and also to Ravello, Salerno and Naples. You can buy tickets and check current schedules at **Bar Il Giardino delle Palme** (Piazza Flavio Gioia), opposite the bus stop.

CAR & MOTORCYCLE
If driving from the north, exit the A3 autostrada at Vietri sul Mare and follow the SS163. From the south, leave the A3 at Salerno and head for Vietri sul Mare and the SS163.

Parking
Parking is a problem in this town, although there are some parking places on Piazza Flavio Gioia near the ferry terminal (€3 per hour), as well as an underground car park accessed from Piazza Municipio with the same hourly rate.

Ravello
POP 2500

Sitting high in the hills above Amalfi, Ravello is a refined, polished town almost entirely dedicated to tourism (and increasingly popular as a wedding venue). Boasting impeccable bohemian credentials – Wagner, DH Lawrence and Virginia Woolf all spent time here – it's today known for its ravishing gardens and stupendous views, the best in the world according to former resident Gore Vidal, and certainly the best on the coast.

Ravello

everything is clearly signposted from the main Piazza Duomo. Explore the narrow backstreets, however, and you will discover glimpses of a quieter, traditional lifestyle: dry-stone walls fronting simple homes surrounded by overgrown gardens, neatly planted vegetable plots and basking cats.

Duomo   CATHEDRAL
(Piazza Duomo; museum €3; ⊙ 8.30am-noon & 5.30-8.30pm) Forming the eastern flank of Piazza Duomo, the cathedral was built in 1086 but has since undergone various makeovers. The facade is 16th century, but the central bronze door, one of only about two dozen in the country, dates from 1179; the interior is a late-20th-century interpretation of what the original must once have looked like.

Of particular interest is the striking pulpit, supported by six twisting columns set on marble lions and decorated with flamboyant mosaics of peacocks and other birds. Note also how the floor is tilted towards the square – a deliberate measure to enhance the perspective effect. Entry is via the cathedral museum, displaying a modest collection of religious artefacts.

Most people visit on a day trip from Amalfi – a nerve-tingling 7km drive up the Valle del Dragone – although, to best enjoy its romantic, otherworldly atmosphere, you'll need to stay here overnight. On Tuesday morning there's a lively street market in Piazza Duomo, where you'll find wine, mozzarella and olive oil, as well as discounted designer clothes.

◎ Sights

Even if you have absolutely no sense of direction and a penchant for going round in circles, it's difficult to get lost in this town;

★ **Villa Rufolo**   GARDENS

(☑ 089 85 76 21; www.villarufolo.it; Piazza Duomo; adult/reduced €5/3; ⊙ 9am-5pm) To the south of Ravello's cathedral, a 14th-century tower marks the entrance to this villa, famed for its beautiful cascading gardens. Created by a Scotsman, Scott Neville Reid, in 1853, they are truly magnificent, commanding divine panoramic views packed with exotic colours, artistically crumbling towers and luxurious blooms. Note that the gardens are at their best from May till October; they don't merit the entrance fee outside those times.

The villa was built in the 13th century for the wealthy Rufolo dynasty and was home to several popes as well as king Robert of Anjou. Wagner was so inspired by the gardens when he visited in 1880 that he modelled the garden of Klingsor (the setting for the second act of the opera *Parsifal*) on them. Today the gardens are used to stage concerts during the town's classical-music festival.

Villa Cimbrone   GARDENS

(☑ 089 85 80 72; www.villacimbrone.com; Via Santa Chiara 26; adult/reduced €7/4; ⊙ 9am-7.30pm summer, to sunset winter) Some 600m south of Piazza Duomo, the Villa Cimbrone is worth a wander, if not for the 11th-century villa itself (now an upmarket hotel), then for the fabulous views from the delightful gardens. They're best admired from the Belvedere of Infinity, an awe-inspiring terrace lined with classical-style statues and busts.

The villa was something of a bohemian retreat in its early days and was frequented by Greta Garbo and her lover Leopold Stokowski as a secret hideaway. Other illustrious former guests included Virginia Woolf, Winston Churchill, DH Lawrence and Salvador Dalí.

Auditorium Oscar Niemeyer   THEATRE

(☑ 346 7378561; Via della Repubblica 12) Located just below the main approach to town, this modern building, which follows the natural slope of the hill, has attracted a love-it-or-hate-it controversy in town. Designed by renowned Brazilian architect Oscar Niemeyer, it is characterised by the sinuous profile of a wave and approached via a rectangular exterior courtyard, which is typically the site of temporary exhibitions of world-class sculpture. The auditorium is a venue for concerts and exhibitions.

🍴 Courses

★ **Mamma Agata**   COOKING COURSE

(☑ 089 85 70 19; www.mammaagata.com; Piazza San Cosma 9; courses Apr-Nov €200, May-Oct €250) Mamma Agata, together with her daughter Chiara, offers private cooking classes in her home, producing simple, exceptional food using primarily organic ingredients. A one-day demonstration class culminates in an interlude on a lovely sea-view terrace, tasting what you've been taught to make and enjoying homemade *limoncello*. There is also a cookbook available for purchase.

Apparently Humphrey Bogart made a tradition out of having Mamma Agata's lemon cake (made with *limoncello*) for breakfast when she was cooking for a wealthy American family here back in the '60s. Other guests of this Hollywood-connected couple included Richard Burton, Frank Sinatra, Audrey Hepburn and, more recently, Pierce Brosnan. Price varies depending on the time of year.

✨ Festivals & Events

Ravello's program of classical music begins in March and continues until late October. It reaches its crescendo in June and September

RAVELLO WALKS

Ravello is the starting point for numerous walks – some of which follow ancient paths through the surrounding Lattari mountains. If you've got the legs for it, you can walk down to **Minori** via an attractive route of steps, hidden alleys and olive groves, passing the picturesque hamlet of Torello en route. This walk kicks off just to the left of Villa Rufolo and takes around 45 minutes. Alternatively, you can head the other way, to Amalfi, via the ancient village of **Scala**. Once a flourishing religious centre with more than a hundred churches, and the oldest settlement on the Amalfi Coast, Scala is now a pocket-sized sleepy place where the wind whistles through empty streets. In the central square, the Romanesque **duomo** (Piazza Municipio; ⊙ 8am-noon & 5-7pm) retains some of its 12th-century solemnity. Ask at the Ravello tourist office for more information on local walks.

with the International Piano Festival and Chamber Music Week. Performances by top Italian and international musicians are world class, and the main venues are unforgettable. Tickets, bookable by phone or online, start at €25 (plus a €2 booking fee). For further information, contact the Ravello Concert Society (www.ravelloarts.org).

★ Ravello Festival   PERFORMING ARTS
(☑ 089 85 83 60; www.ravellofestival.com; ☺ Jun-Sep) Between late June and early September, the Ravello Festival – established in 1953 – turns much of the town centre into a stage. Events range from orchestral concerts and chamber music to ballet performances; film screenings and exhibitions are held in atmospheric outdoor venues, most notably the famous overhanging terrace in the Villa Rufolo gardens.

✖ Eating

Surprisingly, Ravello doesn't offer many good eating options. It's easy enough to find a bar or cafe selling overpriced *panini* and pizza but not so simple to find a decent restaurant or trattoria. There are a few good hotel restaurants, most of which are open to non-

CAMEO MUSEUM

Squeezed between tourist-driven shops and cafes, Camo (☑ 089 85 74 61; Piazza Duomo 9, Ravello; ☺ 9.30am-noon & 3-5.30pm Mon-Sat) is on the face of it a cameo shop – and exquisite they are, too, crafted primarily out of coral and shell. But don't stop here; ask to see the treasure trove of a museum beyond the showroom. It's even more of a treat if cameo creator and shop founder Giorgio Filocamo is here to explain the background to such pieces as a 16th-century crucifix on a crystal cross, a mid-16th-century Madonna, a 3rd-century-AD Roman amphora, gorgeous tortoiseshell combs and some exquisite oil paintings.

This shop is the antithesis of the overpriced ones in the centre of Ravello, though you may think twice about the ethics of buying coral. Giorgio's cameos have been commissioned by all kinds of well-known folk, including Hillary Clinton and actress Susan Sarandon.

guests, and a couple of excellent restaurants, but not much else. The places listed below get very busy in summer, particularly at lunchtime, and prices are universally high.

Caffe Calce   CAFE €
(☑ 089 85 71 52; www.caffecalce.com; Viale Richard Wagner 3; ice creams €2; ☺ 8am-10pm) Located just above the Piazza Duomo, this place has a time-tested feel, with its old-fashioned interior and crusty local clientele. The coffee is famously the best in town, and the sweet treats of pastries and ice creams are good.

★ Babel   CAFE €€
(☑ 089 858 62 15; Via Trinità 13; meals €20; ☺ 11am-11pm) A cool little white-painted deli-cafe serving high-quality, affordable salads, bruschetta, cheese and meat boards and an excellent range of local wines. There's a jazz soundtrack, and a little gallery selling unusually stylish ceramic tiles.

Da Salvatore   ITALIAN €€
(☑ 089 85 72 27; www.salvatoreravello.com; Via della Republicca 2; meals €28; ☺ noon-3pm & 7.30-10pm Tue-Sun) Located just before the bus stop, Da Salvatore has nothing special by way of decor, but the view – from both the dining room and the large terrace – is very special indeed. Dishes include creative options like tender squid on a bed of pureed chickpeas with spicy *peperoncino* (chilli pepper). In the evening, part of the restaurant is transformed into an informal pizzeria, serving some of the best wood-fired pizza you will taste anywhere this side of Naples.

Ristorante Pizzeria Vittoria   PIZZA €€
(☑ 089 85 79 47; www.ristorantepizzeriavittoria.it; Via dei Rufolo 3; pizza from €5, meals €30; ☺ 12.15-3pm & 7.15-11pm; 🖩) Come here for exceptional pizza, with some 16 choices on the menu, including the Ravellese, with cherry tomatoes, mozzarella, basil and zucchini. Other dishes include lasagne with red pumpkin, smoked mozzarella and porcini mushrooms, and an innovative chickpea-and-cod antipasto. The atmosphere is one of subdued elegance, with a small outside terrace and grainy historical pics of Ravello on the walls.

🔒 Shopping

Limoncello and ceramics are the mainstays of the Amalfi Coast souvenir trade and you'll find both here.

Profumi della Costiera
DRINK

(✆089 85 81 67; www.profumidellacostiera.it; Via Trinità 37; ⊙9am-8pm) The *limoncello* produced here is made with local lemons; known to experts as *sfusato amalfitano*, they're enormous – about double the size of a standard lemon. The tot is made according to traditional recipes, so there are no preservatives and no colouring. All bottles carry the Indicazione Geografica Proteta (IGP; Protected Geographical Indication) quality mark. You may see the bottling in progress when you visit; it takes place at the back of the shop.

Wine & Drugs
FOOD

(✆089 85 84 43; Via Trinità 6; ⊙9.30am-9.30pm) Despite the tongue-in-cheek name, no mind-altering substances are sold here, only grappa, organic olive oil, saffron and a good selection of local and international wines. There are also complimentary daily tastings of aged Parmesan dipped into similarly elderly 24-year-old balsamic vinegar.

Check out the owner's collection of baseball caps (over 400 at last count), sent by appreciative customers from around the world in exchange for a Ravello cap, which is routinely included in any shipment.

Cashmere
CLOTHING

(✆089 85 84 67; www.filodautoreravello.it; Via Trinità 8; scarves from €35; ⊙9.30am-9pm) Although you may associate cashmere with more northern climes, this tiny shop in the Ravello backstreets is worth a visit to view the exceptional quality of the locally produced clothing, made primarily from pure cashmere, as well as linen.

ℹ Information

Tourist Office (✆089 85 70 96; www.ravellotime.it; Via Roma 18; ⊙9am-7pm) Can assist with accommodation.

ℹ Getting There & Away

BUS

SITA (✆199 730749; www.sitabus.it) Operates hourly buses from Amalfi departing from the bus stop on the eastern side of Piazza Flavio Gioia.

CAR

Turn north about 2km east of Amalfi.

Parking

Vehicles are not permitted in Ravello's town centre.

> ℹ **PARKING IN RAVELLO**
>
> You may want to consider taking a bus from Amalfi to Ravello instead of driving, as the metered parking around the pedestrianised (ie car-free) centre of town is obviously geared towards Ferrari owners: a costly €5 an hour and only payable by credit card. Alternatively, head for the underground car park at the Auditorium Oscar Niemeyer (p171).

Minori

POP 3000

About 3.5km east of Amalfi, or a steep 45-minute walk down from Ravello, Minori is a small, workaday town, popular with holidaying Italians. Much scruffier than its refined coastal cousins Amalfi and Positano, it's no less dependent on tourism yet seems more genuine, with its festive seafront, pleasant beach, atmospheric pedestrian shopping streets and noisy traffic jams. It is also known for its history of pasta making, dating back to medieval times, the speciality being *scialatielli* (thick ribbons of fresh pasta), featured on many local restaurant menus.

◉ Sights

Villa Roma Antiquarium
HISTORIC BUILDING

(✆089 85 28 93; Via Capodipiazza 28; ⊙8am-7pm) FREE Rediscovered in the 1930s, the 1st-century Villa Roma Antiquarium is a typical example of the splendid homes that Roman nobles built as holiday retreats in the period before Mt Vesuvius' AD 79 eruption. The best-preserved rooms surround the garden on the lower level, the highlight being a floor mosaic depicting a bull. There's also a two-room museum exhibiting various artifacts, including a collection of 6th-century-BC to 6th-century-AD amphorae.

✻ Festivals & Events

Gustaminori
FOOD

(⊙early Sep) Food lovers on the coast gather in Minori for the town's annual food jamboree, with pasta stalls (and the like) as well as live music.

✕ Eating

Gambardella
PASTRIES €

(☑ 089 87 72 99; www.gambardella.it; Piazza Cantilena 7; pastries from €1.50) Tucked to the right facing the pretty buttercup-yellow church, this is the place to come for superb coffee and exemplary pastries – try the *sfogliatella* (ricotta-filled flaky pastry) and *torta di ricotta e pere* (ricotta and pear tart). You can buy *limoncello* and similar boozy delights made with wild strawberries, bilberries, bay leaves and wild fennel.

Il Giardiniello
ITALIAN €€

(☑ 089 87 70 50; www.ristorantegiardiniello.com; Corso Vittorio Emanuele 17; pizza from €8, menu €30; ☺ noon-2.30pm & 7-11.30pm Thu-Tue) Easy to find, just up from the seafront on a bustling pedestrian street, Giardiniello has been pleasing local palates since 1955. Sit on the terrace surrounded by fragrant jasmine and enjoy a 40cm pizza to share (€16) or a girth-expanding menu featuring town speciality *scialatielli* followed by local fish and dessert, plus wine.

ⓘ Information

Tourist Office (☑ 089 87 70 87; www.proloco. minori.sa.it; Via Roma 30; ☺ 9am-noon & 5-8pm Mon-Sat, 9-11am Sun) Head for this small office on the seafront for general information and walking maps.

Cetara

POP 2400

Just beyond **Erchie** and its pleasant beach, Cetara is a picturesque fishing village with a reputation as a gastronomic hot spot. It

has been an important fishing centre since medieval times and today its deep-sea-tuna fleet is considered one of the Mediterranean's most important. At night, fishers set out in small boats armed with powerful lamps to fish for anchovies. Recently, locals have resurrected the production of what is known as *colatura di alici*, a strong anchovy essence believed to be the descendant of *garum*, the Roman fish seasoning.

✲ Festivals & Events

Sagra del Tonno
FOOD

(☺ late Jul/early Aug) Each year the village celebrates *sagra del tonno*, a festival dedicated to tuna and anchovies. If you can time your visit accordingly, there are plenty of opportunities for tasting, as well as music and other general festivities. Further details are available from the tourist office.

If you miss the festival, no worries: you can pick up a jar (never a tin) of the fishy specialities, preserved in olive oil, at local food shops and delis.

✕ Eating

Al Convento
SEAFOOD, PIZZA €€

(☑ 089 26 10 39; www.alconvento.net; Piazza San Francesco 16; meals €25; ☺ 12.30-3pm & 7-11pm summer, closed Wed winter) Al Convento enjoys an evocative setting in former church cloisters with original, albeit faded, 17th-century frescoes. This is an excellent spot to tuck into some local fish specialities: you can eat *tagliata di tonna alle erbe* (lightly grilled tuna with herbs) as an antipasto, and the spaghetti with anchovies and wild fennel is particularly delicious.

For dessert, try the decadent chocolate cake with ricotta and cream.

ⓘ Information

Tourist Office (☑ 328 0156347; Piazza San Francesco 15; ☺ 9am-1pm & 5pm-midnight) For accommodation and general info.

Vietri sul Mare

POP 8600

Marking the end of Amalfi's coastal road, Vietri sul Mare is the ceramics capital of Campania. Production dates back to Roman times, but it took off on an industrial

---

FAVOURITE LOCAL TIPPLE

Wander into a local bar and you may just think you're in rural France. Cetara residents love to accompany their espressos with a tumbler of Pernod instead of plain old water. The aniseed-based *digestif* was introduced to the town by French fishermen several decades ago and the association has continued to the present day. Cetara is twinned with Sète in France and many Italian fishermen have moved there to work in its fishing industry.

scale in the 16th and 17th centuries with the development of high, three-level furnaces. The unmistakable local style – bold brush strokes and strong Mediterranean colours – found favour in the royal court of Naples, which became one of Vietri's major clients. Later, in the 1920s and '30s, the arrival of international artists (mainly Germans) led to a shake-up of traditional designs. The *centro storico* is packed with decorative tiled-front shops selling ceramic wares of every description.

◉ Sights

Museo della Ceramica   MUSEUM

(📞000 21 10 35; Villa Guerriglia, ⏰9am-3pm Tue-Sat, 9.30am-1pm Sun) FREE For a primer on Vietri's ceramics past, head to this museum in the nearby village of Raito. Housed in a lovely villa surrounded by a park, the museum has a comprehensive collection, including pieces from the 'German period' (1929–47), when the town attracted an influx of artists, mainly from Germany.

🛍 Shopping

Ceramica Artistica Solimene   CERAMICS

(📞089 21 02 43; www.ceramicasolimene.it; Via Madonna degli Angeli 7; ⏰9am-7pm Mon-Fri, 10am-1pm & 4-7pm Sat) This vast factory outlet, the most famous ceramics shop in town, sells everything from egg cups to ornamental mermaids, mugs to lamps. Even if you don't go in, it's worth having a look at the shop's extraordinary glass and ceramic facade. It was designed by Italian architect Paoli Soleri, who studied under the famous American 'organic' architect Frank Lloyd Wright.

Ceramiche Sara   CERAMICS

(📞089 21 00 53; www.ceramichesara.it; Via Costiera Amalfitana 14-16) Located at the entrance to town, and with a convenient car park, the showroom here has a great choice of ceramics, including some reasonably priced and colourful tiles (€8) that make terrific hotplates.

ⓘ Information

Tourist Office (📞089 21 12 85; Piazza Matteotti; ⏰10am-1pm & 5-8pm Mon-Fri, 10am-1pm Sat) This moderately helpful office is near the entrance to the *centro storico*.

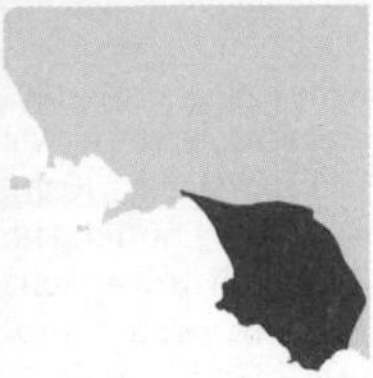

Salerno & the Cilento

Best Places to Eat

➡ La Cantina del Feudo (p181)

➡ Vicolo della Neve (p181)

➡ Anna (p188)

➡ I Tre Gufi (p192)

Best Places to Stay

➡ Agriturismo i Moresani (p213)

➡ Villa Vea (p214)

➡ Marulivo Hotel (p212)

➡ Hotel Calypso (p212)

Why Go?

Salerno may not have the glamorous looks of the Amalfi coast resorts, but its picturesque *centro storico* (historic centre) comprises an intriguing labyrinth of colourful earthy streets, which makes for a refreshing change from the more touristy towns to the west. An enthralling archeological museum and Norman cathedral add depth, and there's also a spacious waterfront promenade lined with palm trees as well as a lively restaurant scene.

The fascinating excavations at nearby Paestum include some of the world's best-preserved Greek temples standing proud among meadows scattered with wildflowers. The museum here holds some captivating ancient frescoes, including the famous Tomba del Truffatore (Tomb of the Diver).

And don't miss the Cilento region, one of this area's lesser-known glories, with a largely undeveloped coastal strip and a beautiful national park famed for its orchids. Villages here have a tangible stuck-in-a-time-warp feel, so be prepared for stares. It's a burgeoning region for walkers, and *agriturismi* (farm-stay accommodation) make perfect bases. The region has some heavyweight sights as well, including an extraordinary monastery, an evocative archeological site, and intriguing grottoes and caves.

When to Go

➡ The Cilento coastal resorts can be crowded with gelato-slurping Italian holidaymakers from July to August, with hotel rooms hard to find.

➡ May and June, and September and October are preferable, when temperatures are pleasant and there's more towel space on the sand.

➡ If you are planning on visiting the Parco Nazionale del Cilento, then springtime is best, when the weather is ideal for strolls or hard-core hiking, and the wildflowers are in bloom.

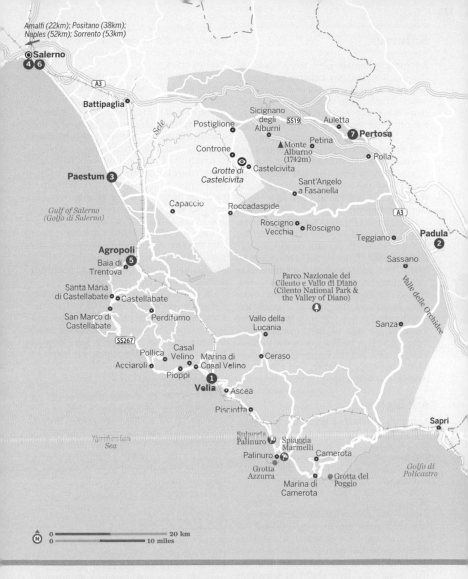

Amalfi (22km); Positano (38km);
Naples (52km); Sorrento (53km)

◎**Salerno**
❹❻

A3

Battipaglia

Sicignano
degli
Alburni   **SS19**

Postiglione

Auletta

Petina

❼**Pertosa**

Controne

▲Monte
Alburno
(1742m)

Castelcivita

Polla

*Grotte di
Castelcivita*

Paestum ❸

Sant'Angelo
a Fasanella

A3

Capaccio

Roccadaspide

*Gulf of Salerno
(Golfo di Salerno)*

Roscigno
Vecchia   Roscigno

Teggiano

Padula

❷

Agropoli ❺

Sassano

Baia di
Trentova

*Parco Nazionale del
Cilento e Vallo di Diano
(Cilento National Park &
the Valley of Diano)*

Santa Maria
di Castellabate

Castellabate

Valle delle Orchidee

San Marco di
Castellabate

Perdifumo

Vallo della
Lucania

Sanza

SS267

Pollica

Casal
Velino

Marina di
Casal Velino

Ceraso

Acciaroli

Pioppi

❶

Velia   Ascea

Piscotta

*Tyrrhenian
Sea*

Sapri

Palinuro ❼   Spiaggia
Marmelli

Palinuro ❼

Camerota

*Grotta
Azzurra*

*Golfo di
Policastro*

Marina di
Camerota

Grotta del
Poggio

Ⓝ 0 ─────── 20 km
     0 ─────── 10 miles

Salerno & the Cilento Coast Highlights

❶ Roaming the ruins of
the Hellenistic town of **Velia**
(p192).

❷ Wondering at the
extraordinary **Certosa di San
Lorenzo** (p186) in Padula.

❸ Taking a trip to the ancient
Greek world at **Paestum**

(p184), one of Europe's most
majestic archaeological sites.

❹ Joining the *passeggiata*
(stroll) through the fascinating
centro storico (historic centre)
in **Salerno** (p178).

❺ Enjoying a sunset walk
along the lovely promenade in
Agropoli (p188).

❻ Marvelling at the heady
views from Salerno's **castle**
(p178).

❼ Visiting the fascinating
Grotte di Pertosa (p185) by
boat.

Salerno

POP 139,000

Salerno may initially seem like a bland big city, but the place has a charming, if gritty, individuality, especially around its vibrant *centro storico*, where medieval churches share space with neighbourhood trattorias, neon-lit wine bars and trendy tattoo parlours. The city recently invested in various urban-regeneration programs centred on this historic neighbourhood, which features a dramatic new ferry terminal designed by Zaha Hadid and a tree-lined seafront promenade widely considered to be one of the most beautiful in Europe.

Originally an Etruscan and later a Roman colony, Salerno flourished with the arrival of the Normans in the 11th century. Robert Guiscard made it the capital of his dukedom in 1076 and, under his patronage, the Scuola Medica Salernitana was renowned as one of medieval Europe's greatest medical institutes. Much later, the city was tragically left in tatters by the heavy fighting that followed the 1943 landings of the American Fifth Army. Part of the historic centre was miraculously spared, but the somewhat featureless wide boulevards elsewhere are a result of postwar reconstruction.

◉ Sights

Although Salerno is a sprawling town, you can easily visit it in one day, and on foot, as the main sights are concentrated in and around the historic centre. Don't miss having a walk along the gracious seafront promenade.

★ **Duomo** CATHEDRAL

(Piazza Alfano; ⊙ 9am-6pm Mon-Sat, 4-6pm Sun) You can't miss the looming presence of Salerno's impressive cathedral, widely considered to be the most beautiful medieval church in Italy. Built by the Normans in the 11th century and later aesthetically remodelled in the 18th century, it sustained severe damage in a 1980 earthquake. It is dedicated

---

BEST BEACHES

Ascea (p191)

Santa Maria di Castellabate (p190)

Spiaggia Palinuro (p193)

Agropoli (p188)

---

to San Matteo (St Matthew), whose remains were reputedly brought to the city in 954 and now lie beneath the main altar in the vaulted crypt.

Take special note of the magnificent main entrance, the 12th-century **Porta dei Leoni**, named after the marble lions at the foot of the stairway. It leads through to a beautiful, harmonious courtyard, surrounded by graceful arches and overlooked by a 12th-century bell tower. Carry on through the huge bronze doors (similarly guarded by lions), which were cast in Constantinople in the 11th century. When you come to the three-aisled interior, you will see that it is largely baroque, with only a few traces of the original church. These include parts of the transept and choir floor and the two raised pulpits in front of the choir stalls. Throughout the church you can see extraordinarily detailed and colourful 13th-century mosaic work.

In the right-hand apse, don't miss the **Cappella delle Crociate** (Chapel of the Crusades), containing stunning frescoes and more wonderful mosaics. It was so named because crusaders' weapons were blessed here. Under the altar stands the tomb of 11th-century pope Gregory VII.

Castello di Arechi CASTLE

(✆ 089 296 40 15; www.ilcastellodiarechi.it; Via Benedetto Croce; adult/reduced €5/2.50; ⊙ 9am-7pm Tue-Sat, to 6.30pm Sun summer, to 5pm Tue-Sun winter) Hop on bus 19 from Piazza XXIV Maggio to visit Salerno's most famous landmark, the forbidding Castello di Arechi, dramatically positioned 263m above the city. Originally a Byzantine fort, it was built by the Lombard duke of Benevento, Arechi II, in the 8th century and subsequently modified by the Normans and Aragonese, most recently in the 16th century.

The views of the Gulf of Salerno and the city rooftops are spectacular; you can also visit a permanent collection of ceramics, arms and coins. If you are here during summer, ask the tourist office for a schedule of the annual series of concerts staged here.

Museo Pinacoteca Provinciale MUSEUM

(✆ 089 258 30 73; www.museibiblioteche.provincia. salerno.it; Via Mercanti 63; adult/reduced €3/1.50; ⊙ 9am-7.45pm Tue-Sun) Art enthusiasts should seek out the Museo Pinacoteca Provinciale, located deep in the heart of the historic quarter. Spread throughout six galleries, the museum houses a collection dating from the

Renaissance right up to the first half of the 20th century.

There are some fine canvases by local boy Andrea Sabatini da Salerno, who was notably influenced by Leonardo da Vinci, plus a diverse selection of works by foreign artists who were permanent residents around the Amalfi Coast. These include intricate etchings by the Austrian-born Peter Willburger (1942–98) and a colourful embroidered picture of a local market by Polish artist Irene Kowaliska. The museum also hosts free classical concerts during the summer months.

Museo Virtuale della Scuola Medica Salernitana
MUSEUM

(☑089 257 61 26; www.museovirtualescuolamedicasalernitana.beniculturali.it; Via Mercanti 74; adult/reduced €3/1; ⊙9.30am-1pm Tue-Wed, 9.30am-1pm & 5-8pm Thu-Sat, 10am-1pm Sun; ⏛) Slap bang in Salerno's historic centre, this engaging museum deploys 3D and touch-screen technology to explore the teachings and wince-inducing procedures of Salerno's once-famous, now-defunct medical institute. Established around the 9th century, the school was the most important centre of medical knowledge in medieval Europe, reaching the height of its prestige in the 11th century. It was closed in the early 19th century.

Museo Archeologico Provinciale
MUSEUM

(☑089 23 11 35; Via San Benedetto 28; adult/reduced €4/2; ⊙9am-7.30pm Tue-Sun) The province's restored and revitalised main archaeological museum is an excellent showcase for a collection of mesmerising grave goods from the surrounding area, dating back to cave dwellers and the colonising Greeks. Don't miss the 4th-century-BC bronze candelabra topped with the figures of a warrior and a woman, his arm around her shoulder.

The upstairs room is dedicated to a stunning 1st-century-BC bronze head of Apollo, discovered in the Gulf of Salerno in 1930, and centuries' worth of findings from nearby Fratte, including a little vase engraved with salacious gossip describing gay and straight relations between the Greek, Roman and indigenous populations.

✗ Eating

Head to Via Roma in the lively medieval centre, where you'll find everything from traditional, family-run trattorias and gelaterias to jazzy wine bars, pubs and expensive restaurants. In summer, the wide seafront promenade is a popular place for the pre-dinner evening *passeggiata*.

THREE PERFECT DAYS IN SALERNO & THE CILENTO

Day 1: Culture & Cuisine
Start off in Salerno by checking out the magnificent **cathedral**, followed by an atmospheric wander around the narrow backstreets of the city's densely packed *centro storico*. Take a cappuccino break in a typical hung-with-washing piazza, buy some deli fodder, then hop on a train to Paestum for a picnic lunch and an afternoon visiting its magical **temples** (p184). In the evening continue south to Agropoli for an ocean-front dinner.

Day 2: Coastal Cilento
Stretch your legs with a morning stroll along Agropoli's sweeping promenade. Visit the **castle** (p188) and historic quarter before continuing south along this dramatic coastline of hidden coves and high cliffs. Stop for a swim, a snack or a walk at small traditional Italian resorts like Acciaroli, a favourite of Ernest Hemingway's; Pioppi, with its pale pebble beach; and medieval Pisciotta, home to a lovely traditional piazza. Carry on along this unspoilt coastline before ending the day in pretty Palinuro.

Day 3: Explore Hidden Caves & Grottoes
It's not half as famous as its Capri cousin, but Palinuro's **Grotta Azzurra** (p193; Blue Grotto) is just as spectacular. Next, head inland into the Parco Nazionale del Cilento and two otherworldly caves, the **Grotte di Castelcivita** (p184), one of the largest cave complexes in Europe, and the equally tantalising **Grotte di Pertosa** (p185), where your tour includes the added adventure of a boat ride. Consider staying overnight at one of the park's superb *agriturismi* (farm-stay accommodation).

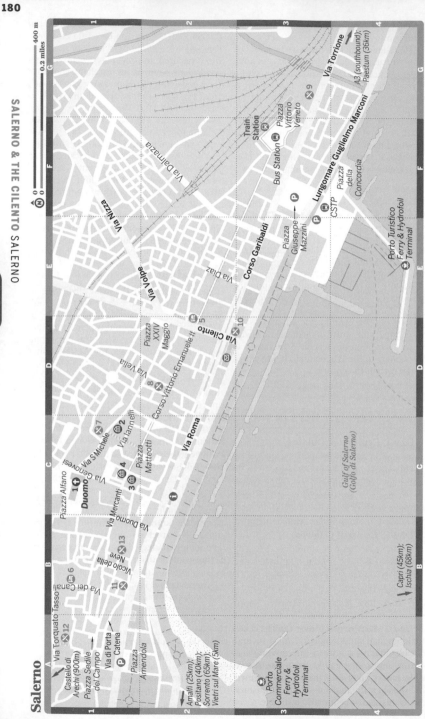

Salerno

Salerno

★ **Vicolo della Neve**　　　ITALIAN €
(☎ 089 22 57 05; www.vicolodellaneve.it; Vicolo della Neve 24; meals €20; ⊗ 7-11.30pm Thu-Tue) A city institution on a scruffy street, this is the archetypal *centro storico* trattoria, with brick arches, fake frescoes and walls hung with works by local artists. The menu is, similarly, unwaveringly authentic, with pizzas and calzones, *peperoni ripieni* (stuffed peppers) and a top-notch *parmigiana di melanzane* (baked aubergine). It can get incredibly busy: book in advance.

Pizza Margherita　　　ITALIAN €
(☎ 089 22 88 80; Corso Garibaldi 201; pizzas/buffet from €5/6.50, lunch menu €8.50; ⊗ 12.30-3.30pm & 7.30pm-midnight; 🧒) It looks like a bland, modern canteen, but this is, in fact, one of Salerno's most popular lunch spots. Locals regularly queue for the lavish lunchtime buffet that, on any given day, might include buffalo mozzarella, salami, mussels in various guises and a range of salads.

If that doesn't appeal, the daily lunch menu (pasta, main course, salad and half a litre of bottled water) is chalked up on a blackboard, or there's the regular menu of pizzas, pastas, salads and main courses.

Pasticceria Romolo　　　PASTRIES €
(☎ 089 23 26 13; www.pasticceriaromolo.it; Corso Garibaldi 33; cakes from €1.50; ⊗ 7.30am-2pm & 3.30-8.30pm Mon & Wed-Sat, 7.30am-8.30pm Sun) This sprawling *pasticceria* (pastry shop) across from the station dates from 1966 and the decor has changed little since. The cakes are legendary, and include *frollini* (fruit and chocolate tarts), *amaretti* (macaroons) and all-time most irresistible treat *sfogliatelle* (flaky pastry filled with ricotta, and warmed and dusted with sugar if you eat in). Fancy chocolates and wine are also available.

Ristorante Santa Lucia　　　SEAFOOD €
(☎ 089 22 56 96; Via Roma 182; pizzas from €5, meals €22; ⊗ noon-2.30pm & 7-11.30pm Tue-Sun) The surrounding Via Roma area may be one of the city's trendiest, but there's nothing remotely flash about the delicious seafood served up here. Dishes such as *linguine ai frutti di mare* (flat spaghetti with seafood) and chargrilled cuttlefish may not be original but taste great – as do the top-notch wood-fired pizzas.

★ **Cicirinella**　　　ITALIAN €€
(☎ 089 22 65 61; Via Genovesi 28; meals €25; ⊗ 6pm-midnight) This place, tucked behind the cathedral, has that winning combination of an earthy and inviting atmosphere and unfailingly good, delicately composed dishes. Exposed stone, shelves of wine and an open-plan kitchen set the scene for traditional Campanian cuisine like pasta with seafood and chickpeas, or a mussel soup that tastes satisfyingly of the sea.

★ **La Cantina del Feudo**　　　ITALIAN €€
(☎ 089 25 46 96; Via Velia 45; meals €28; ⊗ noon-2pm & 7-11pm Tue-Sun; 🧒) Frequented by locals in the know, this restaurant is tucked up a side street off the pedestrian *corso*. The menu changes daily, but the emphasis is on vegetable dishes like white beans with

---

DON'T MISS

SWEET TREAT

Look for *torta ricotta e pera* (ricotta and pear tart), a speciality in Salerno and sold throughout the Cilento region. Just about every *pasticceria* (pastry shop) sells this delicious sweet and fruity delicacy – although it's the locals' favourite as well, so it tends to sell out fast.

chicory, noodles and turnip tops, and ravioli stuffed with cheese. The interior has a rural trattoria feel and there's a terrace for al fresco dining.

Sant'Andrea
ITALIAN €€

(☑ 328 727274; www.ristorantesantandrea.it; Piazza Sedile del Campo 58; meals €25; ☉ 12.30-3pm & 8pm-midnight) There's an earthy southern Italian atmosphere here, with its terrace surrounded by historic houses decorated with washing hung out to dry. Choices are more innovative than you would expect and include such seafood dishes as squid with porcini mushrooms, and cuttlefish accompanied by creamed vegetables. The white-truffle ice cream makes a delicious finale. The owners run the adjacent B&B.

🛍 Shopping

Head for pedestrian Corso Vittorio Emanuele II, which becomes Via Mercanti towards the medieval market square of Piazza Sedile del Campo, where there is an eclectic mix of intriguing ceramic stores, boutiques and idiosyncratic small shops.

ℹ Information

Tourist Office (☑ 089 23 14 32; Lungomare Trieste 7; ☉ 9am-1pm & 3-7pm Mon-Sat) Has limited information.

ℹ Getting There & Away

BOAT

Caremar (p169) runs runs a daily hydrofoil to/from Capri (€18.30, 50 minutes).

Alicost (☑ 089 87 14 83; www.alicost.it) runs several daily hydrofoils to/from Capri (€21, 50 minutes), Amalfi (€8, 20 minutes) and Positano (€12, 30 minutes).

Departures are from the Porto Turistico, 200m down the pier from Piazza della Concordia. You can buy tickets from the booths beside the embarkation point.

BUS

SITA (p269) buses for Amalfi depart at least hourly from Piazza Vittorio Veneto, beside the train station, stopping en route at Vietri sul Mare, Cetara, Maiori and Minori. For Pompeii, take **CSTP** (☑ 089 48 70 01; www.cstp.it) bus 50 from Piazza Vittorio Veneto. There are 15 daily departures. For the south coast and Paestum, take the hourly bus 34 from the CSTP stop on Piazza della Concordia.

CAR & MOTORCYCLE

Salerno is on the A3 between Naples and Reggio di Calabria; the A3 is toll-free from Salerno south. Take the Salerno exit and follow signs to the *centro* (city centre). If you want to hire a car, there's a **Europcar** (☑ 089 258 07 75; www.europcar.com; Via Clemente Mauro 18) agency not far from the train station.

THE SALERNO MUTINY

The Allies invaded Italy on 9 September 1943 in an operation code-named Avalanche, which also became known as the Battle of Salerno. Pitting Allied troops including Lieutenant General Mark Clark's US Fifth Army against the German occupiers, its goal was to gain control of Naples and thus force Italy out of the war, smashing the Axis coalition.

Following the flawed invasion, which resulted in terrible casualties, 600 men staged the biggest mutiny in British military history, refusing to form part of the Fifth Army. They had sailed from Tripoli, many having fought with distinction against Rommel's troops in the desert campaign, and had been informed they were to rejoin comrades in Sicily. It was only on board ship that they were told they were in fact en route to the Battle of Salerno. Once in Salerno, the men were taken to a field by the beach and held for three days; the rebellion continued despite the punishments notoriously meted out to wartime mutineers.

Of the hard core of 300 remaining mutineers, 108 capitulated and 192 continued their refusal to fight. All were then charged with mutiny under the Army Act and sent to Algeria for court martial. The men had only been sent to Salerno in the first place due to clerical error, but the army refused to back down.

All of the men were found guilty, and three sergeants were sentenced to death, commuted to 12 years of forced labour. In time, all the sentences were suspended, but the men had to surrender their war medals and live on reduced pensions.

The battle itself, which reduced parts of Salerno to rubble, was technically a victory for the Allies, though it was far from the swift surgical attack intended, and left them entrenched in a long and difficult fight to conquer Italy.

TRAIN

Salerno is a major stop on southbound routes to Calabria, and the Ionian and Adriatic coasts. From the station in Piazza Vittorio Veneto there are regular trains to Naples (€9, 35 minutes, half-hourly) and Rome (Intercity from €21, three hours, hourly).

Getting Around

CAR & MOTORCYCLE

If you want to hire a car, there's a **Europcar** (089 258 07 75; www.europcar.com; Via Clemente Mauro 18) agency not far from the train station

Parking

Salerno has a reasonable number of car parks. Follow the distinctive blue P sign as you approach the centre of the city. The most convenient car park for the *centro storico* is on Piazza Amendola. Near the train station (and tourist office), other convenient locations are the large car parks on Piazza della Concordia and the adjacent Piazza Giuseppe Mazzini. You can expect to pay around €2 an hour for Salerno car parks.

.

Paestum

Paestum, or Poseidonia as the city was originally called (in honour of Poseidon, the Greek god of the sea), was founded in the 6th century BC by Greek settlers and fell under Roman control in 273 BC. Decline later set in following the demise of the Roman Empire. Savage raids by the Saracens and periodic outbreaks of malaria forced the steadily dwindling population to abandon the city altogether.

Although most people visit Paestum for the day, there is a surprising number of good hotels, and this delightful rural area makes a convenient stopover point for travellers heading for the Cilento region.

Eating

There are various restaurants at Paestum, most serving mediocre food at inflated prices.

Nonna Sceppa   ITALIAN €€
(0828 85 10 64; Via Laura 53; meals €35; 12.30-3pm & 7.30-11pm Fri-Wed;) Seek out the superbly prepared, robust dishes at Nonna Sceppa, a family-friendly restaurant that's gaining a reputation throughout the region

GETTING AROUND THE REGION

Salerno is on the ferry route from Naples, Sorrento and (in summer) the Amalfi Coast resorts and islands. The main Cilento coastal towns can be reached by bus or ferry; however, renting a car will provide the flexibility to explore the smaller villages and the magnificent Parco Nazionale del Cilento e Vallo di Diano inland, where the bus service is sporadic and many smaller villages are only accessible by car. Overall, the roads are good throughout the Cilento region, with well-signposted towns and resorts within easy reach of each other.

for excellence. Dishes are firmly seasonal and, during summer, concentrate on fresh seafood like the refreshingly simple grilled fish with lemon. Other popular choices include risotto with zucchini and artichokes, and spaghetti with lobster.

Information

Tourist Office (0828 81 10 16; www.infopaestum.it; Via Magna Grecia 887; 9am 1.30pm & 2.30-7pm Mon-Sat)

Getting There & Away

BUS

CSTP (089 48 70 01; www.cstp.it) Bus 34 goes to Paestum from Piazza della Concordia in Salerno (€3.80, 80 minutes, 12 daily).

TRAIN

Regular trains link Salerno with Paestum (€2.70, 32 minutes). From Paestum station, walk straight ahead through the stone arch and up Via Porta Sirena; it's a pleasant 10-minute walk.

Parco Nazionale del Cilento e Vallo di Diano

Proving the perfect antidote to the holiday mayhem along the coast, the stunning Parco Nazionale del Cilento e Vallo di Diano (Cilento National Park and the Valley of Diano) is a compelling combination of dense woods, flowering meadows, dramatic mountains, and water – lots of it, with streams, rivers and waterfalls. A World Heritage Site, it is the second-largest national park in Italy, covering a staggering 1810 sq km, including 80 towns and villages.

The park has been inhabited since prehistoric times, and its isolation has attracted waves of refuge-seeking settlers over the ages. The Greeks fled here when the Romans overran the towns of Paestum and Velia. Then early inhabitants of the coastal cities headed inland to escape piracy and pillaging. Benedictine monks later joined the cultural medley, seeking secluded places of worship. Next were the wealthy feudal lords who set up house (or rather castle) here, from where they could impose their power. Centuries later, the park was controlled by the feared *briganti* (bandits), which meant it was a no-go area for Grand Tour visitors. This kept the park out of the tourism loop for decades and helps explain why it remains so pristine today.

◉ Sights

To get the best out of the park, you will, unfortunately, need a car. Allow yourself a full day to visit the grottoes and more if you're intending to hike.

★ **Grotte di Castelcivita**　　　CAVE
(☑0828 77 23 97; www.grottedicastelcivita.com; Piazzale N Zonzi, Castelcivita; adult/reduced €10/8; ◷standard tours 10.30am, noon, 1.30pm & 3pm Mar-Oct, plus 4.30pm & 6pm Apr-Sep; ℗♿) The grottoes are fascinating otherworldly caves that date from prehistoric

---

PAESTUM'S TEMPLES

Paestum's Temples (☑0828 81 10 23; incl museum adult/reduced €10/5; ◷8.45am-7.45pm, last entry 7pm Jun & Jul, as early as 3.35pm Nov) A Unesco World Heritage Site, these temples are among the best-preserved monuments of Magna Graecia, the Greek colony that once covered much of southern Italy. Rediscovered in the late 18th century, the site as a whole wasn't unearthed until the 1950s. Lacking the tourist mobs that can sully better-known archaeological sites, the place has a wonderful serenity. Take sandwiches and prepare to stay at least three hours. In spring the temples are particularly stunning, surrounded by scarlet poppies.

Buy your tickets in the museum, just east of the site, before entering from the main entrance on the northern end. The first structure is the 6th-century-BC **Tempio di Cerere** (Temple of Ceres); originally dedicated to Athena, it served as a Christian church in medieval times.

As you head south, you can pick out the basic outline of the large rectangular forum, the heart of the ancient city. Among the partially standing buildings are the vast domestic housing area and, further south, the amphitheatre; both provide evocative glimpses of daily life here in Roman times. In the former houses you'll see mosaic floors, and a marble *impluvium* that stood in the atrium and collected rainwater.

The **Tempio di Nettuno** (Temple of Neptune), dating from about 450 BC, is the largest and best preserved of the three temples at Paestum; only parts of its inside walls and roof are missing. Almost next door, the so-called **basilica** (in fact, a temple to the goddess Hera) is Paestum's oldest-surviving monument. Dating from the middle of the 6th century BC, it's a magnificent sight, with nine columns across and 18 along the sides. Ask someone to take your photo next to one of the columns: it's a good way to appreciate the scale.

Save time for the **museum** (☑0828 81 10 23; ◷8.30am-7.30pm, last entry 6.45pm, closed 1st & 3rd Mon of month), which covers two floors and houses a collection of fascinating, if weathered, metopes (bas-relief friezes). This collection includes 33 of the original 36 metopes from the Tempio di Argiva Hera (Temple of Argive Hera), situated 9km north of Paestum, of which virtually nothing else remains. The star exhibit is the 5th-century-BC fresco Tomba del Truffatore (Tomb of the Diver), thought to represent the passage from life to death with its frescoed depiction of a diver in mid air. The fresco was discovered in 1968 inside the lid of the tomb of a young man, alongside his drinking cup and oil flasks, which he would perhaps have used to oil himself for wrestling matches. Rare for the period in that it shows a human form, the fresco expresses pure delight in physicalilty, its freshness and grace eternally arresting. Below the diver, a symposium of men repose languidly on low couches and brandish drinking cups.

Parco Nazionale del Cilento e Vallo di Diano

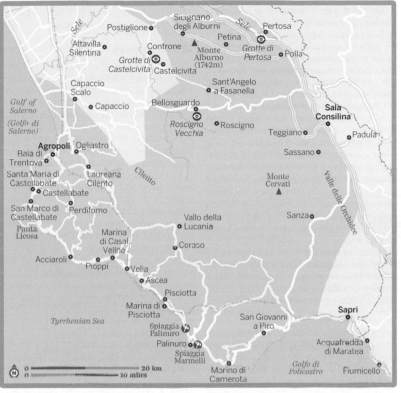

times: excavations have revealed that they were inhabited 42,000 years ago, making them the oldestknown settlement in Europe. Don't forget a jackct, and leave the high heels at home, as paths are wet and slippery. Hard hats, and a certain level of fitness and mobility, are required. Located 40km southeast of Salerno, the complex is refreshingly noncommercial.

Although it extends over 4800m, only around half of the complex is open to the public. The one-hour tour winds through a route surrounded by extraordinary stalagmites and stalactites, and a mesmerising play of colours, caused by algae, calcium and iron that tint the naturally sculpted rock shapes.

The tour culminates in a cavernous lunar landscape – think California's Death Valley in miniature – called the Caverna di Bertarelli (Bertarelli Cavern). The caves are still inhabited – by bats – and visitors are instructed not to take flash photos for fear of blinding them.

Grotte di Pertosa
CAVE

(🖉 0975 39 70 37; www.grottedipertosa-auletta. it; Pertosa; guided visits adult/reduced 100min €20/15, 75min €16/13, 60min €13/10; ⊗ 9am-7pm Apr & May, 10am-7pm Jun-Aug, 10am-6pm Sep, reduced hours rest of year; 🅿 ♿) (Re)discovered in 1932, the Grotte di Pertosa date back 35 million years. Used by the Greeks and Romans as places of worship, the caves burrow for some 2500m, with long underground passages and lofty grottoes filled with stalagmites and stalactites. The first part of the tour takes part as a boat (or raft) ride on the river; you disembark just before the waterfall (phew!) and continue on foot for around 800m, surrounded by marvellous rock formations and luminous crystal accretions.

This grotto is quite commercial, with souvenir shops, bars and a €3 parking fee.

Certosa di San Lorenzo
MONASTERY

(☑ 0975 77 74 45; Padula; adult/reduced €4/2; ☺ 9am-7pm Wed-Mon) One of the largest monasteries in southern Europe, the Certosa di San Lorenzo dates from 1306 and covers 250,000 sq metres. Numerologists can swoon at the following: 320 rooms and halls, 2500m of corridors, galleries and hallways, 300 columns, 500 doors, 550 windows, 13 courtyards, 100 fireplaces, 52 stairways and 41 fountains – in other words, it is *huge*.

As you will unlikely have time to see everything, be sure to visit the highlights, including the vast central courtyard (a venue for summer classical-music concerts), the magnificent wood-panelled library, frescoed chapels, and the kitchen with its grandiose fireplace and famous tale: apparently this is where the legendary 1000-egg omelette was made in 1534 for Charles V. Unfortunately, the historic frying pan is not on view – just how big was it, one wonders?

Within the monastery you can also peruse the modest collection of ancient artefacts at the Museo Archeologico Provinciale della Lucania Occidentale (☑ 0975 7 71 17; ☺ 8am-1.15pm & 2-3pm Tue-Sat, 9am-1pm Sun) FREE.

Roscigno Vecchia
RUIN

Roscigno Vecchia is located in the heart of the national park 28km west of Teggiano. Sudden landslides in the early 20th century caused the population to flee, although most of the original stone houses are still standing, demonstrating the sturdiness of the historic vernacular architecture. These, as well as the church and the central piazza, are all ghostly reminders of a formerly thriving community. The residents were eventually permanently moved to Roscigno Nuovo (now simply known as Roscigno).

🏃 Activities

The park has 15 well-marked nature trails that vary from relatively easy strolls to serious hikes requiring stamina and good knees. The countryside in the park is stunning and dramatic and, in spring, you'll experience real flower power: delicate narcissi, wild orchids and tulips hold their own among blowsier summer drifts of brilliant yellow ox-eye daisies and scarlet poppies.

Thickets of silver firs, wild chestnuts and beech trees add to the sumptuous landscape, as do the dramatic cliffs, pine-clad mountains and fauna, including wild boars, badgers and wolves and, for birdwatchers, the increasingly rare golden eagle.

Even during the busier summer season, the sheer size of the park means that hikers are unlikely to meet others on the trail to swap tales and muesli bars – so getting lost could become a lonely, not to mention dangerous, experience if you haven't done some essential planning before striding out. In theory, the tourist offices should be able to supply you with a guide to the trails. In reality, they frequently seem to have run out of copies. Failing this, you can buy the *Parco Nazionale del Cilento e Vallo di Diano: Carta Turistica e dei Sentieri* (Tourist and Footpath Map; €7) or the excellent *Monte Stella: Walks & Rambles in Ancient Cilento*

GOING WILD FOR ORCHIDS

The Parco Nazionale del Cilento is a rich natural environment for fauna and flora and has been declared part of Unesco's biosphere-preservation program. There are a number of extremely rare plant species here, including the primrose of Palinuro (the symbol of the park). Horticulture enthusiasts will likely trip over their pitchforks when they hear that some 265 varieties of wild orchid flourish annually in the park (the equivalent of 80% of the total number of wild-orchid varieties in Europe).

Concentrated in the appropriately named Valle delle Orchidee (Valley of the Orchids), near the picturesque small town of Sassano (9km west of the Certosa di San Lorenzo in Padula), this annual dazzle of sumptuous colour encompasses 70 orchid species and normally takes place from late April to early May. The surrounding countryside is beautiful, so even if you miss the orchids you can still enjoy the drive and may well glimpse some other wildlife – the park is home to foxes, badgers, wolves, wild boars and the largest otter population in Italy.

Take the sign marked *percorso turistico* on the left just as you enter Sassano; you will pass the medieval bridge of Peglio and woods of silver birches before this blooming event unfolds in all its glory in the valley beyond. You can also join an organised tour with Gruppo Escursionistico Trekking.

published by the Comunita' Montana Alento Monte Stella (€3). Most of the *agriturismi* in the park can also organise guided treks.

A popular self-guided hike, where you are rewarded with spectacular views, is a climb of Monte Alburno (1742m). There's a choice of two trails, both of which are clearly marked from the centre of the small town of Sicignano degli Alburni and finish at the mountain's peak. Allow approximately four hours for either route. The less experienced may prefer to opt for a guide. There are some excellent *agriturismi* here that offer additional activities, including guided hikes, **painting courses** and **horse riding**.

🍴 Eating

There remains a lot of poverty in the small villages that dot the park, but that can mean simple, unadulterated food with hearty meat sauces made from mutton and goat. The flat bread focaccia that you find all over Italy originated in the Cilento region and the *mozzarella di bufala* is similarly famed.

Trattoria degli Ulivi   ITALIAN €
(✉ 334 2595091; www.tavolacaldadegliulivi.it; Viale Certosa, Padula; menus from €12; ⏱ 11am-4pm Sun-Sat) If you've worked up an appetite walking the endless corridors of the Certoza de San Lorenzo, then this restaurant – located just 50m to the west – is the place to come. The decor is canteenlike, but the daily specials are affordable, tasty and generously proportioned. It serves snacks as well as four-course blow-out lunches.

Vecchia Pizzeria Margaret   PIZZA €
(✉ 0975 33 00 00; Via Luigi Curto, Pollo; pizzas from €3) Fabulous wheels of pizza, cooked in a wood-fired oven; it also dishes up antipasti and pasta dishes. Service is fast and friendly, and prices are low. You'll find the restaurant just east of the river, near the hospital. It's great for a fill-up after a walk in the national park.

Antichi Feudi   ITALIAN €€
(✉ 0975 58 73 29; www.antichifeudi.com; Via San Francesco 2, Teggiano; pizzas from €4, meals €25; ⏱ noon-3pm & 7-11pm) This gracious restaurant is located within a swish boutique hotel just off Teggiano's elegant main piazza. The menu varies according to what's in season, but typical dishes include juicy char-grilled meat, grilled mussels with lemon, and seafood soup. The hotel bar-cafe is good for pizza, including tasty *antichi feudi* with

mushrooms, fresh cheese and grilled aubergines (€10). Reservations recommended.

Pasticceria Mery Diano   GELATERIA €
(✉ 0975 7 97 62; Via San Maria, Teggiano; gelato €1.50, cakes from €1.50; ⏱ 8am-9pm) Tucked around the corner from the Chiesa di Santa Maria Maggiore (note the magnificent carved door), this small bar with its couple of outside tables serves the best ice cream in town, as well as drinks and cakes.

Taverna degli Antichi Sapori   ITALIAN €
(✉ 0828 77 25 00; www.tavernadegliantichisapori.it; Via Nazionale 27, Controne; meals from €12; ⏱ 12.30-3pm & 7-11pm) Easy to find on the main road through town, this bright, spacious restaurant with exposed stone walls has a small front terrace flanked by scarlet geraniums and a firmly traditional menu, which is great if you like *fagioli* (white beans). Think *gnocchi e fagioli, pasta e fagioli, lasagne e fagioli, riso* (rice) *e fagioli* and a few grilled-meat dishes.

ℹ Information

Paestum's tourist office (p183) also has some information on the Parco Nazionale del Cilento. **Alpine Rescue** (✉ 118, 338 4351474) For emergencies.

BEST ACTIVITIES IN THE REGION

•••••••••••••••••••••••••••••••••••••

Wreck diving in **Agropoli**

Hiking in the **Parco Nazionale del Cilento** (p187)

Taking a boat trip to the grottoes in **Palinuro** (p193)

Sicignano degli Alburni (☑ 0828 97 37 55; Piazza Plebiscito 13, Sicignano degli Alburni; ⊙ 9am-1.30pm & 2.30-5pm Mon-Sat) Tourist information.

Vallo della Lucania (☑ 0974 71 11 11; www. parks.it/parco.nazionale.cilento/Eindex.html; Via Polombo 16, Palazzo Mainenti, Vallo della Lucania; ⊙ 9am-1.30pm & 2.30-5pm Mon-Sat) Has a useful and fairly comprehensive website.

ℹ Getting There & Around

BUS

Curcio Viaggi (☑ 089 25 40 80; www.curcio viaggi.it) operates services to the park, and SITA (p269) has a daily service from Salerno to Castelcivita and Polla.

CAR

The park is easy to navigate by car, provided you have a detailed map.

TRAIN

It's possible to take the train from Salerno to Battipaglia, and then a bus to Polla and Padula, but services are slow and infrequent, so study timetables in advance.

Agropoli

POP 20,700

Located just south of Paestum, Agropoli is a busy summer resort but otherwise a pleasant, tranquil town that makes a good base for exploring the Cilento coastline and park. While the shell is a fairly faceless grid of shop-lined streets, the kernel, the historic city centre, is a fascinating tangle of narrow cobbled streets with ancient churches, venerable residents and a castle with superb views.

The town has been inhabited since Neolithic times, with subsequent inhabitants including the Greeks, the Romans, the Byzantines and the Saracens. In 915 Agropoli fell under the jurisdiction of the bishops and was subsequently ruled by feudal lords. It was a target of raids from North Africa in the 16th and 17th centuries, when the population dwindled to just a few hundred. Today its residents number closer to 20,000, making it the largest (and most vibrant) town along the Cilento coast.

◉ Sights & Activities

To reach the *centro storico*, head for Piazza Veneto Victoria, the pedestrian-only part of the modern town, where cafes and gelaterie are interspersed with plenty of shopping choice. Head up Corso Garibaldi and take the wide Ennio Balbo Scaloni steps until you reach the fortified *borgo* (medieval town). Follow the signs to the castle. The town is famed for its pristine, golden, sandy beaches.

Il Castello   CASTLE
(⊙ 10am-8pm) **FREE** Built by the Byzantines in the 5th century, the castle was strengthened during the Angevin period, the time of the Vespro War bloodbath. It continued to be modified, and only part of the original defensive wall remains. It's an enjoyable walk here through the historic centre, and you can wander the ramparts and enjoy magnificent views of the coastline and town.

Not just a tourist sight, the castle is utilised by the locals: there's a permanent gallery showcasing the work of contemporary artists and a small open-air auditorium where summer concerts take place.

Cilento Sub Diving Center   DIVING
(☑ 338 2374603; www.cilentosub.com; Via San Francesco 30; single dives from €35; ⛵) Indulge in your favourite watery pursuit here. Courses included snorkelling for beginners, open-water junior dives (from 12 years) and wreck diving; the latter includes the harrowing (for some) viewing of the hulks of ships, tanks and planes that were famously destroyed in the region during WWII.

Diving sites include such tantalising areas as the waters off the coast at Paestum, where – who knows? – you may just come across your very own bronze Apollo.

✕ Eating

★ **Anna**   PIZZA €
(☑ 0974 82 37 63; www.ristorantepizzeriaanna. it; Lungomare San Marco 32; pizzas/meals from €4/15; ⊙ 11am-midnight) At the city-centre end of the promenade, this has been a locals' favourite for decades. Family-run, with a small B&B upstairs, Anna is best known for its pizzas, especially since a British broadsheet

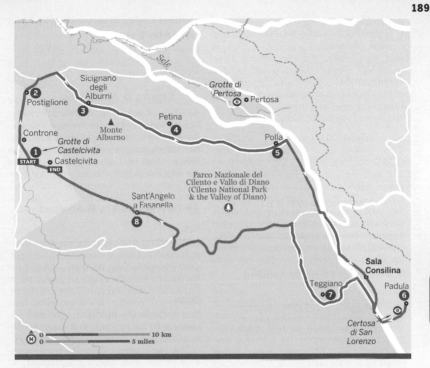

Driving Tour
A Drive in the Park

START GROTTE DI CASTELCIVITA
END CASTELCIVITA
LENGTH 112KM; THREE DAYS

Start this drive after a visit to the otherworld-ly **1 Grotte di Castelcivita** (p184). Take the SS488 through Controne, continuing north on the *strada provinciale* 60; the road passes soaring cliff faces, ancient dry stone walls and lush, arable countryside with wild cherry and fig trees. Put on the brakes at **2 Postiglione**, its medieval town centre crowned by an 11th-century Norman castle. Join the locals for a coffee in one of the Piazza Europa bars before continuing on the SS19 towards Auletta. The countryside here becomes dramatically mountainous, with a wonderful marbled rock face.

Follow signs east on the SS19 to lovely **3 Sicignano degli Alburni**, just south of the road, taking in its 14th-century castle, baroque churches and historic convent. Sicignano is also the kick-off point for the two hiking trails that ascend Monte Alburno. Stay overnight at the nearby Sicinius *agriturismo*.

Next day, continue south on *strada provinciale* 35, passing the village of **4 Petina**, dramatically straddling a high ridge. Note that this is a fairly rough road; if you prefer more reliable tarmac, head north for the SS19, which is similarly scenic and continues southeast, passing the turn-off to the fascinating Grotte di Pertosa en route.

The next stop is **5 Polla**, a strategic town during Roman times and lovely for a stroll, with its riverfront setting, 12th-century castle and brooding dark-stone houses. Pick up picnic fare here and take the SS19 south (the A3 *autovia* is faster but not as scenic), following signs for **6 Padula**, where you can spend the afternoon exploring the extraordinary Certosa di San Lorenzo. Follow the signs to stunning **7 Teggiano**, around 15km northwest, and bristling with churches and museums, as well as a cathedral and a castle.

On day three, head north until you hit the SS166. Follow the signs to **8 Sant'Angelo a Fasanella**, a 13th-century town with a Roman bridge, medieval convents and churches, and an atmospheric *centro storico*. Continue west some 18km to Castelcivita.

named Anna's *sorpresa* the best pizza in Italy in 2010, its seven-slice selection including mussels, aubergines, zucchini, marinated pork, ham, prawns and spicy sausage. More traditional seafood dishes include grilled swordfish. This is also a good place for an energy-stoking start to the day, with more than eight types of *cornetti* (croissants) to choose from, including white chocolate.

Bar Gelateria del Corso GELATERIA €
(Corso Garibaldi 22-24; cakes/ice creams from €1.50/2, cocktails from €2.50; ⌚8am-9pm) The most popular spot for slurping an ice cream, sipping a cocktail or salivating over a cream cake. Wicker chairs are positioned for people-watching on this pedestrian shopping street. There are some unusual ice-cream flavours, including *marron glacé* (candied chestnut) and *limone sicilia* (Sicilian lemon), plus yoghurt-based choices such as *frutti di bosco* (fruit of the forest).

La Brace ITALIAN €
(☎0974 82 16 05; Via A de Gasperi 60; pizzas from €3, meals €15 ; ⌚noon-2.30pm & 7-11.30pm Sat-Thu) There's no sea or historic-centre view from this simple trattoria on a bustling side street, but who cares when the food is this good? It's best for pizza or any of the seafood dishes; eat in the candy-coloured dining room or tranquil back terrace. It's popular with boisterous Italian families on weekends.

Il Gambero SEAFOOD €€
(☎0974 82 28 94; www.gambero.it; Via Lungomare San Marco 234; meals from €25; ⌚12.15-3.30pm & 7pm-midnight, closed Tue winter) Il Gambero is located across from Agropoli's long sandy beach – get here early to grab a table out front and enjoy the sun setting over Sorrento with Capri twinkling in the distance. Specialities include seafood mixed salad, pasta with clams and pumpkin, and fried mixed fish. Although there are some nonseafood dishes, the fish has star billing. Reservations recommended.

ℹ Information

Tourist Office (☎0974 82 74 71; Viale Europa 34; ⌚9.30am-2pm) Not a lot of information, but can provide a basic city map.

ℹ Getting There & Around

CSTP (☎089 48 70 01; www.cstp.it) operates regular buses from Salerno and Paestum to Agropoli. There's a **car-rental outfit** (☎0974 82 80 99; Via A De Gasperi 82; per day from €50).

Cilento Coast

While the Cilento stretch of coastline lacks the gloss and sophistication of the Amalfi Coast, it can afford to have a slight air of superiority when it comes to its beaches: a combination of secluded coves and long stretches of golden sand with a welcome lack of overpriced ice creams and sunbeds. Beyond the options outlined below, the far-southeastern stop along the coastline is **Sapri**, which has two pleasant beaches in the centre of town.

ℹ Getting There & Around

BUS

CSTP (p182) operates regular buses from Salerno and Paestum to several Cilento coastal resorts, including Santa Maria di Castellabate, San Marco di Castellabate and Acciaroli.

TRAIN

Most destinations on the Cilento coast are served by the main rail route from Naples to Reggio di Calabria. Consult Trenitalia (p268) for fares and information.

Agropoli to Castellabate

Around 14km south of Agropoli is the former fishing village of **Santa Maria di Castellabate**. Head for the southernmost point, which still has a palpable southern-Italian feel, with dusky pink-and-ochre sunbaked houses blinkered by traditional green shutters. Santa Maria's golden sandy beach stretches for around 4km, which equals plenty of towel space on the sand, even in midsummer.

Medieval Castellabate clings to the side of a mountain 280m above sea level and is one of the most endearing and historic towns on the Cilento coast. Approached from its coastal sidekick, Santa Maria de Castellabate, the summit is marked by the broad Belvedere di San Costabile, from where there are sweeping coastal views. Flanking this are the shell of a 12th-century castle, with only the defensive walls still standing, and an art gallery. The surrounding labyrinth of narrow pedestrian streets is punctuated by ancient archways, small piazzas and the occasional *palazzo* (mansion). The animated heart and soul of town is the numerological mouthful

Piazza 10 Ottobre 1123, with its panoramic views of the Valle dell'Annunziata.

San Marco di Castellabate to Acciaroli

Heading south from Castellabate, the next stop is the pretty little harbour at San Marco di Castellabate, overlooked by the handsome, ivy-clad Approdo hotel. This was once an important Greek and Roman port, and tombs and other relics have been discovered that are now on view in the museum at Paestum. The area between Santa Maria di Castellabate and San Marco is popular for diving; contact **Galatea** (☑0974 96 67 07, 334 3485643; single dives from €45). San Marco's blue-flag beach is a continuation of the sandy stretch from Santa Maria di Castellabate.

The coastal road heading south lacks the drama (views *and* traffic) of its Amalfi counterpart but is still prettily panoramic. It's an area that Ernest Hemingway apparently rated highly, particularly **Acciaroli**, which – despite the disquieting amount of surrounding concrete – has a charming centre. Head for the sea and the peeling facade of the Parrocchia di Acciaroli church, with its abstract 1920s stained-glass windows. The surrounding streets and piazzas have been tastefully restored using local stone and traditional architecture, and the cafes, bars and restaurants have a buzzing, fashionable appeal.

Pioppi to Pisciotta

A short 10km hop south of Acciaroli is tiny picturesque Pioppi, with its pristine, pale pebble beach and handful of shops and restaurants.

Next stop is **Marina di Casal Velino**, featuring a small, pretty harbour and a family-style stretch of sand, complete with plenty of ice cream opportunities, a playground and pedal boats.

Continuing southeast, **Ascea** – best known as the home of philosophers Parmenides and Zeno of Elea, as well as the famous Eleatic School of Philosophy – boasts some impressive Greek ruins. Fronted by 5km of glorious sandy beach, the town is wonderful for a dip.

Further on, lovely Pisciotta is a medieval town piled high above a ridge. Head straight for the central Piazza Raffaele Pinto, its terraced bars and benches occupied by robust elderly locals. There are a couple of excellent

MOZZARELLA DI BUFALA

A distant cousin of the North American bison (and yes, it is doubtful that cowboys ever topped their T-bone steak with a slice of mozzarella and a couple of basil leaves), the water buffalo was introduced to Italy and, in particular, Cilento by returning Crusaders in the Middle Ages. Today these herds are famed for producing distinctive milk with a far higher fat and protein content than cows' milk. This, in turn, results in that superbly soft, creamy and mildly tangy mozzarella that you taste all over the region and that bears little resemblance to the leathery, bland product you find outside Italy. The *mozzarella di bufala* here is considered to be among the best in the country.

In Cilento there are several farms producing *bufala* milk, but only one organic producer – not just in Cilento but apparently throughout Italy: **Tenuta Vannulo** (☑0828 72 47 65; www.vannulo.it; Via G Galilei 101, Capaccio Scalo; 1hr tour €4, incl lunch €20), located a 10-minute drive from Paestum. 'The mozzarella produced here is generally considered to be the best in the region,' says Franco Coppola, owner of Inn Bufalito restaurant in Sorrento, which specialises in local produce. 'The fact that it is organically produced makes all the difference to the quality and taste.'

Tenuta Vannulo makes its mozzarella exclusively from buffalo milk, unlike most producers who combine it with cows' milk. Its cheese is unpasteurised, and it also produces and serves wonderful ice cream. The farm is open to the public for tours (in English and Italian) of the production facilities, the buffalo stables and an agricultural museum. Visits culminate in that all-important tasting; lunch is an additional option. Advance reservations are essential.

You can also buy fresh mozzarella here, though be warned that demand is such that it generally runs out by early afternoon. And that's despite the considerable daily production of around 408kg, enough for several thousand *caprese* salads....

restaurants in town and one of the region's top boutique hotels. Be sure to stop by the Marina di Pisciotta, lined with seafood restaurants and cafes. Carry on to the far end of the promenade and take a look at the stones and pebbles on the beach, fabulously patterned and in all shades of mauve, grey, cream and ochre.

Sights & Activities

Velia
ARCHAEOLOGICAL SITE

(0974 97 23 96; Ascea; adult/reduced €2/1; 9am-1hr before sunset Mon-Sat) Founded by the Greeks in the mid-6th century BC, Velia subsequently became a resort popular with wealthy Romans. You can wander around the evocative ruins, including parts of the city walls, with traces of one gate and several towers, as well as the remains of thermal baths, an Ionic temple, a theatre and parts of the original Greek streets, paved in limestone blocks and with the gutters intact.

Eating

Arlecchino
SEAFOOD €

(0974 96 18 89; Via Guglielmini, Santa Maria di Castellabate; pizzas from €4, meals €20; noon-2.30pm & 7-11pm Mar-Nov;) Located across from the beach in the pretty southernmost part of Santa Maria, popular Arlecchino has picture windows overlooking the small sweep of sand. Packed to the gills at weekends, the restaurant primarily offers seafood, including a recommended *sepia alla griglia* (grilled cuttlefish). Finish with the calorific delight of local speciality *torta ricotta e pera* (ricotta and pear tart).

Il Capriccio
ITALIAN €

(0974 84 52 41; Corso da Spiafriddo, Castellabate; meals €18) On the road to Perdifumo, this is a favourite local choice. An unassuming place with a terrace, Il Capriccio has a gracious host in owner Enxo. The menu runs the gamut from seafood classics such as *zuppa di cozze* (mussel soup) and *polipetti affogati* (poached octopus) to less fishy options such as *zuppa di ceci* (chickpea soup).

The *crostata della nonna* (grandma's cake) is as promising as it sounds: a delicious confection of puff pastry, almonds and seasonal fruit.

Pizza in Piazza
PIZZA €

(320 0966325; Piazza Vittorio Emanuele, Acciaroli; pizzas from €4; Apr-Nov;) An upper-crust pizza place on a pretty piazza with magnificent rubber trees and wisteria-draped walls. Sit outside or eat on the go. The pizzas include all the standard choices but are excellent, with a crispy base and garden-fresh ingredients. The *caprese* (€7) comes particularly recommended, with its simple topping of cherry tomatoes, *mozzarella di bufala* and basil leaves.

I Tre Gufi
ITALIAN €€

(0974 97 30 42; Via Roma, Pisciotta; meals €25; noon-3pm & 7-11pm) Follow the signs from Pisciotta's sweeping Piazza Raffaele Pinto to this restaurant in a star setting, its long, wide terrace overlooking the pine-forested hillside stretching down to the sea. The menu has plenty of choice, with seafood the speciality. There's also a good choice of salads, plus pasta, *fagiolini* (green beans), risotto and specials like sea bass with porcini mushrooms and olives.

The dining room is lined with jazzy abstract paintings, and there's an adjacent cafe and gelateria (they make their own ice cream).

Cantina Belvedere
ITALIAN €€

(0974 96 70 30; www.cantinabelvedere.it; Castellabate; meals €30; noon-2.30pm & 7-11.30pm Wed-Mon) East of the castle, this restaurant clings limpetlike to the vertiginous cliff, guaranteeing uninterrupted sea views. When you're not gazing at the view, you can enjoy octopus carpaccio, peppered fillet steak or one of the plentiful pasta and pizza choices. This is a popular spot for wedding parties, so be sure to reserve ahead.

Divino
ITALIAN €€

(339 8080457; www.divinoristorantevineria.it; Piazza 10 Ottobre 1123, Castellabate; meals from €25, menus €28-35; noon-3pm & 8.30pm-1.30am) Follow the signs to La Piazzetta from the castle, via a short tunnel, and blink hard when you emerge at this movie-set marvel of a piazza with its terraced restaurants, pastel-coloured houses and stunning situation. The menu here has local favourites like *pasta e fagioli* (pasta and white beans) and grilled swordfish, plus daily well-priced menus.

Divino is fittingly traditional, right down to the chequered tablecloths. Grab the romantic table on the small terrace for the best views.

🍷 Drinking & Nightlife

Il Ciclope   CLUB

(📞 0974 93 03 18; www.ilciclope.com; Marina di Camerota) While the Cilento region may not be well known to your average tourist, it is definitely on the map when it comes to clubbing. An impressive array of big-name DJs have spun their stuff at the club, which occupies four limestone caves.

Palinuro

POP 4800

Despite being hailed as the Cilento coast's main resort, Palinuro remains relatively low-key (and low-rise), with a tangible fishing-village feel. Located in a picturesque bay sheltered by a promontory, and with superb beaches, it gets crowded with Italian holidaymakers in August. Note that the majority of hotels and restaurants are seasonal and are only open from Easter to October.

👁 Sights & Activities

Aside from the grottoes, Palinuro is famous for its beaches. For a quiet cove, head south of town to Spiaggia Marmelli, surrounded by lush banks of greenery. The beach is approached via steep steps, and there's a small car park at the top. The town's main beach is Spiaggia Palinuro, which stretches for around 4km north of the centre. Palinuro's postcard-pretty harbour has colourful fishing boats, several bars and a wide swath of sand.

The epicentre of town is Piazza Virgilio, with a modern octagonal church (which looks transplanted from Salt Lake City), and

main street Via Indipendenza, which is good for shopping and light eats.

Grotta Azzurra   GROTTO

(Palinuro) Although it doesn't have the hype of its Capri counterpart, Palinuro's Grotta Azzurra (Blue Grotto) is similarly spectacular, with a Technicolour play of light and hue. It owes its name to the extraordinary effect produced by the sunlight that filters inside from an underground passage lying at a depth of about 8m. The best time to visit is the afternoon, due to the position of the sun.

Da Alessandro   BOATING

(📞 347 6540931; www.costieradelcilento.it; trips from €15) Da Alessandro, at a kiosk at the harbour, runs trips to Palinuro's Grotta Azzurra as well as four other caves in the area.

🍴 Eating

Pasticceria Egidio   PASTRIES €

(📞 0974 93 14 60; Via Santa Maria 15; sfogliatelle €1.50; ⊗ 9am-8pm) Run by the reassuringly plump Egidio family, this *pasticceria* has a cake display backed by a large bakery where breads (including *integrale*) arrive steaming hot for picnic time. The cakes really are as good as they look: *sfogliatelle* filled with fresh ricotta, *frollini* (mini fruit and chocolate tarts) and the all-time favourite, crumbly *amaretti* (macaroons).

Bar Da Siena   GELATERIA €

(📞 0974 93 10 19; Via Indipendenza 53; ice creams from €1.50; ⊗ 8am-9pm; 🚻) Part of the Albergo Santa Caterina, this L-shaped bar (cocktails from €3) serves the best ice cream in

---

THE MEDITERRANEAN DIET

Pioppi has the right to feel smug: based on initial observations of the town in the late 1950s, American medical researcher Dr Ancel Keys launched his famous study concerning the health benefits of the Mediterranean diet. Of the residents of Pioppi, Keys famously wrote: 'The people were older and vigorous. They were walking up and down the hillside collecting wild grains, and were out fishing before sun-up and going out again in the late afternoon and rowing boats'.

Keys was struck by the low rate of heart disease among poor people here, compared to the rate among well-fed northern Europeans and Americans. He himself adopted the Mediterranean-style diet and lived to be 101 years old. Ironically, you have to be rich to eat healthy foods like a peasant these days, with virgin olive oil, fresh fish and organic fruit and vegetables generally costing far more than processed foods.

Join today's elderly Pioppi residents in their more leisurely pursuit of dozing on the shady benches in lovely Piazza de Millenario with its handy central bar. Then, suitably rested, take a healthy Med-diet picnic to the beach a few steps away.

town with *semi freddi* (semi cold) and yoghurt-based ices, as well as enticing flavours such as *ricotta e pistacchio* (ricotta and pistachio) and the possibly less appealing *zuppa inglese* (literally 'English soup': trifle). The romantic terrace is perfect for a little locked-eyes-over-ice-cream time.

★ **Ristorante Core a Core**   ITALIAN €€
(✆ 0974 93 16 91; www.coreacorepalinuro.it; Via Piano Faracchio 13; meals €30; ⊘ noon-3pm & 7-11pm) Ignore the cheesy heart-shaped sign: with its glorious garden setting and great reputation for seafood, Core a Core is your best bet in Palinuro. The *antipasti al mare* (€19.50) is superb, and there's a menu of proper kids food. Book in advance – it's popular.

Ristorante Miramare   SEAFOOD €€
(✆ 0974 93 09 70; www.miramarepalinuro.it; Corso Pisacane 89; meals from €28; ⊘ noon-3pm & 7-11.30pm) Enjoying a supreme position, with a broad terrace overlooking the turquoise sea and small adjacent sandy cove, this place is part of the same-name hotel. The menu is predominantly seafood based and holds few surprises, although there is the odd nod to the international palate, including roast beef. Otherwise, *spaghetti alla vongole* (spaghetti with clams) is a safe bet.

🍷 Drinking & Nightlife

Babylon   BAR
(✆ 0974 93 14 56; www.babylonpalinuro.it; Via Porto 47; cocktails €5; ⊘ 8am-midnight) A welcome addition to Palinuro's bar scene. The sprawling terrace with perspex furniture and palms creates a glamorous space for live music every Saturday in summer.

ℹ Information

Tourist Office (✆ 0974 93 81 44; Piazza Virgilio; ⊘ 9.30am-1.30pm & 5-7pm Mon-Sat, 9.30am-1.30pm Sun) Can provide a town map and general information.

ℹ Getting There & Away

The nearest train station is Pisciotta, from where there is regular bus service to Palinuro.

Accommodation

Best Places to Sleep

➜ Hotel San Francesco al Monte (p199), Naples

➜ Casa Mariantonia (p202), Capri

➜ Albergo il Monastero (p203), Ischia

Best Luxe Hotels

➜ Grand Hotel Vesuvio (p199), Naples

➜ Grand Hotel Excelsior Vittoria (p206), Sorrento

➜ Hotel Caruso (p211)

Best Guesthouses & B&Bs

➜ Casa D'Anna (p200), Naples

➜ Casale Giancesare (p212), Paestum

➜ Punta Civita (p211), Amalfi Coast

Where to Stay

There's no shortage of satisfying accommodation in Naples and the surrounding region. In the city itself you can sleep under frescoes in a 16th-century *palazzo* (mansion), kick back in a converted candlelit convent or share the home of local artists and intellectuals.

Finding somewhere to stay on the high-profile islands of Capri, Ischia and Procida, in the resort town of Sorrento, and in the Amalfi Coast resorts of Amalfi, Positano and Ravello can be challenging at times. Accommodation tends towards the high end of the market and is generally seasonal. Due to the sheer number of visitors, it is strongly advisable to book ahead as far as possible if you'll be staying in high season.

Agriturismi (farm-stay accommodation) are increasingly opening up inland from the Amalfi Coast and still more in the Cilento region, particularly in and around the Parco Nazionale del Cilento. This can be an option to seriously consider if you prefer to holiday away from camera-wielding tourists and stay in a rural environment, with activities such as trekking and mountain-bike riding readily accessible. Otherwise, the range of accommodation in these areas is similar to that in Naples, running the gamut from sumptuous *palazzi* to idiosyncratic B&Bs, with a sprinkling of budget *pensioni* and campgrounds.

Pricing

The following price indicators refer to the cost of a double room including private bathroom and breakfast, unless otherwise noted.

€ less than €110

€€ €110–200

€€€ more than €200

NAPLES

Centro Storico & Mercato

A World Heritage–listed jumble of hidden ruins, frescoed churches and boisterous street life, the *centro storico* (historic centre) is the city's heart and soul, and a convenient spot to slumber. Options span secret B&Bs, designer dens and converted baroque *palazzi*.

Closer to the train station, Mercato is awash with budget hotels; the options we review were clean and reliable at the time of writing, but be warned that the area is bedlam by day and dodgy by night.

★**Dimora dei Giganti** B&B €
(☑ 081 033 09 77, 338 9264453; www.dimoradeigiganti.it; Vico Giganti 55; s €40-60, d €55-80, tr €70-95, q €85-105; P ❄ 🛜; Ⓜ Piazza Cavour) Run by a warm and personable team, this urbane B&B offers four colour-coordinated bedrooms with specially commissioned sculptural lamps, ethnic-inspired furnishings and designer bathrooms. There's a modern kitchen, a cosy lounge and a charming majolica-tiled terrace. Best of all, its quiet side-street location is only steps away from the buzzing heart of the *centro storico*.

Casa Latina B&B €
(☑ 338 9264453; www.bbcasalatina.it; Vico Cinquesanti 47; s €40-55, d €55-75, tr €70-90, q €85-100; ❄ 🛜; Ⓜ Piazza Cavour) Creativity and style flow through this crisp new B&B, accented with eclectic lighting, boho photography, a fully equipped kitchen and a

tranquil terrace. All four rooms are soothing and contemporary, with original architectural detailing and fetching bathrooms with recycled terracotta basins. One upper-level room features a tatami-style bed and banquettes, the latter transforming into extra bed space (ideal for young families).

Hostel of the Sun HOSTEL €
(☑ 081 420 63 93; www.hostelnapoli.com; Via G Melisurgo 15; dm €18-22, s €30-35, d €60-80; ❄ @ 🛜; Ⓜ Municipio) HOTS is an ultrafriendly hostel near the hydrofoil and ferry terminals. Located on the 7th floor (have €0.05 for the lift), it's a bright, sociable place with multicoloured dorms, a casual in-house bar (with cheap cocktails between 8pm and 11pm) and – a few floors down – a series of hotel-standard private rooms, seven with en suite bathrooms.

Extras include laundry service for stays exceeding four days.

Port Alba Relais B&B €
(☑ 081 564 51 71; www.portalbarelais.com; Via Port'Alba 33; s/d from €72/80; ❄ @; Ⓜ Dante) Located on a street lined with booksellers, this sassy B&B has six rooms channelling an Armani vibe with their muted tones, stainless-steel detailing and mosaic showers; room 216 comes with a jacuzzi. Though windows look out onto lively Piazza Dante, double glazing keeps the noise at bay.

The foyer has soaring bookshelves lined with literature, objets d'art and vintage paraphernalia (including a 1745 edition of Dante's *The Divine Comedy*).

Belle Arti Resort B&B €
(☑ 081 557 10 62; www.belleartiresort.com; Via Santa Maria di Constantinopoli 27; s/d from €72; ❄ @; Ⓜ Dante) More boutique than B&B, this urbane hideaway combines contemporary cool with vintage touches. Four of the impeccable rooms (some as big as a small suite) come with ceiling frescoes, while all feature marble bathrooms. Languid red drapes in the corridor accentuate the airy, glammed-up vibe. Best of all, Piazza Bellini's bustling bar life is a quick walk down the street.

DiLetto a Napoli B&B €
(☑ 081 033 09 77, 338 9264453; www.dilettoanapoli.it; Vicolo Sedil Capuano 16; s €40-50, d €60-70, tr €75-85, q €85-95; ❄ 🛜; Ⓜ Piazza Cavour) In a 15th-century *palazzo*, this modern *centro storico* B&B serves up four rooms with vintage cotto floor tiles, ethnic art and

handmade furniture designed by its architect owners. Bathrooms are equally stylish, while the urbane communal lounge comes with kitchenette and dining table.

Hotel Pignatelli Napoli   HOTEL €
(☑ 081 658 49 50; www.hotelpignatellinapoli.com; Via San Giovanni Maggiore Pignatelli 16; s €40-50, d €50-70; @ 🛜; Ⓜ Università) Cheap yet tasteful, Hotel Pignatelli sits pretty in a restored 15th-century house. Rooms are decorated in a rustic Renaissance style, with wrought-iron beds and bronze wall lamps; some rooms also have original wood-beamed ceilings. Breakfasts are simple and optional, costing an additional €2.50 per guest. Best of all, owner Ciro is warm and hospitable.

Mancini Hostel   HOSTEL €
(☑ 081 553 67 31; www.hostelmancininaples.com; Via PS Mancini 33; dm €15-20, s €40-50, d €50-70, tr €60-80, s without bathroom €30-40, d without bathroom €40-50; ❄ @ 🛜; Ⓜ Garibaldi) The street might be gritty, but this safe, welcoming hostel more than compensates with its close proximity to Stazione Centrale, fantastic staff and modern communal kitchen. All four dorms (one of which is female only) are bright and clean, with updated bathrooms. Also on offer are simple, modern double and triple rooms, some with private bathroom.

Co-owner Margherita cooks up steaming pasta for guests on Saturday night, and free activities include evening walking tours on Thursday and Saturday.

Hotel Zara   HOTEL €
(☑ 081 28 71 25; www.hotelzara.it; 2nd fl, Via Firenze 81; s €39-45, d €46-62, tr €60-80, s without bathroom €30-35, d without bathroom €40-50; ❄ @ 🛜; Ⓜ Garibaldi) An easy walk from the main train station, this spotless hotel is a world away from the grungy street below. Rooms are spartan but clean, with functional modern furniture, TV and double-glazed windows. The in-house book exchange is a nice touch. Don't forget €0.05 to use the lift.

Il Golfo   D&D €
(☑ 081 554 13 98, 330 824330; bbnapolicentrale.com; Piazza Garibaldi 3; d/tr €50/66; 🛜; Ⓜ Garibaldi) This quiet, family-run bargain is ideal for those wanting to crash near Stazione Centrale. The place feels like a family apartment, its four large bedrooms – each with small private bathroom – decked out in modular furniture. The 'Capri' room comes with balcony and impressive views. There's a modern communal kitchen, and a simple

breakfast of *cornetti* (croissants) and coffee. You'll need €0.10 for the lift on weekdays.

Bella Capri Hostel & Hotel   HOSTEL €
(☑ 081 552 94 94; www.bellacapri.it; Via G Melisurgo 4; dm €18-20, s €50-60, d €70-80; ❄ @ 🛜; Ⓜ Municipio) This central, friendly spot offers hostel and hotel options on two separate floors. While the hotel rooms could use a bit more attention, all are clean. The hostel is a little funkier, with bright citrus tones, a kitchen, more beds than bunks, and a bathroom in each dorm. There is no curfew. Bring €0.05 for the lift on weekdays. Laundry service costs €7.

★ Hotel Piazza Bellini   BOUTIQUE HOTEL €€
(☑ 081 45 17 32; www.hotelpiazzabellini.com; Via Santa Maria di Costantinopoli 101; d from €100; ❄ @ 🛜; Ⓜ Dante) Only steps from buzzing Piazza Bellini, this sharp, contemporary hotel occupies a 16th-century *palazzo*, its mint white spaces spiked with original majolica tiles and the work of emerging artists. Rooms offer pared-back cool, with designer fittings, chic bathrooms and mirror frames drawn straight onto the wall. Rooms on the 5th and 6th floors feature panoramic terraces. Check the hotel website for decent discounts.

Decumani Hotel
de Charme   BOUTIQUE HOTEL €€
(☑ 081 551 81 88; www.decumani.it; Via San Giovanni Maggiore Pignatelli 15; s €99-124, d €99-164; ❄ @ 🛜; Ⓜ Università) This classic boutique hotel occupies the former *palazzo* of Cardinal Sisto Riario Sforza, the last bishop of the Bourbon kingdom. Simple, stylish rooms feature high ceilings, parquet floors, 19th-century furniture, and modern bathrooms with spacious showers. Deluxe rooms crank up the dolce vita with personal hot tubs. The pièce de résistance, however, is the property's breathtaking baroque salon.

Costantinopoli 104   BOUTIQUE HOTEL €€
(☑ 081 557 10 35; www.costantinopoli104.it; Via Santa Maria di Costantinopoli 104; s €140 170, d €160-280, ste €200-250; ❄ @ 🛜 ✖; Ⓜ Dante) A chic mix of antique furniture, contemporary art and Liberty stained glass, Costantinopoli 104 occupies a neoclassical villa in the city's bohemian heartland. Although showing a bit of wear, rooms remain understatedly elegant, comfortable and spotlessly clean – those on the 1st floor open onto a terrace, while ground-floor rooms face the small pool. Rooms in the annexe are less desirable.

Caravaggio Hotel
HOTEL €€

(☎ 081 211 00 66; www.caravaggiohotel.it; Piazza Riario Sforza 157; s/d from €80/120; ❄ @ ☎; 🚊 CS5 to Via Duomo, Ⓜ Duomo) Bold abstract paintings face stone arches, yellow sofas line 300-year-old brick walls and original wood-beamed ceilings cap the comfortable bedrooms at Caravaggio. A few rooms come with a hot tub. Wi-fi is free in the communal ground-floor areas.

Toledo & Quartieri Spagnoli

Via Toledo is Naples' main retail strip and a favourite spot for strolling. Directly to the west, the earthy Quartieri Spagnoli (whose reputation for crime is exaggerated) offers an atmospheric mix of razor-thin laneways, lively trattorias and cosy slumber spots spanning homey hotels to a cosy rooftop B&B.

Nardones 48
APARTMENT €

(☎ 338 8818998; www.nardones48.it; Via Nardones 48; small apt €60-72, large apt €80-120; ❄ ☎; 🚊 R2 to Via San Carlo) White-on-white Nardones 48 serves up seven smart mini-apartments in a historic Quartieri Spagnoli building. The five largest apartments, each with mezzanine bedroom, accommodate up to four; the two smallest, each with sofa bed, accommodate up to two. Three apartments boast a panoramic terrace, and all have modern kitchenette, flat-screen TV and contemporary bathroom with spacious shower.

Stays of one week or longer enjoy discounted rates and complimentary laundry service, and the apartment offers nearby parking (€20 per 24 hours).

La Concordia B&B
B&B €

(☎ 081 41 23 49, 338 5040335; www.laconcordia.it; Piazzetta Concordia 5; s/d/tr €50/80/90; ❄ ☎; 🚊 Centrale to Corso Vittorio Emanuele) Your host at this personable B&B is retired literature professor Anna Grappone, whose charming abode features ethnic artefacts, antique furniture, and the work of her artist friends.

All three guestrooms are clean and comfy, and the double room is air-conditioned. The communal lounge is replete with books and a rocking chair. Payment is by cash or PayPal. Three-night minimum stay.

Hotel Toledo
HOTEL €

(☎ 081 40 68 00; www.hoteltoledo.com; Via Montecalvario 15; s/d from €45/85; ❄ @ ☎; Ⓜ Toledo) Snugly situated in an old three-storey building, Hotel Toledo offers comfy, smallish rooms with terracotta tiles and mod cons; the rooms are a little on the dark side, however. Suites come with a stovetop, and breakfast is served on the rooftop terrace when the weather warms up.

Sui Tetti di Napoli
B&B €

(☎ 081 033 09 77, 338 9264453; www.suitettidinapoli.net; Vico Figuerelle a Montecalvario 6; s €35-60, d €45-80, tr €60-95, q €80-105; ❄ ☎; Ⓜ Toledo) A block away from Via Toledo, this well-priced B&B is more like four apartments atop a thigh-toning stairwell. While two apartments share a small terrace, the rooftop option boasts its own, complete with mesmerising views. All apartments include a kitchenette (the cheapest two share a kitchen), simple-yet-funky furnishings and a homey vibe.

★ La Ciliegina Lifestyle Hotel
BOUTIQUE HOTEL €€

(☎ 081 1971 8800; www.cilieginahotel.it; Via PE Imbriani 30; d €150-250, junior ste €200-350; ❄ @ ☎; Ⓜ Municipio) An easy walk from the hydrofoil terminal, this chic, contemporary slumber spot is a hit with fashion-conscious urbanites. Spacious white rooms are splashed with blue and red accents, each with top-of-the-range Hästens bed, flat-screen TV and marble-clad bathroom with water-jet jacuzzi shower (one junior suite has a jacuzzi tub). Breakfast in bed, or on the rooftop terrace, which comes with sunbeds, hot tub and a view of Vesuvius. Complimentary iPad use is a nice touch.

Hotel Il Convento
HOTEL €€

(☎ 081 40 39 77; www.hotelilconvento.com; Via Speranzella 137a; s €50-93, d €65-140; ❄ ☎; Ⓜ Municipio) This lovely hotel in the Quartieri Spagnoli is a soothing blend of antique Tuscan furniture, well-stocked bookshelves and candlelit stairs. Rooms are cosy and elegant, combining creamy tones and dark woods with patches of 16th-century brickwork. For €80 to €180 you get a room with a private roof garden. It's wheelchair accessible.

Santa Lucia & Chiaia

With lavish seaside hotels, Santa Lucia is where presidents and pop stars say goodnight. However, there are still affordable options, some with stunning bay vistas. As a rule, rooms with water views cost a little more. Neighbouring Chiaia is *the* place for designer shopping and bar-hopping, so accommodation is chic rather than cheap, though a funky B&B is keeping it real.

B&B Cappella Vecchia B&B €
(☑ 081 240 51 17; www.cappellavecchia11.it; Vico Santa Maria a Cappella Vecchia 11; s €50-80, d €75-110, tr €90-140, 🖪 🕾 🛜; 🖫 C24 to Piazza dei Martiri) Run by a superhelpful young couple, this B&B is a first-rate choice in the smart, fashionable Chiaia district. Rooms are simple and upbeat, with funky bathrooms, vibrant colours, and Neapolitan themes. There's a spacious communal area for breakfast, and free internet available 24/7. Check the website for special offers.

Chiaja Hotel de Charme BOUTIQUE HOTEL €€
(☑ 081 41 55 55; www.hotelchiaia.it; Via Chiaia 216; s/d from €85/95; 🖫 @ 🛜; 🖫 R2 to Via San Carlo) This renovated marquis' residence is a soothing blend of gilt-framed portraits, restored original furnishings and elegantly draped curtains. Each room is unique, and those facing boutique-flanked Via Chiaia come with a bubbling hot tub. The breakfast buffet showcases Campanian produce. It's worth checking the website for the occasional special offer.

★ Grand Hotel Vesuvio HOTEL €€€
(☑ 081 764 00 44; www.vesuvio.it; Via Partenope 45; s/d €280/310; 🖫 @ 🛜; 🖫 128 to Via Santa Lucia) Known for hosting legends (past guests include Rita Hayworth and Humphrey Bogart) this five-star heavyweight is a decadent mélange of dripping chandeliers, period antiques and opulent rooms. Count your lucky stars while drinking a martini at the rooftop restaurant.

Hotel Excelsior HOTEL €€€
(☑ 081 764 01 11; www.excelsior.it; Via Partenope 48; d €335; 🖫 @ 🛜; 🖫 128 to Via Santa Lucia) Facing yacht-packed Borgo Marinaro, the Excelsior sets the scene for your own *Pretty Woman* moment – think marble columns, dark limousines and apartment-sized fin de siècle rooms. Jaw-dropping water views provide a suitable love-scene backdrop.

Vomero

Middle-class Vomero feels a world apart from the seething sprawl below. It's not exactly bursting with sights, but the views are divine, the streets are leafy and that heady Neapolitan chaos is a funicular ride away.

Casa Tolentino B&B €
(☑ 081 1992 9121, 340 3921011; www.casatolentino.it; Gradini S Nicola da Tolentino 12; s €35-60, d €55-90, tr €70-195; 🛜; 🖫 Centrale to Corso Vittorio Emanuele) Run by a team of young, civic-minded Neapolitans, Casa Tolentino occupies part of a 16th-century monastery, complete with terraced gardens, swoon-inducing views and a soccer field. Rooms are simple and modern, with flat-screen TVs and sparkling blue bathrooms; eight come with bay views, the others face a verdant hillside. Plans include an organic produce garden, an eatery and an exhibition space.

★ Hotel San Francesco al Monte HOTEL €€€
(☑ 081 423 91 11; www.hotelsanfrancesco.it; Corso Vittorio Emanuele I 328; s/d from €135/170; 🅿 🖫 @ 🛜 🏊; 🖫 Centrale to Corso Vittorio Emanuele I) Occupying a 16th-century monastery, this hotel is magnificent. The monks' cells have become classically elegant rooms, the ancient cloisters house an open-air bar, and the barrel-vaulted corridors are lined with contemporary art from the likes of Robert Rauschenberg and Hermann Nitsch. Capping it all is a lofty outdoor swimming pool with views of Capri and Vesuvius.

Grand Hotel Parker's HOTEL €€€
(☑ 081 761 24 74; www.grandhotelparkers.com; Corso Vittorio Emanuele I 35; s/d from €215/250; 🅿 🖫 @ 🛜; 🖫 128, C16 to Corso Vittorio Emanuele I) Darling of the Grand Tour set, this stately pile once hosted the likes of Virginia Woolf and Robert Louis Stevenson. Today Prada-clad guests lounge on Louis XVI armchairs, take *aperitivo* (apéritifs) on the seaview terrace and nibble by candlelight at the George restaurant. The spa retreat is one of the city's best. Check the website for decent deals on room rates.

Capodimonte & La Sanità

While you'll find few slumber options in Capodimonte, there's a growing number of atmospheric, idiosyncratic spots to sleep in La Sanità. Wedged between Capodimonte

ONLINE RESOURCES

Airbnb (www.airbnb.com) Offers shared and private rooms, as well as apartments in Naples, the Bay of Naples islands, the Amalfi Coast and beyond.

Agriturismo.it (www.agriturismo.it) Offers a wide range of *agriturismi* (farmstay accommodation) options with descriptions, reservation details and general information.

Porta Napoli (www.hotel.portanapoli. com) Has a comprehensive list of rental apartments, B&Bs and hotels in Naples, the Bay of Naples, the Amalfi Coast and the Cilento region.

Sorrento Tourism (www.sorrentotourism. com) Includes basic lists of hotels and hostels, B&Bs, apartments and villas, as well as *agriturismi* and campgrounds on the Sorrento Peninsula.

and the *centro storico,* La Sanità is pure old-school Naples, with earthy street life, market stalls, ancient catacombs and some rather famous baroque staircases.

Cerasiello B&B B&B **€**
(☑ 081 033 09 77, 338 9264453; www.cerasiello. it; Via Supportico Lopez 20; s €40-60, d €55-80, tr €70-95, q €85-105; ✶ 🛜 ; Ⓜ Piazza Cavour, Museo) This gorgeous B&B consists of four rooms with private bathroom, an enchanting communal terrace and an ethno-chic look melding Neapolitan art with North African furnishings. The stylish kitchen offers a fabulous view of the Certosa di San Martino, a view shared by all rooms (or their bathroom) except Fuoco (Fire), which looks out at a beautiful church cupola.

Although technically in the Sanità district, the B&B is a short walk from Naples' *centro storico.* Bring €0.20 for the lift.

Casa del Monacone B&B **€**
(☑ 081 744 37 14 , 338 9148012; www.catacombedi-napoli.it/casaDelMonacone.asp; Via Sanità 124; s/d/tr €40/60/80; ✶ @ 🛜 ; 🚌 C51 to Piazza Sanità, Ⓜ Piazza Cavour, Museo) Set in a monastery beside the Basilica Santa Maria della Sanità, this artful B&B is run by 'La Paranza', the inspiring young co-op behind the restoration of the Catacombe di San Gennaro. Complete with communal kitchen, lounge, colourful tiled terrace, and artwork by the prolific

Riccardo Dalisi, the biggest of its six bright rooms comes with its own kitchenette.

Well-sealed windows block out the noisy traffic, and the junior suite costs the same as a standard – so feel free to request one.

La Controra HOSTEL **€**
(☑ 081 549 40 14; www.lacontrora.com; Piazzetta Trinità alla Cesarea 231; dm €15-25, d €50-64; ✶ @ 🛜 ; Ⓜ Salvator Rosa) Recently renovated, this new-school hostel cranks up the cool factor with its stainless-steel lamps, sleek bar, blonde-wood bunks, brightly coloured bathrooms and communal kitchen that's just a little Jamie Oliver. Snooze in the tranquil courtyard, also used for alfresco film screenings (the popcorn is free!). Other freebies include food with any cocktail purchase during happy hour.

★ Casa D'Anna GUESTHOUSE **€€**
(☑ 081 44 66 11; www.casadanna.it; Via dei Cristallini 138; s €84-109, d €120-155; ✶ 🛜 ; Ⓜ Piazza Cavour, Museo) Everyone from artists to Parisian fashionistas adores this elegant guesthouse, lavished with antiques, books and original artwork. Its four guest rooms blend classic and contemporary design features of the highest quality, while the lush communal terrace is perfect for an alfresco tête-à-tête. Breakfast includes homemade baked treats and jams. There's a two-night minimum... though we doubt you'll be hurrying to leave.

Mergellina & Posillipo

With Liberty *palazzi,* anchored yachts and a buzzing seafront scene, Mergellina is well connected to the centre and handy for an early-morning hydrofoil out to the islands.

Hotel Ausonia HOTEL **€€**
(☑ 081 68 22 78; www.hotelausonianapoli.com; Via Francesco Caracciolo 11; s/d/tr €80/100/120; ✶ ; Ⓜ Mergellina) This modest and friendly hotel sits opposite the Mergellina marina, a fact not played down in the decor – think portholes, barometers, and bedheads in the shape of ships' steering wheels. Twee? Sure, but the rooms are clean and comfortable, and the few facing the sea won't cost extra.

THE ISLANDS

Capri

This island is all about lemon trees, pavement cafes, sultry summer evenings and wearing the largest pair of shades you can get your hands on. In other words, accommodation is strictly seasonal, which means bed space is tight and, in general, costly.

Capri Town

★ Hotel La Tosca
PENSION €€

(☎ 081 837 09 89; www.latoscahotel.com; Via Dalmazio Birago 5; s €50-100, d €75-160; ☺ Apr-Oct; ﹟ ⸙) Away from the glitz of the town centre, this charming one-star place is hidden down a quiet back lane overlooking the Certosa di San Giacomo. Rooms are airy and comfortable, with pine furniture, light tiles, striped fabrics and large bathrooms. Several also have private terraces or garden vistas. Breakfast is served on the terrace, with a view of the sea.

★ Hotel Gatto Bianco
HOTEL €€

(☎ 081 837 51 43; www.gattobianco-capri.com; Via Vittoria Emanuele III 32; s €100-170, d €150-230; ☺ Apr-Nov; ﹟ @ ⸙) This gracious hotel dates from 1953 and boasts leafy courtyards and terraces and a fluffy white cat – presumably from a long lineage. The light-filled rooms are decorated in traditional style with stunning blue-and-yellow majolica tiling, a tasteful colour scheme and verdant views.

The hotel is classily placed for your mid-morning coffee, a few minutes' walk from La Piazzetta (Piazza Umberto I). It also runs discount deals with the downstairs Dephina health and beauty salon.

Hotel Esperia
HOTEL €€

(☎ 081 837 02 62; www.esperiacapri.eu; Via Sopramonte 41; €140-190; ☺ Apr-Oct; ﹟ ⸙) The peeling facade, handsome columns and giant urns lend an air of faded elegance to this 19th-century villa. A short uphill walk from the centre of town, the Esperia has large, airy rooms with modern furniture and a floral theme. The best (and priciest) have good-size balconies with sea views. Breakfast, including homemade cakes, is served on a communal terrace.

Hotel Villa Krupp
HOTEL €€

(☎ 081 837 03 62; www.villakrupp.com; Viale Matteotti 12; s €120, d €150-200; ☺ Apr-Oct; P ﹟ ⸙) Housed in the former residence of Russian author Maxim Gorky, this historic hotel oozes old-school charm, with floral tiling, fading antiques and heavy bedsteads. It also commands some fabulous views over the Giardini di Augusto and beyond to the Isole di Faraglioni. If your room doesn't have the view (which costs extra), simply adjourn to the delightful terrace outside reception.

Hotel Villa Sarah
HOTEL €€€

(☎ 081 837 78 17; www.villasarah.it; Via Tiberio 3; s €160-180, d €195-310, tr €265-320, q €295-330; ☺ Easter-Oct; ﹟ ⸙) On the road up to Villa Jovis, a 10-minute walk from the centre of Capri Town, Villa Sarah retains a rustic appeal that so many of the island's hotels have long lost. Surrounded by its own fruit-producing gardens and with a small pool, it has 20 airy rooms, all decorated in local style with ceramic tiles and old-fashioned furniture. The healthy breakfast includes organic produce – and a sea view.

Grand Hotel Quisisana
HOTEL €€€

(☎ 081 837 07 88; www.quisi.com; Via Camerelle 2; r/ste from €330/850; ☺ Easter-Oct; ﹟ ⸙ ⸙) Boasting a five-star luxury rating, the Quisisana is Capri's most prestigious address and just few espadrille-clad steps from La Piazzetta (Piazza Umberto I). A hotel since the 19th century, it's a bastion of unapologetic opulence, with two swimming pools, a fitness centre and spa, restaurants, bars and subtropical gardens. Rooms are suitably palatial, with cool colours and classy furniture.

AGRITURISMI (FARM STAYS)

Live out your bucolic fantasies at one of Italy's growing number of *agriturismi* (farm-stay accommodation). While all are required to grow at least one of the products they serve, options range from rustic country houses with a handful of olive trees to elegant country estates with sparkling pools to fully functioning farms where guests can pitch in.

Agriturismi can be an especially good choice if you're travelling with kids, as they may be able to help with feeding and tending to farm animals.

To find lists of *agriturismi*, ask at any tourist office or check online at one of these sites:

www.agritour.net

www.agriturismo.com

www.agriturismo.it

www.agriturismo.net

www.agriturismo-italia.net

www.agriturismovero.com

www.agriturist.com

Anacapri

★ Casa Mariantonia   BOUTIQUE HOTEL €€

(☑ 081 837 29 23; www.casamariantonia.com; Via Giuseppe Orlandi 80; d €120-280; ☺ Apr-Oct; ⓟ❋⛄❄) This fabulous boutique retreat counts Jean-Paul Sartre and Alberto Moravia among its past guests, which may well give you something to muse over while you are enjoying the tranquil beauty of the surroundings. Rooms deliver restrained elegance in soothing tones and there are private terraces with garden views. The in-house restaurant is set in a lemon grove.

★ Hotel Villa Eva   HOTEL €€

(☑ 081 837 15 49; www.villaeva.com; Via La Fabbrica 8; d €110-180, tr €160-210, apt per person €55-70; ☺ Easter-Oct; ❋@❄⛄) Nestled amid fruit and olive trees in the countryside near Anacapri, Villa Eva is an idyllic retreat, complete with swimming pool, lush gardens and sunny rooms and apartments. Whitewashed domes, terracotta floors, stained-glass windows and vintage fireplaces add character, while the location ensures peace and quiet.

The only drawback is that it's tricky to get to: take the Grotta Azzurra bus from Anacapri and ask the driver where to get off, or cough up for a taxi.

Hotel Bellavista   HOTEL €€

(☑ 081 837 14 63; www.bellavistacapri.com; Via Giuseppe Orlandi 10; s €90-160, d €130-240; ☺ Apr-Oct; ❋@❄) This hotel is more than 100 years old, so it's a grande dame among accommodation here. Rooms are large and have 1960s-style tile floors with enormous flower motifs that you will love (or loathe). It's conveniently positioned near the entrance to Anacapri and has a tennis court, a restaurant with beautiful views, and discounted access to a nearby swimming pool.

There is a minimum four-day stay in July and August.

Hotel Alla Bussola di Hermes   HOTEL €€

(☑ 081 838 20 10; www.bussolahermes.com; Traversa La Vigna 14; s €60-140, d €60-150, tr €90-180, q €120-280; ❋@❄) The sun-filled guestrooms have luxurious drapes, majolica tiles and a cheery blue-and-white colour scheme, while the public spaces have a whiff of Pompeii, with columns, statues and vaulted ceilings. Snag a room with a sea-view terrace, if you can. To get here take the bus up to Piazza Vittoria and call for the hotel shuttle service.

Hotel Carmencita   HOTEL €€

(☑ 081 837 13 60; www.carmencitacapri.com; Via de Tommaso 4; €129-168; ☺ mid-Mar–mid-Nov; ❋@❄⛄) Near the town bus station, the Carmencita is run by a delightful couple who will collect you from the ferry at Marina Grande if you phone ahead. The atmosphere is homey and old fashioned and the rooms are bright – think floral bedspreads and majolica ceramic tiling – big and comfortable. Small terraces overlook the pool and pretty garden.

Hotel Senaria   HOTEL €€

(☑ 081 837 32 22; www.senaria.it; Via Follicara 6; d €100-180; ☺ Apr-Nov; ❋❄) It's quite a trek to this delightful family-run hotel in Anacapri's original town centre, but it's worth the effort. In a whitewashed villa, rooms are decorated in an elegant, Mediterranean style with terracotta tiles and cooling cream tones. It's a very quiet spot and, except for Sunday-morning church bells, you're unlikely to be disturbed by anything other than the breeze.

Capri Palace   HOTEL €€€

(☑ 081 978 01 11; www.capripalace.com; Via Capodimonte 2b; d/ste from €500/1000; ☺ Apr-Oct; ❋❄⛄) A VIP favourite (Gwyneth Paltrow, Liz Hurley and Naomi Campbell have all languished here), the superslick Capri Palace is the hotel of the moment. Its stylish Mediterranean interior is enlivened with eye-catching contemporary art and its guestrooms are never less than lavish – some even have their own terraced garden and private plunge pool.

For stressed guests, the health spa is said to be the island's best. Note that there's a three-night minimum stay in high season.

Marina Grande

Belvedere e Tre Re   HOTEL €€

(☑ 081 837 03 45; www.belvedere-tre-re.com; Via Marina Grande 264; d €150; ☺ Apr-Nov; ❋❄) A five-minute walk from the port and with superb boat-spotting views, this hotel dates from 1900: the 'tre re' in the name refers to the three kings who stayed here in its Grand Tour heyday. A fairly modest two-star today, rooms have been pleasantly modernised and have private covered balconies. There's a sun-bronzing terrace on the top floor.

Relais Maresca   HOTEL €€€

(☑ 081 837 96 19; www.relaismaresca.com; Via Marina Grande 284; d €190-300; ☺ Mar-Nov; ❋❄)

A delightful four-star hotel, this is the top choice in town. The look is classic Capri, with acres of gleaming ceramic in turquoise, blue and yellow, and stylish furniture. There is a range of rooms (with corresponding prices) – the best have balconies and sea views. There's also a lovely flower-filled 4th-floor terrace. Minimum two-day stay at weekends; four-day minimum in August.

Ischia

Like those of its classy little sister, Procida, most of Ischia's hotels close in winter and prices drop considerably at those that stay open. In addition to the hotels we review, there are the spa hotels, most of which only take half- or full-board bookings; the tourist office can supply you with a list. Ischia is the largest island of the trio of Capri, Ischia and Procida, so an overnight stay here to take in the sights makes good sense.

Ischia Porto & Ischia Ponte

Hotel Noris　　　　　　　　　　HOTEL €
(📞 081 99 13 87; www.norishotel.it; Via A Sogliuzzo 2, Ischia Ponte; d €50-85; ⊙ Easter-Oct; ✳🛜) This place has a great price and a great position within easy strolling distance of the Ponte sights. The comfy, decent-size rooms have small balconies and are decked out in fresh colours. Breakfast is the standard, albeit slightly more expansive, continental buffet. Bonus points are due for the special parking deal with the public car park across the way.

★Albergo il Monastero　　　　HOTEL €€
(📞 081 99 24 35; www.albergoilmonastero.it; Castello Aragonese, Rocca del Castello, Ischia Ponte; s €90, d €135-190; ⊙ Easter-Oct; ✳) The former monks' cells still have a certain appealing sobriety about them, featuring dark-wood furniture, white walls, vintage terracotta tiles and no TV (don't worry – the views are sufficiently prime time). Elsewhere there is a pleasing sense of space and style, with vaulted ceilings, chic plush sofas and antiques. The hotel restaurant has an excellent reputation. Bold contemporary art by the late owner and artist Gabriele Mattera adorns the walls.

★Il Moresco　　　　　　　　　HOTEL €€€
(📞 081 98 13 55; www.ilmoresco.it; Via E Gianturco 16, Ischia Porto; d from €340; ⊙ Easter-Oct; 🅿✳🛜) Located in the beating heart of Is-

chia Porto, yet with tall pines and greenery giving a secluded feel, Il Moresco is a truly gorgeous spa hotel, with a Moorish-meets-Med aesthetic. Rooms are wonderfully comfortable, featuring tiled floors and a comfortably old-fashioned vibe. Pampering spa treatments are offered, including wine therapy, where you bathe in water enriched with plant extracts.

Lacco Ameno

Hotel La Sirenella　　　　　　HOTEL €€
(📞 081 99 47 43; www.lasirenella.net; Corso Angelo Rizzoli 41, Lacco Ameno; d €140-180; ⊙ Apr-Oct; ✳🛜) This is a family-owned beachside hotel where you can practically roll out of bed onto the sand. Rooms are bright, with a dazzling blue and lemon-yellow motif and seafront terraces. Sparkling tiled bathrooms and a breezy fun-in-the-sun vibe add to the appeal, as does the downstairs restaurant with its good pizzas.

★Mezzatorre Resort & Spa　　HOTEL €€€
(📞 081 98 61 11; www.mezzatorre.it; Via Mezzatorre 23, Lacco Ameno; d €350-480, ste €490-670; ⊙ mid-Apr–Oct; 🅿✳@🛜🏊) Perched on a bluff above the sea, this luxurious resort is surrounded by a 2.8-hectare pine wood, with sitting rooms and some guest rooms located in a 15th-century defensive tower. An in-house spa centre and tennis courts crank up the luxe factor. Rooms are in sophisticated shades of taupe, peach and ochre, some with private garden and hot tub. Check out the infinity pool above the beach. If you can't afford to stay, just have a long, slow drink in the adjacent bar.

Forio & the West Coast

★Hotel Semiramis　　　　　　HOTEL €€
(📞 081 90 75 11; www.hotelsemiramisischia.it; Spiaggia di Citara, Forio; d €140-180; ⊙ late Apr-Oct; 🅿✳🛜🏊) A few minutes' walk from the Poseidon spa complex, this bright hotel has a tropical-oasis feel with its central pool surrounded by lofty palms. Rooms are large and beautifully tiled in the traditional yellow-and-turquoise pattern, and the garden is glorious, featuring fig trees, vineyards and distant sea views.

Umberto a Mare　　　　　　　HOTEL €€
(📞 081 99 71 71; www.umbertoamare.it; Via Soccorso 2, Forio; d €100-120; ⊙ Apr-Oct; ✳🛜) Easy to find, right next to Forio's emblematic

mission-style church, these 11 quiet rooms ooze understated chic with cool terracotta tiles, modern bathrooms and traditional green shutters. Head out to a sunbed on the terrace with its holiday-brochure-style sea views. You won't have to stray far to eat well: the hotel is tucked under one of Ischia's finest restaurants.

Sant'Angelo & the South Coast

Camping Mirage   CAMPGROUND €
(☑081 99 05 51; www.campingmirage.it; Via Maronti 37, Spiaggia dei Maronti, Barano d'Ischia; camping per 2 people, car & tent €45; ⊘ Easter-Oct; ℗) Located on Spiagga dei Maronti, one of Ischia's best beaches, and within walking distance of Sant'Angelo, this shady campground offers 50 places, showers, laundry facilities, a bar and a restaurant dishing up local special *tubettoni, cozze e pecorino* (pasta with mussels and sheep cheese).

Hotel Casa Celestino   HOTEL €€
(☑081 99 92 13; www.casacelestino.it; Via Chiaia di Rose 20, Sant'Angelo; d €150-230; ⊘ Jan-Oct; ✳@�🖤) Hugging the headland, this chic little number is a soothing blend of creamy furnishings, whitewashed walls, contemporary art and bold paintwork. The uncluttered bedrooms sport majolica-tiled floors, modern bathrooms and enviable balconies overlooking the sea. There's a good, unfussy restaurant across the way.

Procida

The island returns to the locals after the day trippers have gone and takes on a palpable and tranquil Med-island feel. Fittingly, accommodation tends to be of the small-scale variety: B&Bs and family-run hotels. Many places close over winter and are booked out in August, so check ahead during these periods.

Marina Grande

Bed & Breakfast La Terrazza   B&B €
(☑081 896 00 62; Via Faro 26, Marina Grande; s €50-70, d €75-90; ⊘ Easter-Oct) An extremely attractive budget option, where the rooms are decked out with paintings, metal lamps, tiles and antiques. Take time out on the terracotta-floored terrace – thus the B&B's name – where you can lie back on a lounger and enjoy the sunset. Homemade breakfasts are served up here.

Marina Corricella

⭐**Hotel La Vigna**   BOUTIQUE HOTEL €€
(☑081 896 04 69; www.albergolavigna.it; Via Principessa Margherita 46, Terra Murata; d €150-180, ste €180-230; ⊘ Easter-Oct; ✳@🖤) Enjoying a fabulous cliffside location with a delightful garden and in-house spa, this 18th-century villa is a delight. Five of the spacious, simply furnished rooms offer direct access to the garden. Superior rooms (€180 to €200) feature family-friendly mezzanines, while the main perk of the suite is the bedside hot tub: perfect for romancing couples.

⭐**Casa Sul Mare**   HOTEL €€
(☑081 896 87 99; www.lacasasulmare.it; Salita Castello 13, Marina Corricella; r €125-170; ⊘ Easter-Oct; ✳🖤) A fabulous place with the kind of evocative views that helped make *The Talented Mr Ripley* such a memorable film. Overlooking the picturesque Marina Corricella, near the ruined Castello d'Avalos, the rooms are elegant, with exquisite tiled floors, wrought-iron bedsteads and a warm Mediterranean colour scheme.

The hotel treats its guests well: during summer there's a boat service to the nearest beaches, and the morning cappuccino, courtesy of Franco, may be the best you've ever had.

Casa Giovanni da Procida   B&B €€
(☑081 896 03 58; www.casagiovannidaprocida. it; Via Giovanni da Procida 3, Marina Corricella; d €110-170; ⊘ Easter-Oct; ℗✳🖤) This chic converted-farmhouse B&B features split-level, minimalist rooms with low-rise beds and contemporary furniture. Bathrooms are small but slick, with mosaic tiling, cube basins, huge showerheads and the occasional vaulted ceiling. In the lush garden, chilled-out guests read and eat peaches under the giant magnolia tree.

Hotel La Corricella   HOTEL €€
(☑081 896 75 75; www.hotelcorricella.it; Via Marina Corricella 88, Marina Corricella; d €100-140; ⊘Apr-Oct; 🖤) It's hard to miss the peach-and-yellow candy-cane colour scheme of this place, which bookends Marina Corricella. Low-fuss rooms with fan and TV feature modular-style furniture. The large shared terrace boasts top-notch harbour views, the restaurant serves decent seafood and a boat service will take you to the nearby beach.

Marina di Chiaiolella

Hotel Crescenzo
HOTEL €€

(☑ 081 896 72 55; www.hotelcrescenzo.it; Via Marina di Chiaiolella 33, Marina di Chiaiolella; d €120; ⊘ Easter-Oct; ❄) The Crescenzo has just 10 smallish rooms; choose between a bay window and a balcony with sea view. The decor is a suitably nautical blue and white, with sparkling-clean bathrooms. The hotel is fronted by a restaurant that's generally bursting with an affable local crowd, and you can enjoy breakfast here after a long lie-in: unusually, it's served until noon.

Check the website for good deals on longer stays.

THE AMALFI COAST

Sorrento

Accommodation is thick on the ground in this town, although if you're arriving in high summer (July and August), you'll need to book ahead. Most of the big city-centre hotels are geared towards package tourism and prices are correspondingly high. There are, however, some excellent choices, particularly on Via Capo, the coastal road west of the centre. This area is within walking distance of the city centre, but if you're carrying luggage it's easier to catch a SITA bus for Sant'Agata or Massa Lubrense.

★ Ulisse
HOSTEL €

(☑ 081 877 47 53; www.ulissedeluxe.com; Via del Mare 22; dm €30, d €60-120; P❄☎) Although it calls itself a hostel, the Ulisse is about as far from a backpackers' pad as a hiking boot from a stiletto. Most rooms are plush, spacious affairs with swish if rather bland fabrics, gleaming floors and large en-suite bathrooms. There are two single-sex dorms, and quads for sharers. Breakfast is included in some rates but costs €10 with others.

Facilities include an adjacent Wellness Centre where guests can use the pool for just €5 and enjoy free fitness sessions and reasonably priced treatments.

Casa Astarita
B&B €

(☑ 081 877 49 06; www.casastarita.com; Corso Italia 67; d €90-130, tr €110-150; ❄☎) Housed in a 16th-century *palazzo* on Sorrento's main strip, this charming B&B has a colourful, eclectic look with original vaulted ceilings, brightly painted doors and majolica-tiled floors. Its six simple but well-equipped rooms surround a central parlour, where breakfast is served on a large rustic table.

Hotel Desiré
HOTEL €

(☑ 081 878 15 63; www.desireehotelsorrento.com; Via Capo 31b; s/d €64/87; ⊘ Mar-Dec; P❄) One of a cluster of hotels along Via Capo, the Desiré is a top budget choice. It's not so much the simple, sunny rooms (although they're fine) or the facilities (a TV lounge and panoramic roof terrace) as the relaxed atmosphere, friendly owner and beautiful views.

The lift down to the rocky beach below is a further plus, even if you still have to pay for the umbrellas and deck chairs.

Seven Hostel
HOSTEL €

(☑ 081 878 67 58; www.sevenhostel.com; Via lommella Grande 99, Sant'Agnello; dm/d from €15/50; ⊘ year-round; ❄@☎) The ethos of the owners here is to offer the best hostel in the world, and the first *ostello di design*. Located in an 8th-century former convent surrounded by olive and lemon trees, the hostel has chic rooftop terraces with decking and loungers, weekend live music and the more down-to-earth perk of an on-site laundry. Rooms are contemporary and spacious.

Nube d'Argento
CAMPGROUND €

(☑ 081 878 13 44; www.nubedargento.com; Via Capo 21; camping per 2 people, car & tent €38, 2-person bungalows €60-85, 4-person bungalows €90-120; ⊘ Mar-Dec; @❄) This inviting campground is an easy 1km drive west of

ACCOMMODATION SORRENTO

WHERE TO STAY ON THE AMALFI COAST

If you are planning to explore beyond the coast, Sorrento has the best transport connections and is a good base. Positano, Amalfi and Ravello feature some of the classiest accommodation in Italy, ranging from sumptuous *palazzi* to exquisite B&Bs. Book ahead in summer and remember that most hotels close over the winter.

While Salerno doesn't have a great choice of accommodation, the Cilento coast and park have a diverse range of places to lay your head. You'll find mountaintop hostels, discreet *palazzi*, breezy beachfront hotels and ecofriendly *agriturismi* here, with prices considerably lower than those on the Amalfi Coast.

the Sorrento city centre. Pitches and wooden chalet-style bungalows are spread out beneath a canopy of olive trees – a source of much-needed summer shade – and the facilities are excellent. Kids in particular will enjoy the open-air swimming pool, table-tennis table, slides and swings.

Hotel Rivage
HOTEL €

(☎ 081 878 18 73; www.hotelrivage.com; Via Capo 11; d €70; ✆ Mar-Nov; ☑ P @ 🖨) A low-rise, modern hotel just beyond the shops on the western edge of town, the Rivage has a slight tour-group feel but is well located and priced. There's a roof terrace you can lounge on, and a reasonable bar and restaurant. Rooms are bland hotel-style but have good-size balconies.

★ Hotel Cristina
HOTEL €€

(☎ 081 878 35 62; www.hotelcristinasorrento.it; Via Privata Rubinacci 6, Sant'Agnello; s/d/tr/q €130/150/180/200; ✆ Mar-Oct; 🌡🖨🏊) Located high above Sant'Agnello, this hotel has superb views, particularly from the swimming pool. The spacious rooms have seaview balconies and combine inlaid wooden furniture with contemporary flourishes like Philippe Starck chairs. There's an in-house restaurant and a free shuttle bus to/from Sorrento's Circumvesuviana train station.

Hotel Astoria
HOTEL €€

(☎ 081 807 40 30; www.hotelastoriasorrento.com; Via Santa Maria delle Grazie 24; s €50-110, €70-170; 🌡🖨) This renovated classic has the advantage of being located in the heart of the *centro storico*. Overall, it's an excellent choice. The interior sparkles with colourful glossy tiles and blue and buttercup-yellow paintwork. The large enclosed back terrace is a delight, with seats set under orange and lemon trees and colourful tiled murals lining the back wall.

Il Giglio Bianco
B&B €€

(☎ 0334 123 3 064; www.bbgigliobiancosorrento.it; Via Parsano 25; d $45-99, tr $65-114, q $75-129; 🌡) Il Giglio Bianco has nicely soothing white and cream decor, wrought-iron beds and a wraparound balcony that gives each of the three rooms a portion of terrace. It's a little off the main drag, so it's nice and quiet, and the friendly owner brothers will help with taking your luggage up the stairs. The breakfast is particularly good.

Mignon
HOTEL €€

(☎ 081 807 38 24; www.sorrentohotelmignon.com; Via Sersale 9; s €50-85, d €60-139, tr €90-159; ✆ Apr-Oct & Christmas; 🌡🖨) The interior designer here had a serious fit of the blues. From the striking dark-blue-and-white floor tiles to the pale-blue walls and bedcovers, it's the predominant colour. Contemporary artwork and black-and-white historic photos of Sorrento complete the decor. The rooms are spacious and there is a rooftop solarium for catching the rays.

La Tonnarella
HOTEL €€

(☎ 081 878 11 53; www.latonnarella.com; Via Capo 31; d €120-140, ste €240-350; ✆ Apr-Oct & Christmas; P 🌡 @ 🖨) A splendid choice (but not for minimalists) La Tonnarella is a dazzling canvas of majolica tiles, antiques, chandeliers and statues. Rooms, most with their own balcony or small terrace, continue the sumptuous classical theme with traditional furniture and discreet mod cons. The hotel also has its own private beach, accessible by lift, and a highly regarded terrace restaurant.

Villa Elisa
APARTMENT €€

(☎ 081 878 27 92; www.villaelisasorrento.com; Piazza Sant'Antonino 19; d €70-120 plus €15 for extra bed, ste €70-120; ✆ year-round; 🌡🖨) Rooms come with cooking facilities and overlook a central courtyard. Up a steep staircase, the self-contained suite has a pint-sized living room, bathroom, bedroom and kitchen, but the washing machine's a definite plus. It's in a terrific central location. Parking costs an additional €15 per day.

★ Grand Hotel Excelsior Vittoria
HOTEL €€€

(☎ 081 807 10 44; www.exvitt.it; Piazza Tasso 34; s/d/ste from €350/400/700; P 🌡🖨🏊) A hotel for over 170 years, the grand old dame of Sorrento oozes belle époque elegance. Huge potted palms adorn gilded public rooms awash with antique furniture. Rooms vary in size and style, ranging from tasteful simplicity to extravagant, frescoed opulence, but all have views of the hotel's gardens dripping with crimson bougainvillea or over the sea to Vesuvius. Past guests have included Pavarotti, Wagner, Goethe, Sophia Loren and British royalty.

Plaza Hotel
HOTEL €€€

(☎ 081 878 28 31; www.plazasorrento.com; Via Fuorimura 3; d from €220; P 🌡 @ 🖨) This is one of the newer hotels in town: the whole place sports a bright, contemporary look with dazzling white contrasting with earthy parquet floors, accented by splashes of colour. Abstracts adorn the walls, and the rooftop sky bar (round the corner from the infinity pool) is perfect for a sundowner, with its scenic views of town and sea.

Massa Lubrense

Mainly frequented by Italian tourists in the know, pretty Massa Lubrense makes a good base and offers a quieter location than some of its higher-profile Amalfi Coast neighbours.

★ **Casale Villarena** APARTMENT €
(☑081 808 17 79; www.casalevillarena.it; Via Cantone 3, Nerano; 2-/4-person apt from €70/170; ☺Easter-Oct; P❄) These family-friendly apartments have good facilities, including a shared pool, a playground and a lovely beach within easy strolling distance. There are landscaped terraces with lemon trees, shady pergolas and such practical necessities as a laundry. The original property dates from the 18th century, but the apartments are comfortable, spacious and simply, yet elegantly, furnished.

★ **Hotel Ristorante Primavera** HOTEL €
(☑081 878 91 25; www.laprimavera.biz; Via IV Novembre 3g; d €100; ☺Easter-Oct; ❄☎) A welcoming, family-run two-star hotel, the Primavera has spacious, airy rooms with traditional Vietri tiles, light wood and white paint. Several rooms have terraces with sunbeds, plus table and chairs (rooms 101 to 103 are good choices). The bath tubs, in most rooms, are an unexpected treat. The bright terrace restaurant, with views stretching over orchards to the sea, serves typical local fare.

Sant'Agata sui due Golfi

In a superb position overlooking the two gulfs of Salerno and Naples, Sant'Agata is fast gaining a reputation for its *agriturismi* as well as its restaurants. Book ahead if you are planning to visit in high season.

Agriturismo Le Tore AGRITURISMO €
(☑081 808 06 37; www.letore.com; Via Pontone 43; s €60-70, d €90-130, dinner €25-35; ☺Easter-early Nov; P❄☎) A working organic farm amid 14 hectares of olive groves, producing olive oil, sundried tomatoes (and paste) and marmalade (among other products), La Tore is

a wonderful place to stay. Decidedly off the beaten track, it offers seven barnlike rooms within a lovely rustic farmhouse hidden among fruit trees. Terracotta tiles and wooden furniture add to the rural appeal.

Children between two and six years of age are offered a 50% discount (30% discount for seven- to 10-year-olds) if they sleep in their parents' room. During winter there is the option of a self-contained apartment. Additional meals are available.

Agriturismo Fattoria Terranova AGRITURISMO €
(☑081 533 02 34; www.fattoriaterranova.it; Via Pontone 10; d €85; ☺Mar-Dec; P❄) Stone floors, dried flowers hanging from heavy wooden beams and large wine barrels artfully positioned – this great *agriturismo* is the epitome of rural chic. The accommodation is in small apartments spread over the extensively cultivated grounds. The apartments are fairly simple, but the setting is delightful and the swimming pool is a welcome luxury.

Marina del Cantone

You should have little problem finding accommodation in this delightful, low-key place – aside from in August when the tidal wave of holidaying Italians swamps the hotels in this hot spot of the Sorrento Peninsula.

Villaggio Residence Nettuno CAMPGROUND, APARTMENT €
(☑081 808 10 51; www.villaggionettuno.it; Via A Vespucci 39; camping per 2 people, tent & car €41, bungalows €130-185, apt €190; ☺Mar-early Nov; P❄@☎❄) Marina's campground – in the terraced olive groves by the entrance to the village – offers an array of accommodation options, including campsites, mobile homes and (best of all) apartments in a 16th-century tower for two to five people. It's a friendly, environmentally sound place with excellent facilities and a comprehensive list of activities.

Positano

Positano is a glorious place to stay, but be aware that prices are, overall, high. Like everywhere on the Amalfi Coast, it gets very busy in summer, so book ahead, particularly on weekends and in July and August. Ask at the tourist office about rooms or apartments in private houses.

★Villa Nettuno HOTEL €

(☎089 87 54 01; www.villanettunopositano.it; Viale Pasitea 208; s/d €70/85; ⊙year-round) Hidden behind a barrage of perfumed foliage, Villa Nettuno oozes charm. Go for one of the original rooms in the 300-year-old part of the building with heavy rustic decor and a communal terrace. Rooms in the renovated part of the villa lack the same character.

★Pensione Maria Luisa PENSION €

(☎089 87 50 23; www.pensionemarialuisa.com; Via Fornillo 42; d €70-80, with sea view €95; ⊙Mar-Oct; @📶) The Maria Luisa is a friendly old-school *pensione*. Rooms feature shiny blue tiles and simple, no-frills decor; those with private balconies are well worth the extra €15 for the bay views. If you can't bag a room with a view, there's a small communal terrace offering the same sensational vistas. Breakfast is an additional €5.

Casa Celeste PENSION €

(☎089 87 53 63; www.casaceleste.net; Via Fornillo 10; s €45, d €80-90; ⊙Easter-Oct) First of all, a warning: owner Celeste's homemade *limoncello* (lemon liqueur) has more alcohol in it than most – her coffee is excellent too. In her 80s, she's a gem, and also makes all the breakfast preserves and cakes. Son Marco is behind the tasteful restoration of the 17th-century rooms, attractively furnished with bright tilework and dark-wood furniture. If you have a choice, go for room 5 with its atmospheric vaulted ceiling.

Hostel Brikette HOSTEL €

(☎089 87 58 57; www.hostel-positano.com; Via Marconi 358; dm €24-50, d €65-145, apt €80-220; ⊙year-round; ❄📶) The Brikette is a bright, cheerful place with wonderful views and a range of sleeping options, from dorms to doubles and apartments. Conveniently, it also offers a daily hostelling option that allows day trippers use of the hostel's facilities, including showers, wi-fi and left luggage, for €10. Breakfast isn't included.

The English owner is a great source of information if you're planning walks in the area, providing maps and sound advice.

★La Fenice B&B €€

(☎089 87 55 13; www.lafenicepositano.com; Via Guglielmo Marconi 4; d €140; ⊙Easter-Oct; 🏊) With hand-painted Vietri tiles, white walls and high ceilings, the rooms here are simple but stylish; most have their own balcony or terrace. The views are stunning, but it feels very smartly homely and not super posh. As with everywhere in Positano, you'll need to be good at stomping up and down steps to stay here. There's a delightful pool and hot tub, with even a little waterfall splashing from the rocks above.

★Hotel California HOTEL €€

(☎089 87 53 82; www.hotelcaliforniapositano.it; Via Cristoforo Colombo 141; d €160-195; ⊙Easter-Oct; P❄📶) Ignore the incongruous name: this Hotel California is housed in a grand 18th-century palace, its facade washed in soothing pinks and yellows. The rooms in the older part of the house are magnificent, with original ceiling friezes; new rooms are spacious and luxuriously decorated. Breakfast is served on a glorious and leafy front terrace.

Florida Residence B&B €€

(☎089 87 58 01; www.floridaresidence.net; Viale Pasitea 171; d €90-120; ⊙Apr-Oct; P❄📶) There are two rarities here: free parking and boiled eggs for breakfast. This friendly, family-owned place has good-size rooms that, although starting to look mildly scuffed, are well equipped, with fridge and hairdryer. Several rooms have bath tubs as well as showers. There is plenty of communal space, including a rooftop solarium and garden, complete with gazebo.

★Hotel Palazzo Murat HOTEL €€€

(☎089 87 51 77; www.palazzomurat.it; Via dei Mulini 23; d €180-270; ⊙May–mid-Jan; ❄@📶) Shielded behind an ancient wall from the tourists who surge along its pedestrian thoroughfare daily, this magnificent hotel occupies the 18th-century *palazzo* that the one-time king of Naples used as his summer residence. Rooms – five (more expensive) in the original part of the building, 25 in the newer section – are decorated with sumptuous antiques, original oil paintings and glossy marble. The lush gardens contain banana trees, bottlebrush, Japanese maple and pine trees.

★San Pietro HOTEL €€€

(☎089 87 54 55; www.ilsanpietro.it; Via Laurito 2; d from €420-580; ⊙Apr-Oct; P❄📶🏊) For such a talked-about hotel, the San Pietro is remarkably discreet. Built into a rocky headland 2km east of Positano, it's almost entirely below road level; if driving, look for an ivy-clad chapel and a black British telephone box by the side of the road. All the individually decorated rooms have sea views, private terrace and hot tub. Other facilities include a semicircular swimming pool, a Michelin-starred restaurant, and a private beach (accessible by lift) with an adjacent lawn and sunbeds, plus tennis court. The vast lobby is a suitably swish introduction and draped with brilliantly coloured bougainvillea – an unusual touch. There's a 24-hour complimentary shuttle service to Positano.

Hotel Villa Gabrisa BOUTIQUE HOTEL €€€
(☑ 089 81 14 98; www.villagabrisa.it; Via Pasitea 219-227; d €250-320; ☺ year-round; ❄ 🛜)
This lovely four-star hotel occupies an 18th-century *palazzo* near the top of town. Rooms exude Italian style, with painted furniture from Tuscany coupled with traditional wrought-iron beds, Murano-glass chandeliers and majolica tiles. There's also an elegant wine bar and restaurant serving sophisticated regional cuisine.

Villa Franca HOTEL €€€
(☑ 089 87 56 55; www.villafrancahotel.it; Viale Pasitea 318; d €160-220; ☺ Apr–mid-Oct; 🅿 ❄)
This immaculate boutique hotel has a sparkling blue-and-white Mediterranean feel, while the rooftop pool has some of the best views in town. Rooms are white and bright with classical-themed tiled frescoes. Downstairs there's a bar, plus a gym (as if you didn't get enough exercise in this town) and a Wellness Centre offering Turkish bath, massages and treatments.

An additional annexe houses nine more rooms with similar decor.

Positano to Amalfi

The stretch of road between Positano and Amalfi is one of the most stunning on the coast. Accommodation here is centred on Praiano.

★**Agriturismo Serafina** AGRITURISMO €
(☑ 089 83 03 47; www.agriturismoserafina. it; Via Picola 3, Loc Vigne; s/d/tr €50/80/100; ☺ year-round; ❄) It's difficult to get more off the beaten track than this superb *agriturismo*. But make it up here and you'll find one of the best deals on the coast. Accommodation is in seven spruce, air-conditioned rooms in the main farmhouse, each with its own small balcony and views over the lush green terraces below.

The food is quite special, virtually everything made with the farm's own produce (which includes salami, pancetta, wine, olive oil, fruit and veg).

★**Ercole di Amalfi**
Bed & Breakfast B&B €€
(☑ 089 83 18 43; www.ercolediamalfi.it; Via Giovanni d'Amalfi 29, Amalfi; d €145; ☺ year-round)
Located five minutes' drive west of Amalfi towards Conca dei Marini, this newish hillside B&B has a lovely rustic terrace with sweeping sea views to enhance your breakfast, and lemons hanging overhead. The stylish rooms feature vaulted ceilings, locally made tiles and swish modern bathrooms. It's a good spot for mountain strolls.

Hotel Onda Verde HOTEL €€
(☑ 089 87 41 43; www.hotelondaverde.com; Via Terramare 3, Praiano; d €110-230; ☺ Apr-Nov; ❄ 🛜) This hotel enjoys a stunning cliffside position overlooking the picturesque Marina de Praiano. The interior is tunnelled into the stone cliff face, which makes it wonderfully cool in the height of summer. Rooms have lashings of white linen, satin bedheads, elegant Florentine-style furniture and majolica-tiled floors. Some have terraces with deckchairs for contemplating that view. The restaurant comes highly recommended.

Hotel Villa Bellavista HOTEL €€
(☑ 089 87 40 54; www.villabellavista.it; Via Crado 47, Praiano; r €80-120; ☺ Apr-Oct; ❄ 🛜 🏊) Amid lush gardens that include a vast vegetable plot, this Praiano hotel has an old-fashioned charm with its slightly stuffy furniture in the public areas and large, cool but fairly bare rooms. The appeal lies in the fabulous views from the spacious, flower-festooned terrace; the delightful pool, surrounded by greenery; and the tranquil setting.

Located on a narrow lane that leads to the Spiaggia della Gavitelli, the (signposted) hotel is accessed from Via Rezzolo from the SS163 that runs through town.

Villa Maria Bed and Breakfast B&B €€
(☑ 089 87 28 02; www.villamariaamalfi.it; Piazza Gaetano Amodio 1, Pogerola; d €110-135; ☺ Easter-Oct) Located a short bus ride west of Amalfi on the main square of tiny Pogerola, this elegantly decorated lemon-yellow villa is backed by mountain vistas and has rooms with wonderful beamed ceilings and cool tiled floors. Views towards Amalfi are stunning, and stepped walkways take you off on mountainside explorations.

Amalfi

Despite its reputation as a day-trip destination, Amalfi has plenty of places to stay. It's not especially cheap, though, and most hotels are in the midrange to top-end price bracket. Always try to book ahead, as the summer months are very busy and many places close over winter. Note that if you're coming by car, consider a hotel with a car park, as finding on-street parking could lead to an attack of the vapours.

★ Albergo Sant'Andrea   HOTEL €

(☑089 87 11 45; www.albergosantandrea.it; Via Duca Mansone I; s/d €60/90; ☺Mar-Oct; ❄🤖) Enjoy the atmosphere of busy Piazza del Duomo from the comfort of your own room. This modest two-star hotel has basic rooms with brightly coloured tiles and coordinating fabrics. Double glazing has helped cut down the piazza hubbub, which can reach fever pitch in high season – this is one place to ask for a room with a (cathedral) view.

★ Residenza del Duca   HOTEL €€

(☑089 873 63 65; www.residencedelduca.it; Via Duca Mastalo II 3; s €70, d €130; ☺Mar-Oct; ❄) This family-run hotel has just six rooms, all of them light, sunny, and prettily furnished with antiques, majolica tiles and the odd chintzy cherub. The Jacuzzi showers are excellent. Call ahead if you are carrying heavy bags, as it's a seriously puff-you-out-climb up some steps to reach here and a luggage service is included in the price.

Room 2 is a particular winner, with its French windows and stunning views.

Hotel Lidomare   HOTEL €€

(☑089 87 13 32; www.lidomare.it; Largo Duchi Piccolomini 9; s/d €65/145; ☺year-round; ❄🤖) Family run, this old-fashioned hotel has real character. The large, luminous rooms have an air of gentility, with their appealingly haphazard decor, vintage tiles and fine antiques. Some have Jacuzzi bathtubs, others have sea views and a balcony, some have both. Rather unusually, breakfast is laid out on top of a grand piano.

Hotel Amalfi   HOTEL €€

(☑089 87 24 40; www.hamalfi.it; Vico dei Pastai 3; s €70-120, d €100-120; ☺Easter-Oct; ℗❄🤖) Located in the backstreets just off Amalfi's main pedestrian thoroughfare, this family-run three-star hotel is elegant and central. Rooms, some of which have their own balconies, sport pale-yellow walls, majolica-tiled flooring and stencilling. The glossily tiled, albeit small, bathrooms have a choice of bath tub or shower. The roof garden is a relaxing place to idle over a drink.

Hotel Centrale   HOTEL €€

(☑089 87 26 08; www.amalfihotelcentrale.it; Largo Duchi Piccolomini 1; d €100-120; ☺Easter-Oct; ❄@🤖) This is one of the best-value hotels in Amalfi. The entrance is on a tiny little piazza in the *centro storico,* but many of the small but tastefully decorated rooms overlook Piazza del Duomo. The aquamarine ceramic tiling lends it a vibrant, fresh look and the views from the rooftop terrace are magnificent.

DieciSedici   B&B €€

(www.diecisedici.it; Piazza Municipio 10-16; d €150; ☺Easter-Oct; ❄) Brand new and brilliantly positioned, DieciSedici is located in a swishly renovated medieval palace. The bright rooms have tiled floors, whitewashed walls and – mostly – sea views. The friendly owners go out of their way to point you to good restaurants and attractions in the town. Satellite TV, air con and sound systems make it great value for money.

★ Hotel Luna Convento   HOTEL €€€

(☑089 87 10 02; www.lunahotel.it; Via Pantaleone Comite 33; s €250-300, d €270-320, ste €460-620; ☺Easter-Oct; ℗❄@🤖🏊) This former convent was founded by St Francis in 1222 and has been a hotel for some 170 years. Rooms in the original building are in the former monks' cells, but there's nothing poky about the bright tiles, balconies and seamless sea views. The newer wing is equally beguiling, with religious frescoes over the bed. The cloistered courtyard is magnificent.

★ Hotel Santa Caterina   HOTEL €€€

(☑089 87 10 12; www.hotelsantacaterina.it; Strada Amalfitana 9; d €315-770, ste from €480; ☺Mar-Oct; ℗❄🤖🏊) Situated west of town on the coastal road – and boasting fabulous views – this Amalfi landmark is is one of Italy's most famous hotels. Everything here oozes luxury, from the discreet service to the fabulous gardens, the private beach to the opulent rooms. Built in 1880 by the Gambardella family, the hotel is run by the third generation of the same family.

For honeymooners, the Romeo and Juliet suite (€1000 to €3200 per night) is the one to go for, a private chalet in the colourful grounds.

Ravello

Ravello is an upmarket town and the accommodation reflects this, both in style and in price. There are some superb top-end hotels, several lovely midrange places and a fine *agriturismo* nearby. Book well ahead for summer – especially if you're planning to visit during the music festival.

Affittacamere Il Roseto
PENSION €

(📞 089 858 64 92; www.ilroseto.it; Via Trinità 37; s €60-70, d €80-90; ☺year-round) If you're after a no-frills, clean room within easy walking distance of everything, come here. There are only two rooms, both of which have white walls, white sheets and white floors. But what they lack in charm they make up for in value, and, if you want colour, you can always sit outside under the lemon trees.

The owners also run the Profumi della Costiera *limoncello* shop.

Agriturismo Monte Brusara
AGRITURISMO €

(📞 089 85 74 67; www.montebrusara.com; Via Monte Brusara 32; s/d €45/90; ☺year-round) An authentic working farm, this mountainside *agriturismo* is located a tough half-hour walk of about 1.5km from Ravello's centre (call ahead to arrange to be picked up). It is especially suited to families – children can feed the pony while you sit back and admire the views – or to those who simply want to escape the crowds.

The three rooms are comfy but basic, the food is fabulous and the owner is a charming, garrulous host. Half-board is also available.

★ Punta Civita
B&B €€

(📞 089 872 326; www.puntacivita.it; Via Civita 4; d €110; ☺Mar-Oct; 🛜) Located on the road up to Ravello and accessible via a 15-minute walk from Atrani, this spruce little B&B has a bougainvillea-wreathed terrace with heavenly views of the sea and surrounding lemon groves, and bright tiled rooms that also look seaward. The warm, friendly owners serve an excellent Continental breakfast on – of course – the terrace.

Albergo Ristorante Garden
HOTEL €€

(📞 089 85 72 26; www.gardenravello.com; Via Giovanne Boccaccio 4; s/d €140/160; ☺mid-Mar–late Oct; ❄🛜) Look at the photos behind reception to see the current owners playing with the Jackie Kennedy brood many years ago. Although no longer the celebrity magnet that it once was, this family-run three-star

is a good bet. The smallish rooms leave little impression (clean with nondescript decor), but the views are superb and fridges are a welcome touch.

Apparently Gore Vidal was a regular at the terrace restaurant (meals from around €30).

Hotel Toro
BOUTIQUE HOTEL €€

(📞 089 85 72 11; www.hoteltoro.it; Via Wagner 3; s/d €85/125; ☺Easter-Nov; ❄🛜) This has been a hotel since the late 19th century; the Dutch artist Escher stayed in room 6 here and was possibly inspired by the dizzily patterned tiles. The rooms are decked out in traditional Amalfi Coast style, with terracotta or light marble tiles, soothing cream furnishings and tasteful landscape paintings; several rooms have fridges.

It's located just off Piazza del Duomo within easy range of the clanging cathedral bells. The walled garden is a delightful place to sip your sundowner.

Hotel Villa Amore
PENSION €€

(📞 089 85 71 35; www.villaamore.it; Via dei Fusco 5; s/d €65/120; ☺May-Oct; 🚗) This welcoming family-run *pensione* is the best choice in town for price. Tucked down a quiet lane, it has modest, homey rooms and sparkling bathrooms. All rooms have a balcony and some have bath tubs. The restaurant is a further plus, its terrace boasting fabulous views: the food's good and prices are reasonable (around €25 for a meal).

★ Hotel Caruso
HOTEL €€€

(📞 089 85 88 01; www.hotelcaruso.com; Piazza San Giovanni del Toro 2; s €575-720, d €757-976; ☺Apr-Nov; 🅿❄🛜🏊) There can be no better place to swim than the Caruso's sensational infinity pool. Seemingly set on the edge of a precipice, its blue waters merge with sea and sky to magical effect. Inside, the sublimely restored 11th-century *palazzo* is no less impressive, with Moorish arches doubling as window frames, 15th-century vaulted ceilings and high-class ceramics.

Rooms are suitably mod-conned: the TV/DVD system slides sexily out of a wooden cabinet at the foot of the bed.

Palazzo Avino
HOTEL €€€

(Palazzo Sasso; 📞 089 81 81 81; www.palazzosasso.com; Via San Giovanni del Toro 28; d from €320, with sea view €530; ☺Mar-Oct; ❄🛜🏊) One of three luxury hotels on Ravello's millionaires' row, Palazzo Sasso has been a hotel since 1880, sheltering many 20th-century luminaries – General Eisenhower planned the Allied attack on Monte Cassino here, and Roberto Rossellini and Ingrid Bergman flirted over dinner in the restaurant. A stunning pale-pink 12th-century palace, it combines tasteful antiques with Moorish colours and modern sculpture.

The 20m swimming pool commands great views, and its Michelin-starred restaurant, Rossellinis, has a superb reputation. There is a small spa.

SALERNO & THE CILENTO

Salerno

The little accommodation that Salerno offers is fairly uninspiring, although, conveniently, there are several reasonable hotels in the town centre. Prices tend to be considerably lower than on the Amalfi Coast.

★ **Ostello Ave Gratia Plena**   HOSTEL €
(☑ 089 23 47 76; www.ostellodisalerno.it; Via dei Canali; dm/s/d €16/45/65; ☉year-round; @ 🛜)
Housed in a 16th-century convent, Salerno's excellent HI hostel is right in the heart of the *centro storico*. Inside there's a charming central courtyard and a range of bright rooms, from dorms to great bargain doubles with private bathroom. The 2am curfew is for dorms only.

Hotel Montestella   HOTEL €€
(☑ 089 22 51 22; www.hotelmontestella.it; Corso Vittorio Emanuele II 156; s/d/tr €75/100/110; ☉year-round; 🌀 @ 🛜) Within walking distance of just about anywhere worth going to, the Montestella is on Salerno's main pedestrian thoroughfare, halfway between the *centro storico* and train station. The rooms are spacious and comfortable, with blue carpeting and patterned wallpaper, while the public spaces have a fresh, modern look. It's one of the best midrange options in town.

There is a handy underground car park a couple of blocks away (€25 for 24 hours).

Paestum

Despite the fact that most people visit Paestum for one day, there is a surprising number of hotels here. Aside from the inevitable three-star hotels geared towards coach tours, there are some excellent options.

★ **Casale Giancesare**   B&B €
(☑ 0828 72 80 61, 333 1897737; www.casale-giancesare.it; Via Giancesare 8; s €65-120, d €65-120, apt per week €600-1300; ☉year-round; 🅿 🌀 @ 🛜 🏊)
A 19th-century former farmhouse, this elegantly decorated stone-clad B&B is run by the delightful Voza family, who will happily ply you with their homemade wine and *limoncello*. It's located 2.5km from the glories of Paestum and surrounded by vineyards and olive and mulberry trees; views are stunning, particularly from the swimming pool.

Villaggio dei Pini   CAMPGROUND €
(☑ 0828 81 10 30; www.campingvillaggiodeipini.com; camping per 2 people, car & tent €45, 2-person cabins per week €450-800; ☉year-round; 🛜)
Paestum has numerous campgrounds, but this is where you should hammer in those tent pegs. Set in a mature landscaped area with lofty pines, facilities include restaurant, pizzeria, mini market, football pitch, private beach and children's playground. Cabins are simply furnished but have all the essentials.

★ **Hotel Calypso**   HOTEL €€
(☑ 0828 81 10 31; www.calypsohotel.com; Via Mantegna 63; s €50-75, d €100-150; ☉year-round; 🅿 🌀 @) This is a top choice for artistically or alternatively inclined folk. The large, tastefully decorated rooms have private balconies and some choice handcrafted decor pieces, and a sandy beach is a short stroll away. Owner Roberto is a world traveller who can advise on the local area. Concerts, ranging from folk to classical, are regularly staged during summer.

There's a macrobiotic restaurant (the hotel is a member of the Slow Food movement), which can cater for vegans. Rooms without TV are available for guests concerned about electromagnetic fields.

Agropoli & the Cilento Coast

A popular destination for Italian tourists in the summer months, Agropoli and the main coastal resorts have a good range of accommodation.

★ **Marulivo Hotel**   BOUTIQUE HOTEL €
(☑ 0974 973 792; www.marulivohotel.it; Via Castello, Pisciotta; d €85-100; ☉Easter-Oct; 🌀 🛜)
Great for romance, or just a stress-free break in idyllic surroundings. Located in the narrow web of lanes behind medieval Pisciotta's main piazza, rooms feature earthy colours,

antique furnishings, crisp white linen and exposed stone walls. The rooftop terrace with sea views and an adjacent small bar is unbeatable for lingering over a cold drink.

Anna
B&B, APARTMENT €

(☑ 0974 82 37 63; www.bbanna.it; Via S Marco 28-30, Agropoli; d €75-90; ☺ year-round; P ✳) A great location, across from the town's sweeping sandy beach, this trim budget choice is known locally for its restaurant, where you can salivate over homemade morning *cornetti*. The rooms are large and plain with small balconies; specify a sea view to enjoy the sun setting over Sorrento. Sunbeds and bicycles can be hired for a minimal price.

La Lanterna
AGRITURISMO €

(☑ 089 79 02 51; www.cilento.it/lanterna; Via della Lanterna 8, Agropoli; dm €16, d €34-45, tr €51-55, q €68-72; ☺ Easter-Oct; P @) Ivo and Tiziana are great hosts at this friendly place, 1km from the centre. The homey cabin accommodation is great value, set in the large terraced gardens. Dorms are clean with lockers, while the communal breakfast of rolls with cream cheese or jam and homemade cake is better than most. Internet €3 per hour.

Raggio di Sole
AGRITURISMO €

(☑ 0974 96 73 56; www.agriturismoraggiodisole.it; Via Terrate, Castellabate; d €80; ☺ Apr-Nov; P ✳) Situated on the outskirts of town coming from Santa Maria di Castellabate, this welcoming *agriturismo* is just one mountain peak away from the town, so the views are superb, with the sea and the island of Capri beyond. The 200-year-old farmhouse has been thoroughly updated, and rooms are plain and modern with balconies. The main house is surrounded by greenery, including lofty eucalyptus, citrus and olive trees, while below there is a small farmyard.

La Corallina
HOTEL €

(☑ 0974 96 68 61; www.hotellacorallina.it; Via Porto, San Marco di Castellabate; d €75-120; ☺ Easter-Oct; P ✳ 🛜) This small hotel has a beautiful facade painted in dark ochre with traditional green shutters and flower-filled windowboxes. Overlooking the fishing boats in the harbour, the rooms are a dazzle of white tiles with colourful Vietri-tile trim, contrasting with dark-blue fabrics.

Albergo il Castello
HOTEL €

(☑ 0974 96 71 69; www.hotelcastello.co.uk; Via Amendola, Agropoli; d €90-100; ☺ Easter-Oct; P ✳) This ivy-clad old-fashioned hotel is housed in an early-19th-century building with large rooms, still with the original floor tiles, plus exposed stone walls and spacious private terraces. The courtyard is a delight, with its lemon trees and abundance of plants: the perfect place to enjoy a sundowner or the bountiful breakfast.

Antico Maniero Palinuro
B&B €€

(☑ 0974 93 30 38; www.anticomanieropalinuro.it; Colle San Sergio, Centola; d €110; ☺ Easter-Oct) Located in a stone mansion with a gorgeous terrace and sweeping sea views, Antico Maniero Palinuro features unashamedly romantic rooms – with drapes, lace bedspreads and dark wood furniture – that stay on the right side of kitsch. Located between Centola and Palinuro, it's a good option if you're driving around the Cilento or along the coast.

Albergo Santa Caterina
HOTEL €€

(☑ 0974 93 10 19; www.albergosantacaterina.com; Via Indipendenza 53, Palinuro; d €100-155; ☺ Easter-Oct; P ✳ @ 🛜) At this superb hotel on the main street, guestroom colour schemes vary from brilliant canary yellow to deep Mediterranean blue. All have good-size bathrooms, with tubs as well as showers, and private terraces. Sea views cost €20 more. The satellite TV here is a rare treat in these parts: great if you are suffering from international-news withdrawal.

Villa Sirio
HOTEL €€

(☑ 0974 96 01 62; www.villasirio.it; Via Lungomare de Simone 15, Santa Maria di Castellabate; d €130-220; ☺ Apr-Nov; P ✳) Dating from 1912, this family-owned hotel has a classic, elegant facade with ochre paintwork and traditional green shutters. The rooms are brightly furnished with a yellow, blue and turquoise colour scheme; shiny marble clad bathrooms come complete with hot tub. The small balconies have forfeited the plastic for tasteful marble tables and have seamless sea views with Capri in the distance.

Parco Nazionale del Cilento

Unsurprisingly, the dramatic and lush scenery in the park makes it an excellent place to stay in an *agriturismo*.

★ Agriturismo I Moresani
AGRITURISMO €

(☑ 0974 90 20 86; www.imoresani.com; Località Moresani; d €90-110; ☺ Mar-Oct; ✳ 🛜 ⛲) If you are seeking utter tranquility, head to this *agriturismo* 1.5km west of Casal Velino. The setting is bucolic: rolling hills in every direction, interspersed with grapevines, grazing pastures and olive trees. Family run, the 18-hectare farm produces its own *caprino* goat cheese, wine, olive oil and preserves. Rooms have cream- and earth-coloured decor and surround a pretty private garden.

The restaurant uses primarily homegrown organic products and has a terrace that fronts onto vineyards. Horse riding, cooking and painting courses are regularly held; check the website or contact the friendly owners for a schedule.

Villa Vea
AGRITURISMO €

(☑ 0828 196 22 37; www.agriturismovillavea. it; C da Soubaddei 10, Bellosguardo; d €74; ☺year-round; 🛜�ⓘ) Surrounded by olive trees and vines with distant pine-covered mountains, this superb *agriturismo* is run by an American-Italian family. Enjoy distant views of Capri while savouring delicious traditional food prepared by Angela, who also conducts cooking classes. The rooms are rustic with chunky furniture and bright walls. Dating from 1978, this was the first *agriturismo* to open in the area.

Homemade olive oil, wine and jam are on the menu and breakfasts are a cut above the standard *cornetti*, with cooked breakfasts available on request (a rarity in these parts).

Agriturismo La Loggia degli Alburni
AGRITURISMO €

(☑ 334 3204398; www.laloggiadeglialburni.it; Sicignano degli Alburni; d €45; ☺year-round; 🅿✳) Popular with walkers, this place is more country hotel than true *agriturismo*, but the setting is sublime: high up in a grove of chestnut trees overlooking a magnificent castle. Follow the signs from the village along a rough track, backed by steep, forested slopes. The rooms are large, modern and comfortable. The dining room (meals €25), complete with colourful hunting mural, serves good traditional fare like homemade tagliolini pasta in a *ragù*.

Antichi Feudi
BOUTIQUE HOTEL €

(☑ 0975 58 73 29; www.antichifeudi.com; Via San Francesco 2, Teggiano; s €35-65, d €70-90; ☺year-round; ✳🛜) Just off the picturesque main Piazza San Cono, this former palace is distinguished by its sumptuous burnt-sienna exterior. An atmospheric and inexpensive option, the rooms are all different but share careful attention to detail, with painted wardrobes, canopy beds and even the occasional chandelier. The public spaces include a small courtyard with its original well and an excellent restaurant.

Casale San Martino
B&B €

(☑ 0974 83 22 13; www.casalesanmartino.eu; Contrada Vignali 5; d €85; ☺Mar-Oct; 🅿✳) At this exquisite B&B, boasting stunning panoramic views of Agropoli and the coast to the west and rolling countryside to the east, you can sleep under the beams in tasteful stone-walled bedrooms, decorated in earth colours and featuring five-star-quality bathrooms with mosaic marble tiles. To get here, take the SP172 east off the main coastal road south of Agropoli.

The family menagerie includes goats and ducks. If you time your visit right, breakfast will include fresh figs from the pretty garden, complete with wisteria-draped arbour.

La Congiura dei Baroni
HOTEL €

(☑ 0975 7 90 44; www.lacongiuradeibaroni.it; Via Castello 16, Teggiano; s/d €35/75; ☺Easter-Oct) This inviting small hotel has a wonderful position overlooking a castle and moat. Cute, comfortable accommodation has a reassuring spare-room feel, with private terraces, while owner Anna Maria will extend a warm welcome (but speaks no English).

★ Zio Cristoforo
AGRITURISMO €€

(☑ 0974 90 75 52; www.agriturismoziocristoforo. com; Via Chiuse 24, Casal Velino; d €130-160; ☺year-round; 🅿✳💺💺) If *agriturismi* had stars, this would have five. That said, it's more boutique hotel than farmstay: no one seems to be trudging around in muddy boots here, although there *is* a surrounding farm and the animals raised do feature in the popular restaurant menu. The rooms are rustic yet elegant, with wrought-iron bedheads, terracotta tiles and a soothing green-and-white colour scheme.

Cooking classes are available during winter (€150 for three days), and there are regular wine-tasting courses.

Park Hotel Cilento
HOTEL €€

(☑ 0974 93 26 62; www.parkhotelcilento. it; Via Sirene 26, Marina di Camerota; d €140; ☺year-round; 🅿) An excellent and comfortable family-friendly base for park hikes and coastal trips, located south round the bay from Palinuro. The rooms are plain rather than characterful, but it's spotless and efficient. There's a pool and a restaurant, where you can enjoy gigantic buffet breakfasts. Reception staff will arrange boat trips.

Understand Naples, Pompeii & the Amalfi Coast

Naples, Pompeii & the Amalfi Coast Today

Berlin, Portland, Melbourne, Napoli? It might be better known for the old and classic than the cool and cutting edge, but Italy's third-largest city is finally finding its hipper side. A fresh, youthful energy is sweeping through Naples' ancient streets, driven by young, globe-hopping Neapolitans who are giving the style, innovation and thinking of trend-setting cities a local flavour.

Best on Film

L'oro di Napoli (Vittorio De Sica; 1954) An anthology of stories set in Naples and featuring Sophia Loren.
Passione (John Turturro; 2010) Turturro's tribute to Naples' hypnotic music and traditions.
Gomorra (Matteo Garrone; 2008) A fast-paced feature exposing the city's violent underbelly.
E poi c'è Napoli (Gianluca Migliarotti; 2014) Neapolitan fashion, style and tailoring are the focus of this refreshing documentary.

Best in Print

Capri and No Longer Capri (Raffaele La Capria; 1991, English translation 2001) La Capria presents a slightly melancholic vision of modern Capri.
Falling Palace: A Romance of Naples (Dan Hofstadler; 2005) Naples' electric streets are brought to life in this evocative love story.
Naples '44: An Intelligence Officer in the Italian Labyrinth (Norman Lewis; 1978) An engrossing account of postwar Naples.
The Ancient Shore: Dispatches from Naples (Shirley Hazzard & Francis Steegmuller; 2008) Eloquent musings on Neapolitan life and history.

Winds of Change

In the *centro storico* (historic centre), a new generation of cafes and bars is embracing a less-is-more aesthetic, ditching chintzy, kitsch interiors for pared-back tufa-stone walls and quirky designer detailing *Monocle* magazine would approve of. Even old-school coffee-bar chain Mexico is in on the act, its newest branch a past-meets-present combo of retro barista caps, recycled timber cladding, post-industrial steel and sit-down tables dotted with laptop-tapping clients.

Keywords such as sustainable, organic and locally sourced are peppering a growing number of menus, including those of new-gen eateries and wine bars like Eccellenze Campane, Salumeria and Jamón. Here, chances are your *prosciutto crudo* (cured ham) is made using cognoscente *maialino nero casertano* (a speciality breed of pig from Caserta), your cinnamon-infused *mortadella* comes from organic pork and your *birra* (beer) is of the craft variety.

This burgeoning interest in all things artisanal, local and creative extends beyond the table. Naples' hoard of street art – which includes Banksy's only Italian creation – is finally getting the recognition it deserves thanks to local street-art fan Federica Belmonte and her friends. Thirty-something Belmonte sparked the idea for Napoli Paint Stories, whose walking tours showcase the city's vibrant street art and graffiti scene to both locals and visitors.

Meanwhile, at San Caterina in Formiello on the eastern edge of the *centro storico*, grassroots project Made in Cloister is steadily transforming a historic cloister and wool factory into a thriving cultural hub for artisans, artists and musicians. Among its venues is Lanificio 25, a live-music venue already drawing reinvigorated crowds of cosmopolitan, forward-thinking Neapolitans.

After a period of stagnation, it seems that southern Italy's biggest city is itching to write its next kicking chapter.

Green City

When Luigi de Magistris took over the reins at city hall in 2011, his vision for Naples was of a greener, cleaner metropolis. The challenge was nothing short of formidable. Only a few years earlier, a major waste-disposal crisis saw Neapolitan streets piled high with uncollected garbage. Footage of fed-up locals setting fire to mounds of refuse was beamed across the globe, a PR nightmare for a city all too well aware of its dirty-and-dangerous tag.

But de Magistris was determined. In September 2011 the ZTL (limited-traffic zone) was introduced in Naples' *centro storico* to slash carbon emissions, improve traffic flow and curb the illegal use of lanes reserved for public transport. Following this, a stretch of Naples' famous Lungomare (seafront) was pedestrianised in time for the city's hosting of the World Series of the America's Cup in spring 2012. Where cars and scooters once spewed exhaust, locals and visitors now stroll, jog, cycle and take in a panorama that includes the island of Capri. It's what de Magistris proudly calls *il Lungomare liberato* (the liberated seafront).

The growing presence of peddling Neapolitans is itself revolutionary in a city where, not that long ago, riding a bike on city streets would have been considered little more than a bemusing environmentalist statement. In June 2015, Naples hosted its fourth annual Napoli Bike Festival. A year earlier, it launched a trial bike-sharing scheme, Bike Share Napoli. Initiated by CleaNap – an award-winning grassroots association well known for cleaning up the city's garbage-strewn streets and squares – the scheme had clocked up over 4000 users by early 2015, a figure widely considered indicative of a city ripe for a permanent bike-sharing system.

Not that cycling is Naples' only form of sustainable transport. In 2015, the city launched its latest starchitect-designed Line 1 metro stations, Duomo and Municipio. The latter is the centrepiece of a major – and much-needed – redevelopment of Piazza Municipio, the city's veritable welcome mat for cruise-ship and ferry passengers. When completed, the area is set to become one of Europe's largest pedestrianised urban zones, not to mention another source of civic pride in a place too often the victim of negative coverage.

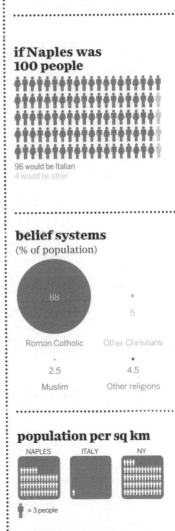

POPULATION: **5.87 MILLION**

AREA: **13,590 SQ KM**

UNEMPLOYMENT: **21.7% (2015)**

FOREIGN RESIDENTS: **3% OF TOTAL POPULATION**

NUMBER OF UNESCO WORLD HERITAGE SITES: 5

if Naples was 100 people

96 would be Italian
4 would be other

belief systems
(% of population)

88 — Roman Catholic
5 — Other Christians
2.5 — Muslim
4.5 — Other religions

population per sq km

NAPLES   ITALY   NY

= 3 people

History

With almost 3000 candles on its birthday cake, Naples and its sparkling coastline have seen it all, from pleasure-seeking Roman emperors and Spanish conquests to plagues, eruptions, revolutions, even uninvited Nazis. Whoever said history was boring has clearly never known this city.

Top Ancient Sites

Paestum

Pompeii

Herculaneum

Museo Archeologico Nazionale, Naples

Anfiteatro Flavio, Pozzuoli

The Early Years

The ancient Greeks were the first major players on the scene, setting up a trading post on Ischia and another settlement at Cumae (Cuma) in the 8th century BC. As their main foothold in Italy, Cumae became the most important city in the Italian peninsula's southwest during the next 200 years, a rich commercial centre whose sibyl was said to be Apollo's mouthpiece.

According to legend, the traders also established Naples on the island of Megaris, current home of the Castel dell'Ovo, in about 680 BC. Christened Parthenope, its namesake was a suicidal siren. Unable to lure the cunning Ulysses with her songs, she drowned herself, washing up on shore.

Failure also stalked the Tuscany-based Etruscans, who twice invaded Cuma and were twice repelled. After the second of these clashes, in 474 BC, the Cumaeans founded Neapolis (New Town) where Naples' *centro storico* (historic centre) stands.

Despite the Cumaeans' resilience, the Etruscan battles had taken a toll, and in 421 BC the Greeks fell to the Samnites. They, in turn, proved no match for the Romans, who took Neapolis in 326 BC. Not long after, in 273 BC, the Romans conquered Paestum, a Greek city dating back to the 5th century BC.

Togas, Triumph & Terror

Under the Romans, the Bay of Naples sparkled with lavish villas, thermal spas and cashed-up out-of-towners. Farmland and forests covered Vesuvius' lower slopes, while VIPs indulged by the coast. Notables holi-

TIMELINE	8th century BC	680 BC	474 BC
	Greeks establish a colony at Cuma in the Campi Flegrei. The area becomes the most important Greek settlement on the Italian mainland and a strategic part of Magna Graecia.	The Cuman Greeks establish Parthenope on the island of Megaris, naming it in honour of a suicidal siren whose song failed to seduce the cunning Ulysses.	The Cumans found Neapolis (New Town) on the site of Naples' *centro storico* (historic centre). The original Greek street plan can still be seen today.

dayed in Stabiae (Castellammare di Stabia), Nero's second wife, Poppea, entertained in upmarket Oplontis and Julius Caesar's father-in-law kept a home at Herculaneum. West of Naples, Puteoli (Pozzuoli) became a major international port, docking everything from Alexandrian grain ships to St Paul, who reputedly stepped ashore in AD 61. Further west, Misenum (Miseno) boasted the ancient world's largest naval fleet.

Despite the Romans' stranglehold on the region, the citizens of Neapolis never completely gave in to their foreign occupiers, refusing (among other things) to relinquish their language. While the Romans may have tolerated the linguistic snub, the Neapolitans' opposition to Rome during the Roman Civil War (88–82 BC) was another story, prompting Cornelius Sulla to take the city and slaughter thousands. Equally catastrophic was the unexpected eruption of Mt Vesuvius in AD 79, which drowned nearby Pompeii and Herculaneum in molten lava, mud and ash. Coming just 17 years after a massive earthquake, it was a devastating blow for the rural people already struggling in the region.

Inside the city walls, Neapolis was booming: General Lucullus built an enviable villa where the Castel dell'Ovo now stands, and even Virgil moved to town. Offshore, Capri became the centre of Emperor Tiberius' famously debauched operations.

Yet, as Neapolis' welfare was by now tied to that of the Roman Empire, the death of the last Roman emperor, Romulus Augustus, in AD 476 saw the city pass into barbarian hands.

The Normans & the Angevins

By the beginning of the 11th century, Naples was a prospering duchy. Industry and culture were thriving and Christianity was the dominant religion. Outside the city, however, the situation was more volatile, as

Get to grips with the history, peoples and wars of ancient Greece by logging on to www. ancientgreece. com, which gives compact histories of all the key characters and places. It also has an online bookstore.

AMALFI: THE GOLDEN DAYS

Musing on the fabled town of Amalfi, 19th-century scribe Renato Fucini declared that when the town's inhabitants reach heaven on Judgement Day, it will be just like any other day for them. It must have been a view shared by the Roman patricians shipwrecked on its coast in AD 337. Seduced by the area's beauty, they decided to ditch their long-haul trip to Constantinople and stay put.

Despite these early fans, Amalfi's true golden era would arrive in the 9th century, when centuries of Byzantine rule were ditched for Marine Republic status. Between this time and the ruinous Pisan raids of 1135 and 1137, its ever-expanding fleet brought a little bit of Amalfi to the far reaches of the Mediterranean, from churches named in honour of Sant'Andrea (Amalfi's patron saint) to a 'Little Amalfi' quarter in 10th-century Constantinople, complete with expat shops and schools.

326 BC	AD 79	305	536
The Romans conquer Neapolis and the city is absorbed into the Roman Empire. Despite this, locals cling to their Greek heritage and language.	At 10am on 24 August, Mt Vesuvius erupts after centuries of slumber, startling the Neapolitans and burying Pompeii, Herculaneum and other towns on the mountain's slopes.	San Gennaro, patron saint of Naples, becomes a victim of Emperor Diocletian's anti-Christian campaign. The martyr is arrested and beheaded at Solfatara Crater in Pozzuoli.	Byzantine chief general Delisarius and his fighters sneak into the city through its ancient aqueduct and lay siege. Conquered, Naples becomes a Byzantine duchy.

the Normans were beginning to eye up the Lombard principalities of Salerno, Benevento, Capua and Amalfi.

The Normans had arrived in southern Italy in the 10th century, initially as pilgrims en route from Jerusalem, later as mercenaries attracted by the money to be made fighting for the rival principalities and against the Arab Muslims in Sicily. And it was to just such a mercenary, Rainulfo Drengot, that the duke of Naples, Sergio IV, gave the contract to drive the Lombards out of Capua. Capua duly fell in 1062, followed by Amalfi in 1073 and Salerno four years later. By 1130 most of southern Italy, including Sicily, was in Norman hands and, inevitably, Naples joined them in 1139. The Kingdom of the Two Sicilies was thus complete.

The Normans maintained their capital in Sicily, and Palermo began to outshine Naples. The Neapolitans seemed happy with their lot, but when the last of the Norman kings, Tancred, was succeeded by his enemy Henry Hohenstaufen of Swabia in 1194, the mood turned ugly. The Neapolitans despised their new Swabian rulers and were delighted when Charles I of Anjou routed them at the battle of Benevento in February 1265.

Under the French Angevins, Naples' artistic and intellectual credentials grew. Charles built the Castel Nuovo in 1279, the port was enlarged, and in the early 14th century Robert of Anjou constructed Castel Sant'Elmo. Alas, nasty politicking between rival factions marked the last century of Angevin rule. Queen Joan I was suspected of murdering her husband and fled the city between 1348 and 1352, leaving her vengeful Hungarian in-laws to occupy Naples. Some 70-odd years later her namesake, Queen Joan II, only stopped her husband from stealing the crown thanks to substantial popular support.

With the royals tangled up in soap-style angst, the time was ripe for the Spanish Aragonese to launch their attack.

Aragonese Angst

Taking control of Naples in 1442, Alfonso of Aragon – dubbed Il Magnanimo (The Magnanimous) – did much for the city, promoting art and science and introducing institutional reforms. What he couldn't do was live down the fact that he'd overthrown the popular Angevins.

In 1485 the city's barons took up arms against Alfonso's successor, Ferdinand I. Within a year, however, the ringleaders had been executed (in the Sala dei Baroni inside Castel Nuovo) and peace restored. In 1495 Charles VIII of France invaded. Fiercely opposed by the Neapolitan masses, the French monarch was forced out four months later and replaced by Aragonese Ferdinand II.

After Ferdinand's death in 1496, the mutinous barons crowned his uncle, Frederick, as king. This angered everyone; the Neapolitans, the French and the Spanish had all wanted Ferdinand II's widow, Joan, to

1139	1265	1343	1414
Naples joins the Norman-ruled Kingdom of the Two Sicilies after the Norman conquest of Capua, Amalfi and Salerno. The city plays second fiddle to the kingdom's capital, Palermo.	Charles I of Anjou beats Naples' hated Swabian rulers, heralding the city's tenure as the capital of the French Anjou dynasty. The port is expanded and Castel Nuovo is built in 1279.	On 25 November, a major earthquake in the Tyrrhenian Sea triggers a tsunami. Ports along the Amalfi Coast, including the town of Amalfi, suffer heavy damage and loss of life.	Joan II is crowned Queen of Naples. In 1432, faced with the growing political ambitions of her lover, Giovanni Caracciolo, Joan plots his murder; on 19 August Caracciolo is fatally stabbed at Naples' Castel.

succeed him. The upshot was the joint Franco-Spanish invasion of 1501. Frederick tried to hang onto power, but, facing almost total opposition, he skulked off, leaving Naples to the Spanish. Thus Ferdinand of Spain became Ferdinand III of Naples.

Don Pedro & the Spanish Years

As part of the cashed-up Spanish empire, 16th-century Naples prospered. By 1600 it was Europe's largest city, with a population of 300,000. The boom heralded urban expansion, with viceroy Don Pedro de Toledo moving the city walls westward and creating the Quartieri Spagnoli (Spanish Quarter). Hundreds of new churches and monasteries sprang up, giving artistic greats like Caravaggio, Giuseppe de Ribera and Luca Giordano the chance to show off their skills. The most prolific of all Naples' architects was Cosimo Fanzago (1591–1678), whose work on the Certosa di San Martino is a highlight of Neapolitan baroque.

Less welcome were the ever-increasing tax hikes, resulting from the economic depression that descended in the early 17th century. When the

For a wide-ranging general site on Italian history, check out www.arcaini.com. It covers, in potted form, everything from prehistory to the post–WWII period, and includes a brief chronology.

JOAN II: QUEEN OF LUST

Had tabloids existed in the middle ages, Joan II (1373–1435) would have been a fixture. Six centuries after her reign as Queen of Naples, Neapolitans still point out the various settings for her 'man-eating' antics. It was at the Castel Nuovo that she apparently threw her lovers to a hungry crocodile and at the Palazzo Donn'Anna that she threw them straight off a cliff. One can only assume they had underperformed at the queen's infamous orgies.

While the line separating fact and fiction is a very fine one indeed, it is widely accepted that the daughter of Charles III and Margherita di Durazzo was no stranger to the company of men, many of them powerbrokers. At the time of her coronation in 1414, she was already the widow of William, Duke of Austria, the rejected fiancé of her cousin, Hedwig of Poland. As queen, Joan wasted little time appointing her lover Pandolfello Alopo grand chamberlain, and she was briefly engaged to John of Aragon in 1415.

That same year she married James II of Bourbon, but the honeymoon was short-lived: refused the title of Prince of Taranto, jealous James had Alopo murdered and forced Joan to bestow on him the title of King of Naples. As king, James was determined to assume complete power, imprisoning Joan in the royal household. The king's behaviour provoked rioting in Naples in 1416, forcing him to hang up his crown.

If Joan needed any consolation, she found it in the arms of nobleman Giovanni Caracciolo. Yet the position of prime minister of Naples wasn't enough for Caracciolo, whose increasingly ruthless ambition drove his royal lover to plot his assassination in 1432. His tomb lies in the Chiesa di San Giovanni a Carbonara, not far from cunning Joan's own resting place, the Basilica della Santissima Annunziata.

1442	**1503**	**1532–53**	**1600**
Alfonso of Aragon drives out René of Anjou to become Naples' new king; a long period of Spanish control begins.	Two years after a Franco-Spanish invasion of Naples, Spanish general Consalvo di Cordoba enters the city and Ferdinand of Spain becomes Ferdinand III of Naples.	Don Pedro de Toledo rules as Spanish viceroy, moving the city walls westwards and constructing the Quartieri Spagnoli (Spanish Quarter).	Naples is the biggest city in Europe, boasting a population of more than 300,000. Among its growing number of residents is renegade artist Caravaggio, who arrives in 1606.

Spanish introduced a levy on fresh fruit in January 1647, it was one tax too many, and on 7 July violence broke out on Piazza del Mercato. Nine days later, the rebellion's illiterate leader – Amalfi fisherman Tommaso Aniello (aka Masaniello) – was murdered in the Chiesa di Santa Maria del Carmine. The culprits were extremists from within his own camp: they wanted to drive out the Spanish, but their leader had been happy with cheaper fruit. Local lore has it that Masaniello lies buried in an unmarked tomb in the church.

The French then tried to cash in by sending the duke of Giusa to take the city; the duke failed and on 6 April 1648 was captured by the new Spanish viceroy, the count of Oñate. Order was soon reestablished, the rebel leaders were executed and life in Naples returned to a semblance of normality.

Putting a spanner in the works was the plague of 1656, which wiped out more than half of Naples' population and much of the economy. The horror that infected the city's squalid streets is graphically depicted in the paintings that hang in room 37 of the Certosa di San Martino (p63).

Bourbon Brilliance & Habsburg Cunning

With the death of the childless Charles V of Naples (Charles II of Spain) in 1700, Spain's European possessions were up for grabs. Despite Philip, grandson of Charles V's brother-in-law, taking the Spanish throne (and therefore the Neapolitan throne) as Philip V, Austrian troops nabbed Naples in 1707. Waiting in the wings, however, was Philip's Bourbon son Charles, who followed his ambitious mother Elisabetta Farnese's advice to take the city. Between his ascension to the Neapolitan throne in 1734 and Italian unification in 1860, Naples was transformed into Europe's showpiece metropolis. The Palazzo Reale di Capodimonte hit the skyline, central Palazzo Reale was enlarged and the Teatro San Carlo became Europe's grandest opera house.

In 1759 Charles returned to Spain to succeed his father as Charles III. As European law prohibited the simultaneous holding of three crowns (in this case it would have been Naples, Sicily and Spain), Naples was left to Charles' eight-year-old son, Ferdinand, though, in effect, power was held by Charles' conscientious prime minister, Bernardo Tanucci.

When in 1768 Austrian Maria Carolina arrived in town to marry Ferdinand, Tanucci's days were numbered. Maria was one of the 16 children of the Habsburg Empress of Austria (the very person whom Tanucci had opposed in the 1740 crisis of Austrian succession). She was beautiful, clever and ruthless – a ready match for Tanucci and an unlikely partner for the famously dim, dialect-speaking Ferdinand.

In accordance with her marriage agreement, Maria Carolina joined the Council of State on the birth of her first son in 1777. It was the posi-

Between January and August 1656, the bubonic plague wiped out more than half of Naples' 300,000-plus inhabitants. The city would take almost two centuries to return to its preplague population.

1656	1707	1734	1737
A devastating plague hits Naples. Within six months, more than half of the city's population is dead and buried in mass graves.	Austrian viceroys begin their 27-year rule of Naples. Tax and university reforms are introduced and coastal roads connecting the city to the slopes of Mt Vesuvius are built.	Encouraged by his ambitious mother and backed by his army, Spanish king Philip V's son Charles takes control from the Austrians and becomes the first Bourbon king of Naples.	The original Teatro San Carlo is built in a swift eight months. Designed by Giovanni Medrano, it is rebuilt in 1816 after a devastating fire.

tion she'd been waiting for to oust Tanucci, and into his shoes stepped a French-born English aristocrat, John Acton. Acton had won Maria over with his anti-Bourbon politics and wish to forge closer links with Austria and Britain. But just as things began to go smoothly with the English, France erupted in revolution.

The Parthenopean Republic

While the Neapolitan court naturally disapproved of the 1789 French Revolution, it would take the beheading of Maria Carolina's sister, Marie Antoinette, to prompt Naples to join the anti-French coalition.

Troops from Naples and revolutionary France clashed in French-occupied Rome in 1798. The Neapolitans claimed the city but within 11 days were scurrying back south with the French in hot pursuit. Panicked, Ferdinand and Maria Carolina headed for Palermo, leaving Naples to its own devices.

Bitterly opposed by most of the population, the French were welcomed by the Neapolitan nobility and bourgeoisie, many of whom had adopted fashionable republican ideas. And it was with the full backing of the French that the Parthenopean Republic was declared on 23 January 1799.

But it wasn't a success. The leaders were an ideologically rather than practically minded lot, and they were soon in dire financial straits. Their efforts to democratise the city failed and the army was a shambles.

Over the water in Palermo, the royal exiles had not been sitting idle. Ferdinand and Maria Carolina dispatched Cardinal Fabrizio Ruffo to Calabria to organise an uprising. On 13 June he entered Naples and all hell broke loose as his men turned the city into a slaughterhouse. With a score to settle, Ferdinand and Maria Carolina returned from Sicily on 8 July and embarked on a systematic extermination of republican sympathisers. More than 200 were executed.

Bourbon Decline & Nationalist Fervour

Despite the Parthenopean Republic's failure, French forces marched again into Naples in 1806. The royal family once more fled to Sicily, and in 1808 Joachim Murat, Napoleon's brother-in-law, became king of Naples. Despite his abolishment of feudalism and kick-starting of local industry, Murat could do no right in the eyes of the royalist masses.

With Murat finally ousted in 1815, Ferdinand returned to claim his throne. But the French Revolution had stirred up too many ideas for a return to the age of absolutism, and the ruthless Carbonari society forced Ferdinand to grant the city a constitution in 1820. A year later, however, it was abandoned as Ferdinand called in Austrian troops.

GOETHE

Of Naples, Goethe wrote: 'I can't begin to tell you of the glory of a night by full moon when we strolled through the streets and squares to the endless promenade of the Chiaia, and then walked up and down the seashore. I was quite overwhelmed by a feeling of infinite space'.

1768	1799	1806	1848
Marie Antoinette's sister, Maria Carolina, marries the uncouth Ferdinand IV. Nine years later she enters the Council of State and ousts prime minister and enemy Bernardo Tanucci.	The Parthenopean Republic is proclaimed on 23 January. It quickly fails, royal rule is reinstalled and more than 200 republican sympathisers are executed.	Joseph Bonaparte occupies the city and declares himself king of Naples. Two years later, Bonaparte is crowned king of Spain.	Pressured by rebellions sweeping across Europe, Ferdinand reintroduces a constitution in January. A dispute with the parliament, however, sees the king dissolve parliament altogether in March 1849.

Pressured by rising rebellion across Europe, Ferdinand reintroduced a constitution in 1848, only to dissolve the parliament altogether. He was as blind to the changing times as his equally obstinate son, who succeeded him in 1859.

More popular was nationalist fighter Giuseppe Garibaldi, whose goal was a united Italy. Buoyed by the victory of Piedmontese rebels against the Austrian army, he set sail for Sicily in May 1860 with a volunteer army of 1000 Red Shirts. Although Ferdinand's 25,000-strong Neapolitan army was waiting in Sicily, the Bourbons' repression of liberalism was beginning to cost it goodwill. With an army that had swelled to 5000 men, Garibaldi defeated the half-hearted Bourbon forces, declaring himself dictator in the name of King Vittorio Emanuele II.

In a case of too little too late, Ferdinand's son and successor, Francesco II, agreed to a constitution in June 1860, but Garibaldi had crossed over to the Italian mainland and was Naples bound. True to tradition, Francesco fled the city, taking refuge with 4000 loyalists behind the Volturno River, north of Naples. On 7 September Garibaldi marched unopposed into Naples, welcomed as a hero.

After a series of last-ditch attacks on the rebels, the Bourbon loyalists were defeated at the Battle of Volturno and on 21 October the city voted overwhelmingly to join a united Italy under the Savoy monarchy.

A seasoned royal city, Naples was a serious contender for capital of Italy. But when Rome was wrested from the French in 1870, the newly formed Italian parliament transferred from its temporary home in Florence to the Eternal City. From being the grand capital of a Bourbon kingdom, Naples suddenly became a lowly regional centre – something the city has never forgotten.

Between 1876 and 1913, 11.1 million Italians left their homeland in search of a better life in the New World. Of these, at least four million are believed to have come from Naples and the surrounding area. By 1927, 20% of the Italian population had emigrated.

War & Peace

A poorer shadow of its former self, post-unification Naples suffered two major blows: mass emigration and a cholera outbreak in 1884. In response to the cholera epidemic, a citywide clean-up was launched. The worst slums near the port were razed, Corso Umberto I was bulldozed through the city centre, and a sparkling new residential quarter appeared on the Vomero.

The Fascists continued the building spree: an airport was built in 1936, railway and metro lines were laid, and the Vomero funicular opened for business. No sooner had many of these projects been completed than the strategic port city was hit by the full force of WWII. Savage aerial bombing by the Allies left over 20,000 people dead and much of the city in tatters.

Although the Nazis took Naples in 1943, they were quickly forced out by a series of popular uprisings between 26 and 30 September, famously

1860	1884	1889	1906
Garibaldi enters the city to a hero's welcome and Naples votes overwhelmingly to join a united Italy under the Savoy monarchy.	A cholera epidemic strikes the city, prompting the closure of Naples' ancient aqueduct system and the launch of a major urban-redevelopment project.	Raffaele Esposito invents pizza margherita in honour of Queen Margherita, who takes her first bite of the Neapolitan staple on a royal visit to the city.	Mt Vesuvius erupts on 7 April, killing over 100 people. The Italian government diverts funds from Rome's planned 1908 Summer Olympics to the relief effort and London hosts the games instead.

known as the Quattro Giornate di Napoli (Four Days of Naples). Led by locals, especially by young *scugnizzi* (Neapolitan for 'street urchins') and ex-soldiers, the street battles paved the way for the Allied 'liberators' to enter the city on 1 October.

Despite setting up a provisional government in Naples, the Allies were confronted with an anarchic mass of troops, German prisoners of war and bands of Italian fascists all competing with the city's starving population for food. Then, to make matters worse, in 1944 Mt Vesuvius erupted.

Overwhelmed, Allied authorities turned to the underworld for assistance. As long as the Allies agreed to turn a blind eye to their black-market activities, the Mafia was willing to help. And so the Camorra (Neapolitan Mafia) began to flourish.

Rocked by Quake & Scandals

On 23 November 1980, an earthquake registering 6.83 on the Richter scale left over 2700 people dead and thousands more homeless. The opportunistic Camorra made the most of the disaster, siphoning off billions of lire poured into the devastated region.

In the decade that followed, *abusivismo* (illegal construction) flourished, profiteering mobsters partied publicly with the city's football icon, Argentine Diego Armando Maradona, and public services virtually ceased to exist. The situation was not unique to Naples – corruption and cronyism were rife across Italy.

It couldn't go on, and in 1992 the Mani pulite (Clean Hands) campaign kicked into gear. What had started as an investigation into bribery at a retirement home in Milan quickly grew into a nationwide crusade against corruption. Industry bosses and politicians were investigated, some were imprisoned, and former prime minister Bettino Craxi fled Italy to avoid prosecution.

In Naples, the city indicated its approval by electing as mayor former communist Antonio Bassolino, whose promises to kick-start the city and fight corruption were music to weary Neapolitan ears. In the seven years that followed, a burst of urban regeneration gave Naples a refreshing sense of hope and pride, one that included the commissioning of world-renowned artists to design new metro stations and the G7 summit in 1994.

Despite winning a second term in 1997, Bassolino couldn't keep up the impressive momentum and in 2000 he was elected president of the Campania region, which meant that he was no longer involved in the day-to-day running of the city. Into his shoes stepped Rosa Russo Iervolino, a former interior minister and Naples' first female mayor. Elected on a centre-left ticket first in 2001 and then for a second term in May

Although much has happened since it was written, Paul Ginsborg's *A History of Contemporary Italy: Society and Politics 1943–1988* remains one of the single most readable and insightful books on postwar Italy.

1943	1980	1987	1992
Allied bombing raids wreak havoc on the city, destroying the 14th century Basilica di Santa Chiara. A year later, Mt Vesuvius erupts.	At 7.34pm on 23 November, a powerful earthquake rocks Campania, causing widespread damage and killing almost 3000 people.	Under Maradona, Napoli wins both the Serie A championship (*lo scudetto*) and the Coppa Italia. Mass elation sweeps across the city.	The anticorruption campaign known as Mani pulite ('Clean Hands') is launched. The following year, Antonio Bassolino is voted mayor and a major city clean up begins.

2006, her time in office was not free of controversy. In April 2002 political chaos ensued after eight police officers were arrested on charges of torturing antiglobalisation protestors arrested at a 2001 government conference. Even more damaging were the waste-disposal crises of 2003, 2006 and 2008, which saw numerous city streets and squares reduced to festering rubbish tips. The 2008 crisis prompted the EU to take legal action against Italy for its ineffective management of the issue.

Beleaguered by years of humiliating headlines involving litter-strewn streets and gun-wielding *camorristi* (Camorra members), voters elected the city's current mayor, Luigi de Magistris, in 2011. For many disillusioned Neapolitans, the youthful former public prosecutor represented a glimmer of hope in a city deeply tarnished and abused.

2003	2004–05	2013	2015
The Campanian regional government launches Progetto Vesuvia in an attempt to clear Mt Vesuvius' heavily populated lower slopes. The €30,000 offered to relocate is rejected by most in the danger zone.	Tension between rival Camorra (Neapolitan Mafia) clans explodes on the streets of suburban Scampia and Secondigliano. In only four months almost 50 people are gunned down in retributive attacks.	Naples hosts the fourth Universal Forum of Cultures. The 101-day event sees further rejuvenation of the industrial Coroglio area between Naples and Pozzuoli.	After lengthy delays, Naples' showcase Municipio metro station opens to the public, featuring uncovered ancient ruins and a specially commissioned video painting by Israeli artist Michal Rovner.

The Arts

Dramatic, surprising and deliciously contradictory, Naples and its coast have long been a fertile ground for creativity. Caravaggio, Ribera, Scarlatti, Totò, De Sica: the region's list of homegrown and adopted talent spans some of the world's finest painters, composers, playwrights and film-makers. Indeed, some of Italy's most internationally recognisable cultural icons hail from Campanian soil, among them *commedia dell'arte* protagonist Pulcinella, the disconcertingly catchy tune 'Funiculì, Funiculà' and celluloid goddess Sophia Loren. Welcome to southern Italy's cultural powerhouse.

Brush-Clutching Greats

While Naples has produced great paintings throughout the centuries, none compare to the works created in the golden 17th and 18th centuries. High on wealth and power, the booming city had become the New York of its time, a magnet for talented, ambitious artists desperate to put their stamp on Naples' grand new churches and palaces.

The main influence on 17th-century Neapolitan art was Milan-born Michelangelo Merisi da Caravaggio (1573–1610), who fled to the city in 1606 after killing a man in Rome. Although he only stayed for a year, his naturalist style and dramatic depiction of light and shade (termed chiaroscuro) in paintings like *The Seven Acts of Mercy* (inside Pio Monte della Misericordia) and *Flagellation* (inside the Palazzo Reale di Capodimonte) had an electrifying effect on Naples' younger artists.

Among these was Giuseppe (or Jusepe) de Ribera (1591–1652), an aggressive, bullying Spaniard who arrived in Naples in 1616 after a seven-year stint in Rome. Ribera's combination of shadow, colour and gloomy naturalism proved hugely popular, best captured in his *capo lavoro* (masterpiece), the *Pietà* inside the Certosa di San Martino.

A fledgling apprentice to Ribera, Naples-born Luca Giordano (1632–1705) found great inspiration in the luminous brushstrokes of Mattia Preti (1613–99), not to mention the pomp of Venetian artist Paolo Veronese and the flounce of Rome-based artist and architect Pietro da Cortona. By the second half of the 17th century, Giordano would become the single most prolific baroque artist in Naples, his many commissions including wall frescoes in the Duomo's nave and a ceiling painting in the adjacent Basilica di Santa Restituta. The Chiesa del Gesù Nuovo boasts several Giordano creations, including vault and wall frescoes in the Cappella della Visitazione and canvases in the Cappella di San Francesco Saverio. Upstaging them all is his *Triumph of Judith*, a ceiling fresco in the treasury of the church of the Certosa di San Martino.

Giordano's contemporary Francesco Solimena (1657–1747) was also influenced by Ribera, although his use of shadow and solid form showed a clearer link with Caravaggio. Solimena would also become an icon of Neapolitan baroque, and his lavish compositions – among them the operatic fresco *Expulsion of Eliodoro from the Temple* in the Chiesa del

The region's diaspora turned Neapolitan tunes into the most internationally recognisable form of Italian music. When the sheet music to the Italian national anthem was lost at the 1920 Olympic Games in Antwerp, the orchestra broke into 'O Sole Mio' instead. It was the only Italian melody that everyone knew.

Gesù Nuovo – represented an accumulation of more than half a century of experimentation and trends, spanning Preti and Giordano himself.

The Neapolitan Score

Culture-Vulture Musts
....

Teatro San Carlo, Naples
....

Ravello Festival, Ravello
....

Napoli Teatro Festival, Naples
....

Centro di Musica Antica Pietà de' Turchini, Naples
....

La Mortella, Ischia

In the 1700s, Naples was the world's opera capital, with industry heavyweights flocking south to perform at the Teatro San Carlo. Locally trained greats like Francesco Durante (1684–1755), Leonardo Vinci (1690–1730) and Tommaso Traetta (1727–79) wowed conservatories across Europe. Naples' greatest composer, Alessandro Scarlatti (1660–1725), trained at the esteemed conservatory at the Chiesa della Pietà dei Turchini on Via Medina, which also gave birth to the renowned music group Pietà de' Turchini.

Creator of around 100 operatic works, Scarlatti also played a leading role in the development of *opera seria* (serious opera), giving the world the three-part overture and the *aria da capo*.

Running parallel to the high-brow *opera seria* was *opera buffa* (comic opera). Inspired by the Neapolitan *commedia dell'arte*, the genre began life as light-hearted, farcical interludes – *intermezzi* – performed between scenes of heavier classical operas. Kick-started by Scarlatti's *Il Trionfe Dell'onore* (The Triumph of Honour) in 1718, the contemporary interludes soon developed into a major, crowd-pleasing genre, with homegrown favourites including Giovanni Battista Pergolesi's *La Serva Padrona* (The Maid Mistress) and Domenico Cimarosa's *Il Matrimonio Segreto* (The Clandestine Marriage).

The following century saw the rise of the *la canzone napoletana* (Neapolitan song), its roots firmly planted in the annual Festa di Piedigrotta folk-song festival. Some tunes celebrated the city – among them the world-famous 'Funiculì, Funiculà', an ode to the funicular that once scaled Mt Vesuvius – and others lamented one's distance from it. Either way, the songs deeply resonated with the locals, especially the millions who boarded ships in search of a better life abroad.

The arrival of the American Allies in 1943 sparked another Neapolitan musical predilection: jazz, rhythm and blues. As music journalist Francesco Calazzo puts it: 'As a port city, Naples has always absorbed foreign influences. Musically, the result is a fusion of styles, from Arab laments and Spanish folk to African percussion and American blues'.

This fusion came to the fore in the late 1970s. A defining moment for Neapolitan music, it saw new-wave pioneers like Eugenio Bennato, Enzo Avitabile and Pino Daniele revive Neapolitan folk and cross it with rock, roots and hypnotic African beats. Singing many of his songs in Neapolitan, Daniele wrote bittersweet lyrics about his beloved hometown. Epitomised by songs like 'Napule è' (Naples Is), his work struck a particularly deep chord with the public. The singer-songwriter's fatal heart attack in January 2015 prompted widespread grief and camaraderie, with commuters even joining together in song on the metro. Even though

---

RIBERA: THE RUTHLESS SPANIARD
• •

Even though he was the leading light of Naples' mid-17th-century art scene, success did little to brighten Giuseppe de Ribera's dark side. Along with the Greek artist Belisario Corenzio and local painter Giambattista Caracciolo, Lo Spagnoletto (The Little Spaniard, as Ribera was known) formed a cabal to stamp out any potential competition. Merciless in the extreme, they stopped at nothing to get their way. Ribera reputedly won a commission for the Cappella di San Gennaro in the Duomo by poisoning his rival Domenichino (1581–1641) and wounding the assistant of a second competitor, Guido Reni (1575–1642). Much to the relief of other nerve-wracked artists, the cabal eventually broke up when Caracciolo died in 1642.

he's taken his final bow, Daniele's music lives on as an indelible part of Naples' rich musical heritage, one that forms the focus of John Turturro's film *Passione* (2010), a self-proclaimed 'cinematic love letter' to the city and its sounds.

Theatrical Legacies

Rivalling Naples' musical prowess is its theatrical tradition, considered one of Italy's oldest. Its most famous contribution to the world stage is the *commedia dell'arte*, dating back to the 16th century and rooted in the earthy ancient-Roman comedy theatre of *fabula Atellana* (Atellan farce). Like its ancient inspiration, this highly animated genre featured a set of stock characters in masks acting out a series of semistandard situations. Performances were often used to satirise local situations and were based on a tried-and-tested recipe of adultery, jealousy, old age and love.

Not only did *commedia dell'arte* give birth to a number of legendary characters, including the Harlequin and Punchinello, it provided fertile ground for the development of popular theatre in Naples and was a tradition in which the great dramatist Raffaele Viviani (1888–1950) was firmly rooted. Viviani's focus on the regional dialect and the Neapolitan working class won him local success and the enmity of the Mussolini regime.

The most important figure in modern Neapolitan theatre remains Eduardo de Filippo (1900–84). The son of a famous Neapolitan actor, Eduardo Scarpetta (1853–1925), De Filippo made his stage debut at the age of four and over the next 80 years became a hugely successful actor, impresario and playwright. His body of often-bittersweet work, which includes the classics *Il sindaco del Rione Sanità* (The Mayor of the Sanità Quarter) and *Sabato, domenica e lunedì* (Saturday, Sunday and Monday), encapsulated struggles well known to Neapolitans, from the injustice of being forced to live beyond the law to the fight for dignity in the face of adversity.

The *furbizia* (cunning) for which Neapolitans are famous is celebrated in De Filippo's play *Filumena Marturano*, in which a clever ex-prostitute gets her common-law husband to marry her by declaring him to be the father of one of her three *bambini*. The film adaptation, *Matrimonio all'italiana* (Marriage, Italian Style; 1964), stars homegrown siren Sophia Loren (1934–) alongside the great Marcello Mastroianni (1924–96).

Roberto de Simone (1933–) is another great Neapolitan playwright, not to mention a renowned composer and musicologist. While he is lesser known than De Filippo abroad, his theatrical masterpiece *La gatta cenerentola* (The Cat Cinderella) enjoyed a successful run in London in 1999. Artistic director of the Teatro San Carlo in the 1980s and later

THEATRE

THE ARTS THEATRICAL LEGACIES

While Naples' contemporary theatre scene remains fairly hit and miss, one of its leading talents is Enzo Moscato (1948–), whose work fuses a vibrant physicality with skilful use of dialect and music. His most famous production is the 1991 multiple-award-winning *Rasoi* (Razors).

A PUPPET WITH PUNCH

His aliases are many, from Punchinello or Mr Punch in Britain to Petruska in Russia. In his home town of Naples, however, he's simply Pulcinella: the best-known character of the *commedia dell'arte*.

In his white costume and black hook-nosed mask, this squeaky-voiced clown is equally exuberant and lazy, optimistic and cynical, melancholic and witty. As a street philosopher, he is anti-authoritarian and is often seen beating the local copper with a stick (hence the term slapstick). At home, however, his wife's the beater and he's the victim.

While some trace his creation to a 16th-century actor in the town of Capua, others believe he has been dancing and stirring since the days of togas...or even longer. In fact, his iconic hook-nosed mask appears on frescoed Etruscan tombs in Tarquinia, north of Rome. The mask belongs to Phersu, a vicious Etruscan demon known as the Queen of Hell's servant.

director of the Naples Conservatory, his extensive research into the city's folkloric tales and tunes has seen him revive rare comic operas, and create a cantata for 17th-century Campanian revolutionary Masaniello as well as the oratorio *Eleonora,* in honour of the heroine of the Neapolitan revolution of 1799.

The Silver Screen

In this corner of Italy, locations read like a red-carpet roll call: 'La Loren' wiggled her booty through Naples' Sanità district in *Ieri, oggi, domani* (Yesterday, Today, Tomorrow; 1963), Julia Roberts did a little soul-searching in its *centro storico* (historic centre) in *Eat Pray Love* (2010), and Jude Law and Gwyneth Paltrow toasted and tanned on Ischia and Procida in *The Talented Mr Ripley* (1999).

Naples' homemade offerings have often been intense and darkly comic, holding a mirror to the city's harsh realities. Feted for his 1948 neo-realist masterpiece *Ladri di biciclette* (Bicycle Thieves), Vittorio de Sica (1901–74) was a master at depicting the bittersweet struggle at the heart of so much Neapolitan humour. His two Neapolitan classics, *L'oro di Napoli* (The Gold of Naples; 1954) and *Ieri, oggi, domani,* delighted audiences across the world.

Appearing with Loren in both *L'oro di Napoli* and the slapstick farce *Miseria e nobilità* (Misery and Nobility; 1954) was the city's other screen deity, Antonio de Curtis (1898–1967), aka Totò. Dubbed the Neapolitan Buster Keaton, Totò depicted Neapolitan cunning like no other. Born in the working-class Sanità district, he appeared in over 100 films, typically playing the part of a hustler living on nothing but his quick wits. It was a role that ensured Totò's cult status in a city where the art of *arrangiarsi* (getting by) is a way of life.

Inheriting Totò's mantle, Massimo Troisi (1953–94) was best known internationally for his role in *Il postino* (The Postman; 1994). In his 1980 debut film, *Ricomincio da tre* (I'm Starting from Three), he humorously tackled the problems faced by Neapolitans forced to head north for work. Troisi's cameo in the schlock murder mystery *No grazie, il caffè mi rende nervoso* (No Thanks, Coffee Makes Me Nervous; 1982) – arguably one of his funniest – saw a rambling, pyjama-clad Troisi hopelessly attempting to convince Funiculì, Funiculà (an unseen, helium-pitched psychopath set on sabotaging Naples' new jazz festival) that he is loyal only to the city's traditional cultural offerings.

A new wave of Neapolitan directors, including Antonio Capuano (1940–), Mario Martone (1959–), Pappi Corsicato (1960–) and Antonietta de Lillo (1960–), have also turned their cameras on the city in films such as Capuano's critically acclaimed *Luna rossa* (Red Moon) of 2001. While Corsicato's queer-centric classics *Libera* (Free; 1993) and *I bucchi neri* (The Black Holes; 1995) evoke the ever-present link between the ancient and modern sides of Naples, De Lillo's finest offering to date, *Il resto di niente* (The Remains of Nothing; 2003), explores the psychological complexities of revolutionary Eleonora de Fonseca Pimentel; it's also the inspiration for De Simone's aforementioned oratorio. A much more recent offering is *E poi c'è Napoli* (And Then There is Naples; 2014), a documentary film directed by Gianluca Migliarotti (1974–). An ode to classic Neapolitan style and tailoring, its depiction of an elegant, cultured metropolis of Kiton suits and modern-day dandies is a refreshing counterpoint to the ruthless, blood-stained Naples portrayed in the multi-award-winning feature film *Gomorra* (Gomorrah; 2008). Directed by Rome's Matteo Garrone (1968–) but based on the explosive book by Neapolitan Roberto Saviano, *Gomorra* intertwines five stories of characters affected by Naples' notorious organised-crime syndicate, the Camorra.

Neapolitan Playlist

························

James Senese
Sax man and jazz icon
························

Enzo Avitabile
(www.enzoavitabile.it) Funk and world-music artist
························

Marcello Colasurdo
(www.marcellocolasurdo.it) Folk-music legend
························

99 Posse
(www.novenove.it) Topical rap-dub-trip-hop outfit

The Neapolitan Way of Life

There is nowhere more theatrical than Naples, a city in which everyday transactions become minor performances and traffic jams give rise to impromptu car-horn concerts. Neapolitans often wear their hearts on their sleeves, and the streets and squares are a stage on which to play out quotidian dramas. Indeed, nowhere else in Italy are the people so conscious of their role in the theatre of everyday life and so addicted to its intensity.

Language & Identity

Neapolitans have a very strong sense of their own identity, one which includes their very particular dialect. Though not recognised as an official minority language by the Italian government, the Neapolitan dialect (known locally as *napulitano*) is considered one of the world's endangered languages by Unesco. Influenced by centuries of foreign domination (there are an estimated 400 Spanish loanwords alone), it features its own distinct vocabulary, grammar, orthography and pronunciation. The official language of the Kingdom of Naples between 1442 and 1458, Neapolitan lives on in the region's streets, as well as in a bounty of literature and music written in the language, from Giovanni Boccaccio's 14th-century *Epistola napoletana* (Neapolitan Epistle) to the contemporary folk-rock anthems of the late singer-songwriter Pino Daniele. You'll even hear the occasional Neapolitan quip from Sophia Loren in classic Italian films like *L'oro di Napoli* (The Gold of Naples; 1954) and *Matrimonio all'italiana* (Marriage Italian Style; 1964). As the homegrown actor once famously declared, 'I'm not Italian, I am Neapolitan! It's another thing'.

Neapolitans know that many of the stereotypes foreigners hold of Italians – noisy, theatrical, food-loving, passionate and proud – refer to them. And many revel in it. Everyone has an opinion to give, a line to deliver or a sigh to perform. Eavesdropping is a popular pastime and knowing everyone else's business is a veritable sport. Neapolitans joke that if you were to collapse on the street a local would first want to know all the juicy details, and only after that would they think of calling an ambulance. In a city with a population density of 8566 people per square kilometre (45 times higher than the national average), this penchant for curiosity is understandable.

And yet, Neapolitans are far more complex than any earthy, streetwise hallmark can convey. After all, theirs is a city of aristocratic palaces and art collections, a world-renowned opera house, and one of Europe's oldest universities. Naples gave the world pizza and Pulcinella, but it has also given it composer Alessandro Scarlatti, playwright Roberto de Simone, and contemporary artist Francesco Clemente. To the world's fashion elite, Neapolitan tradition means meticulous tailoring and inimitable male elegance. This is the home town of hand-stitched Kiton suits, dashing E Marinella ties, and handcrafted Talarico umbrellas. It's an oft-overlooked side of the city beautifully captured in Gianluca

Neapolitans' fierce and famous individuality goes back to ancient times. Despite Roman conquest, Neapolis held fast to its Greek language and Hellenic customs.

Migliarotti's *E poi c'è Napoli* (And Then There is Naples; 2014), which portrays an erudite, elegant metropolis. As the locals will quickly remind you, Napoli is more than *pizza e mandolini* (pizza and mandolins).

Wanted: Opportunity

While Neapolitans may be rightly passionate about their city, a scarcity of jobs sees many forced to bid it a bittersweet *arrivederci*. Figures released by Istat (Italy's Bureau of Statistics) in early 2015 put Campania's unemployment rate at 21.7%, compared to the national average of around 13%. In Naples itself, the figure is an even higher 24.6%. Even more disconcerting is the youth unemployment rate, with 42.7% of those aged 15 to 24 jobless.

Such dire statistics are driving the region's – indeed, the country's – ongoing *fuga dei cervelli* (brain drain), in which an ever-growing number of young university-educated Italians are heading abroad in search of a better future. In a 2012 study of Italians under 30 by Milan's Instituto Toniolo, 48.9% of participants claimed that they were ready and willing to bid their country farewell to improve their job prospects. Of those with both a university degree and a job, only 33% were employed in an area that reflected their formal training.

For many young, educated and ambitious Campanians wanting to develop their careers, there is little incentive to remain in Italy. Relatively low government investment in research and development (about 1.3% of GDP, compared to 3% in France and Germany) has stunted economic innovation and opportunity. The country's ingrained culture of nepotism prevents many of the country's brightest, most promising talent from obtaining positions they truly deserve. It's a problem well documented in *La fuga dei talenti* (Flight of the Talented; www.fugadeitalenti.word press.com), a book-turned-blog by Italian journalist Sergio Nava aimed at reversing the country's loss of human capital. As Nava puts it, Italy is a country where 'the value of merit is largely disregarded', where 'it doesn't help to have a good CV, or an international profile: corporative interests and family relations come before anything else'. Over 60% of Italian companies recruit through personal introductions and recommendations. In a landscape so riddled with nepotism, putting in a good word is not simply a thoughtful gesture, it's essential to help someone get ahead.

At the bottom end of the job chain are Campania's migrant communities. While a growing number of Chinese, Sri Lankans and Eastern Europeans are opening their own small businesses – mostly restaurants, grocery shops and cheap clothing outlets – the majority of immigrants in the region work on construction sites and in private homes. Indeed, around 70% of immigrants in Naples work as housekeepers, babysitters or domestic carers for the elderly. In the 1970s and 1980s, housekeeping was a veritable dream job for the newly arrived. Having a maid was the

Over 60% of Neapolitans aged 18 to 34 live at home. This is not because Naples is a city of *mammoni* (mamma's boys) and *figlie di papa* (daddy's girls) – at least, not entirely. High rents make independent living prohibitively expensive for many young locals.

THE OLD PROVERBIAL

They may be clichés, but proverbs can be quite the cultural revelation. Here are five of Naples' well-worn best:

➡ *A léngua nun tène òsso ma ròmpe ll'òssa* (The tongue has no bone, but it breaks bones).

➡ *A mughièra 'e ll'àte é sèmpe cchiù bbòna* (Other people's wives are always more beautiful).

➡ *Ògne scarrafóne è bèllo 'a màmma sóia* (Even a beetle is beautiful to its mother).

➡ *E pariénte so còmme 'e scàrpe: cchiù so strìtte e cchiù te fànno màle* (Relatives are like shoes: the tighter they are the more they hurt).

➡ *L'amico è come l'ombrello, quando piove non lo trovi mai* (The friend is like the umbrella: when it's raining, you never find it).

THE NORTH–SOUTH DIVIDE

While countless *meridionali* (southern Italians) have headed abroad in search of greener pastures, just as many have settled in Italy's wealthier north – a situation comically captured in *Ricomincio da tre* (I'm Starting from Three; 1980), a film starring late Neapolitan actor Massimo Troisi. Punchlines aside, the film reveals Italy's very real north–south divide.

From the Industrial Revolution to the 1960s, millions fled to the industrialised northern cities for factory jobs. As the saying goes, *Ogni vero milanese ha un nonno pugliese* (Every true Milanese has a Pugliese grandparent). For most of these homegrown migrants, the welcome they received north of Rome was anything but warm. Disparagingly nicknamed *terroni* (peasants), many faced discrimination from everyone from landlords to baristas.

Although such overt discrimination is now practically nonexistent, historical prejudices linger. Many northerners resent their taxes being used to 'subsidise' the 'lazy', 'corrupt' south – a sentiment that takes political form in the right-wing, Veneto-based Lega Nord (Northern League) party.

Yet negative attitudes can work both ways. One well-worn southern joke tells how God invented the north of Italy, realised his mistake, and consequently added its infamous fog.

ultimate status symbol for the city's rich, and as a result many immigrant workers enjoyed long-term job security and friends in high places. Since the 1990s, however, increased demand has come from the time-pressed middle classes. Unlike their upper-class counterparts, many of these more modest clients cannot afford to offer workers the same economic and legal perks. What was once a secure job is now fraught with insecurity.

Even more precarious is the life of the street sellers, many of whom are *clandestini* (illegal immigrants) from Senegal. Known as *vù cumprà* – named for their catchphrase, 'Do you want to buy?' – they sell counterfeit goods displayed on sheets along the pavement. When the police cruise by, the vendors swoop up their stock and flee, fearing arrest and possible deportation.

Outside the city the situation is worse for *clandestini*, who mostly find short-term seasonal work in the agricultural sector. The work is hard and poorly paid, and some employers are more than happy to exploit their illegal employees' vulnerable position. Many illegal African immigrants are smuggled into Italy by Mafia-run operatives. Once on Italian soil, they are hired out as farmhands, their Mafia handlers demanding a percentage of the labourers' below-minimum wages. Most workers receive no more than €25 for up to two weeks' work on southern-Italian farms. Resentment caused by this exploitation exploded in January 2010, when the small Calabrian town of Rosarno became the scene of violent race riots that sent shock waves through Italy and the world.

Family Life & Gender Battles

While Neapolitans pride themselves on their spontaneity and flexibility, Sunday *pranzo* (lunch) with the family is usually non-negotiable. Rain, hail or shine, this time of the week is sacred to Neapolitan families a time to catch up on each others' lives, pick over the latest news about politicians, footballers and celebrities, and eat like royalty. Indeed, the sacred status of Sunday lunch is a reminder that family remains the bedrock of Neapolitan life. Loyalty to family and friends is deeply engraved in the Neapolitan psyche. As Luigi Barzini (1908–84), author of *The Italians,* noted, 'A happy private life helps tolerate an appalling public life'. This chasm between the private arena and the public one is a noticeable aspect of the southern mentality, and has evolved over years of intrusive foreign domination. Some locals mightn't think twice about littering in the street, but step inside their home and you'll find floors clean enough

Focus on the positives. Although Neapolitans regularly lament their city's shortcomings, jibes from a *straniero* (foreigner) can cause offence.

to eat off. After all, you'd never want someone dropping in and thinking you're a *barbone* (tramp), right?

Maintaining a *bella figura* (beautiful image) is very important to the average Neapolitan, and how you and your family appear to the outside world is a matter of honour, respectability and pride. To many southern Italians, you are better than your neighbour if you own more and better things. This mentality is rooted in the past, when one really did need to own lots of things to attain certain social roles, and ultimately sustain your family. Yet *fare bella figura* (making a good impression) goes beyond a well-kept house, extending to dressing well, behaving modestly, performing religious and social duties and fulfilling all essential family obligations. In the context of the extended family, where gossip is rife, a good image protects one's privacy.

Families in Campania remain among the country's largest, with an average size of 2.73 compared to 2.23 in Lazio, 2.27 in Lombardy and 2.20 in Piedmont. It's still the norm to live at home until you marry, and one-third of husbands still visit their mothers every day. While many of these will have a bowl of their favourite pasta waiting for them, some will also have their laundry freshly washed and ironed. According to a 2009 report by the Uomini Casalinghi (The Italian Association of Househusbands), 95% of Italian men have never turned on a washing machine, and 70% of them have never used a stove. Figures released by the Organisation of Economic Co-Operation and Development (OECD) in 2013 indicate that Italian women spend 36 hours a week on domestic duties, compared to 14 hours for Italian men. The report also found that only 47% of Italian women are in the workforce, a significantly lower proportion than the OECD average of 60%.

> Steer clear of chrysanthemums when buying flowers for a local. In Italy they're only used to decorate graves.

Men continue to receive roughly 10% more in their pay packet than their female colleagues, while some employers still view female candidates as a risk, likely to give up their jobs to raise a family. Add a largely ineffective child care system, and the juggling of work and motherhood becomes a rather stressful act for many Campanian women.

IN FOOTBALL WE TRUST

Catholicism may be Italy's official faith, but its true religion is *calcio* (football). On any given weekend from late August to May, you'll find millions of *tifosi* (football fans) at the *stadio* (stadium), glued to the television or checking the score on their phone. Naples is no exception: the city is home to southern Italy's most successful team (Napoli) and the country's third-largest stadium (Stadio San Paolo), not to mention a small shrine dedicated to Napoli's greatest-ever on-field hero, Diego Maradona.

Swiped from Barcelona for a record-breaking €12 million in 1984, the Argentine star would lead Napoli to its greatest ever glory in the 1986–87 football season, winning both the Serie A title and the Coppa Italia. A first for any mainland southern-Italian team, the twin win transformed Maradona into a Neapolitan demigod.

While captaining Argentina in the 1990 FIFA World Cup, Maradona infamously encouraged the city to cheer on Argentina in the semifinals against Italy in Naples. Tapping into Italy's north–south tension, Maradona controversially declared: 'I don't like the fact that now everybody is asking Neapolitans to be Italian and to support their national team. Naples has always been marginalised by the rest of Italy. It is a city that suffers the most unfair racism'.

Thankfully, any north–south resentment was relegated to the sidelines in 2006, when Neapolitan pin-up Fabio Cannavaro led Italy to victory in the World Cup. Nine months after the win, hospitals in northern Italy reported a baby boom.

Saints & Superstitions

Naples is Europe's esoteric metropolis par excellence: a Mediterranean New Orleans with less voodoo and more Catholic guilt. Here, miracles pack out cathedrals, dreams channel lottery numbers, and horn-shaped charms ward off the dreaded *mal'occhio* (evil eye). Despite the contemporary feel of blaring pop and ringtones, Neapolitan streets are littered with well-worn myths and legends, from Santa Maria Francesca's miraculous chair in the Quartieri Spagnoli to an alchemist prince's bizarre anatomical models deep in the *centro storico* (historic centre).

Friends in High Places

Headlining the city's supernatural scene are the saints, who are veritable celebrities. Fireworks explode in their honour, fans flock to kiss their marble feet and newborn *bambini* (children) take their names. That Gennaro is the most common male name in Naples is no coincidence: San Gennaro is the city's patron saint. As in much of southern Italy, Neapolitans celebrate their *giorno omastico* (name day) with as much gusto as they do their birthday. Forgetting a friend's name day is a bigger faux pas than forgetting their birthday because everyone knows (or should know) the most important saints' days.

For the religiously inclined, these haloed helpers play a more significant role in their spiritual life than the big 'G' himself. While the Almighty is perceived as authoritative and distant – just like many old-school Italian *papà* (dads) – the saints enjoy a more familial role as intercessor and confidant.

Topping the list of go-betweens is the Virgin Mary, whose status as maternal protector strikes a deep chord in a society where mothers have always fiercely defended the rights of their precious sons. Festival days in honour of the Madonna are known to whip up mass hysteria, best exemplified by the annual Feast of the Madonna dell'Arco. Held on Easter Monday, it sees thousands of pilgrims called *fujenti* (Neapolitan for 'those who run') walk barefoot to the Santuario della Madonna dell'Arco, located near the village of Sant'Anastasia at the foot of Mt Vesuvius. The focus of their devotion is an unusual image of the Virgin Mary, in which her cheek is wounded. According to legend, the wound's origins go back to Easter Monday in 1500, when a disgruntled mallet player hit the Virgin's image with a wooden ball. Miraculously, the image began to bleed, leading to the spoilsport's hanging and the construction of the sanctuary on the site of the event. As they approach the sanctuary, the *fujenti* run towards it. Some fall into a trance, with many more shouting, crying and walking on their knees towards the image in what can be described as a collective purging of guilt and pain. In Naples, the lead-up to the festival is an event in itself. From the week following the Epiphany (6 January) to Easter Monday, hundreds of neighbourhood *congreghe* (instrument-playing congregations) parade through the streets, carrying a statue of the Madonna, collecting offerings for the big day and playing an incongruous medley of tunes (think 'Ave Maria' followed by a 1970s Raffaella Carrà pop hit).

So popular was the cult of the *anime pezzentelle* (poor souls) that a special tram – packed with flower-laden locals each Monday, the day dedicated to visiting souls in limbo – ran to the Cimitero delle Fontanelle. Involving the veneration of skulls (each representing a soul trapped in purgatory), the cult was banned by the Church in 1969.

In Naples, it is still possible to see elaborate, coach-style hearses drawn by as many as eight horses. It seems that when people die, the obsession with *fare bella figura* (keeping up appearances) does not die with them.

Exactly which saint you consult can depend on what you're after. If it's an addition to the family, chances are you'll head straight to the former home of Santa Maria Francesca delle Cinque Piaghe to sit on the saint's miraculous chair. It's the closest thing to a free fertility treatment in Naples. On the opposite side of Via Toledo, in the Chiesa del Gesù Nuovo, entire rooms are dedicated to Dr Giuseppe Moscati (1880–1927), a much-loved local medic canonised in 1987. Here, *ex-votos* decorate the walls, each one testament to the MD's celestial intervention.

Despite the Madonna's popularity, the city's ultimate holy superhero is San Gennaro. Every year in May, September and December thousands of Neapolitans cram themselves into the Duomo to pray for a miracle: that the blood of Naples' patron saint, kept here in two phials, will liquefy and save Naples from any potential disaster.

According to scientists, the so-called miracle has a logical explanation. Apparently, it's all to do with thixotrophy, the property of certain compounds to liquefy when shaken and then to return to their original form when left to stand. To verify this, however, scientists would have to analyse the blood, something the Church has effectively blocked by refusing permission to open the phials.

And while many locals acknowledge the scientific line, the fact remains that when the blood liquefies the city breathes a sigh of relief. After all, when the miracle failed in 1944 Mt Vesuvius erupted, and when it failed again in 1980, a catastrophic earthquake hit the city.

> For centuries, locals believed that a crocodile lurked below the Castel Nuovo. Some said the reptile lunched on Queen Joan II's ex-lovers. Others swore that political prisoners were on the menu. According to writer and intellectual Benedetto Croce, the crocodile was eventually caught using a horse's thigh as bait.

Beware the Evil Eye

The concept of luck plays a prominent role in the Neapolitan mindset. Curse-deterring amulets are as plentiful as crucifix pendants, and the same Neapolitan who makes the sign of the cross when passing a church will make the sign of the horns (by extending their thumb, index finger and little finger and shaking their hand to the ground) to keep the *mal'occhio* (evil eye) at bay.

A common belief throughout Italy, though particularly strong in the country's south, *mal'occhio* refers to misfortune cast upon an individual by a malevolent or envious person. In fact, Neapolitans often refer to this bad luck as *jettatura*, a derivative of the Italian verb *gettare* (to throw or cast).

Ready to deflect the negative energy is the city's most iconic amulet-souvenir: the *corno*. Usually red and shaped liked a single curved horn, its evil-busting powers are said to lie in its representation of the bull and its sexual vigour.

Another traditional, though rare, deflector of bad luck is the *'o Scartellat*. Usually an elderly man, he can occasionally be spotted burning incense through the city's older neighbourhoods, clearing the streets of bad vibes and inviting good fortune. The title itself is Neapolitan for those suffering from kyphosis (overcurvature of the upper back), as the

> A knight who lay down on St Patrizia's tomb was inexplicably cured of all his ills. Seized by religious fervour, he opened her tomb and tore out one of her teeth. Blood flowed miraculously and the knight captured it in two phials, now safely stored in the Chiesa di San Gregorio Armeno.

DEATH & THE CITY

It makes sense that Neapolitans – rattled by earthquakes and the odd volcanic eruption – are a fatalistic lot. Indeed, the city's intense passion for life is only matched by its curious attachment to death. Here, contemporary culture's death-defying delusions are constantly undermined, whether by death-notice–plastered walls, shrines dedicated to the dearly departed or edible treats with names like *torrone dei morti* (nougat of the dead), the latter merrily gobbled on All Saints' Day. Carved skulls decorate churches and cloisters, such as those adorning the Chiostro Grande (Great Cloister) inside the Certosa di San Martino – a constant reminder of one's mortal status.

LOTTERY DREAMS

In every visible aspect the Neapolitan lottery is the same as every other lottery: tickets are bought, numbers are marked and the winning combination is pulled out of a closely guarded hat. It differs, however, in the way that some Neapolitans select their numbers. They dream them – or rather they interpret their dreams with the aid of *La Smorfia*, a kind of dream dictionary.

According to the good book, if you dream of God or Italy, you should pick number one. Other symbols include dancing (37), crying (21), fear (90) and a woman's hair (55).

Some leave the interpreting to the lotto-shop expert by whispering their dreams into the shop-owner's ear (no-one wants to share a winning combination) and letting them choose the numbers. According to the locals, the city's luckiest *ricevitoria* (lotto shop) is the one at Porta Capuana. Run by the same family for more than 200 years, the current owner's grandmother was considered a dream-theme expert. To this day, people bring their dreams here from as far afield as the US, Spain and Switzerland.

While *La Smorfia's* origins are obscure, links are often made to the number-word mysticism of the Jewish Kabbalah. The term itself most likely derives from Morpheus, the Greek god of dreams, suggesting that the tradition is linked to Naples' ancient Greek origins and to the Hellenic tradition of oneirocriticism (dream interpretation).

task was once the domain of the posture challenged. According to Neapolitan lore, touching a hunchback's hump brings good luck, as does stepping in dog poop and having wine spilt on you accidentally.

Scandalous Souls

One figure who could have used some good luck was Donna Maria d'Avalos, who in October 1590 met a gruesome end in the Palazzo dei Di Sangro on Piazza San Domenico Maggiore. Her murderer was Carlo Gesualdo, one of the late Renaissance's most esteemed composers, not to mention d'Avalos' husband. Suspecting her of infidelity, Gesualdo tricked his wife into thinking that he was away on a hunting trip. Instead, Gesualdo was waiting in the wings, ready to catch d'Avalos and her lover, Don Fabrizio Carafa, red-handed. According to eyewitnesses, Gesualdo entered the apartment with three men, shouting 'Kill the scoundrel, along with this harlot!'. Officials investigating the crime scene described finding a mortally wounded Carafa lying on the floor, covered in blood and wearing a woman's nightgown adorned with ruffs of black silk. On the bed was d'Avalos, nightgown drenched in blood and throat slit.

Gesualdo's jealous rage would not have been helped by Carafa's enviable good looks – it's said that the younger nobleman was so devastatingly handsome that he was known around town as *l'angelo* (the Angel). As a nobleman himself, Gesualdo was immune from prosecution, though a fear of retribution for the murders saw him flee to his hometown, Venosa.

In the decades that followed Gesualdo's own death, the Prince of Venosa became a semimythical figure, his name associated with ever more lurid tales of bloody revenge. Some say that 'the Angel's' death wasn't enough for the betrayed husband, who subsequently murdered his own infant son for fear that he really belonged to Carafa. According to other accounts, Gesualdo's victims included his father-in-law, who had come seeking his own revenge.

And then there is the beautiful Maria d'Avalos herself, whose scantily dressed ghost is said to haunt Piazza San Domenico Maggiore when the moon is full, desperately searching for her slaughtered sweetheart.

The Palazzo dei Di Sangro was built for the noble Di Sangro family, a member of which, Raimondo Di Sangro (1710–71), remains one of Naples' most rumour-ridden characters. Inventor, scientist, soldier

Mythical Musts in Naples

Festa di San Gennaro

Casa e Chiesa di Santa Maria Francesca delle Cinque Piaghe

Cimitero delle Fontanelle

Madonna del Carmine festival

Complesso Museale di Santa Maria delle Anime del Purgatorio ad Arco

VICTORY OF THE SHRINES

It only takes a quick stroll through the *centro storico* (historic centre), Quartieri Spagnoli or Sanità district to work out that small shrines are a big hit in Naples. A kitschy combo of electric votive candles, Catholic iconography and fresh or plastic flowers, they adorn everything from *palazzo* (mansion) facades to courtyards and staircases. Most come with an inscription, confirming the shrine as a tribute *per grazie ricevute* (for graces received) or *ex-voto* (in fulfilment of a vow).

The popularity of the shrines can be traced back to the days of Dominican friar Gregorio Maria Rocco (1700–82). Determined to make the city's dark, crime-ridden laneways safer, he convinced the Bourbon monarch to light them up with oil lamps. The lamps were promptly trashed by the city's petty thieves, who relied on darkness to trip up their victims with rope. Thankfully, the quick-thinking friar had a better idea. Banking on the city's respect for its saints, he encouraged locals to erect illuminated shrines. The idea worked and the streets became safer, for even the toughest of petty thieves wouldn't dare upset an adored celestial idol.

Across from the Solfatara Crater – reputed site of San Gennaro's beheading in 305 – is the Santuario di San Gennaro alla Solfatara, home to the marble slab said to have been used for his murder. Legend has it that, when the saint's blood liquefies, dark bloodstains reappear on the slab.

and alchemist, the Prince of Sansevero came up with some nifty inventions, among them a waterproof cape for Charles III of Bourbon and a mechanical land-and-water carriage 'drawn' by life-size cork horses. He also introduced freemasonry into the Kingdom of Naples, resulting in a temporary excommunication from the Catholic Church.

Yet even a papal rethink couldn't quell the salacious stories surrounding Raimondo, which included castrating promising young sopranos and knocking off seven cardinals to make furniture with their skin and bones. Even fellow freemason Count Alessandro Cagliostro – who went on trial before the Inquisition court in Rome in 1790 – confessed that everything he knew about alchemy and the dark arts he learned from Di Sangro. According to Italian philosopher Benedetto Croce (1866–1952), who wrote about Di Sangro in his book *Storie e leggende napoletane* (Neapolitan Stories and Legends), the alchemist held a Faustian fascination for the *centro storico's* masses. To them, his supposed knack for magic saw him master everything from replicating the miracle of San Gennaro's blood to reducing marble to dust with a simple touch.

For centuries rumours surrounded the two perfect anatomical models in the crypt of the Di Sangro funerary chapel, the Cappella Sansevero. One popular legend suggested that the bodies were those of his domestics. Even taller was the tale that the servants were far from dead when the prince got started on the embalming. It's cruel fiction, undoubtedly, but even today the models' realistic detail leaves many questions unanswered.

The Campanian Table

Sampling Campania's larder is a mouthwatering experience, reflecting the locals' own seasoned seductiveness. Everything seems to taste that little bit better here – the tomatoes are sweeter, the mozzarella is silkier and the *caffè* (coffee) is richer and stronger. Some put it down to the rich volcanic soil, others to the region's sun and water. Complementing these natural perks is the advantage of well-honed traditions, passed down through the generations and still faithfully venerated. Here, food, identity and pride are inseparable.

A Historical Melting Pot

The region's culinary line-up is an exotic culmination of foreign influence and local resourcefulness. In its 3000-year history, Naples has played countless roles, from Roman holiday resort and medieval cultural hot spot to glittering European capital. As the foreign rulers have come and gone, they've left their mark – on the art and architecture, on the local dialect and on the food. The ancient Greeks turned up with the olive trees, grapevines and durum wheat. Centuries later, the Byzantines and Arab traders from nearby Sicily brought in the pine nuts, almonds, raisins and honey that they used to stuff their vegetables. They also brought what was to become the mainstay of the Neapolitan diet and, in time, Italy's most famous food – pasta.

Although it was first introduced in the 12th century, pasta really took off in the 17th century when it established itself as the poor man's food of choice. Requiring only a few simple ingredients – just flour and water at its most basic – pasta proved a lifesaver as the city's population exploded. The nobility, however, continued to shun pasta until Gennaro Spadaccini invented the four-pronged fork in the early 18th century.

During Naples' Bourbon period (1734–1860), two parallel gastronomic cultures developed: that of the opulent Spanish monarchy; and that of the streets, the *cucina povera* (cuisine of the poor). As much as the former was elaborate and rich, the latter was simple and healthy.

The food of the poor, the so-called *mangiafoglie* (leaf eaters), was largely based on pasta, and vegetables grown on the fertile volcanic plains around Naples. Aubergines (eggplants), artichokes, courgettes (zucchini), tomatoes and peppers were among the staples, while milk from sheep, cows and goats was used to make cheese. Flat breads imported from Greek and Arab lands, the forebears of pizza, were also popular. Meat and fish were expensive and reserved for special occasions.

Meanwhile, in the court kitchens, the top French cooks of the day were working to feed the insatiable appetites of the Bourbon monarchy. The headstrong queen Maria Carolina, wife of King Ferdinand I, was so impressed by her sister Marie Antoinette's court in Versailles that she asked to borrow some chefs. These Gallic imports obviously took to the Neapolitan air, creating among other things highly elaborate *timballi di pasta* (pasta pies), the *gattò di patate* (potato tart) and the iconic *babà*, a mushroom-shaped sponge cake soaked in rum and sugar.

The excellent food and travel portal www.deliciousitaly.com lists culinary courses and tours. Another useful website for lovers of Italian food and wine is www.gambero-rosso.it, which offers a plethora of information on Italian food, wine, culinary events and courses.

DIY LIMONCELLO

Campania's celebrated *limoncello* (lemon-flavoured liqueur) is remarkably easy to make; there's a good recipe at www.bbcgoodfood.com. Just make sure you use good unwaxed lemons, even if they are not the sun-kissed variety from Capri. If you speak Italian, you'll find another good recipe at www.limoncellodiprocida.it (and they also ship...).

More contentious are the origins of Naples' most famous pastry: the flaky, seashell-shaped *sfogliatella*. Filled with cinnamon-infused ricotta and candied fruit, it was created, some say, by French chefs for the king of Poland in the 18th century. Others say that it was invented by 18th-century nuns in Conca dei Marini, a small village on the Amalfi Coast. Nowadays its two most popular forms are the soft and doughy shortcrust *frolla* and the crispy, filo-style '*riccia*' version.

Campanian Culinary Icons

Pizza

Despite the Bourbons' lavish legacy, Campania's no-nonsense attitude to food – keep it simple, keep it local and keep it coming – remains deeply rooted in the traditions of the poor. This is especially true in its predilection for pizza, a mainstay of *cucina povera* and one of the foundations on which Naples' gastronomic reputation stands.

A derivation of the flat breads of ancient Greece and Egypt, pizza was already a common street snack by the time the city's 16th-century Spanish occupiers introduced the tomato to Italy. The New World topping cemented pizza's popularity and in 1738 Naples' first pizzeria opened its doors on Port'Alba, where it still stands. Soon after, the city's *pizzaioli* (pizza makers) began to enjoy minor celebrity status.

There is no seafood on a Neapolitan pizza marinara – just tomato, garlic, oregano and extra-virgin olive oil. The pizza's name stems from its popularity with local fishermen, who'd take it out to sea for lunch.

To this day, the city's most famous dough-kneader remains Raffaelle Esposito, inventor of the classic pizza margherita. As the city's top *pizzaiolo*, Esposito was summoned to fire up a treat for a peckish King Umberto I and his wife, Queen Margherita, on a royal visit in 1889. Determined to impress the Italian royals, Esposito based his creation of tomato, mozzarella and basil on the red, white and green flag of the newly unified Italy. The resulting topping met with the queen's approval and was subsequently named in her honour.

More than a century later, pizza purists claim that you really can't top Esposito's classic combo when it's made by a true Neapolitan *pizzaiolo*. Not everyone is in accordance, and Italians are often split between those who favour the thin-crust Roman variant and those who go for the thicker Neapolitan version.

According to the official Associazione Verace Pizza Napoletana (Real Neapolitan Pizza Association), genuine Neapolitan pizza dough must be made using highly refined type 00 wheat flour (a small dash of type 0 flour is permitted), compressed or natural yeast, salt, and water with a pH level between six and seven. While a low-speed mixer can be used for kneading the dough, only hands can be used to form the *disco di pasta* (pizza base), which should not be thicker than 3mm. The pizza itself should be cooked at 485°C (905°F) in a doubled-domed, wood-fired oven using oak, ash, beech or maple timber.

Pasta

Pizza's bedfellow, pasta, arrived in Naples via Sicily, where it had been introduced by Arab merchants. The windy Campanian climate was later found to be ideal for drying pasta, and production took off in a big way, especially after the 1840 opening of Italy's first pasta plant in Torre Annunziata.

The staple itself is divided into *pasta fresca* (fresh pasta), devoured within a few days of purchase, and *pasta secca* (dried pasta), handy for long-term storage. One of the top varieties of local *pasta fresca* is Amalfi's own *scialatielli*, a flat noodle both longer and thicker than tagliatelle and often 'pinched' in the middle. Its name stems from the Neapolitan term *sciglià* (to tousle), and it's a perfect match for delicate tomato and seafood *sughi* (sauces).

This said, Naples is more famous for its *pasta secca,* the most obvious examples of which are spaghetti, macaroni, penne (smallish tubes cut at an angle) and rigatoni (similar to penne but with ridges on them). Made from *grano duro* (durum wheat) flour and water, it's often served (al dente, of course) with vegetable-based *sughi,* which are generally less rich than the traditional *pasta fresca* varieties.

The best of the region's artisanal pastas comes from the small town of Gragnano, some 30km southeast of Naples. A pasta-producing hub since the 17th century, its main street was specifically built along the sun's axis so that the pasta put out to dry by the town's *pastifici* (pasta factories) would reap a full day's sunshine.

As for the queen of the region's pasta dishes, it's hard to beat the mouth-watering *pasta al forno* (baked pasta), a decadent combination of macaroni, tomato sauce, mozzarella and, depending on the recipe, hard-boiled egg, meatballs and sausage. No less than a gastronomic 'event', it's often cooked for Sunday lunch and other special occasions.

Vegetables & Fruit

Poverty and sunshine also helped develop Campania's prowess with vegetables. Dishes like *zucchine fritte* (panfried zucchini), *parmigiana di melanzane* (fried aubergines layered with hard-boiled eggs, mozzarella, onion, tomato sauce and basil) and *peperoni sotto aceto* (marinated peppers) are common features of both antipasto buffets and the domestic kitchen table.

Some of the country's finest produce is grown in the mineral-rich volcanic soil of Mt Vesuvius and its surrounding plain, including tender *carciofi* (artichokes) and *cachi* (persimmons), as well as Campania's unique green *friarielli* – a bitter broccoli-like vegetable *saltata in padella* (panfried), spiked with *peperoncino* (red chilli) and often served with diced *salsiccia di maiale* (pork sausage).

Although some producers find these official Italian classifications unduly costly and creatively constraining, the DOCG (Denominazione di Origine Controllata e Garantita) and DOC (Denominazione di Origine Controllata) designations are awarded to food and wine that meet regional quality-control standards.

THE CAMPANIAN TABLE CAMPANIAN CULINARY ICONS

APPETISING READS

Pique your appetite with the following insightful guides to Campania's culinary riches:

➡ *Italian Kitchen: Family Recipes from the Old Country* (David Ruggerio) Filled with the secrets of a Neapolitan kitchen.

➡ *Foods of Naples and Campania* (Giuliano Bugialli) A culinary journey through the region led by a prolific Italian cookery writer.

➡ *La Pizza: The True Story from Naples* (Nikko Amandonico, Natalia Borri and Ian Thomson) Sumptuously illustrated history of pizza, set in Naples' kaleidoscopic streets.

➡ *Naples at Table: Cooking in Campania* (Arthur Schwartz) Local food trivia and 250 recipes.

➡ *The Food Lover's Companion to Naples and the Campania* (Carla Capalbo) An encyclopedic guide to Campania's food producers and nosh spots.

In June, slow-food fans should look out for *albicocche vesuviana* (Vesuvian apricots), known locally as *crisommole* and given IGP (Indicazione Geografica Protetta; Protected Denomination of Origin) status.

DOC (Denominazione di Origine; Certified Designation of Origin) status is granted to another lauded local, the *pomodoro San Marzano* (San Marzano plum tomato). Grown near the small Vesuvian town of the same name, it's Italy's most famous and cultivated tomato, best known for its low acidity and intense, sweet flavour. Its sauce, *conserva di pomodoro*, is made from super-ripe tomatoes, cut and left to dry in the sun for at least two days to concentrate the flavour. This is the sauce that adorns so many of Naples' signature pasta dishes, including the colourfully named *spaghetti alla puttanesca* (whore's spaghetti), the sauce of which is a lip-smacking blend of tomatoes, black olives, capers, anchovies and (in some cases) a dash of red chilli.

A richer tomato-based classic with aristocratic origins is the Neapolitan *ragù,* whose name stems from the French ragout. A tomato and meat sauce, it is left to simmer for about six hours before being served with macaroni.

Mozzarella di Bufala

So you think the *fior di latte* (cow-milk mozzarella) served in Capri's *insalata caprese* (a salad made of mozzarella, tomatoes, basil and olive oil) is delicious? Taste Campania's *mozzarella di bufala* (buffalo-milk mozzarella) and you'll move on to an entirely different level of deliciousness. Made on the plains surrounding Caserta and Paestum, it's best eaten when freshly made that morning, its rich, sweet flavour and luscious texture nothing short of a revelation. You can find it fresh at *latterie* (dairies), sold lukewarm in a plastic bag filled with a slightly cloudy liquid: the run-off from the mozzarella making. You'll also find it served in trattorias (informal restaurants) and restaurants across the region. You'll even find dedicated mozzarella eateries in Naples and Sorrento; **Muu Muzzarella Lounge** (p78) and **Inn Bufalito** (p149), respectively.

As for that irresistible taste, it's the high fat content and buffalo-milk protein that give the cheese the distinctive, pungent flavour so often absent in the versions sold abroad. Even more luscious is the *burrata,*

LA DOLCE VITA

Fragrant *sfogliatelle* (sweetened ricotta pastries) and trickling *babà* (rum-soaked sponge cake) aren't the only *pasticceria* staples you'll find on a Campanian table. Savour the sweet life with the following local favourites:

➜ **Cassatina** The Neapolitan version of the Sicilian *cassata*, this mini cake is made with *pan di Spagna* (sponge), ricotta and candied fruit, and covered in glazed sugar.

➜ **Pastiera** Traditionally baked at Easter (but available year-round), this latticed tart is made of shortcrust pastry and filled with ricotta, cream, candied fruit and cereals flavoured with orange-blossom water.

➜ **Torta caprese** A flourless almond and chocolate torte from Capri. Naples *pasticceria* Scaturchio (p77) offers a twist with its lemon version.

➜ **Torta di ricotta e pera** A light, tangy ricotta-and-pear torte.

➜ **Delizia al limone** A light, tangy lemon cake made with *limoncello* (lemon liqueur).

➜ **Paste reali** Cleverly crafted miniatures of fruit and vegetables, these sweets are made of almond paste and sugar (marzipan) and gobbled up at Christmas.

➜ **Raffioli** A yuletide biscuit made with sponge and marzipan, and sprinkled with icing sugar.

TABLE RULES

....

➡ Make eye contact when toasting and never clink using plastic cups; it's bad luck!

➡ Pasta is eaten with a fork only.

➡ Bread is not eaten with pasta – unless you're cleaning up the sauce afterwards.

➡ It's fine to eat pizza with your hands.

➡ If in doubt, dress smartly.

➡ If invited to someone's home, take a tray of *dolci* (sweets) from a *pasticceria* (pastry shop).

a mozzarella filled with a wickedly buttery cream. *Burrata* itself was invented in the neighbouring region of Puglia.

Campania's most decadent mozzarella dish is *mozzarella in carrozza*. Literally translating as 'mozzarella in a carriage', it sees fresh mozzarella sliced, sandwiched in white bread, coated in flour and egg yolk, and fried to golden perfection. Although many Italian pizzerias make it using cheaper *fior di latte* these days, the classic Campanian recipe demands the use of *mozzarella di bufala*; the higher fat and lower water content prevents the cheese from seeping out when fried. The classic recipe also specifies the use of stale bread, bought straight from the *panificio* (bakery).

Local Specialities

Campania's regional specialities are testament to the locals' obsession for produce with a postcode. Beyond the STG (Specialità Tradizionale Garantita; Guaranteed Traditional Speciality)–protected *pizza napoletana*, surprisingly light *fritture* (fried snacks) and fragrant pastries, Naples' bounty of staples includes *pizzu di scarole* (escarole pie), 'Napoli' salami, wild-fennel sausages and *sanguinaccio* (a cream of candied fruits and chocolate made during Carnevale).

West of Naples, in the Campi Flegrei, Pozzuoli's lively fish market attests to the town's reputation for superlative seafood. Another Campi Flegrei local is the IGP-status Annurca apple, ripened on a bed of straw to produce the fruit's distinctive stripy red hue.

Seafood revelations are also the norm on the island of Procida, where local concoctions include *volamarina* (moonfish) tripe with tomato and chilli and anchovy-stuffed squid. And while neighbouring Ischia is equally seafood-savvy, the island's agricultural history shines through in classics like *coniglio all'ischitana* (rabbit cooked in wine and herbs), made using locally bred rabbits.

Southeast of Naples, the Sorrento Peninsula heaves with local specialities, from the ubiquitous *gnocchi alla sorrentina* (gnocchi in a tomato, basil and pecorino cheese sauce) to refreshing *limoncello* (lemon liqueur) sorbet. Feast on *burrino incamiciato* (*fior di latte* mozzarella wickedly filled with butter) and pizza by the metre in Vico Equense, or ricotta-stuffed cannelloni in Sorrento, whose famous walnuts are used to make *nocino* liqueur. Almonds and chocolate are the key ingredients in the sugar-dusted *torta caprese* (Caprese cake), which, alongside seafood dishes like linguine in scorpion-fish sauce, and the refreshing *insalata caprese,* call the island of Capri home.

Predictably, fish features strongly on Amalfi Coast menus, from cod and monkfish to *coccio* (rockfish) and grey mullet. You'll also find two

During spring, summer and early autumn, towns across southern Italy celebrate *sagre,* the festivals of local foods in season. Scan www.prodottit-ipici.com/sagre (in Italian) for a lip-smacking list.

THE CULT OF CAFFÈ

The Neapolitan coffee scene trades hipsters, soy and siphons for retro-vested baristas, chintzy fit-outs and unhyped java brilliance. Here, velvety, lingering espresso is not a fashion statement – it's a birthright. In most cases, it's also a quick, unceremonious swill standing at local bars. But don't be fooled: the speed with which it's consumed does not diminish the importance of its quality.

According to Neapolitans, it's the local water that makes their coffee stronger and better than any other in Italy. To drink it like a local, keep milky options like caffe latte and cappuccino for the morning. After 11am, espresso and *caffè macchiato* (an espresso with a drop of milk) are the norm. For a weaker coffee (shame on you!) ask for a *caffè lungo* (a watered-down espresso in a larger cup) or a *caffè americano* (an even weaker version of the *caffè lungo*).

Another ritual is the free *bicchiere d'acqua* (glass of water), offered either *liscia* (uncarbonated) or *frizzante* (sparkling) with your coffee. Drink it before your coffee to cleanse your palate. Just don't be surprised if you're not automatically offered one. After all, what would a heathen *straniero* (foreigner) know about coffee? Don't be shy – smile sweetly and ask for *un bicchiere d'acqua, per favore.*

larder staples down here: *colatura di alici* (an intense anchovy essence) in Cetara and Colline Salernitane DOP olive oil in Salerno.

Nearby, the Cilento region expresses its earthy tendencies in hearty peasant grub like *cuccia* (a soup of chickpeas, lentils, beans, chickling, maize and wheat) and *pastorelle* (fried puff pastry filled with chestnut custard).

Menu Lowdown

➡ **Antipasto** A hot or cold appetiser. For a tasting plate of different appetisers, request an *antipasto misto* (mixed antipasto).

➡ **Contorno** Side dish, usually *verdura* (vegetable).

➡ **Dolce** Dessert, including *torta* (cake).

➡ **Frutta** Fruit; usually the epilogue to a meal.

➡ **Menù a la carte** Choose whatever you like from the menu.

➡ **Menù di degustazione** Degustation menu, usually consisting of six to eight 'tasting size' courses.

➡ **Menù turistico** The 'tourist menu' usually signals mediocre fare for gullible tourists – steer clear!

➡ **Nostra produzione** Made in-house; used to describe anything from bread and pasta to *liquori* (liqueurs).

➡ **Piatto del giorno** Dish of the day.

➡ **Primo** First course, usually a substantial pasta, rice or *zuppa* (soup) dish.

➡ **Secondo** Second course, often *pesce* (fish) or *carne* (meat).

➡ **Surgelato** Frozen; usually used to denote fish or seafood that has not been caught fresh.

The word *melanzana* (aubergine) comes from 'mela insana', meaning crazy apple. In Latin it was called *solanum insanum*, as it was thought to cause madness.

The Campanian Vine Revival

Revered by the ancients and snubbed by modern critics, Campanian wine is once again hot property, with a new generation of winemakers creating some brilliant drops. Lauded producers such as Feudi di San Gregorio, Mastroberardino, Villa Matilde, Pietracupa and Terredora have returned to their roots, cultivating ancient grape varieties like the red

PICK YOUR PLONK

To help you navigate Campania's ever-growing wine list, here are some of the region's top drops:

→ **Taurasi** A DOCG since 1991, this dry, intense red goes well with boiled and barbecued meat.

→ **Fiano di Avellino** A dry, fresh DOCG white that's one of Campania's historic wines. Ideal with seafood.

→ **Greco di Tufo** Another long-standing favourite, this DOCG white comes in both dry and sparkling versions.

→ **Aglianico del Taburno** A rich, dense DOCG red that pairs perfectly with succulent cuts of meat.

→ **Falerno del Massico** Its red and white versions originate from the volcanic slopes of Mt Massico in the north of the region.

Aglianico (thought to be the oldest cultivated grape in Italy) and the whites Falanghina, Fiano and Greco (all growing long before Mt Vesuvius erupted in AD 79). Keeping them company is a lengthening list of reputable organic and biodynamic wineries, among them Terre Stregate, I Cacciagalli, Colli di Lapio and Cautiero. It's all a far cry from 1990, when wine critic Burton Anderson humiliatingly wrote that Campania's noteworthy winemakers could be 'counted on one's fingers'.

Campania's three main wine-producing zones are centred on Avellino, Benevento and Caserta. And it's in the high hills east of Avellino that the region's best red is produced. Taurasi – a full-bodied Aglianico wine – is considered one of southern Italy's finest drops. Sometimes called the Barolo of the south, its notes range from dark berries and leather to roasted coffee and Mediterranean herbs. The wine is also one of only four in the region to carry Italy's top quality rating, DOCG (Denominazione di Origine Controllata e Garantita; Controlled and Guaranteed Denomination of Origin). The other three wines to share this honour are Aglianico del Taburno, a full-bodied red from the Benevento area, as well as Fiano di Avellino and Greco di Tufo, both whites and both from the Avellino area. The province of Caserta is well known for producing Falerno del Massico, a DOC-designated wine grown in the very same area as Falernum, the most celebrated wine in ancient Roman times.

Other vino-producing areas include the Campi Flegrei (home to DOC-labelled Piedirosso and Falanghina vines), Ischia (whose wines were the first to receive DOC status) and the Cilento region, home to the DOC Cilento *bianco* (Cilento white) and to the Aglianico Paestum. Mt Vesuvius' most famous drop is the Lacryma Christi (Tears of Christ), a blend of locally grown Falanghina, Piedirosso and Coda di Volpe grapes.

And while vines also lace the Amalfi Coast, the real speciality here are fruit and herbal liqueurs, with flavours spanning mandarin, myrtle and wild fennel, and the ubiquitous *limoncello* – a simple yet potent concoction of lemon peel, water, sugar and alcohol traditionally served in a frozen glass after dinner. *Limoncello* fans take note: the greener the tinge, the better the drop.

Don't believe the hype about espresso. One diminutive cup packs less of a caffeine wallop than a large cup of French-pressed or American-brewed coffee. It also leaves drinkers less jittery.

Food & Drink Glossary
Places to Eat & Drink

enoteca	wine bar
friggitoria	fried-food kiosk
osteria	informal restaurant
pasticceria	patisserie; pastry shop
ristorante	restaurant
trattoria	informal restaurant

At the Table

cameriere/a	waiter (m/f)
carta dei vini	wine list
conto	bill/cheque
spuntini	snacks
tovagliolo	napkin/serviette
vegetaliano/a	vegan (m/f)
vegetariano/a	vegetarian (m/f)

Staples

aglio	garlic
fior di latte	cow-milk mozzarella
insalata	salad
limone	lemon
mozzarella di bufala	buffalo-milk mozzarella
oliva	olive
panna	cream
peperoncino	chilli
pizza margherita	pizza topped with tomato, mozzarella and basil
pizza marinara	pizza topped with tomato, garlic, oregano and olive oil
rucola	rocket

Fish & Seafood

acciughe	anchovies
carpaccio	thin slices of raw fish (or meat)
granchio	crab
merluzzo	cod
pesce spada	swordfish
polpi	octopus
sarde	sardines
seppia	cuttlefish
sgombro	mackerel
vongole	clams

Meat

bistecca	steak
capretto	kid (goat)

coniglio	rabbit
fegato	liver
prosciutto cotto	cooked ham
prosciutto crudo	cured ham
salsiccia	sausage
vitello	veal

Cooking Methods

arrosto/a	roasted
alla griglia	grilled (broiled)
bollito/a	boiled
cotto/a	cooked
crudo/a	raw
fritto/a	fried

Fruit

ciliegia	cherry
fragole	strawberries
melone	cantaloupe; musk melon; rockmelon
pera	pear

Vegetables

asparagi	asparagus
carciofi	artichokes
fagiolini	green beans
finocchio	fennel
friarielli	Neapolitan broccoletti
melanzane	aubergine; eggplant
peperoni	capsicums; peppers
tartufo	truffle

Gelato

Amarena	wild cherry
bacio	chocolate and hazelnut
cioccolata	chocolate
cono	cone
coppa	cup
crema	cream
frutta di bosco	fruit of the forest (wild berries)
nocciola	hazelnut
vaniglia	vanilla
zuppa inglese	'English soup', trifle

Drinks

amaretto	almond-flavoured liqueur
amaro	dark liqueur prepared from herbs
espresso	short black coffee

Architecture

Campania's architectural cachet is epic and illustrious. Given the region's rich and ancient history, that makes perfect sense. Millenniums of political conquests and struggles, of human ingenuity, creativity and ambition, have bestowed the place with a built legacy few corners of Europe can match. This is a land of muscular Greek temples and lavish Roman villas, of storybook Angevin castles, medieval Moorish cloisters and oversized Bourbon palaces. It's an overwhelming heap, so why not start with the undisputed highlights?

Graeco-Roman Legacies

The breadth and depth of Campania's ancient architecture is superlative, its jumble of temples, towns and engineering feats delivering a crash course in classical aesthetics and talent.

The Greeks invented the Doric architectural order and used it to great effect at the 6th-century-BC temples of Paestum, confirming not only the ancient Greeks' power but also their penchant for harmonious proportion. In Naples, Piazza Bellini has remnants of the city's 4th-century-BC walls, while traces of Greek fortifications linger at the acropolis of Cuma.

Having learned a few valuable lessons from the Greeks, the Romans refined architecture to such a degree that their building techniques, designs and mastery of harmonious proportion underpin most of the world's architecture and urban design to this day. The Greeks may have created Naples' first aqueduct, but it was the Romans who extended and improved it. The aqueduct led to the glorious Piscina Mirabilis, a cathedrallike cistern once complete with sophisticated hydraulics.

The space below Pozzuoli's Anfiteatro Flavio is also testament to Roman ingenuity. Here, an elliptical corridor is flanked by a series of low *cellae* set on two floors and capped by trapdoors that open straight to the arena above. The *cellae* on the upper floor held the caged wild animals used in the stadium games. Hoisted up through the trap doors, the animals could then spring immediately from darkness into the bright light of the arena with rock-star effect.

Across the bay, it's a case of *Vogue Ancient Living* in Pompeii, home to many of Italy's best-preserved classical abodes. Here, buildings like the Villa dei Misteri, the Casa del Fauno and the Casa del Menandro illustrate the trademarks of classical domestic architecture, from an inward-facing design (for maximum privacy) to the light-filled atrium (the focal point of domestic life) and the ornamental peristyle (colonnaded garden courtyard). The finest villas were adorned with whimsical mythological frescoes, stunningly exemplified at the Villa dei Misteri, as well as Villa Oplontis, located in nearby Torre Annunziata.

In *Medieval Naples: An Architectural & Urban History 400–1400*, Caroline Bruzelius, William Tronzo and Ronald G Musto deliver a thoroughly researched review of Naples' architecture and urban development from late antiquity to the high and late Middle Ages. Topics include the Angevins' ambitious reconfiguration of the city.

Medieval Icons

Following on from the Byzantine style and its mosaic-encrusted churches was Romanesque, a style that found four regional forms in Italy: Lombard, Pisan, Florentine and Sicilian Norman. All displayed an emphasis on width and the horizontal lines of a building rather than its height, and featured church groups with *campanili* (bell towers) and baptisteries that were separate to the church. Surfacing in the 11th century, the Sicilian Norman style encompassed an exotic mix of Norman, Saracen and Byzantine influences, from marble columns to Islamic-inspired pointed arches to glass tesserae detailing. This style is clearly visible in the two-toned masonry and 13th-century bell tower of the Cattedrale di Sant'Andrea in Amalfi. It's also echoed in the 12th-century bell tower of Salerno's Duomo, not to mention in its bronze, Byzantine-style doors and Arabesque portico arches.

For Naples, its next defining architectural period would arrive with the rule of the French House of Anjou in the 13th century. As it was the new capital of the Angevin kingdom, suitably ambitious plans were announced for the city. Land was reclaimed, and bold new churches and monasteries built. This was the age of the 'Gothic', a time of flying buttresses and grotesque gargoyles. While enthusiastically embraced by the French, Germans and Spanish, the Italians preferred a more restrained and sombre interpretation of the style, defined by wide walls, a single nave, a trussed ceiling and horizontal bands. One of its finest examples is Naples' Basilica di San Lorenzo Maggiore, its pared-back elegance also echoed in the city's Chiesa di San Pietro a Maiella and Basilica di Santa Chiara.

That both the facade of the Basilica di San Lorenzo Maggiore and the coffered ceiling of the Chiesa di San Pietro a Maiella are later baroque add-ons remind us that much of the period's original architecture was altered over successive centuries. A case in point is the Chiesa di San Domenico Maggiore, whose chintzy gilded interior betrays a neo-Gothic makeover. The church's main entrance, in a courtyard off Vico San Domenico, also bears witness to a series of touch-ups. Here, a delicate 14th century portal is framed by an 18th-century *pronaos* (the space in front of the body of a temple) surmounted by a 19th-century window, and flanked by two Renaissance-era chapels and a baroque bell tower. Indeed, even the Angevins' Castel Nuovo wasn't spared, with only a few sections of the original structure surviving, among them the Pa-

ARCHITECTURE SPEAK 101

Do you know your transept from your triclinium? Demystify some common architectural terms with the following bite-size list:

Apse Usually a large recess or niche built on a semicircular or polygonal ground plan and vaulted with a half dome. In a church or temple, it may include an altar.

Baldachin (*baldacchino*) A permanent, often elaborately decorated canopy of wood or stone above an altar, throne, pulpit or statue.

Balustrade A stone railing formed of a row of posts (called balusters) topped by a continuous coping, and commonly flanking baroque stairs, balconies and terraces.

Impluvium A small ornamental pool, often used as the centrepiece of atriums in ancient Roman houses.

Latrine A Roman-era public convenience, lined with rows of toilet seats and often adorned with frescoes and marble.

Narthex A portico or lobby at the front of an early Christian church or basilica.

Necropolis Burial ground outside the city walls in antiquity and the early Christian era.

Oratory A small room or chapel in a church reserved for private prayer.

Transept A section of a church running at right angles to the main body of the church.

Triclinium The dining room in a Roman house.

latina Chapel. The castle's striking, white triumphal-arch centrepiece – a 15th-century addition – is considered one of Naples' most notable early-Renaissance creations.

The Baroque

While the Renaissance all but transformed Italy's north, its impact on southern streetscapes was much less dramatic. In Naples, one of the few buildings to page the Florentine style is the Palazzo Cuomo, now home to the Museo di Filangieri. Featuring typically Tuscan rusticated walls, the late-15th-century building was created for wealthy Florentine merchant Angelo Como ('Cuomo' in Neapolitan) before finding new life as a monastery in 1587.

Yet, what Naples missed out on during the Renaissance it more than made up for in the baroque of the 17th and 18th centuries. Finally, the city had found an aesthetic to suit its exhibitionist streak: a style that celebrated the bold, the gold and the over-the-top. Neapolitan baroque rose out of heady times. Under 17th-century Spanish rule, the city became one of Europe's biggest. Swelling crowds and counter-Reformation fervour sparked a building boom, with taller-than-ever *palazzi* (mansions) mixing it with glittering showcase churches. Ready to lavish the city with new landmarks was a brash, arrogant and fiery league of architects and artists, who brushed aside tradition and rewrote the rulebooks.

A Neapolitan Twist

Like the Neapolitans themselves, the city's baroque architecture is idiosyncratic and independently minded. Architects working in Naples at the time often ignored the trends sweeping through Rome and northern Italy. Pilasters may have been all the rage in late-17th-century Roman churches, but in Naples, architects like Dionisio Lazzari (1617–89) and Giovanni Battista Nauclerio (1666–1739) went against the grain, reasserting the value of the column and effectively paving the way for Luigi Vanvitelli's columnar architecture and the neoclassicism that would spread across Europe in the mid-18th century.

In domestic Neapolitan architecture, a *palazzo*'s *piano nobile* (principal floor) was often on the 2nd floor (not the 1st floor, as was common), encouraging the creation of the epic *porte-cochères* (coach porticoes) that distinguish so many Neapolitan buildings.

Equally grandiose were the city's open staircases, which reached perfection in the hands of Naples-born architect Ferdinando Sanfelice (1675–1748). His double-ramped creations in the Palazzo dello Spagnuolo and the Palazzo Sanfelice exemplify his ability to transform humble domestic staircases into operatic statements.

Another star on the building scene was Domenico Antonio Vaccaro (1678–1745), who originally trained as a painter under Francesco Solimena. Vaccaro's architectural legacy includes the redesign of the cloisters at the Basilica di Santa Chiara, the decoration of three chapels of the church inside the Certosa di San Martino, and the design of the soaring *guglia* (obelisk) on Piazza San Domenico Maggiore. With the help of his father, Lorenzo (himself a renowned sculptor), Vaccaro also contributed a bronze monument dedicated to Philip V of Spain, which topped the Guglia dell'Immacolata on Piazza del Gesù Nuovo. Alas, the work was later toppled by Charles III and replaced with a much less controversial Madonna, which still stands.

While Greek Doric columns are short, heavy and baseless, with plain, round capitals (tops), Ionic columns are slender and fluted, with a large base and two opposed *volutes* (scrolls) below the capital. Corinthian columns are fancier still, with ornate capitals featuring scrolls and acanthus leaves.

Marble Mavericks

Piazza del Gesù Nuovo is one of the very few sweeping squares in the city, a fact that led many baroque architects to invest less time on show-stopping exteriors and more time on what the people could actually see: the interiors. A case in point is the Chiesa di San Gregorio Armeno, whose facade gives little indication of the opulence glowing inside.

Indoor splendor also defines the Certosa di San Martino's on-site church, its glorious inlaid marble a common feature of Neapolitan baroque. This mix-and-match marble is the work of Cosimo Fanzago (1591–1678), the undisputed master of the craft. A revered sculptor, decorator and architect, the fiery Fanzago would cut the stone into the most whimsical of forms, producing a luscious, polychromatic spectacle that is one of Italy's true baroque highlights. The church is not Fanzago's only contribution at the Certosa; the artist had previously completed the charterhouse's Chiostro Grande (Great Cloister), adding to Giovanni Antonio Dosio's original design the statues above the portico, the ornate corner portals and the white balustrade around the monks' cemetery.

Fanzago took the art of marble inlay to a whole new level of complexity and sophistication, as also seen in the Cappella di Sant'Antonio di Padova and the Cappella Cacace, both inside the Basilica di San Lorenzo Maggiore. The latter chapel is considered to be his most lavish expression of the form. His altarpieces were equally influential. Exemplified by his beautiful high altar in the Chiesa di San Domenico Maggiore, his creations inspired the work of other sculptors, including Bartolomeo and Pietro Ghetti's altar in the Chiesa di San Pietro a Maiella, Bartolomeo Ghetti and siblings Giuseppe and Bartolomeo Gallo's altar in the Chiesa del Gesù Nuovo, and Giuseppe Mozzetti's exquisite choir in the Chiesa di Santa Maria del Carmine.

Another chisel-wielding genius was Giuseppe Sanmartino (1720–93). Arguably the finest sculptor of his time, his ability to turn cold stone into sensual, soul-stirring revelations is exemplified in the baroque Chiesa dei Girolamini. It's in this church that you'll find his celebrated pair of Carrara-marble angels, their curls and robes imbued with extraordinary softness and fluidity. Sanmartino's talent for breathing life into his creations won him a legion of fans, among them the city's Bourbon rulers and alchemist prince Raimondo di Sangro. The latter's family chapel, the Cappella Sansevero, is home to Sanmartino's undisputed masterpiece,

Best Baroque Surprises

....

Church, Certosa e Museo di San Martino, Naples

....

Farmacia Storica, Ospedale degli Incurabili, Naples

....

Sacristy, Basilica di San Paolo Maggiore, Naples

....

Palazzo dello Spagnuolo, Naples

....

THE NOT-SO-BRILLIANT LIFE OF COSIMO FANZAGO

Like many stars of the Neapolitan baroque, Cosimo Fanzago (1591–1678) was not actually Neapolitan by birth. Born in the small town of Clusone in northern Italy, the budding sculptor-decorator-architect ventured to Naples at the tender age of 17 and quickly earned a reputation for his imaginative way with marble. Alas, it wasn't the only reputation he acquired. According to legal documents, Fanzago was partial to the odd violent outburst, attacking his mason Nicola Botti in 1628 and reputedly knocking him off completely two years later. His alleged involvement in the 1647 Masaniello revolt saw him flee to Rome for a decade to avoid the death sentence on his head.

Yet Fanzago's ultimate downfall would come from his notorious workplace practices, which included missing deadlines, disregarding clients' wishes and using works created for one client for completing other clients' projects. Responsible for giving him his enviable commissions at the Certosa di San Martino, the Carthusian monks would ultimately learn to loathe the man revamping their hilltop home, suing the artist in a long, arduous legal battle that ultimately affected Fanzago's health and the number of his commissions. By the time of his death in 1678, the greatest baroque master Naples had ever seen cut a poor, neglected figure.

Reggia di Caserta (Royal Palace), north of Naples (p74)

the 1753 *Cristo velato* (Veiled Christ). Considered the apogee of his technical brilliance, it's quite possibly the greatest sculpture of 18th-century Europe. Even the great neoclassical sculptor Antonio Canova wished it were his own.

End of an Era

Canova may have wished the same of the Reggia di Caserta. Officially known as Caserta's Palazzo Reale, the epic royal residence was one of several grand-scale legacies of the Bourbon years. Designed by late-baroque architect Luigi Vanvitelli (1700–73), son of Dutch landscape artist Gaspar van Wittel (1653–1736), the Reggia not only outsized Versailles but would go down in history as Italy's great baroque epilogue.

Ironically, while it does feature many of the genre's theatrical hallmarks, from acres of inlaid marble to allegorical statues set into wall niches, its late-baroque style echoed a classical style more indebted to contemporary French and Spanish models than to the exuberant playfulness of the homegrown brand. According to the Bourbon blue bloods, the over-the-top Neapolitan baroque was *plutôt vulgaire* (rather vulgar). And as the curtain began to fall on Naples' baroque heyday, a more restrained neoclassicism was waiting in the wings.

Greek geographer, philosopher and historian Strabo (63 BC–AD 24) wrote that the stretch of Italian coast from Capo Miseno (in the Campi Flegrei) to Sorrento resembled a single city, so strewn was it with elegant villas and suburbs sprawling from central Naples.

The Subterranean City

Sacred shrines, secret passageways, forgotten burial crypts: it might sound like the set of an Indiana Jones film, but we're actually talking about what lurks beneath Naples' loud and greasy streets. Subterranean Naples is one of the world's most thrilling urban other-worlds: a silent, mostly undiscovered sprawl of cathedral-like cisterns, pin-width conduits, catacombs and ancient ruins. Speleologists (cave specialists) estimate that about 60% of Neapolitans live and work above this network, known in Italian as the *sottosuolo* **(underground).**

An Action-Packed History

Since the end of WWII, some 700 cavities have been discovered, from original Greek-era grottoes to palaeo-Christian burial chambers and Bourbon escape routes. According to the experts, this is simply a prelude, with another 2 million sq metres of troglodytic treats still to unfurl.

Naples' dedicated caving geeks are quick to tell you that their underworld is one of the largest and oldest on earth. Sure, Paris might claim a catacomb or two, but its subterranean offerings don't come close to this giant's 2500-year history.

And what a history it is: from buried martyrs and foreign invaders to wife-snatching spirits and drug-making mobsters. Naples' most famous saint, San Gennaro, was interred in the Catacombe di San Gennaro in the 5th century BC. A millennium later, in AD 536, Belisario and his troops caught Naples by surprise by storming the city through its ancient tunnels. According to legend, Alfonso of Aragon used the same trick in 1442, undermining the city walls by using an underground passageway leading into a tailor's shop and straight into town.

Inversely, the 18th-century Bourbons had an escape route built beneath the Palazzo Reale di Capodimonte. A century later they commissioned a tunnel to connect their central Palazzo Reale (Royal Palace) to their barracks in Chiaia: a perfect crowd-free route for troops or a fleeing royal family.

Even the city's underworld has got in on the act. In 1992 Naples' dreaded Stolder clan was busted for running a subterranean drug lab, with escape routes heading straight to the clan boss's pad.

From Ancient Aqueduct to Underground Tip

While strategic tunnels and sacred catacombs are important features of Naples' light-deprived other-world, the city's subterranean backbone is its ancient aqueduct system. Naples' first plumbing masterpiece was built by Greek settlers, who channelled water from the slopes of Mt Vesuvius into the city's cisterns. The cisterns themselves were created as builders dug out the pliable *tufo* sandstone on which the city stands. At street level, well shafts allowed citizens to lower their buckets and quench their thirst.

Not to be outdone, the Romans wowed the plebs (abbreviated term for 'plebeians', common Roman citizens) with their new, improved 70km aqueduct, transporting water from the River Serino near Avellino to Naples, Pozzuoli and Baia, where it filled the enormous Piscina Mirabilis.

The next update came in 1629, with the opening of the Spanish-commissioned 'Carmignano' aqueduct. Expanded in 1770, it finally met its Waterloo in the 1880s, when cholera outbreaks heralded the building of a more modern, pressurised version.

Dried up and defunct, the ancient cisterns went from glorious feats of ancient engineering to handy in-house rubbish tips. As refuse clogged the well shafts, access to the *sottosuolo* became ever more difficult and, within a few generations, the subterranean system that had nourished the city was left bloated and forgotten.

The WWII Revival

It would take the wail of air-raid sirens to reunite the city's sunlit and subterranean sides once more. With Allied air attacks looming, Mussolini's UMPA (civil-defence program) ordered that the cisterns and former quarries be turned into civilian shelters. The lakes of rubbish were compacted and covered, old passageways were enlarged, toilets were built and new staircases were erected. As bombs showered the city above, tens of thousands took refuge in the dark, damp spaces below.

The fear, frustration and anger of those days lives on in the historic graffiti that covers some of the old shelters, from hand-drawn caricatures of Hitler and 'Il Duce' to poignant messages like '*Mamma, non piangere*' (Mum, don't cry). Many families spent weeks living underground, often emerging to find their homes and neighbourhoods nothing more than rubble. For the many whose homes were destroyed, these subterranean hideouts became semipermanent dwellings. Entire families cohabited in cisterns, partitioning their makeshift abodes with bedsheets and furnishing them with the odd ramshackle bed. Traces of this rudimentary domestication survive to this day, from tiled 'kitchen' walls and showers to evidence of DC battery power.

Alas, once rebuilding began, the aqueducts once again became subterranean dumpsters, with everything from wartime rubble to scooters and Fiats thrown down the shafts. And in a case of history repeating itself, the historic labyrinth and its millennia-old secrets faded from the city's collective memory.

MYTH OF THE LITTLE MONK

It's only natural that a world as old, dark and mysterious as Naples' *sottosuolo* (underground) should breed a few fantastical urban myths. The best known and most loved is that of the *municello* (little monk), a Neapolitan leprechaun of sorts known for being both naughty and nice. Said to live in a wine cellar, the hooded sprite was reputedly a regular sight in the 18th and 19th centuries. Some spoke of him as a kindred soul, a bearer of gifts and good fortune. To others, the *municello* spelt trouble, sneaking into homes to misplace objects, steal precious jewels and seduce the odd lonely housewife.

While a handful of Neapolitans still curse the imp whenever the car keys go missing, most now believe that the cheeky *municello* was actually the city's long-gone *pozzari* (aqueduct cleaners). Descending daily down the wells, the small-statured *pozzari* fought off the damp, cool conditions with a heavy, hooded mantel. Naturally, most would pop back up for a breath of fresh air, sometimes finding themselves in people's very homes. For some, the temptation of scouring drawers in search of valuables was all too strong. For others, it was a way of making new acquaintances – or of bringing a little company to the odd neglected homemaker. Regardless, it quickly becomes clear just how the tale of the 'mini monk' began.

INTERVIEW: FULVIO SALVI & LUCA CUTTITTA

Naples' subterranean world has been dubbed everything from 'the parallel city' to 'the negative city', but Neapolitan speleologists (cave specialists) Fulvio and Luca prefer to call it *la macchina del tempo'* (the time machine). As Fulvio explains, 'In 30m to 40m you're transported from the 21st century to 2000 BC. Some of the axe marks on the *tufo* stone predate Christ himself'.

For Fulvio and Luca, the constant possibility of new discoveries is addictive: 'We can descend into the same cistern 30 times and still find new objects, like oil lamps used by the Greek and Roman excavators'.

One of their most memorable finds to date was made after stumbling across an unusual-looking staircase behind an old chicken coop in a *palazzo* in the district of Arinella.

As Fulvio recalls, 'I headed down the stairs and through a hole in the wall. Reaching the bottom, I switched on my torch and was quickly dumbstruck to find carved columns and frescoes of the ancient Egyptian deities Isis, Osiris and Seth on the walls. We believe we've found part of the Secretorum Naturae Accademia, the laboratory used by scholar, alchemist and playwright Giambattista della Porta (c 1535–1615) after the Inquisition ordered an end to his experiments'.

Speleological associations like Napoli Underground group (NUg) play a vital role in preserving Naples' heritage: 'There are between 10 and 15 NUg members, each with a specific role to play on our expeditions, from photographer or filmmaker to medical support. We're like a well-oiled machine whose role is to sew up the little tears in our city's history. It's a bit like a puzzle and each new passageway or cistern we find is a piece of that puzzle that we're trying to put together. It's too enormous for us to finish in our lifetimes, but at least we will have contributed to what are important scientific, historical and archaeological discoveries'.

Speleologists Fulvio Salvi and Luca Cuttitta prefer dark cisterns to southern sunshine any day.

Speleological Saviours & Rediscovered Secrets

Thankfully, all is not lost, as a passionate league of professional and volunteer speleologists continues to rediscover and render accessible long-lost sites and secrets – a fact not overlooked by the likes of *National Geographic* and the BBC, both of which have documented the work of these subterranean experts. The city's most prolific speleological association today is the aptly named La Macchina del Tempo (The Time Machine). Led by speleologist Luca Cuttitta, it manages the fascinating **Museo del Sottosuolo** (Map p66; Museum of the Underground; ☑347 6455332; www.comeonaples.it/macchinadeltempo; Piazza Cavour 140, adult/reduced €10/4; ☉10am, noon, 3.30pm & 5.30pm Sat & Sun; MPiazza Cavour, Museo), a DIY ode to speleologists and the treasures they uncover. Hidden away on Naples' Piazza Cavour, between the *centro storico* (historic centre) and the Sanità district, its series of restored underground cisterns recreates real-life sites inaccessible to the public, from a phallocentric shrine to the Graeco-Roman god of fertility, Priapus, to a luridly hued Hellenic-era *hypogeum* (underground chamber). Precious debris that once filled the voids is now displayed, from rare majolica tiles to WWII-era domestic objects. The museum was founded by veteran cave crusader Clemente Esposito, lovingly nicknamed *il Papa del sottosuolo* (the Pope of the Underground) in local speleological circles.

Even more thrilling are La Macchina del Tempo's speleological **tours** (www.comeonaples.it/macchinadeltempo; guided tour adult/reduced €35/25), which take in unexplored nooks few locals will ever see. On these journeys, surprise discoveries are far from rare, whether it's a secret wartime hideout, an early-Christian engraving or an even older Greek urn. A minimum number of six participants is required for these adventures, which run on weekends and last three hours.

Minimum numbers are not an issue for the city's more touristy underground tours, run by **Napoli Sotterranea** (p48) and Borbonica Sotterranea. While Borbonica Sotterranea's **Tunnel Borbonico** (p59) conducts tours of the Bourbon tunnel running beneath Mt Echia (home to Naples' earliest settlement), Napoli Sotterranea takes a steady stream of visitors below the *centro storico* for a look at remnants of a Roman theatre frequented by madcap Emperor Nero, as well as to a cistern returned to its original, water-filled splendour.

To dig deeper into the region's subterranean scene, check out the information-packed www.napoliunderground.org.

Mixed Blessings

And yet, not even the infectious enthusiasm of Naples' speleologists is enough to secure the protection and preservation of the city's *sottosuolo*. The golden era of the 1990s, which saw the city council provide generous funding to speleological research, has since been supplanted by standard Italian bureaucracy and political bickering. As a result, many precious sites uncovered by the city's speleologists remain indefinitely abandoned, with little money to salvage and restore them. As Fulvio Salvi from NUg (Napoli Underground group) laments: 'The problem with Naples is that it's almost too rich in historical treasure. It creates a certain amount of indifference to such marvels because they are almost a dime a dozen here'.

A more positive outcome involved NUg's discovery of a long, ring-shaped corridor beneath the Quartieri Spagnoli. Part of the ancient Largo Baracche district, the unearthing called for its transformation into a much-needed community centre – a wish that fell on deaf ears at city hall. Destined to become a squat, its saving grace was a gung-ho group of young community activists called SABU. Giving the space a mighty scrub, the group opened it as a nonprofit art lab and gallery in 2005, headed by archaeology students Giuseppe Ruffo and Pietro Tatafiore. As Giuseppe explains, 'The gallery is an open space where emerging artists can exhibit their work, amongst them young graduates from Naples' Accademia delle Belle Arti. Unfortunately, such spaces are lacking in Naples.' The space is also well known for its permanent mural, created by Naples' best-known street artists, cyop&kaf (www.cyopekaf.org). To see it, you'll need to ask the guys to turn off the lights – it's the only way you'll catch the glow-in-the-dark creation.

Naples' original Graeco-Roman city was covered by a great mudslide in the 6th century. The excavations to open the Roman market beneath the Complesso Monumentale di San Lorenzo Maggiore took 25 years.

The Camorra

Alongside Calabria's 'Ndrangheta, Sicily's Cosa Nostra and Puglia's Sacra Corona Unita, Campania's Camorra is one of Italy's four main organised-crime syndicates. According to *Fortune* magazine, the Camorra is the most successful of these groups, its illegal dealings in drug and firearms trafficking, prostitution, waste disposal, racketeering and counterfeiting securing the organisation an estimated US$4.9 billion annually. Even more astounding is the human cost: in the past 30 years, the Camorra has claimed more than 3000 lives, more than any other mafia in the country.

Origins

It is widely believed that the Camorra emerged from the criminal gangs operating among the poor in late-18th-century Naples. The organisation would get its first big break after the failed revolution of 1848. Desperate to overthrow Ferdinand II, pro-constitutional liberals turned to *camorristi* to help garner the support of the masses. The Camorra's political influence was sealed. Given a serious blow by Mussolini, the organisation would get its second wind from the invading Allied forces of 1943, which turned to the flourishing, influential underworld, believing it to be the best way to get things done.

The Value of Vice

With annual profits running into the billions, the modern Camorra is a far cry from the days of roguish characters bullying shopkeepers into paying the *pizzo* (protection money). As journalist Roberto Saviano writes in his Camorra exposé *Gomorra:* 'Only beggar Camorra clans inept at business and desperate to survive still practice the kind of monthly extortions seen in Nanni Loy's film *Mi manda Picone'*. While small-time extortion still exists, the Mafia big guns are where the serious bucks lie, from the production and sale of counterfeit goods to the construction and waste-disposal industries.

One of the Camorra's biggest money-spinners is the drug trade. Indeed, the Camorra-ravaged suburbs of Secondigliano and Scampia in northern Naples have the dubious claim of being Europe's largest open-air drug market, supplying addicts from across the country with cheap, low-grade heroin and cocaine. Needless to say, disputes between rival clans over this lucrative trade have seen the spilling of much blood.

One of the most serious clan battles in recent history was the so called 'Scampia Feud', ignited by *camorrista* Cosimo Di Lauro in late 2004. As the newly appointed head of the powerful Di Lauro clan, the 30-year-old decided to centralise the area's drug trade, giving himself more power and the clan's long-respected franchisees much less. This did not go down well with many of Di Lauro's associates. Among them were Raffaele Amato and Cesare Pagano, who broke away to form a rival clan dubbed the Scissionisti (Secessionists). What followed was a long and ruthless series of murders and retributions between the opposing groups, one that would claim over 50 lives in 2004–05 alone.

Arrested in 2009, Ugo Gabriele broke the mould like no other. Beefy and cunning, the then 27-year-old would go down in history as Italy's first cross-dressing mobster. In between shaping his eyebrows, dabbing on lipstick and dyeing his hair platinum blonde 'Kitty' found time to manage prostitution and drug rackets for Naples' Scissionisti clan.

A TOXIC LEGACY

According to Italian environmentalist association Legambiente, the Camorra has illegally dumped, buried or burned close to 10 million tons of garbage in Campania since 1991. Alarmingly, this includes highly toxic waste, collected from northern Italian and foreign manufacturers lured by the cut-price rates of Camorra-owned waste-disposal companies. Despite widespread knowledge of the practice, many local politicians have turned a blind eye, testament to the Mafia's powerful influence in local government. This systematic negligence has had devastating effects on the region. Abnormally high rates of cancer and congenital malformations of the nervous and urinary systems led medical journal *Lancet Oncology* to nickname an area in Naples' northeast hinterland 'the triangle of death' in 2004. In 2008 a public-health survey by the US Navy concluded that water contamination in certain areas of the region posed unacceptable risks, while Campania now lays claim to Italy's highest infertility rate.

Fighting Back

The Camorra on Screen

Gomorra (Matteo Garrone; 2009)

Il camorrista (The Professor; Giuseppe Tornatore; 1986)

Mi manda Picone (Picone Sent Me; Nanni Loy; 1983)

Luna rossa (Red Moon; Antonio Capuano; 2001)

Over the years, the law has captured many Camorra kingpins, among them Cosimo Di Lauro, his father, Paolo, Giuseppe Dell'Aquila, and Pasquale Scotti. The latter – a fugitive Scissionisti boss convicted in absentia of over 20 murders – was arrested in Brazil in 2015 after 30 years on the run. Authorities have also seized millions of euros worth of assets: in February 2015, police in Naples confiscated €320 million in real estate and business ventures linked to the city's Contini clan.

Despite these victories, the war against the Camorra remains an uphill battle. Its presence in Campanian society spans centuries, and, for many, the Camorra – known locally as *Il sistema* (The System) – has provided everything Italy's official avenues have not, from employment and business loans to a sense of order in local communities. The Camorra's weekly drug-trade rates range from €100 for lookouts to €1000 for those willing to hide the drugs at home. Driving a shipment of drugs from Milan to Naples can pay as much as €2500.

Italy's enduring financial lull has proven another boon. With liquidity in short supply, hard-pressed companies have become more susceptible to questionable money. Camorra-affiliated loan sharks commonly offer cash with an average interest rate of 10%. An estimated 50% to 70% of shops in Naples are run with dubiously sourced money. Mafia profits are also reinvested in legitimate real estate, credit markets and businesses around the world.

Although too many Neapolitans shrug their shoulders in resignation, others are determined to loosen the Camorra's grip. In the Sanità district, people like parish priest Don Antonio Loffredo and renowned artist Riccardo Dalisi offer youth the opportunity to learn artistic and artisanal skills and help restore local heritage sites, including the Catacombe di San Gennaro.

Across the city in Ercolano, elderly shopkeeper Raffaella Ottaviano made international headlines for her refusal to pay the *pizzo*. Her courage has influenced other traders to say no, which in turn has led the local council to offer tax breaks to those who report threats of extortion instead of giving in to the Camorra.

The Greater Naples region is home to over 100 Camorra clans, with an estimated 10,000 immediate associates, and an even larger number of clients, dependants and supporters.

Survival Guide

Directory A–Z

Customs Regulations

Duty-free sales within the EU no longer exist (but goods are sold tax-free in European airports). Visitors coming into Italy from non-EU countries can import the following items duty free:

Alcohol 1L of spirits, 4L of wine and 16L of beer

Tobacco 200 cigarettes

Other goods Up to a total of €430

Anything over these limits must be declared on arrival and the appropriate duty paid. On leaving the EU, non-EU citizens can reclaim any Value Added Tax (VAT) on expensive purchases.

Discount Cards

Free admission to many galleries and cultural sites is available to people under 18 or over 65; in addition, visitors aged between 18 and 25 often qualify for a 50% discount. In some cases, free admission and discounts only apply to EU citizens.

If travelling to Naples and Campania, consider buying a **Campania artecard** (www.campaniaartecard.it; three/seven days €32/34), which offers free public transport and free or reduced admission to many museums and archaeological sites. For more on discount cards see p262.

Embassies & Consulates

For foreign embassies and consulates not listed here, look under 'Ambasciate' or 'Consolati' in the telephone directory. Alternatively, tourist offices generally have a list.

French Consulate (☎081 598 07 11; www.ambafrance-it.org; Via Francesco Crispi 86, Naples; Ⓜ Amedeo)

US Consulate (☎081 583 81 11; italy.usembassy.gov; Piazza della Repubblica 2, Naples; Ⓜ Mergellina)

Food

In reviews, 'meals' denotes the average price for two courses and a glass of wine. Reviews are listed by budget category as follows:

€ less than €20

€€ €25-45

€€€ more than €45

For more information on food in Naples and Campania, see p239.

PRACTICALITIES

➤ **Weights and measures** Italy uses the metric system.

➤ **Smoking** Smoking in all closed public spaces (from bars to elevators, offices to trains) is banned.

➤ **Newspapers** If your Italian is up to it, try reading Naples' major daily newspapers *Il Mattino* or *Corriere del Mezzogiorno*. The latter is the southern spin-off of Italy's leading daily, *Corriere della Sera*. The national *La Repubblica* also has a Neapolitan section.

➤ **Radio** Tune into state-owned Italian RAI Radio 1, RAI Radio 2 and intellectual heavyweight RAI Radio 3 (www.rai.it), which broadcast all over Italy and abroad. The region's plethora of contemporary-music stations includes Radio Kiss Kiss (www.kisskiss.it).

➤ **Television** Switch on the box to watch the state-run RAI-1, RAI-2 and RAI-3 (www.rai.it), and the main commercial stations (mostly run by Silvio Berlusconi's Mediaset company): Canale 5 (www.mediaset.it/canale5), Italia 1 (www.mediaset.it/italia1), Rete 4 (www.mediaset.it/rete4) and La 7 (www.la7.it).

Electricity

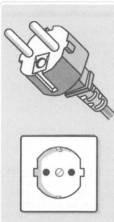

230V/50Hz

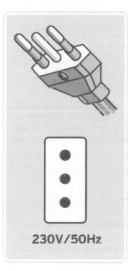

230V/50Hz

Gay & Lesbian Travellers

Homosexuality is legal in Italy and well tolerated in Naples, perhaps less so in smaller towns on the Amalfi Coast. Resources include the following:

→ **Arcigay Napoli** (www. arcigaynapoli.org, in Italian) Website for Naples' main GLBTI organisation, listing special events as well as gay and gay-friendly venues in town.

→ **Criminal Candy** (www. criminalcandy.com, in Italian) Organises one-off queer dance parties in Naples.

→ **Gay-Friendly Italy** (www. gayfriendlyitaly.com) English-language site featuring information on everything from hotels to homophobia issues and the law.

→ **Gay.it** (www.gay.it, in Italian) Lists gay venues and hotels across the country.

→ **Pride** (www.prideonline.it, in Italian) National monthly magazine of art, music, politics and gay culture.

Health

Availability of Health Care

Good health care is readily available throughout Campania. In major centres such as Naples you are likely to find English-speaking doctors or a translator service.

Pharmacists can give you valuable advice and sell over-the-counter medication for minor illnesses. Pharmacies generally keep the same hours as other shops, closing at night and on Sunday. However, a handful remain open on a rotation basis (*farmacie di turno*) for emergency purposes. Closed pharmacies display a list of the nearest ones open.

If you need an ambulance anywhere in Italy, call ☎118. For emergency treatment, head straight to the *pronto soccorso* (casualty) section of a public hospital, where you can also get emergency dental treatment.

Health Insurance

If you're an EU citizen (or from Switzerland, Norway or Iceland), a European Health Insurance Card (EHIC) covers you for most medical care in public hospitals free of charge, but not for emergency repatriation home or non-emergencies. The card is available from health centres and (in the UK) from post offices. Citizens from other countries should find out if there is a reciprocal arrangement for free medical care between their country and Italy (Australia, for instance, has such an agreement; carry your Medicare card).

If you do need health insurance, make sure you get a policy that covers you for the worst possible scenario, such as an accident requiring an emergency flight home. Find out in advance if your insurance plan will make payments directly to providers or reimburse you later for overseas health expenditures.

Recommended Vaccinations

No jabs are required to travel to Italy. The World Health Organization (WHO), however, recommends that all travellers should be vaccinated against diphtheria, tetanus, measles, mumps, rubella, polio and hepatitis B.

Insurance

A travel-insurance policy to cover theft, loss and medical problems is a good idea. It may also cover you for cancellation or delays to your travel arrangements. Paying for your ticket with a credit card can often provide limited travel accident insurance and you may be able to reclaim the payment if the operator doesn't deliver. Ask your credit-card company what it will cover. Worldwide travel insurance is available at www.lonelyplanet.com/travel-insurance. You can buy, extend and claim online any time – even if you're already on the road.

Legal Matters

Despite its mafia notoriety, Campania is relatively safe, and the average tourist will only have a brush with the law if robbed by a bag-snatcher or pickpocket.

Police

Contact details for police stations (questure) are given throughout this book. If you run into trouble in Italy, you're likely to end up dealing with the *polizia statale* (state police) or the *carabinieri* (military police). The former wear powder blue trousers with a fuchsia stripe and a navy blue jacket; the latter wear black uniforms with a red stripe and drive dark-blue cars with a red stripe. The following list outlines Italian police organisations and their jurisdictions.

Carabinieri (military police) General crime, public order and drug-law enforcement (often overlapping with the *polizia statale*).

Guardia di finanza Tax evasion, drug smuggling.

Guardia forestale (aka Corpo Forestale) Environmental protection.

Polizia statale (state police) Theft, visa extensions and permits.

Vigili urbani (local traffic police) Parking tickets, towed cars.

Drugs & Alcohol

Under Italy's tough drug laws, possession of any controlled substances, including cannabis or marijuana, can get you into hot water. Those caught in possession of 5g of cannabis can be considered traffickers and prosecuted as such. The same applies to tiny amounts of other drugs. Those caught with amounts below this threshold can be subject to minor penalties.

The legal limit for blood-alcohol levels is 0.05% and random breath tests do occur.

Your Rights

If you're detained, your arresting officers should give you verbal and written notice of the charges laid against you within 24 hours. You have no right to a phone call upon arrest. The prosecutor must apply to a magistrate for you to be held in preventative custody awaiting trial (depending on the seriousness of the offence) within 48 hours of your arrest. You have the right not to respond to questions without the presence of a lawyer. If the magistrate orders preventative custody, you have the right to contest this within 10 days.

Money

The seven euro notes come in denominations of €500, €200, €100, €50, €20, €10 and €5. The eight euro coins are in denominations of €2 and €1, and €0.50, €0.20, €0.10, €0.05, €0.02 and €0.01.

For the latest exchange rates, check out www.xe.com.

Credit & Debit Cards

Bancomats (ATMs) are widely available throughout Campania and are the best way to obtain local currency. International credit and debit cards can be used in any Bancomat displaying the appropriate sign. Cards are also good for payment in most hotels, restaurants, shops, supermarkets and tollbooths.

Check any charges with your bank. Most banks now build a fee of around 2.75% into every foreign transaction. In addition, ATM withdrawals can attract a further fee, usually around 1.5%.

If your card is lost, stolen, or swallowed by an ATM, you

YOUTH, STUDENT & TEACHER CARDS

The European Youth Card offers thousands of discounts on Italian hotels, museums, restaurants, shops and clubs, while a student, teacher or youth travel card can save you money on flights to Italy. The European Youth Card is available from the **Centro Turistico Studentesco e Giovanile** (CTS; www.cts.it, in Italian), a youth travel agency with branches throughout southern Italy. The final three cards in the table below are available worldwide from student unions, hostelling organisations and youth travel agencies such as STA Travel (www.statravel.com).

Card	Website	Cost (€)	Eligibility
European Youth Card (Carta Giovani)	www.europeanyouthcard.org	10	under 30yr
International Student Identity Card (ISIC)	www.isic.org	10	full-time student
International Teacher Identity Card (ITIC)	www.isic.org	10	full-time teacher
International Youth Travel Card (IYTC)	www.isic.org	10	under 30yr

can telephone toll free to have an immediate stop put on its use:

Amex ☑800 268 9824

MasterCard ☑800 870 866

Visa ☑800 819 014

Moneychangers

You can change money in banks, at the post office or in a *cambio* (currency-exchange bureau). Post offices and banks tend to offer the best rates; currency-exchange bureaus keep longer hours, but watch for high commissions and inferior rates.

Taxes & Refunds

A value-added tax of around 20%, known as Imposta di Valore Aggiunto (IVA), is slapped onto just about everything in Italy. If you are a non-EU resident and spend more than €155 (€154.94 to be more precise!) on a purchase, you can claim a refund when you leave. For information, visit **Tax Refund for Tourists** (www.taxrefund.it) or pick up a pamphlet on the scheme from participating stores, which usually display a 'Tax Free for Tourists' (or similar) sign.

Tipping

You are not expected to tip on top of restaurant service charges, but you can leave a little extra if you feel the service warrants it. If there is no service charge, consider leaving a 10% tip, but this is not obligatory. In bars, Italians often leave small change as a tip (usually €0.10 to €0.20). Tipping taxi drivers is not common practice, but you are expected to tip the porter at top-end hotels a couple of euros.

Opening Hours

➡ Standard hours for businesses:

Banks 8.30am-1.30pm and 2.45-3.45pm or 4.15pm Monday to Friday

Cafes and bars 7.30am-8pm or later

Clubs 11pm-5am

Post offices 8am-6pm Monday to Friday, 8.30am-1pm Saturday; smaller branch offices close 1.30pm weekdays

Restaurants noon-3pm and 7.30-11pm or midnight

Shops 9am-1pm and 3.30-7.30pm (or 4-8pm) Monday to Saturday; some close Monday morning and some open Sunday

➡ The opening hours of museums, galleries and archaeological sites vary enormously. Many museums are closed on Monday or (less commonly) Tuesday or Wednesday.

➡ Currency-exchange offices usually keep longer hours, though these are hard to find outside major cities and tourist areas.

➡ Restaurant kitchens often shut an hour earlier than final closing time. Most places close at least one day a week. Many restaurants are closed in August, while those in coastal resort towns are usually closed in the low season, between November and Easter.

➡ In larger cities, supermarkets may stay open at lunchtime or on Sunday.

Post

Poste Italiane (www.poste.it), Italy's postal system, is reasonably reliable.

Francobolli (stamps) are available at *uffici postali* (post offices) and authorised tobacconists (look for the big white-on-black 'T' sign). Since letters often need to be weighed, what you get at the tobacconist for international airmail will occasionally be an approximation of the proper rate. Tobacconists keep regular shop hours.

Postal Service Rates

The cost of sending a letter by *via aerea* (airmail) depends on its weight and size

and where it is being sent. Most people use *posta prioritaria* (priority mail), Italy's most efficient mail service, guaranteed to deliver letters sent to European destinations within three days and to the rest of the world within four to nine days. Letters up to 20g cost €0.65 within Europe and the Mediterranean basin, and €0.85 to the rest of the world. Packets weighing up to 350g cost €2 within Europe and the Mediterranean basin, €4.50 to Africa, Asia and the Americas, and €4.80 to Australia and New Zealand.

Receiving Mail

Poste restante (general delivery) is known as *fermoposta* in Italy. Letters marked thus will be held at the counter of the same name in the main post office in the relevant town.

You'll need to pick up your letters in person and you must present your passport as ID.

Public Holidays

Most Italians take their annual holiday in August, with the busiest period occurring around 15 August, known locally as Ferragosto. As a result, many businesses and shops close for at least part of that month.

National public holidays:

New Year's Day (Capodanno) 1 January

Epiphany (Epifania) 6 January

Easter Monday (Pasquetta) March/April

Liberation Day (Giorno della Liberazione) 25 April

Labour Day (Festa del Lavoro) 1 May

Republic Day (Festa della Repubblica) 2 June

Feast of the Assumption (Assunzione or Ferragosto) 15 August

All Saints' Day (Ognisanti) 1 November

Feast of the Immaculate Conception (Festa della Immacolata Concezione) 8 December

Christmas Day (Natale) 25 December

Boxing Day (Festa di Santo Stefano) 26 December

Safe Travel

Naples has a reputation for being unsafe. The following are some basic safety tips:

➡ Pickpockets are highly active on crowded transport and in crowds. Avoid keeping money, credit cards and other valuables in easy-to-reach pockets, especially coat and back pockets.

➡ Never leave your bags unattended on a train. At cafes and bars, loop your bag's strap around your leg while seated.

➡ Be cautious of strangers who want your attention, especially at train stations and ports.

➡ Wear bags and cameras across your body, on the side away from the street to avoid scooter-riding petty thieves.

➡ At archaeological sites, watch out for touts posing as legitimate guides.

Scams

Avoid buying mobile phones and other discounted electrical goods from vendors on Piazza Garibaldi in Naples and at street markets. It's not unusual to get home and discover that you've bought a box with a brick in it. At Naples' Stazione Centrale, ignore touts offering taxis; use only registered white taxis with a running meter.

On the Road

Car theft is a problem in Naples, so it pays to leave your car in a supervised car park. If you leave your car on the street, you'll often be approached by an unofficial (illegal) parking attendant asking for money. Clearly, you don't have to pay them,

but if you refuse you run the risk of returning to a damaged car. In case of theft or loss, always report the incident to the police within 24 hours; ask for a statement, as otherwise your travel-insurance company won't pay out.

Traffic

Neapolitan traffic requires some getting used to. Drivers are not keen to stop for pedestrians, even at pedestrian crossings, and are more likely to swerve. Locals simply step off the footpath and walk through the (swerving) traffic with determination. It is a practice that seems to work, but if you feel uncertain, wait and cross with a local.

In many cities, roads that appear to be for one-way traffic have lanes for buses travelling in the opposite direction – always look both ways before stepping onto the road.

Telephone

Domestic Calls

Italian telephone area codes all begin with 0 and consist of up to four digits; the Naples area code is ☑081. The area code is followed by a number of anything from four to eight digits. The area code is an integral part of the telephone number and must always be dialled, even when calling from next door. Mobile-phone numbers begin with a three-digit prefix such as 330. Toll-free (free-phone) numbers are known as *numeri verdi* and usually start with 800. Nongeographical numbers start with 840, 841, 848, 892, 899, 163, 166 or 199. Some six-digit national-rate numbers are also in use (such as those for Alitalia, and rail and postal information).

As elsewhere in Europe, Italians choose from a host of phone-plan providers, with a resultant galaxy of price options.

International Calls

The cheapest options for calling internationally are free or low-cost computer programs such as Skype, cut-price call centres, or an international calling card (*scheda telefonica internazionale*), sold at newsstands and tobacconists. Cut-price call centres can be found in the main cities, and rates can be considerably lower than from Telecom payphones for international calls. You simply place your call from a private booth inside the call centre and pay for it when you've finished. Direct international calls can also easily be made from public telephones with a phonecard. Dial ☑00 to get out of Italy, then the relevant country and area codes, followed by the telephone number.

To call Italy from abroad, call the international access number (☑011 in the USA, ☑00 from most other countries), Italy's country code (☑39) and then the area code of the location you want, including the leading 0.

To make a reverse-charge (collect) international call, dial ☑170. All operators speak English. Alternatively, use the direct-dialling (Country Direct) service provided by your home-country phone company (such as AT&T in the USA and Telstra in Australia). You simply dial the relevant access number and request a reverse-charge call via the operator in your country. Numbers for this service include the following:

Australia (Telstra) ☑800 172 610

Canada ☑800 172 213

New Zealand ☑800 172 641

USA (AT&T) ☑800 172 444

Directory Enquiries

National and international phone numbers can be requested at ☑1254 (or online at 1254.virgilio.it).

Mobile Phones

Italy uses GSM 900/1800, which is compatible with

the rest of Europe and Australia but not with North American GSM 1900 or the totally different Japanese system (though some GSM 1900/900 phones do work here). If you have a GSM phone, check with your service provider about using it in Italy and beware of calls being routed internationally (very expensive for a 'local' call).

Italy has one of the highest levels of mobile-phone penetration in Europe, and you can get a temporary or prepaid account from several companies if you already own a GSM, dual- or tri-band mobile phone. You will usually need your passport to open an account. Always check with your service provider in your home country to ascertain whether your handset allows use of another SIM card. If yours does, it can cost as little as €10 to activate a local prepaid SIM card (sometimes with €10 worth of calls on the card). To recharge a card, simply pop into the nearest outlet or buy a charge card (*ricarica*) from a tobacconist. Alternatively, you can buy or lease an inexpensive Italian phone for the duration of your trip.

Of the main mobile-phone companies, TIM (Telecom Italia Mobile), Wind and Vodafone have the densest networks of outlets across the country.

Phonecards

You'll find Telecom Italia silver payphones on the streets, in train stations, in some stores and in Telecom offices. Most payphones accept only *carte/schede telefoniche* (telephone cards), although some still accept credit cards and coins.

Phonecards (in denominations of €3 and €5) are available at post offices, tobacconists and newsstands.

Time

Italy is one hour ahead of GMT. Daylight-saving time, when clocks are moved forward one hour, starts on the last Sunday in March. Clocks are put back an hour on the last Sunday in October. Italy operates on a 24-hour clock.

Toilets

➜ Public toilets are rare in Naples.

➜ Bars and cafes usually have toilets, although you may need to buy a coffee before you can use them. Public toilets are readily available at museums, and there are public toilets at the main bus and train stations.

➜ Several public toilets have attendants, who'll expect a small tip – €0.50 should do.

➜ There are free toilets at Pompeii and Herculaneum.

Tourist Information

The quality of tourist offices varies dramatically. One office might have enthusiastic staff, another might be indifferent. Most offices can offer you a plethora of brochures, maps and leaflets, even if staff are uninterested in helping in any other way.

Campania's **main tourist office** (☑081 410 72 11; www.in-campania.com; Piazza dei Martiri 58; ◷9am-2pm Mon-Fri) is in the Naples district of Chiaia. It is generally more concerned with planning, budgeting, marketing and promotion than with offering a public information service. However, it maintains a useful tourist website.

Local & Provincial Tourist Offices

Main tourist offices are generally open Monday to Friday; some also open on weekends, especially in urban areas or during the peak summer season. Affiliated information booths (at train stations and airports, for example) may keep slightly different hours.

Tourist Offices Abroad

ENIT (www.enit.it), the Italian National Tourist Office, maintains offices in over two dozen cities on five continents. Contact information for all offices can be found on its website.

Travellers with Disabilities

Campania is not an easy destination for travellers with disabilities. Cobbled streets, hair-raising traffic, blocked pavements and tiny lifts make life difficult for the wheelchair-bound, and those with sight or hearing difficulties. The uneven surfaces at archaeological sites like Pompeii virtually rule out wheelchairs, and the steep slopes of many Amalfi Coast towns pose a considerable obstacle. However, some city buses, including R2 and R3 in Naples, are set up with access ramps and space for a wheelchair.

The website www.turismoaccessibile.it gives a rundown on the facilities at Naples' museums and hotels and on its transport services.

The ENIT office in your country may be able to provide advice on Italian associations for the disabled, and information on what help is available.

Italy's national rail company, **Trenitalia** (www.trenitalia.com), offers a national helpline for disabled passengers at ☑199 303060 (7am to 9pm daily). To secure assistance at Naples' Stazione Centrale, you should call this number 24 hours prior to your departure.

For more information and help, try the following organisations:

Accessible Italy (www.accessibleitaly.com) A San Marino–based company that specialises in holiday services for the disabled. This is the best first port of call.

Cooperative Integrate Onlus (www.coinsociale.it) Based in Rome, CO.IN provides information on the capital (including transport and access) and is happy to share its contacts throughout Italy.

Tourism for All (www.tourismforall.org.uk) This UK-based group has information on hotels with access for disabled guests, where to hire equipment, and tour operators who cater to disabled travellers.

Visas & Permits

Italy is one of 25 member countries of the Schengen Convention, under which 22 EU countries (all but Bulgaria, Cyprus, Ireland, Romania and the UK), plus Iceland, Norway and Switzerland, have abolished permanent checks at common borders.

Legal residents of one Schengen country do not require a visa for another. Residents of 28 non-EU countries, including Australia, Brazil, Canada, Israel, Japan, New Zealand and the USA, do not require visas for tourist visits of up to 90 days (this list varies for those who want to travel to the UK and Ireland).

All non-EU and non-Schengen nationals entering Italy for more than 90 days, or for any reason other than tourism (such as study or work), may need a specific visa. For details, visit www.esteri.it/visti/home_eng.asp or contact an Italian consulate. You should also have your passport stamped on entry as, without a stamp, you could encounter problems when trying to obtain a residence permit *(permesso di soggiorno)*. If you enter the EU via another member state, get your passport stamped there.

Study Visas

Non-EU citizens who want to study at a university or language school in Italy must have a study visa. These can be obtained from your nearest Italian embassy or consulate. You will normally require confirmation of your enrolment, and proof of payment of fees and adequate funds to support yourself. The visa covers only the period of the enrolment. This type of visa is renewable within Italy but, again, only with confirmation of ongoing enrolment and proof that you are able to support yourself (bank statements are preferred).

Work

EU citizens do not require any permits to live or work in Italy but, after three months' residence, are supposed to register themselves at the municipal registry office where they live and offer proof of work or sufficient funds to support themselves. Non-EU foreign citizens with five years' continuous legal residence may apply for permanent residence.

Transport

GETTING THERE & AWAY

A plethora of airlines link Italy to the rest of the world, and numerous carriers fly directly to Naples' international airport, Capodichino. Naples is southern Italy's main transport hub, with excellent rail and bus connections to other parts of Campania and beyond. Naples is also a key port, hosting international cruise ships and operating car and passenger ferries to destinations throughout the Mediterranean.

Flights, tours and rail tickets can be booked online at lonelyplanet.com/bookings.

Entering the Region

EU and Swiss citizens can travel to Italy with their national identity card alone. All other nationalities must have a valid passport, and may be required to fill out a landing card at airports.

By law you should have your passport or ID card with you at all times. You'll need one of these documents for police registration every time you check into a hotel.

Air

Airports

Capodichino airport (☑081 789 61 11; www.aeroportodi-napoli.it), 7km northeast of central Naples, is southern Italy's main airport, linking Naples with most Italian and several major European cities, as well as New York.

The **Alibus** (☑800 639525; www.anm.it) airport shuttle (€3, or $4 if bought on board, 45 minutes, every 20 to 30 minutes) connects the airport to Piazza Garibaldi (Stazione Centrale) and Molo Beverello (the main ferry terminal).

Set taxi fares to the airport are as follows: €19 from a seafront hotel or from Mergellina hydrofoil terminal, €9.50 from Piazza Municipio and €12.50 from Stazione Centrale.

Curreri (☑081 801 54 20; www.curreriviaggi.it) runs seven services daily between the airport and Sorrento. Journey time is 75 minutes; tickets (available on board) cost €11.

Tickets

The internet is the easiest way of locating and booking reasonably priced seats. Full-time students and those under 26 may qualify for discounted fares at agencies such as **STA Travel** (www.statravel.co.uk). Many of these fares require a valid International Student Identity Card (ISIC).

CLIMATE CHANGE & TRAVEL

Every form of transport that relies on carbon-based fuel generates CO_2, the main cause of human-induced climate change. Modern travel is dependent on aeroplanes, which might use less fuel per kilometre per person than most cars but travel much greater distances. The altitude at which aircraft emit gases (including CO_2) and particles also contributes to their climate change impact. Many websites offer 'carbon calculators' that allow people to estimate the carbon emissions generated by their journey and, for those who wish to do so, to offset the impact of the greenhouse gases emitted with contributions to portfolios of climate-friendly initiatives throughout the world. Lonely Planet offsets the carbon footprint of all staff and author travel.

Land

Reaching Campania overland involves traversing three-quarters of the entire length of Italy, which can either be a big drain on your time or, if you have plenty to spare, a wonderful way of seeing the country.

Bus

Buses are the cheapest overland option to Italy, but services are less frequent, less comfortable and significantly slower than the train.

Eurolines (www.eurolines. com) A consortium of coach companies with offices throughout Europe. Italy-bound buses head to Milan, Venice, Florence, Siena and Rome, from where Italian train and bus services continue south to Naples.

Miccolis (✆081 563 03 20; www.miccolis-spa.it) Runs several services a day from Naples to Potenza, Taranto, Brindisi and Lecce.

Marino (✆080 311 23 35; www.marinobus.it) Runs daily services from Naples to Bari and Matera.

SAIS (www.saistrasporti.it) Operates long-haul services to Sicily from Naples and Rome.

Car & Motorcycle

If you are planning to drive to Naples, bear in mind the cost of toll roads and the fact that fuel prices in Italy are among the highest in Europe. Most importantly, however, if you are spending time in Naples, it is unlikely that you will be tempted to drive and you will also have to pay for secure parking. Although your own car is a definite bonus when it comes to visiting more remote areas of Campania, like west of Sorrento and the Parco Nazionale del Cilento, given the cost of driving here, renting a car is a wiser option.

Train

Regular trains on two western lines connect Italy with France (one along the coast and the other from Turin into the French Alps). Depending on distances covered, rail can be highly competitive with air travel: those travelling from neighbouring countries to northern Italy will find it is frequently more comfortable, less expensive and only marginally more time-consuming than flying.

Those travelling longer distances (say, from London, Spain, northern Germany or Eastern Europe) will doubtless find flying cheaper and quicker. Bear in mind, however, that the train is a much greener way to go – a trip by rail can contribute up to 10 times fewer carbon-dioxide emissions per person than the same trip by air.

The national rail company, **Trenitalia** (✆892021; www. trenitalia.com), has a comprehensive network in Italy, and also operates long-distance trains throughout Europe. Within Italy, direct trains run from Milan, Florence and Rome to Naples. From Naples, trains continue south to Reggio di Calabria and to Messina, Sicily. Naples is served by *regionale* (regional), *diretto* (direct), Intercity and high-speed Frecciarossa trains. They arrive at and depart from Naples' **Stazione Centrale** (✆081 554 31 88; Piazza Garibaldi) or **Stazione Garibaldi** (on the lower level). There are up to 30 trains daily to and from Rome.

➡ The comprehensive European Rail Timetable (UK£15.99), updated monthly, is available from Thomas Cook Publishing (www.europeanrailtimetable. eu).

➡ Reservations on international trains to/from Italy are always advisable and sometimes compulsory.

➡ Some international services include transport for private cars.

➡ Consider taking long journeys overnight, as the supplemental fare for a sleeper costs substantially less than a stay in an Italian hotel.

GETTING AROUND

Bicycle

Cycling is a dangerous option in Naples – a city where all road rules are seemingly disregarded. Most drivers speed, chat on their mobile phones and ignore traffic lights. Bicycle and motorcycle theft is rife.

Bicycle hire is costly in Naples (from €20 per day), so if you are staying for some time and are dead set on taking to the saddle, it may be cheaper to buy a bike. Taking your bicycle to the Amalfi Coast is also a fraught option: think blind corners and sheer, precipitous drops.

Boat

Naples, the bay islands and the Amalfi Coast are served by a comprehensive ferry network. Catch fast ferries and hydrofoils for Capri, Sorrento, Ischia (both Ischia Porto and Forio) and Procida from Molo Beverello in front of Castel Nuovo; hydrofoils for Capri, Ischia and Procida also sail from Mergellina.

Ferries for Sicily, the Aeolian Islands and Sardinia sail from Molo Angioino (right beside Molo Beverello) and neighbouring Calata Porta di Massa. Slow ferries to Ischia and Procida also depart from Calata Porta di Massa.

Fares are for a one-way, high-season deck-class single, unless otherwise stated. Services are pared back considerably in winter, and adverse sea conditions may affect schedules.

Tickets for shorter journeys can be bought at the ticket booths on Molo Beverello and at Mergellina. For longer journeys, try the offices of the ferry companies or a travel agent.

Alilauro (☑081 497 22 01; www.alilauro.it)

Caremar (☑081 551 38 82; www.caremar.it)

Gescab (☑081 807 18 12; www.gescab.it)

Medmar (☑081 333 44 11; www.medmargroup.it)

Navigazione Libera del Golfo (NLG; ☑081 552 07 63; www.navlib.it)

Siremar (☑081 497 29 99; www.siremar.it)

SNAV (☑081 428 55 55; www.snav.it)

Tirrenia (☑892123; www.tirrenia.it)

Bus

ANM (☑800 639525; www.anm.it) operates city buses in Naples. There's no central bus station, but most buses pass through Piazza Garibaldi. Useful routes:

140 Santa Lucia to Posillipo via Mergellina.

154 From Via Volta to Via Vespucci, Via Marina, Via Depretis,

Via Acton, Via Morelli, Piazza Vittoria and Via Santa Lucia.

C24 From Via Mergellina to Corso Vittorio Emanuele, Via Crispi, Via Colonna, Via Carducci, Riviera di Chiaia, Piazza Vittoria, Via Santa Lucia, Via Morelli, Piazza dei Martiri, Via Filangieri, Via dei Mille, Via Colonna, Via Crispi, Corso Vittorio Emanuele, Via Piedigrotta and back to Via Mergellina.

C55 Circles the *centro storico* (historic centre), travelling from Piazza Cavour to Via Enrico Pessina, Piazza Dante, Via Toledo, Piazza Bovio, Corso Umberto I and Via Duomo.

R1 From Piazza Medaglie d'Oro to Piazza Carità, Piazza Dante and Piazza Bovio.

R2 From Stazione Centrale, along Corso Umberto I, to Piazza Bovio, Piazza del Municipio and Piazza Trento e Trieste.

R4 From Capodimonte down past Via Dante to Piazza Municipio and back again.

➡ Hop-on, hop-off tourist bus **City Sightseeing Napoli** (☑081 551 72 79; www.napoli.city sightseeing.it; adult/reduced €22/11) operates four routes: routes A and R cover the *centro storico* (route A also reaches Capodimonte), route B follows the

Lungomare seafront and the scenic Posillipo road, and route C heads up to Vomero. Tickets (adult/child €22/11) are valid for 24 hours.

➡ Regional bus services are operated by a number of companies, the most useful of which is **SITA** (☑199 730749; www.sitasudtrasporti.it), which runs frequent daily services from Sorrento and Salerno to the Amalfi Coast.

➡ Other useful companies:

Marino (☑080 311 23 35; www.marinobus.it) Destinations include Bari (€22, three hours).

Miccolis (☑081 563 03 20; www.miccolis-spa.it) Runs to Taranto (€19, three to four hours), Brindisi (€32, five hours) and Lecce (€32, six hours).

CLP (☑081 531 17 07; www.clpbus.it) Services Foggia (€12, two hours), Perugia (€32, 3½ hours) and Assisi (€35, 4½ hours).

Car & Motorcycle

Driving in Naples is not encouraged. The *centro storico* is off-limits to nonresident vehicles, and anarchic traffic conditions make for highly stressful situations. Parking

HYDROFOILS & HIGH-SPEED FERRIES

Destination (from Naples' Molo Beverello)	Ferry company	Price (€)	Duration (min)	Daily frequency (high season)
Capri	Caremar	13.50	50	4
Capri	Navigazione Libera del Golfo	20	45	9
Capri	SNAV	20	45	13
Ischia (Casamicciola Terme)	Caremar	19	45	7
Ischia (Forio)	Alilauro	19	60	4
Ischia (Casamicciola Terme)	SNAV	19	60	4
Procida	Caremar	15	25	4
Procida	SNAV	19	25	4
Sorrento	Gescab	17	20	18
Sorrento	Caremar	13	25	4

is also a nightmare. A scooter is quicker and easier to park but even more nerve-racking to ride. Car/bike theft is also a major problem.

If you're determined to drive, there are some simple guidelines to consider: get used to tailgaters; worry about what's in front of you, not behind; watch out for scooters; give way to pedestrians no matter where they appear from; approach all junctions and traffic lights with extreme caution; and keep cool.

For more detailed information, check the website www.comune.napoli.it (in Italian).

Away from the city, a car becomes more practical. However, be aware that driving along the Amalfi Coast can be quite a hair-raising experience as buses careen around impossibly tight hairpin bends and locals brazenly overtake anything in their path. On the bay islands – Capri, Ischia and Procida – hiring a scooter is an excellent way of getting around.

Naples is on the north–south Autostrada del Sole, the A1 (north to Rome and Milan) and the A3 (south to Salerno and Reggio di Calabria). The A30 skirts Naples to the northeast, while the A16 heads across to Bari.

When approaching Naples, the motorways meet the Tangenziale di Napoli, a major ring road around the city. The ring road hugs the city's northern fringe, meeting the A1 for Rome and the A2 to Capodichino airport in the east, and continuing towards Campi Flegrei and Pozzuoli in the west.

Automobile Associations

Italy's automobile association, the **Automobile Club d'Italia** (ACI; www.aci.it; Piazzale Tecchio 49/d), is the best source of motoring information. It also operates a 24-hour **recovery service** (☑ from landline 803 116, from mobile phone 800 116800).

Bringing Your Own Car

If you are determined to bring your own car to Naples, ensure that all the paperwork is in order and that you carry a hazard triangle and a reflective jacket in your car – and don't forget that Italians drive on the right-hand side! Arriving in Naples, you should be prepared for heavy traffic jams, particularly at commuter times and at lunchtime. Familiarise yourself with important road signs like *uscita* (exit) and *raccordo* (ring road surrounding a city).

Driving Licence & Documentation

An EU driving licence is valid for driving in Italy. However, if you've got an old-style green UK licence or a licence issued by a non-EU country, you'll need an International Driving Permit (IDP). Valid for 12 months, these are inexpensive (about US$21 or UK£5.50) and are easily available from your national automobile association – take along a passport photo and your driving licence. When driving you should always carry the IDP with your home licence, as it's not valid on its own.

Fuel & Spare Parts

Petrol stations located along the main highways are open 24 hours. In smaller towns, the opening hours are generally 7am to 7pm Monday to Saturday, with a lunchtime break. The cost of *benzina senza piombo* (unleaded petrol) and *gasoil* (diesel) is about €1.825 and €1.725 per litre, respectively.

An increasing number of petrol stations are self-service. At these, simply key in the number of the pump

FERRIES

Destination (from Naples' Calata Porta di Massa & Molo Angioino)	Ferry company	Price (€)	Duration	Frequency (high season)
Aeolian Islands	SNAV (Jul-Sep only)	from 65	4-6hr	1 daily
Aeolian Islands	Siremar	from 50	30min	2 weekly
Cagliari (Sardinia)	Tirrenia	from 45	16hr 15min	2 weekly
Capri	Caremar	11	75min	7 daily
Ischia	Caremar	12	90min	7 daily
Ischia	Medmar	12	75min	6 daily
Milazzo (Sicily)	Milazzo (Siremar)	from 50	16hr	2 weekly
Palermo (Sicily)	SNAV	from 35	10hr 15min	1-2 daily
Palermo (Sicily)	Tirrenia	from 45	11hr 45min	1 daily
Procida	Caremar	11	60min	7 daily

and the amount you require and then insert the necessary bill (only acceptable in denominations of €5, €10, €20 and €50).

If you run into car trouble, the nearest petrol station should be able to advise on a reliable mechanic, although few have workshops on-site and they are, overall, very poor at stocking car parts. If you are driving a hire car and run into any serious problems, your car-hire company will probably have an emergency tow service with a toll-free call. You will need to report which road you are on, which direction you are heading, the make of the car and your licence-plate number (targa).

Car Hire

➡ If hiring a car, expect to pay around €60 per day for an economy car or a scooter. Prebooking via the internet often costs less than hiring a car after you arrive in Italy.

➡ Renters must generally be aged 25 or over, with a credit card and a home-country driving licence or IDP.

➡ Consider hiring a small car, which will reduce your fuel expenses and help you negotiate narrow city lanes and tight parking spaces.

➡ Check with your credit-card company to see if it offers a collision-damage waiver, which covers you for additional damage if you use the card to pay for the car.

Multinational car-hire agencies:

Avis (☑081 28 40 41; www. avisautonoleggio.it; Corso Novara 5, Naples)

Europcar (☑081 780 56 43; www.europcar.it; Capodichino airport)

Hertz (☑081 20 28 60; www. hertz.it; Corso Arnaldo Lucci 171, Naples) Also at Via Marina Varco Pisacane Calata Piliero, beside the ferry terminal.

Maggiore (☑081 28 78 58; www.maggiore.it; Stazione Centrale, Naples)

Rent Sprint (☑081 764 34 52; www.rentsprint.it; Via Santa Lucia 32, Naples) Scooter hire only.

Parking

Parking in Naples is no fun. Blue lines by the side of the road denote pay-and-display parking – buy tickets at the meters or from tobacconists – with rates around €2 per hour. Elsewhere street parking is often overseen by illegal attendants who will expect a €2 to €3 fee for their protection of your car. It's usually easier to bite the bullet and pay them than attempt a moral stance.

East of the city centre, there's a 24-hour car park at Via Brin (€1.30 for the first four hours, €7.20 for 24 hours). It is also the safer option, as thieves often tar-

get hire or foreign-registered cars.

Elsewhere in the region, parking can be similarly problematic, especially at the main resorts on the Amalfi Coast and, even more especially, in August.

Road Rules

Contrary to appearances, there are road rules in Italy. Here are some of the most essential:

➡ Cars drive on the right side of the road and overtake on the left.

➡ Seat-belt use (front and rear) is mandatory.

➡ You must give way to cars entering an intersection from a road on your right, unless otherwise indicated.

➡ In the event of a breakdown, a warning

triangle is compulsory, as is use of an approved yellow or orange safety vest if you leave your vehicle.

➡ Italy's blood-alcohol limit is 0.05%. Random breath tests occur and penalties can be severe.

➡ Speed limits for cars are 130km/h to 150km/h on *autostrade* (freeways), 110km/h on other main highways, 90km/h on minor, nonurban roads, and 50km/h in built-up areas.

➡ The speed limit for mopeds is 40km/h.

➡ Helmets are required on all two-wheeled transport.

➡ Headlights are compulsory day and night for all vehicles on the *autostrade*, and advisable for motorcycles even on smaller roads.

Toll Roads

There are tolls on most motorways, payable by cash or credit card as you exit. For information on traffic conditions, tolls and driving distances, see www.auto-strade.it.

Funicular

Three of Naples' four *funic-ulare* (funicular) railways connect the city centre with Vomero. The fourth, **Funicu-lare di Mergellina** (⊙7am-10pm), connects the water-front at Via Mergellina with Via Manzoni. Unico Napoli tickets are valid on board.

Funiculare Centrale (⊙6.30am-10pm Mon & Tue, to 12.30am Wed-Sun & holidays) Travels from Piazzetta Augusteo to Piazza Fuga.

Funiculare di Chiaia (⊙7am-10pm Tue & Wed, to 12.30am Thu, Sun & Mon, to 2am Fri & Sat) Travels from Via del Parco Margherita to Via Domenico Cimarosa.

Funiculare di Montesanto (⊙7am-10pm) Travels from Piazza Montesanto to Via Raffaele Morghen.

Local Transport

Metro

Naples' **metro** (p88) is, in fact, mostly above ground. Metro journeys are covered by Unico Napoli tickets.

Taxi

Official taxis are white and metered and bear the Naples symbol, the Pulcinella (with his distinctive white, cone-shaped hat and long, hooked nose) on their front doors. Always ensure the meter is running.

The minimum starting fare is €3, with a baffling range of additional charges, all of which are listed at www.consorziotaxinapoli.it/who-we-are/rates/. These extras include the following:

➡ €1 for a radio taxi call

➡ €2.50 extra on Sunday, holidays and between 10pm and 7am

➡ €3 for an airport run, €4 for trips starting at the airport and €0.50 per piece of luggage in the boot (trunk). Guide dogs and wheelchairs are carried free of charge.

There are taxi stands at most of the city's main piazzas.

Train

Circumvesuviana (☎800 211388; www.eavsrl.it) trains connect Naples and Sorrento (€4.50, 65 minutes, around 40 daily). Stops along the way include Ercolano (€2.50, 15 minutes) and Pompeii (€3.20, 35 minutes). From Naples, trains depart from Stazione Circumvesuviana, which is attached to Stazione Centrale.

Trains between Naples and the Campi Flegrei depart from Naples' Stazione Cuma-na di Montesanto on Piazza Montesanto, 500m south-west of Piazza Dante. Stops include Pozzuoli (€1.40, 20 minutes, every 25 minutes).

Trams

The following Naples trams may be useful:

Tram 1 Operates from east of Stazione Centrale, through Piazza Garibaldi, the city centre and along the waterfront to Piazza Vittoria.

Tram 29 Travels from Piazza Garibaldi to the city centre along Corso Giuseppe Garibaldi.

Language

Standard Italian is taught and spoken throughout Italy. Dialects are an important part of regional identity, but you'll have no trouble being understood anywhere if you stick to standard Italian, which we've also used in this chapter.

The sounds used in spoken Italian can all be found in English. If you read our coloured pronunciation guides as if they were English, you'll be understood. The stressed syllables are indicated with italics. Note that ai is pronounced as in 'aisle', ay as in 'say', ow as in 'how', dz as the 'ds' in 'lids', and that r is a strong and rolled sound. Keep in mind that Italian consonants can have a stronger, emphatic pronunciation – if the consonant is written as a double letter, it should be pronounced a little stronger, eg *sonno* son·no (sleep) versus *sono* so·no (I am).

BASICS

Italian has two words for 'you' – use the polite form *Lei* lay if you're talking to strangers, officials or people older than you. With people familiar to you or younger than you, you can use the informal form *tu* too.

In Italian, all nouns and adjectives are either masculine or feminine, and so are the articles *il/la* eel/la (the) and *un/una* oon/oo·na (a) that go with the nouns.

In this chapter the polite/informal and masculine/feminine options are included where necessary, separated with a slash and indicated with 'pol/inf' and 'm/f'.

WANT MORE?

For in-depth language information and handy phrases, check out Lonely Planet's *Italian Phrasebook*. You'll find it at **shop.lonelyplanet.com**, or you can buy Lonely Planet's iPhone phrasebooks at the Apple App Store.

Hello.	*Buongiorno.*	bwon·jor·no
Goodbye.	*Arrivederci.*	a·ree·ve·der·chee
Yes.	*Sì.*	see
No.	*No.*	no
Excuse me.	*Mi scusi.* (pol)	mee skoo·zee
	Scusami. (inf)	skoo·za·mee
Sorry.	*Mi dispiace.*	mee dees·pya·che
Please.	*Per favore.*	per fa·vo·re
Thank you.	*Grazie.*	*gra*·tsye
You're welcome.	*Prego.*	*pre*·go

How are you?
Come sta/stai? (pol/inf) ko·me sta/stai

Fine. And you?
Bene. E Lei/tu? (pol/inf) be·ne e lay/too

What's your name?
Come si chiama? pol ko·me see kya·ma
Come ti chiami? inf ko·me tee kya·mee

My name is ...
Mi chiamo ... mee kya·mo ...

Do you speak English?
Parla/Parli par·la/par·lee
inglese? (pol/inf) een·gle·ze

I don't understand.
Non capisco. non ka·pee·sko

ACCOMMODATION

Do you have a ... room?	*Avete una camera ...?*	a·ve·te oo·na ka·me·ra ...
double	*doppia con letto matrimoniale*	do·pya kon le·to ma·tree·mo·nya·le
single	*singola*	seen·go·la
How much is it per ...?	*Quanto costa per ...?*	kwan·to kos·ta per ...
night	*una notte*	oo·na no·te
person	*persona*	per·so·na

Is breakfast included?
La colazione è compresa?
la ko·la·*tsyo*·ne e kom·*pre*·sa

air-con	*aria condizionata*	*a*·rya kon·dee·tsyo·*na*·ta
bathroom	*bagno*	*ba*·nyo
campsite	*campeggio*	kam·*pe*·jo
guesthouse	*pensione*	pen·*syo*·ne
hotel	*albergo*	al·*ber*·go
youth hostel	*ostello della gioventù*	os·*te*·lo de·la jo·ven·*too*
window	*finestra*	fee·*nes*·tra

DIRECTIONS

Where's ...?
Dov'è ...?
do·ve ...

What's the address?
Qual'è l'indirizzo?
kwa·*le* leen·dee·*ree*·tso

Could you please write it down?
Può scriverlo, per favore?
pwo *skree*·ver·lo per fa·*vo*·re

Can you show me (on the map)?
Può mostrarmi (sulla pianta)?
pwo mos·*trar*·mee (soo·la *pyan*·ta)

at the corner	*all'angolo*	a·*lan*·go·lo
at the traffic lights	*al semaforo*	al se·*ma*·fo·ro
behind	*dietro*	*dye*·tro
far	*lontano*	lon·*ta*·no
in front of	*davanti a*	da·*van*·tee a
left	*a sinistra*	a see·*nee*·stra
near	*vicino*	vee·*chee*·no
next to	*accanto a*	a·*kan*·to a
opposite	*di fronte a*	dee *fron*·te a
right	*a destra*	a *de*·stra
straight ahead	*sempre diritto*	*sem*·pre dee·*ree*·to

EATING & DRINKING

What would you recommend?
Cosa mi consiglia?
ko·za mee kon·*see*·lya

What's in that dish?
Quali ingredienti ci sono in questo piatto?
kwa·li een·gre·*dyen*·tee chee so·no een *kwe*·sto *pya*·to

What's the local speciality?
Qual'è la specialità di questa regione?
kwa·*le* la spe·cha·lee·*ta* dee *kwe*·sta re·*jo*·ne

That was delicious!

Era squisito!
e·ra skwee·*zee*·to

Cheers!
Salute!
sa·*loo*·te

Please bring the bill.
Mi porta il conto, per favore?
mee *por*·ta eel *kon*·to per fa·*vo*·re

I'd like to reserve a table for ...	*Vorrei prenotare un tavolo per ...*	vo·*ray* pre·no·*ta*·re oon *ta*·vo·lo per ...
(two) people	*(due) persone*	*(doo*·e) per·*so*·ne
(eight) o'clock	*le (otto)*	le (*o*·to)

I don't eat ...	*Non mangio ...*	non *man*·jo ...
eggs	*uova*	*wo*·va
fish	*pesce*	*pe*·she
nuts	*noci*	*no*·chee
(red) meat	*carne (rossa)*	*kar*·ne (*ro*·sa)

SIGNS

Entrata/Ingresso	Entrance
Uscita	Exit
Aperto	Open
Chiuso	Closed
Informazioni	Information
Proibito/Vietato	Prohibited
Gabinetti/Servizi	Toilets
Uomini	Men
Donne	Women

Key Words

bar	locale	lo·ka·le
bottle	bottiglia	bo·tee·lya
breakfast	prima colazione	pree·ma ko·la·tsyo·ne
cafe	bar	bar
cold	freddo	fre·do
dinner	cena	che·na
drink list	lista delle bevande	lee·sta de·le be·van·de
fork	forchetta	for·ke·ta
glass	bicchiere	bee·kye·re
grocery store	alimentari	a·lee·men·ta·ree
hot	caldo	kal·do
knife	coltello	kol·te·lo
lunch	pranzo	pran·dzo
market	mercato	mer·ka·to
menu	menù	me·noo
plate	piatto	pya·to
restaurant	ristorante	ree·sto·ran·te
spicy	piccante	pee·kan·te
spoon	cucchiaio	koo·kya·yo
vegetarian (food)	vegetariano	ve·je·ta·rya·no
with	con	kon
without	senza	sen·tsa

Meat & Fish

beef	manzo	man·dzo
chicken	pollo	po·lo
duck	anatra	a·na·tra
fish	pesce	pe·she
herring	aringa	a·reen·ga
lamb	agnello	a·nye·lo
lobster	aragosta	a·ra·gos·ta
meat	carne	kar·ne
mussels	cozze	ko·tse
oysters	ostriche	o·stree·ke
pork	maiale	ma·ya·le
prawn	gambero	gam·be·ro
salmon	salmone	sal·mo·ne
scallops	capasante	ka·pa·san·te
seafood	frutti di mare	froo·tee dee ma·re
shrimp	gambero	gam·be·ro
squid	calamari	ka·la·ma·ree
trout	trota	tro·ta
tuna	tonno	to·no
turkey	tacchino	ta·kee·no
veal	vitello	vee·te·lo

Fruit & Vegetables

apple	mela	me·la
beans	fagioli	fa·jo·lee
cabbage	cavolo	ka·vo·lo
capsicum	peperone	pe·pe·ro·ne
carrot	carota	ka·ro·ta
cauliflower	cavolfiore	ka·vol·fyo·re
cucumber	cetriolo	che·tree·o·lo
fruit	frutta	froo·ta
grapes	uva	oo·va
lemon	limone	lee·mo·ne
lentils	lenticchie	len·tee·kye
mushroom	funghi	foon·gee
nuts	noci	no·chee
onions	cipolle	chee·po·le
orange	arancia	a·ran·cha
peach	pesca	pe·ska
peas	piselli	pee·ze·lee
pineapple	ananas	a·na·nas
plum	prugna	proo·nya
potatoes	patate	pa·ta·te

QUESTION WORDS

How?	Come?	ko·me
What?	Che cosa?	ke ko·za
When?	Quando?	kwan·do
Where?	Dove?	do·ve
Who?	Chi?	kee
Why?	Perché?	per·ke

spinach	spinaci	spee·*na*·chee
tomatoes	pomodori	po·mo·*do*·ree
vegetables	verdura	ver·*doo*·ra

Other

bread	pane	*pa*·ne
butter	burro	*boo*·ro
cheese	formaggio	for·*ma*·jo
eggs	uova	*wo*·va
honey	miele	*mye*·le

Drinks

beer	birra	*bee*·ra
coffee	caffè	ka·*fe*
(orange) juice	succo (d'arancia)	*soo*·ko (da·*ran*·cha)
milk	latte	*la*·te
red wine	vino rosso	*vee*·no *ro*·so
soft drink	bibita	*bee*·bee·ta
tea	tè	te
(mineral) water	acqua (minerale)	*a*·kwa (mee·ne·*ra*·le)
white wine	vino bianco	*vee*·no *byan*·ko

EMERGENCIES

Help!
Aiuto! — a·*yoo*·to

Leave me alone!
Lasciami in pace! — la·sha·mee een *pa*·che

I'm lost.
Mi sono perso/a. (m/f) — mee *so*·no *per*·so/a

There's been an accident.
C'è stato un incidente. — che *sta*·to oon een·chee·*den*·te

Call the police!
Chiami la polizia! — *kya*·mee la po·lee·*tsee*·a

Call a doctor!
Chiami un medico! — *kya*·mee oon *me*·dee·ko

Where are the toilets?
Dove sono i gabinetti? — *do*·ve *so*·no ee ga·bee·*ne*·tee

I'm sick.
Mi sento male. — mee *sen*·to *ma*·le

It hurts here.
Mi fa male qui. — mee fa *ma*·le kwee

I'm allergic to ...
Sono allergico/a a ... (m/f) — *so*·no a·*ler*·jee·ko/a a ...

SHOPPING & SERVICES

I'd like to buy ...
Vorrei comprare ... — vo·*ray* kom·*pra*·re ...

I'm just looking.
Sto solo guardando. — sto *so*·lo gwar·*dan*·do

Can I look at it?
Posso dare un'occhiata? — *po*·so *da*·re oo·no·*kya*·ta

How much is this?
Quanto costa questo? — *kwan*·to *kos*·ta *kwe*·sto

It's too expensive.
È troppo caro/a. (m/f) — e *tro*·po *ka*·ro/a

Can you lower the price?
Può farmi lo sconto? — pwo *far*·mee lo *skon*·to

There's a mistake in the bill.
C'è un errore nel conto. — che oo·ne·*ro*·re nel *kon*·to

ATM	Bancomat	*ban*·ko·mat
post office	ufficio postale	oo·*fee*·cho pos·*ta*·le
tourist office	ufficio del turismo	oo·*fee*·cho del too·*reez*·mo

TIME & DATES

What time is it?	*Che ora è?*	ke *o*·ra e
It's one o'clock.	*È l'una.*	e *loo*·na
It's (two) o'clock.	*Sono le (due).*	*so*·no le (*doo*·e)

NUMBERS		
1	uno	*oo*·no
2	due	*doo*·e
3	tre	tre
4	quattro	*kwa*·tro
5	cinque	*cheen*·kwe
6	sei	say
7	sette	*se*·te
8	otto	*o*·to
9	nove	*no*·ve
10	dieci	*dye*·chee
20	venti	*ven*·tee
30	trenta	*tren*·ta
40	quaranta	kwa·*ran*·ta
50	cinquanta	cheen·*kwan*·ta
60	sessanta	se·*san*·ta
70	settanta	se·*tan*·ta
80	ottanta	o·*tan*·ta
90	novanta	no·*van*·ta
100	cento	*chen*·to
1000	mille	*mee*·lel

Half past (one).	(L'una) e mezza.	(loo·na) e me·dza
in the morning	di mattina	dee ma·tee·na
in the afternoon	di pomeriggio	dee po·me·ree·jo
in the evening	di sera	dee se·ra
yesterday	ieri	ye·ree
today	oggi	o·jee
tomorrow	domani	do·ma·nee
Monday	lunedì	loo·ne·dee
Tuesday	martedì	mar·te·dee
Wednesday	mercoledì	mer·ko·le·dee
Thursday	giovedì	jo·ve·dee
Friday	venerdì	ve·ner·dee
Saturday	sabato	sa·ba·to
Sunday	domenica	do·me·nee·ka
January	gennaio	je·na·yo
February	febbraio	fe·bra·yo
March	marzo	mar·tso
April	aprile	a·pree·le
May	maggio	ma·jo
June	giugno	joo·nyo
July	luglio	loo·lyo
August	agosto	a·gos·to
September	settembre	se·tem·bre
October	ottobre	o·to·bre
November	novembre	no·vem·bre
December	dicembre	dee·chem·bre

TRANSPORT

Public Transport

At what time does the ... leave/arrive?	A che ora parte/ arriva ...?	a ke o·ra par·te/ a·ree·va ...
boat	la nave	la na·ve
bus	l'autobus	low·to·boos
ferry	il traghetto	eel tra·ge·to
metro	la metropolitana	la me·tropo·lee·ta·na
plane	l'aereo	la·e·re·o
train	il treno	eel tre·no
... ticket	un biglietto ...	oon bee·lye·to
one-way	di sola andata	dee so·la an·da·ta
return	di andata e ritorno	dee an·da·ta e ree·tor·no

bus stop	fermata dell'autobus	fer·ma·ta del ow·to·boos
platform	binario	bee·na·ryo
ticket office	biglietteria	bee·lye·te·ree·a
timetable	orario	o·ra·ryo
train station	stazione ferroviaria	sta·tsyo·ne fe·ro·vyar·ya

Does it stop at ...?
Si ferma a ...? see fer·ma a ...

Please tell me when we get to ...
Mi dica per favore mee dee·ka per fa·vo·re
quando arriviamo a ... kwan·do a·ree·vya·mo a ...

I want to get off here.
Voglio scendere qui. vo·lyo shen·de·re kwee

Driving & Cycling

I'd like to hire a/an ...	Vorrei noleggiare un/una ... (m/f)	vo·ray no·le·ja·re oon/oo·na ...
4WD	fuoristrada (m)	fwo·ree·stra·da
bicycle	bicicletta (f)	bee·chee·kle·ta
car	macchina (f)	ma·kee·na
motorbike	moto (f)	mo·to
bicycle pump	pompa della bicicletta	pom·pa de·la bee·chee·kle·ta
child seat	seggiolino	se·jo·lee·no
helmet	casco	kas·ko
mechanic	meccanico	me·ka·nee·ko
petrol/gas	benzina	ben·dzee·na
service station	stazione di servizio	sta·tsyo·ne dee ser·vee·tsyo

Is this the road to ...?
Questa strada porta a ...? kwe·sta stra·da por·ta a ...

(How long) Can I park here?
(Per quanto tempo) (per kwan·to tem·po)
Posso parcheggiare qui? po·so par·ke·ja·re kwee

The car/motorbike has broken down (at ...).
La macchina/moto si è la ma·kee·na/mo·to see e
guastata (a ...). gwas·ta·ta (a ...)

I have a flat tyre.
Ho una gomma bucata. o oo·na go·ma boo·ka·ta

I've run out of petrol.
Ho esaurito la o e·zow·ree·to la
benzina. ben·dzee·nat

GLOSSARY

Albergo (alberghi) – hotel (hotels)

alimentari – grocery shop

allergia – allergy

archeologica – archaeology

autostrada (autostrade) – motorway, highway (motorways, highways)

bagno – bathroom; also toilet

bancomat – Automated teller machine (ATM)

bassi – one-room, ground-floor apartments mostly found in the traditionally poorer areas of Naples

benzina – petrol

biblioteca (biblioteche) – library (libraries)

biglietto – ticket

biglietto giornaliero – daily ticket

caffettiera – Italian coffee percolator

calcio – football (soccer)

camera – room

cambio – currency-exchange bureau

canzone (canzoni) – song (songs)

cappella – chapel

carabinieri – police with military and civil duties

carta d'identità – identity card

carta telefonica – phone-card

casa – house; home

casareccio – home style

castello – castle

catacomba – underground tomb complex

centro – city centre

centro storico – historic centre; old city

chiesa (chiese) – church (churches)

chiostro – cloister

cimitero – cemetery

colle/collina – hill

colonna – column

commissariato – local police station

comune – equivalent to a municipality or county; town or city

council; historically, a commune (self-governing town or city)

concerto – concert

corso – main street

cripta – crypt

cupola – dome

Dio (Dei) – God (Gods)

faraglione (faraglioni) – rock tower; rock pinnacle (rock towers; rock pinnacles)

farmacia – pharmacy

ferrovia – train station

festa – feast day; holiday

fiume – river

fontana – fountain

forno – bakery

forte/fortezza – fort

forum (fora) – (Latin) public square (public squares)

francobollo (francobolli) – stamp (stamps)

gabinetto – toilet; WC

gasolio – diesel

gelateria – ice-cream parlour

giardino (giardini) – garden (gardens)

golfo – gulf

gratis – free (no cost)

isola – island

lago – lake

largo – small square

lavanderia – laundrette

libreria – bookshop

lido – beach

lungomare – seafront; esplanade

mare – sea

medicina (medicine) – medicine (medicines)

mercato – market

monte – mountain

mura – city wall

museo – museum

nazionale – national

nuovo/a – new (m/f)

orto botanico – botanical gardens

ospedale – hospital

ostello – hostel

palazzo (palazzi) – mansion; palace; large building of any type (including an apartment block)

panetteria – bakery

panino (panini) – sandwich (sandwiches)

parcheggio – car park

parco – park

passeggiata – a stroll

pasticceria – cake shop

pastificio – pasta-making factory

pensione – small hotel or guesthouse, often offering board

pescheria – fish shop

piazza (piazze) – square (squares)

pinacoteca – art gallery

piscina – pool

polizia – police

ponte – bridge

porta – city gate

porto – port

presepe (presepi) – nativity scene (nativity scenes)

questura – police station

reale – royal

ruota – wheel

sala – room in a museum or a gallery

salumeria – delicatessen

santuario – sanctuary

scavi – archaeological ruins

scheda telefonica – phone-card

sedia a rotelle – wheelchair

sentiero – path; trail; track

servizio – service charge in restaurants

sole – sun

sottosuolo – underground

spiaggia – beach

statua – statue

stazione – station

strada – street; road

tabaccheria – tobacconist's shop

teatro – theatre

tempio – temple

terme – baths

torre – tower

treno – train

via – street, road

vecchio – old

vicolo – alley, alleyway

Behind the Scenes

SEND US YOUR FEEDBACK

We love to hear from travellers – your comments keep us on our toes and help make our books better. Our well-travelled team reads every word on what you loved or loathed about this book. Although we cannot reply individually to your submissions, we always guarantee that your feedback goes straight to the appropriate authors, in time for the next edition. Each person who sends us information is thanked in the next edition – the most useful submissions are rewarded with a selection of digital PDF chapters.

Visit **lonelyplanet.com/contact** to submit your updates and suggestions or to ask for help. Our award-winning website also features inspirational travel stories, news and discussions.

Note: We may edit, reproduce and incorporate your comments in Lonely Planet products such as guidebooks, websites and digital products, so let us know if you don't want your comments reproduced or your name acknowledged. For a copy of our privacy policy visit lonelyplanet.com/privacy.

OUR READERS

Many thanks to the travellers who used the last edition and wrote to us with helpful hints, useful advice and interesting anecdotes:
Bernie Kingsley, Donald Brooks, Jacqueline DiGiovanni, Louise Coad, Nick Parkes, Norbert Happé, Richard Monk, Roger Butler, Sabine Gerull

AUTHOR THANKS

Cristian Bonetto

As always, *grazie infinite* to my 'Re e Regina di Napoli', as well as to Alfonso Sperandeo, Andrea Maglio, Susy Galeone and La Paranza, Bonnie Alberts, Luca Coda and Harriet Driver, Alfredo Cefalo and Malgorzata Gajo, Giancarlo Di Maio, Gigi Crispino and Valentina Vellusi. At LP, a big thanks to Anna Tyler for the commission and to my diligent co-writer Helena Smith.

Helena Smith

Many thanks to everyone who helped with advice along the way, most particularly Matteo, Daniele, Angela and Francesco.

ACKNOWLEDGMENTS

Climate map data adapted from Peel MC, Finlayson BL & McMahon TA (2007) 'Updated World Map of the Köppen-Geiger Climate Classification', Hydrology and Earth System Sciences, 11, 163344.

Illustration pp102-103 by Javier Zarracina.

Cover photograph: Marina Corricella, Procida Island, Italy, Frank Chmura/Corbis ©

THIS BOOK

This 5th edition of Lonely Planet's *Naples, Pompeii & the Amalfi Coast* guidebook was researched and written by Cristian Bonetto and Helena Smith. Cristian Bonetto and Josephine Quintero wrote the previous two editions. This guidebook was produced at Lonely Planet by the following:

Destination Editor
Anna Tyler

Coordinating Editor
Sarah Bailey

Product Editors
Paul Harding, Briohny Hooper

Senior Cartographer
Anthony Phelan

Cartographer Julie Dodkins

Book Designer
Wendy Wright

Assisting Editors Charlotte Orr, Gabrielle Stefanos

Cover Research
Naomi Parker

Thanks to Sasha Baskett, Bruce Evans, Corey Hutchison, Andi Jones, Anne Mason, Claire Murphy, Karyn Noble, Martine Power, Samantha Russell-Tulip, Dianne Schallmeiner, Angela Tinson, Lauren Wellicome., Tony Wheeler

Index

Map Legend

Sights

- Beach
- Bird Sanctuary
- Buddhist
- Castle/Palace
- Christian
- Confucian
- Hindu
- Islamic
- Jain
- Jewish
- Monument
- Museum/Gallery/Historic Building
- Ruin
- Shinto
- Sikh
- Taoist
- Winery/Vineyard
- Zoo/Wildlife Sanctuary
- Other Sight

Activities, Courses & Tours

- Bodysurfing
- Diving
- Canoeing/Kayaking
- Course/Tour
- Sento Hot Baths/Onsen
- Skiing
- Snorkelling
- Surfing
- Swimming/Pool
- Walking
- Windsurfing
- Other Activity

Sleeping

- Sleeping
- Camping

Eating

- Eating

Drinking & Nightlife

- Drinking & Nightlife
- Cafe

Entertainment

- Entertainment

Shopping

- Shopping

Information

- Bank
- Embassy/Consulate
- Hospital/Medical
- Internet
- Police
- Post Office
- Telephone
- Toilet
- Tourist Information
- Other Information

Geographic

- Beach
- Gate
- Hut/Shelter
- Lighthouse
- Lookout
- Mountain/Volcano
- Oasis
- Park
- Pass
- Picnic Area
- Waterfall

Population

- Capital (National)
- Capital (State/Province)
- City/Large Town
- Town/Village

Transport

- Airport
- Border crossing
- Bus
- Cable car/Funicular
- Cycling
- Ferry
- Metro station
- Monorail
- Parking
- Petrol station
- S Bahn/Subway station
- Taxi
- T-bane/Tunnelbana station
- Train station/Railway
- Tram
- Tube station
- U-Bahn/Underground station
- Other Transport

Routes

- Tollway
- Freeway
- Primary
- Secondary
- Tertiary
- Lane
- Unsealed road
- Road under construction
- Plaza/Mall
- Steps
- Tunnel
- Pedestrian overpass
- Walking Tour
- Walking Tour detour
- Path/Walking Trail

Boundaries

- International
- State/Province
- Disputed
- Regional/Suburb
- Marine Park
- Cliff
- Wall

Hydrography

- River, Creek
- Intermittent River
- Canal
- Water
- Dry/Salt/Intermittent Lake
- Reef

Areas

- Airport/Runway
- Beach/Desert
- Cemetery (Christian)
- Cemetery (Other)
- Glacier
- Mudflat
- Park/Forest
- Sight (Building)
- Sportsground
- Swamp/Mangrove

Note: Not all symbols displayed above appear on the maps in this book

OUR STORY

A beat-up old car, a few dollars in the pocket and a sense of adventure. In 1972 that's all Tony and Maureen Wheeler needed for the trip of a lifetime – across Europe and Asia overland to Australia. It took several months, and at the end – broke but inspired – they sat at their kitchen table writing and stapling together their first travel guide, *Across Asia on the Cheap*. Within a week they'd sold 1500 copies. Lonely Planet was born.

Today, Lonely Planet has offices in Franklin, London, Melbourne, Oakland, Beijing and Delhi, with more than 600 staff and writers. We share Tony's belief that 'a great guidebook should do three things: inform, educate and amuse'.

OUR WRITERS

Cristian Bonetto

Naples, Pompeii & Around, Plan Your Trip & Understand chapters Despite being the son of northern Italians, Cristian has an enduring weakness for Naples and Campania. It took one visit as a young backpacker to get him hooked, and the Australian-born writer has been covering the region's food, culture and lifestyle for over a decade. According to Cristian, no Italian city quite matches Naples' complexity and intrigue, and its ability to constantly surprise and contradict makes it a thrill to write about. The writer's musings have appeared in publications across the globe, and his Naples-based play *Il Cortile* (The Courtyard) has toured numerous Italian cities. Cristian has contributed to over 30 Lonely Planet guides, including *Venice & The Veneto*, *New York City*, *Denmark*, and *Singapore*. You can follow Cristian's adventures on Twitter (@Cristian Bonetto) and on Instagram (rexcat75). Cristian also contributed to the Accommodation chapter.

Helena Smith

The Islands, The Amalfi Coast, Salerno & the Cilento, Outdoor Activities, Survival Guide Helena Smith has been visiting Italy since she was five years old. At that time chocolate spread on toast was the main draw – now she goes back for the food, the warmth, the art and the atmosphere. Researching this edition took her from mountain walks with sea views to the stunning Greek temples of Paestum. Helena also contributed to the Accommodation chapter.

Published by Lonely Planet Publications Pty Ltd
ABN 36 005 607 983
5th edition – Jan 2016
ISBN 978 1 7432 155 17
© Lonely Planet 2016   Photographs © as indicated 2016
10 9 8 7 6 5 4 3 2 1
Printed in China

32953012487726